Rock on Record

Rock on Record

Albin J. Zak

Cover image: © Bob Carlin.

Published by State University of New York Press, Albany

© 2022 State University of New York

All rights reserved

Printed in the United States of America

No part of this book may be used or reproduced in any manner whatsoever without written permission. No part of this book may be stored in a retrieval system or transmitted in any form or by any means including electronic, electrostatic, magnetic tape, mechanical, photocopying, recording, or otherwise without the prior permission in writing of the publisher.

For information, contact State University of New York Press, Albany, NY
www.sunypress.edu

Library of Congress Cataloging-in-Publication Data

Name: Zak, Albin, author.
Title: Rock on record / Albin J. Zak.
Description: Albany : State University of New York Press, 2022. | Includes bibliographical references and index.
Identifiers: LCCN 2021021222 | ISBN 9781438487533 (pbk. : alk. paper) | ISBN 9781438487540 (ebook)
Subjects: LCSH: Rock music—Analysis, appreciation. | Popular music—Analysis, appreciation. | Music appreciation.
Classification: LCC MT146 .Z35 2022 | DDC 781.66/117—dc23
LC record available at https://lccn.loc.gov/2021021222

10 9 8 7 6 5 4 3 2 1

*to
my students
and
Richard Carlin*

CONTENTS

Introduction	1
1. Fundamentals	5
1.1. Sound: Acoustic • Electric	5
1.2. From Sound to Song: Scales • Melody • Rhythm • Harmony • Form	7
1.3. Songs on Record: Arrangement • Stereo • Voice • Lyrics • Shaping the Mix	27
2. New Sounds: Mainstream Pop	34
2.1. "That Lucky Old Sun (Just Rolls around Heaven All Day)" (1949): Frankie Laine	37
2.2. "Lover" (1952): Peggy Lee	39
2.3. "Vaya con Dios" (1953): Les Paul and Mary Ford	43
3. Rhythm and Blues for the Kids: Doo Wop	48
3.1. "It's Too Soon to Know" (1948): The Orioles	50
3.2. "Why Do Fools Fall in Love" (1955): Frankie Lymon and the Teenagers	54
3.3. "In the Still of the Nite" (1956): The Five Satins	58
4. Rocking Country: Rockabilly	62
4.1. "Crazy Man, Crazy" (1953): Bill Haley and His Comets	63
4.2. "Blue Moon of Kentucky" (1954): Elvis Presley	66
4.3. "I Gotta Know" (1956): Wanda Jackson	69
5. Lo-Fi Rave-Up: Recasting the Blues, Reinventing Song	74
5.1. "Tutti Frutti" (1955): Little Richard	76
5.2. "Hound Dog" (1956): Elvis Presley	79
5.3. "Peggy Sue" (1957): Buddy Holly	82
5.4. "Rock and Roll Music" (1957): Chuck Berry	86

6.	R&B with Strings: Sweet Soul	90
	6.1. "Blueberry Hill" (1956): Fats Domino	91
	6.2. "There Goes My Baby" (1959): The Drifters	93
	6.3. "A Change Is Gonna Come" (1963): Sam Cooke	97
7.	Easy Listening and Slow Dancing: Rockaballad	102
	7.1. "Only You (And You Alone)" (1955): The Platters	103
	7.2. "All I Have to Do Is Dream" (1958): The Everly Brothers	106
	7.3. "Crying" (1961): Roy Orbison	109
8.	Brill Building Pop: Girl Groups	115
	8.1. "Will You Love Me Tomorrow" (1960): The Shirelles	117
	8.2. "Be My Baby" (1963): The Ronettes	121
	8.3. "Remember (Walking in the Sand)" (1964): The Shangri-Las	125
9.	Affirming a New Pop Tradition: The Beatles	129
	9.1. "A Hard Day's Night" (1964)	131
	9.2. "Nowhere Man" (1965)	134
	9.3. "Eleanor Rigby" (1966)	136
	9.4. "While My Guitar Gently Weeps" (1968)	140
	9.5. "Sun King"/"Mean Mr. Mustard"/"Polythene Pam"/"She Came In through the Bathroom Window" (1969)	143
10.	London Blues: The Rolling Stones	152
	10.1. "Paint It Black" (1966)	153
	10.2. "Ruby Tuesday" (1967)	157
	10.3. "Jumpin' Jack Flash" (1968)	158
	10.4. "You Can't Always Get What You Want" (1969)	161
	10.5. "Wild Horses" (1971)	165
11.	The California Vibe: The Beach Boys	169
	11.1. "I Get Around" (1964)	171
	11.2. "God Only Knows" (1966)	173
	11.3. "Good Vibrations" (1966)	177
12.	Urban Folk: Folk Rock	182
	12.1. "Like a Rolling Stone" (1965): Bob Dylan	184
	12.2. "My Back Pages" (1967): The Byrds	189
	12.3. "America" (1968): Simon and Garfunkel	192

13. Berry Gordy's Empire: Motown — 198
    13.1. "Stop! In the Name of Love" (1965): The Supremes — 200
    13.2. "The Tracks of My Tears" (1965): The Miracles — 203
    13.3. "I Heard It through the Grapevine" (1967): Marvin Gaye — 206
    13.4. "Superstition" (1972): Stevie Wonder — 209

14. Rock's Gospel Strain: Southern Soul — 214
    14.1. "In the Midnight Hour" (1965): Wilson Pickett — 215
    14.2. "Chain of Fools" (1967): Aretha Franklin — 218
    14.3. "(Sittin' on) The Dock of the Bay" (1967): Otis Redding — 222
    14.4. "I Got the Feelin'" (1968): James Brown — 225

15. Counterculture: Psychedelic Rock — 230
    15.1. "White Rabbit" (1966): Jefferson Airplane — 231
    15.2. "The End" (1966): The Doors — 234
    15.3. "Sunshine of Your Love" (1967): Cream — 238
    15.4. "Purple Haze" (1967): Jimi Hendrix — 240

16. Back to the Roots: Country Rock — 245
    16.1. "Lay Lady Lay" (1969): Bob Dylan — 246
    16.2. "Chest Fever" (1968): The Band — 248
    16.3. "Fortunate Son" (1969): Creedence Clearwater Revival — 252

17. Troubadours: The Singer-Songwriter — 257
    17.1. "Both Sides Now" (1969): Joni Mitchell — 258
    17.2. "Fire and Rain" (1969): James Taylor — 260
    17.3. "Heart of Gold" (1971): Neil Young — 263

18. Grand Ambition: Progressive Rock — 267
    18.1. "The Court of the Crimson King" (1969): King Crimson — 268
    18.2. "Roundabout" (1972): Yes — 272
    18.3. "Money" (1973): Pink Floyd — 277

19. Heavy Sounds: Hard Rock — 281
    19.1. "Black Dog" (1971): Led Zeppelin — 282
    19.2. "Sweet Emotion" (1975): Aerosmith — 285
    19.3. "Highway to Hell" (1979): AC/DC — 288

20. Everybody Dance: Disco ... 292
  20.1. "Bad Luck" (1975): Harold Melvin and the Blue Notes ... 294
  20.2. "He's the Greatest Dancer" (1979): Sister Sledge ... 298
  20.3. "I Feel Love" (1977): Donna Summer ... 301

21. Scuffing It Up: Punk and New Wave ... 305
  21.1. "Sheena Is a Punk Rocker" (1977): Ramones ... 306
  21.2. "Call Me" (1980): Blondie ... 309
  21.3. "London Calling" (1979): The Clash ... 313

22. A Whole New Thing: Hip-Hop ... 319
  22.1. "The Adventures of Grandmaster Flash on the Wheels of Steel" (1981): Grandmaster Flash ... 321
  22.2. "Fight the Power" (1989): Public Enemy ... 324
  22.3. "Let Me Ride" (1993): Dr. Dre ... 328

Glossary ... 333

Index ... 341

Song Index ... 363

INTRODUCTION

Rock on Record is meant to enhance what is already a pleasurable experience: listening to music. Listening, of course, is its own reward. There is no requirement beyond letting the music into your ears. You don't need to know who's singing, who's in the band, who wrote the song, or who produced the record. You don't need to dance, and you certainly don't need to analyze the music. But if you pause for a while amid your million-song playlist and spend some time with a single track, allowing yourself the luxury of paying close attention, you may find a new level of enjoyment.

ROCK?

The term "rock" is pretty vague. It can mean a genre, as in rock vs. pop vs. R&B. But if Run-DMC can proclaim themselves kings of rock, the word clearly has other connotations. I use it here as a catchall to represent popular music (represented by another catchall: pop music) since World War II. What all of this music has in common is its birthplace: the recording studio. Records of earlier eras were meant literally to record a musical event in order to render it as accurately as possible. The goal was to make listeners feel they were in the presence of live musicians. But in the postwar years, even before there was a hint of rock and roll, record making became more like movie making. Records were intended to be not mere representations of real-world performances but listening experiences—sonic worlds—unto themselves. The tracks covered here, from rockabilly to disco, are all creations of the recording studio.

HISTORY

Rock on Record is not primarily a history book, but all the tracks are situated in a historical context and the book is organized according to a chronology of genre. Whenever we hear music, we put it into a context informed by our listening experience. Consciously or not, we hear records in relation to other records. Most pop music fans have a general awareness of genre, which is defined by the collection of stylistic features that certain bands and records have in common. Our awareness of genre leads us to instinctively recognize a surprise if we hear an ABBA record with a death metal arrangement or a hardcore punk record with vocals by Celine Dion.

Rock music developed as a series of genres, each unprecedented. Yes, all had precursors. But there was no doo wop, or rockabilly, or surf, or psychedelic, or folk rock until there was. And once a genre came into being, it never went away. Fashions wax and wane, but every genre represented in this book is still with us today. Genres continue to evolve. They are bent and blended according to artists' whims. Exploring the origins of rock's principal formative genres can give us a fuller appreciation not only of music past but also of music today.

Rock is a democratic musical idiom. It developed in a commercial marketplace where audience opinions helped shape the landscape. The music covered in this book emerged as a haphazard cultural collaboration between artists and audience. No master plan produced rock and roll. Hit records—the ones that got the most "votes" at record stores and in juke boxes—pointed the way forward. In presenting this particular set of genres and artists, I have followed the map left by history. Selecting specific tracks within genres, however, has been more subjective on my part. Any number of tracks might be substituted. My goal is to present a collection of tracks sufficiently diverse that they represent a wide range of aesthetic and practical approaches to making records.

THEORY

Whenever someone says, "Talking about music is like dancing about architecture," they seem to mean it pejoratively. I don't know why. Dancing about architecture shows imagination. And every music lover talks about music, sometimes a lot. But it is difficult to describe music's sound and sensory effect with precision using only adjectives. That's where theory and detailed analytic description come in. Music theory—which for records encompasses principles of sound engineering—gives us tools to better apprehend, understand, and communicate what the music makes us feel.

The first chapter of *Rock on Record* is devoted to some basic theory concepts and language, but those concepts are not intended for abstract speculation. They will be put to practical use. They will help make track descriptions more precise and streamlined. In guiding listeners through the tracks, some technical language will actually simplify the process.

THE GUIDES

How should you use the listening guides? First, just listen. Familiarize your ears with the track, and then read the description. It will highlight key elements of the track's character, but the explanation will need sonic illustration. Use the guide's time markers to locate the specific moments referred to in the track description and familiarize your ear with that sound or concept. Get to know the track in detail. Its words and melody are easily apprehended and can serve as a map. Listen to how the words and melody articulate the narrative structure, the form. Is there a chorus that repeats periodically? Is there a bridge that takes the music momentarily in a different direction? Is there a refrain that recurs through the track?

Listen to the arrangement of the instruments. What sounds do you hear? What "color" are they? Are they bright? Dull? Mellow? Strident? Do they stand out or blend together? Listen to the mix. Are the instruments balanced? Are some more prominent than others? Is the range of frequencies balanced? Or are some mixes heavy in the low-end (the bass), while others favor the high-end for a brighter overall sound? If the track is stereo, where in the stereo field are the sounds located? Do they move around?

Listen to the groove. A track's rhythmic character accounts for much of its feel. Listen to the words. They tell some sort of story, but they are also sounds in themselves. Sometimes their "song sense" may sound like nonsense in a more literal context. But songs change the function of words and can change their meaning as well. Listen to the voice. It is the focal point for most records. What sort of character does it portray? What is its emotional tone?

Once you have absorbed the details, follow the guide as the track plays through, like a musical score. It will remind you of the things you've been studying and thinking about. Finally, put the guide away and just listen. Listen closely, but go with the music's flow. You'll find that you are more attuned to what the track offers. The recorded musical image is dynamic and ever fluid. The sensory experience, even for a relatively simple track, is complex when heard in full. When we really *listen* to records, our ears take in a web of sound made up of words, voices, melody, rhythm, harmony, timbre, reverb (space), and myriad effects of electronic processing all unfolding interactively. It's a lot. It requires skill. Crossing the perceptive threshold from hearing to listening demands that we pay attention. Take some time to do that. The effort will easily pay for itself.

The numbers in parentheses in the listening guides refer to numbers of bars. The chart numbers are all *Billboard* charts. The changing names reflect the magazine's different chart terminology over time, but all refer to retail sales. These are the ones referred to here.

Pop Charts	R&B Charts	Country Charts
Popular Records: Best Sellers in Stores Hot 100 Top LP's Top Pop Albums Billboard 200 (album)	Best Selling Retail Race Records R&B Records: Best Sellers in Stores Hot R&B Sides Hot R&B Singles Hot R&B LP's Top Selling R&B Singles Top Selling R&B LP's Best Selling Soul Singles Best Selling Soul LP's Hot Soul Singles Soul LP's Hot Rap Songs Top R&B Albums	Country and Western (C&W) Territorial Best Sellers, Memphis C&W Best Sellers in Stores

1
FUNDAMENTALS

1.1. SOUND: ACOUSTIC • ELECTRIC

Sound is conveyed to our ears by fluctuations in air pressure caused by vibration. When a guitar string is plucked, for example, it begins to vibrate and sets air in motion. The effect of the changing air pressure on our ears is what we perceive as sound. The speed of the vibration, or **frequency**, determines our perception of **pitch**: The faster the vibration, the higher the pitch. Another way to think of it is the higher the number of vibrations, the higher the pitch. Vibration speed is measured in cycles per second, or **hertz** (**Hz**). Generally speaking, humans can discern frequencies between 18 Hz and 22k Hz. We hear this continuum in terms of distinct subsets called **ranges**, or **registers**. A choir, for example, consists of bass, tenor, alto, and soprano voices, each filling a particular pitch range from low to high.

In the electronic realm of records, frequency is represented as alternating current (AC) voltage. So a microphone capsule that "hears" the vibrating guitar string translates the information into an analogous electric current and sends it to the recording medium. Loudspeakers reverse this process, turning the current back into sound as the speaker cone vibrates. If the guitar string vibrates at 440 Hz, so will the speaker cone, reproducing the same pitch. Electronic frequency ranges are referred to as **low-end**, **mid-range**, and **high-end**.

Another fundamental property of sound is loudness, or **amplitude**. There are two ways to think about loudness: as an element of musical expression and as a function of electronic amplification. In musical performance, degrees of loudness are called **dynamics**. Musicians use dynamics to shape their performances expressively. However, there is no absolute scale of dynamics as there is for pitch. The ear is extremely sensitive to fine gradations in loudness and there is no fixed point at which we cross a threshold from soft to loud. In the electronic realm, on the other hand, a measurement system based on a logarithmic unit called the **decibel** (**dB**) tracks loudness more objectively. This method of electronic measurement allows for precise control of audio signals.

We identify sounds by their characteristic qualities. We can tell the difference between a passing car and a barking dog and a bird's song because each has a distinct quality of sound, called **timbre**. Similarly, each musical instrument has its own sonic character, or its own tone color. This is why we can tell the difference between a clarinet and a trumpet, for example, even if both are playing the same pitch at the same amplitude.

Several factors affect timbre but two are universal.

1. Overtones

    Almost all sounds are made up of many frequencies sounding at the same time. If we can discern a particular pitch in a sound (as opposed to random noise) it is because that frequency—called the **fundamental**—is louder than the rest. But there are also higher frequencies—called **overtones**—present in the sound at much lower amplitudes. Our perception of timbre depends on which overtones are present and at what amplitude.

    Timbre can be altered by manipulating a sound's overtone content. In the recording studio this is done with an **equalizer** (**Eq**), which allows the user to select specific frequency ranges to either amplify (emphasize) or attenuate (weaken). We see this at a basic level in the "bass" and "treble" controls on audio playback devices.

2. Envelope

    A sound's **envelope** describes the shape of its amplitude over time. Four parameters describe this shape: attack, decay, sustain, and release (**ADSR**). The initial onset of a sound is its *attack*, which brings the sound to its maximum amplitude. This is followed immediately by *decay*, during which the amplitude falls to a level at which it *sustains* until it begins to die away in the *release* phase. The attack phase is especially important in identifying timbre (see figure 1.1).

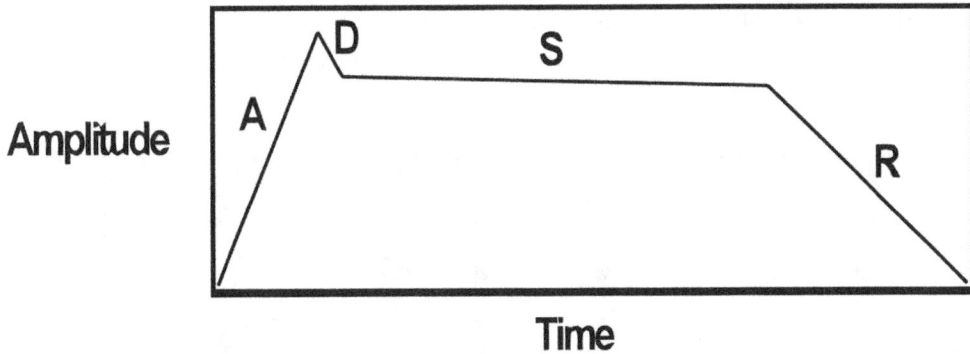

Figure 1.1. Envelope.

1.2. FROM SOUND TO SONG: SCALES • MELODY • RHYTHM • HARMONY • FORM

Records are rock music's primary medium of musical composition and **songs** are the essential ingredient of most records. (Purely instrumental rock music comprises only a tiny portion of the rock universe.) Songs are usually written (though often not finished) prior to recording. They can be arranged for various instrumental combinations and performed in a range of styles. In other words, songs have their own identity apart from any specific recording. In fact, they can be represented without any sound at all in the form of sheet music. Let's take a look at songwriters' basic musical resources.

SCALES

From the thousands of pitches in the audible frequency spectrum (18–22k Hz), only a relative few are used for expressing musical ideas. These are named with the alphabet letters A, B, C, D, E, F, G and organized into a system of **scales**. The easiest way to hear and see a scale is to play only the white keys on the piano. Start anywhere and press eight adjacent keys in succession. You've just played a scale of some kind. Notice that in every case the eighth note sounds very similar to the first note. This is the phenomenon of the **octave**. An octave has a frequency relationship of two to one. So if we begin on the pitch at 262 Hz (the frequency referred to as "middle C"), traveling up our scale leads us to 524 Hz at the octave destination. These two pitches, although in different registers, sound somehow alike. This special property has made the octave the basis for our system of scales. Once we arrive at the octave, the scale simply repeats (see figure 1.2).

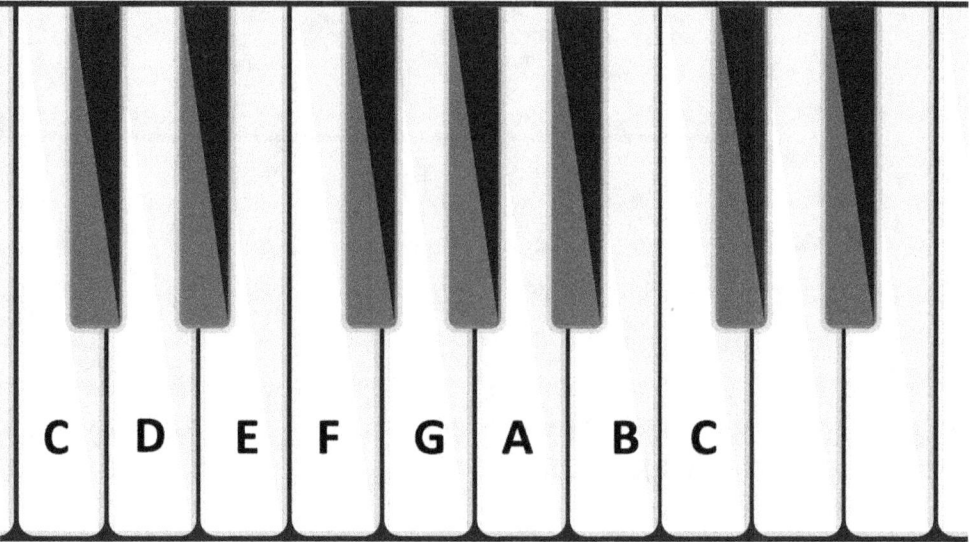

Figure 1.2. C Major Scale.

Although any series of adjacent white notes makes a scale, two scales are fundamental: **major** and **minor**. To make these scales using only the white notes, we must begin on specific pitches. My choice of C as a starting point was intentional. This is the only note from which a white-note major scale can be launched.

Similarly, playing successive white notes starting on A will produce a minor scale (see figure 1.3).

Note that each scale is named for the pitch it begins on. These pitches identify the scale and the **key**, a system of relationships among the scale's seven different pitches. The first pitch is called the **tonic**, and it is the key's center of gravity.

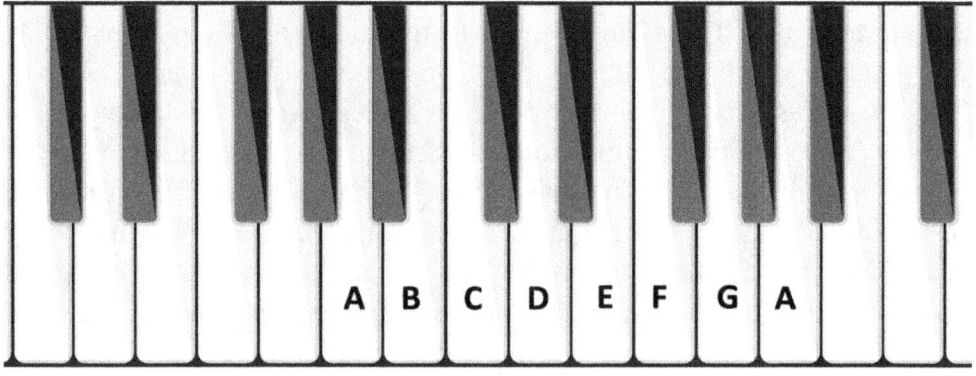

Figure 1.3. A Minor Scale.

MUSIC NOTATION

We can and do refer to letter names when talking about music, but it's often easier to use a picture (see figure 1.4).

Figure 1.4. The Grand Staff.

Pitch notation is written on a five-line **staff**, where each line and each space represents a note. A **clef** at the left-hand margin of each staff indicates how the staff is to be read. The same lines and spaces can represent different notes depending on which clef is indicated. The two most common clefs are treble (figure 1.5) and bass (figure 1.6).

Figure 1.5. Treble Clef.   Figure 1.6. Bass Clef.

INTERVALS

The distance between any two notes is called an **interval**. If we move between two successive letters of the alphabet—A to B, say—we traverse an interval of a second. A distance of three letters—A to C—is a third. A to D, four letters, is a fourth, and so on until we reach the octave, A to A. The interval between successive notes in a scale is a second because scales always move to the next letter in the alphabet. But notice on the piano keyboard that there are two kinds of seconds. Moving from A to B requires jumping over a black note, while B to C does not. So A to B is a larger interval than B to C. These two kinds of seconds are called whole steps (from A to B) and half steps (from B to C). Half steps, the smallest interval in our tuning system, are the units by which all intervals are measured.

Interval Chart

Interval Name	Half Steps
Half step	1
Whole step	2
Minor third	3
Major third	4
Perfect fourth	5
Augmented fourth/diminished fifth	6
Perfect fifth	7
Minor sixth	8
Major sixth	9
Minor seventh	10
Major seventh	11
Octave	12

Let's return to our major (figure 1.7) and minor (figure 1.8) scales. Looking at the keyboard, notice that each scale has a specific sequence of whole (W) and half (H) steps.

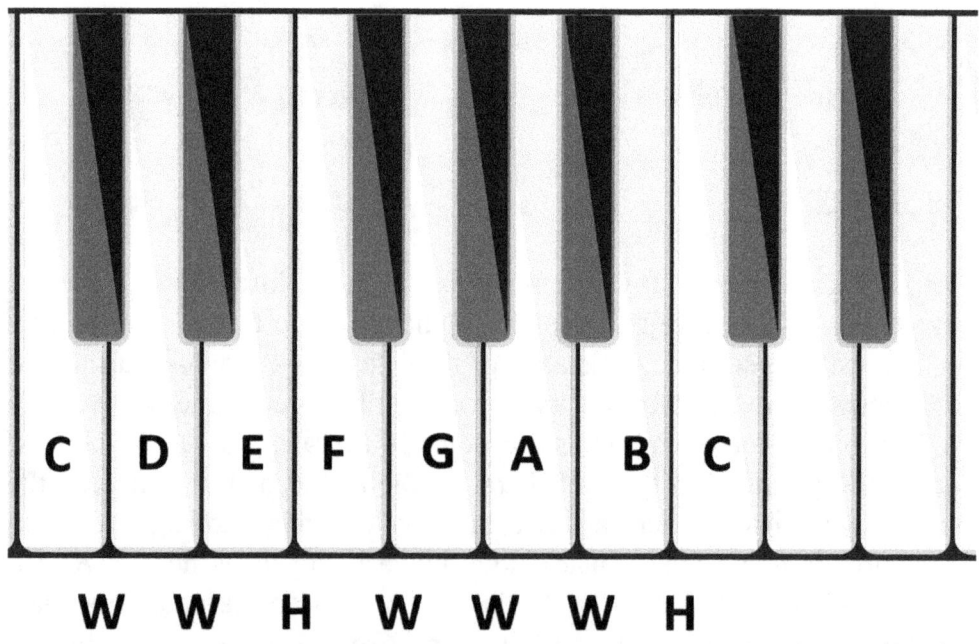

Figure 1.7a. C Major.

Figure 1.7b. C Major.

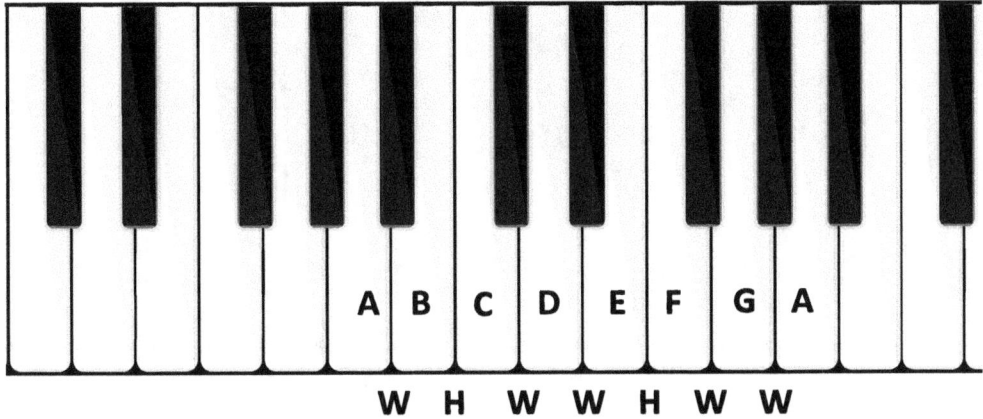

Figure 1.8a. A Minor.

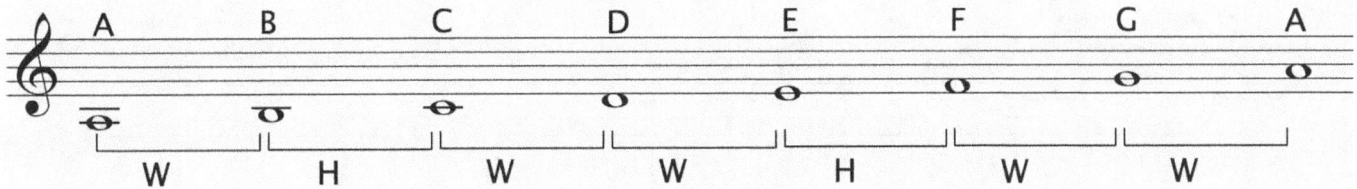

Figure 1.8b. A Minor.

What about the Black Keys?

Our tuning system in Western music divides the octave into twelve notes, each separated by a half step. Notice, however, that there are only seven white keys. The five black keys give us the full set of twelve pitches that we need. (The distance between any two adjacent keys on a piano, or one fret on a guitar, is a half step.)

As we have seen, we use only seven of these notes to make our major and minor scales. But since a scale may be built starting on any note in the octave, the white keys alone do not provide enough resources to follow our scale patterns for any scales except C major and A minor. Moving a whole step up from E, for example, requires that we move past the white key F to land on the black key above it: F♯. We use the same letter to name this note but modify it with the symbol ♯ to indicate that it is one half step higher than the white note F. The symbol is called a **sharp**.

Black keys may attach to the white note on either side, so the black key that gives us F♯ also gives us G♭. The ♭ symbol is called a **flat**, indicating that the named note has been lowered by a half step. Whether the note is F♯ or G♭ depends on the musical context. As far as making scales is concerned, just remember that every alphabet letter must be used. Given seven letters to name seven scale degrees, none may be repeated or omitted. So if the next letter in the scale is F and the scale pattern lands us on F♯, there's no way we could call it a G♭, even though it's the same piano key.

Canceling a sharp or a flat to make the note a **natural** is indicated with the symbol ♮.

Because scales are defined by their interval patterns, we can begin on any note, and if we follow the major scale pattern, the scale will sound the same as C major. Moving the pattern to another note is called transposition. Let's **transpose** the pattern to G and build a G major scale (see figures 1.9a and 1.9b).

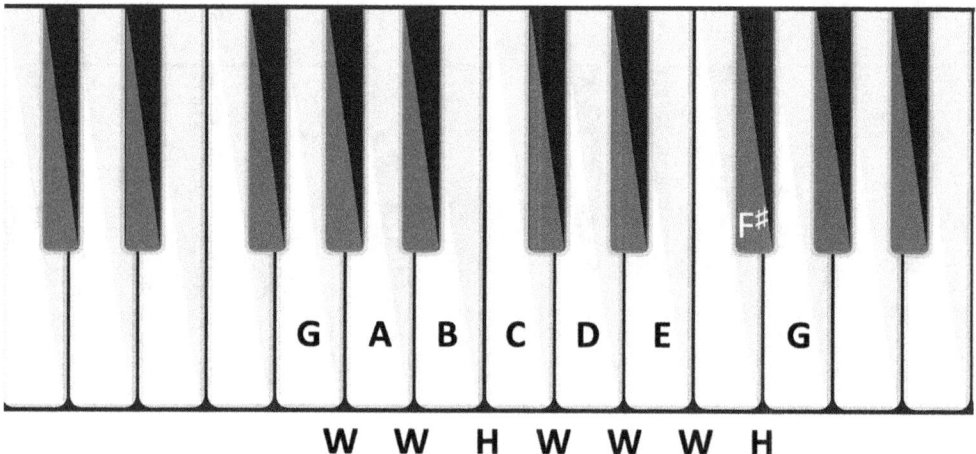

Figure 1.9a. G Major.

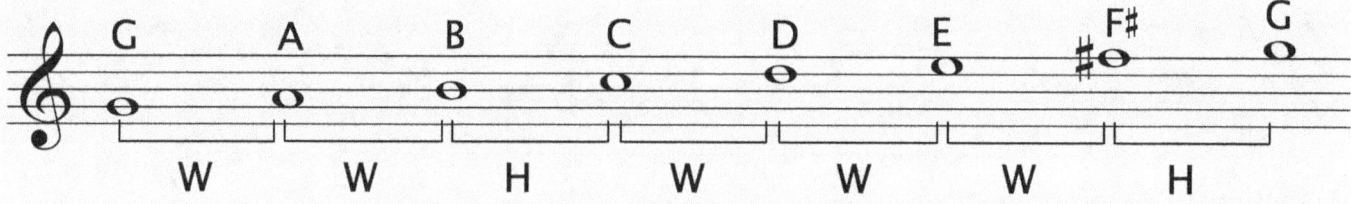

Figure 1.9b. G Major.

Notice that in order to maintain the pattern we have to add a black key. We still follow the alphabet, but when it becomes necessary to include a black key, we alter the pitch name from F to F♯.

Let's build a major scale starting on F (see figures 1.10a and 1.10b).

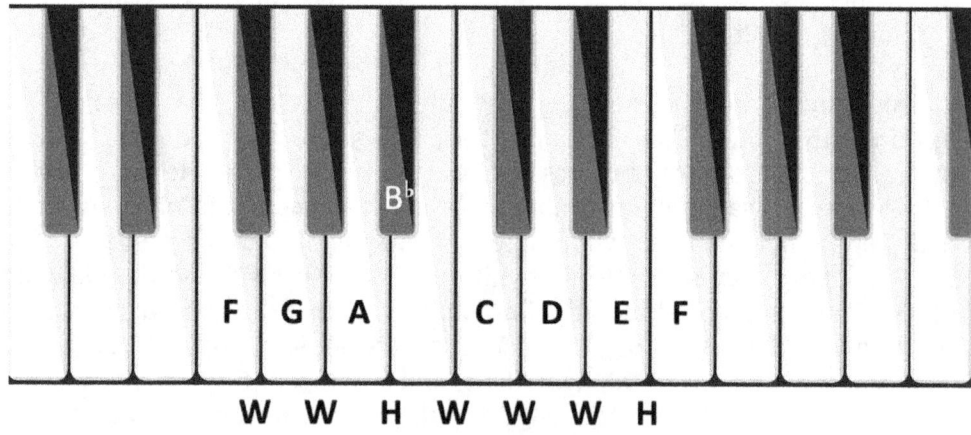

Figure 1.10a. F Major.

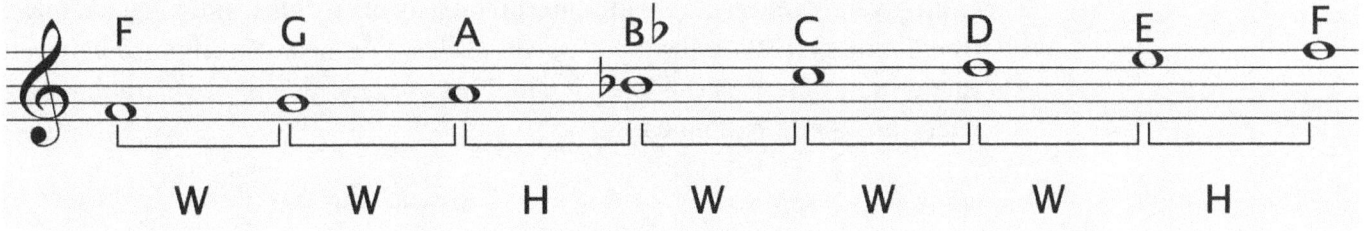

Figure 1.10b. F Major.

This time the scale pattern required lowering the B by a half step to B♭.

Similarly, if we want to make a minor scale, we simply follow the minor scale interval sequence of W–H–W–W–H–W–W. Let's make a minor scale starting on C (see figures 1.11a and 1.11b).

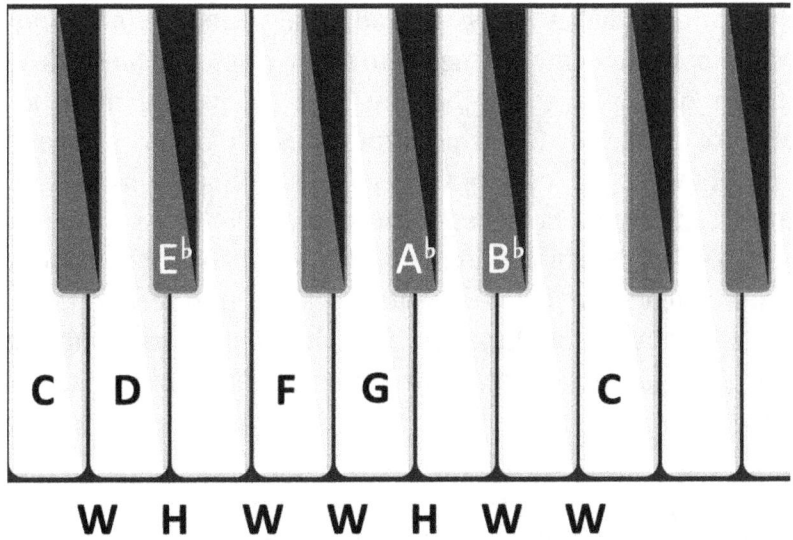

Figure 1.11a. C Minor.

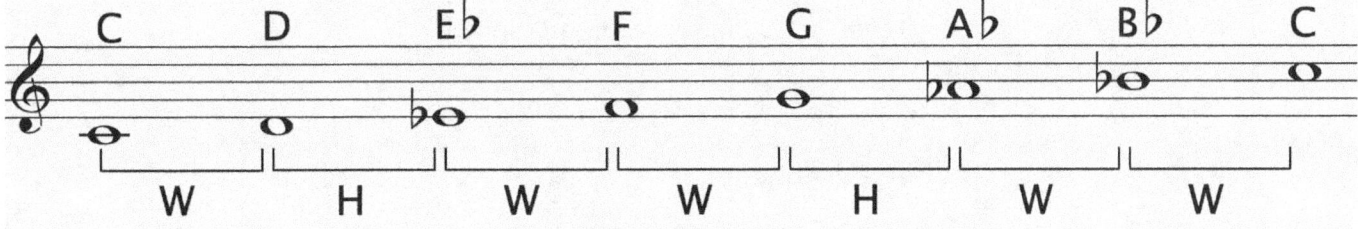

Figure 1.11b. C Minor.

Notice that the scales for major and minor keys have a different overall quality, or a different mood. Describing these is subjective. Even though it may be generally accurate to say that major keys seem brighter whereas minor keys seem more melancholy, there are many exceptions.

And given listeners' differing interpretations of "bright" and "melancholy," the distinction is tough to pin down. Still, we do hear a difference between major and minor. Perhaps their qualities are best defined by actual songs. Here are some examples.

Major Key Songs
Chuck Berry, "Rock and Roll Music"
Everly Brothers, "All I Have to Do Is Dream"
Beach Boys, "I Get Around"
Miracles, "The Tracks of My Tears"

Minor Key Songs
Rolling Stones, "Paint It Black"
Stevie Wonder, "Superstition"
Beatles, "Eleanor Rigby"
Marvin Gaye, "I Heard It through the Grapevine"

Blues

Rock music uses various pitch resources in addition to major and minor scales, the most important being pitches borrowed from the blues. The blues is an African American genre that has had a powerful influence on popular music of all sorts. Blues performers use a complex palette of pitches, many of which do not correspond to any notes on a piano keyboard. Roughly speaking, however, if we lower the third, fifth, or seventh scale degrees of a major scale by a half step, we get a blues feeling. These new pitches do not necessarily replace the normal third, fifth, and seventh. But whether they appear on their own or alongside the normal major scale pitches, these **"blue notes"** create a bluesy flavor (see figure 1.12).

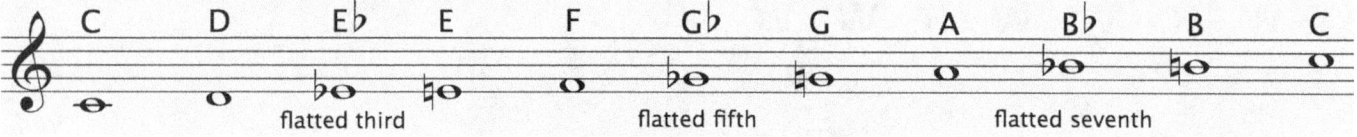

Figure 1.12. Blue Notes in a C Scale.

PENTATONIC

Another scale commonly used in rock is the **pentatonic**, which has a major and a minor version. As the *penta* suggests, these are five-note scales. Both the major and minor pentatonic omit half steps. In the case of the major, that means leaving out scale degrees four and seven (see figure 1.13). The minor pentatonic omits scale degrees two and six (see figure 1.14).

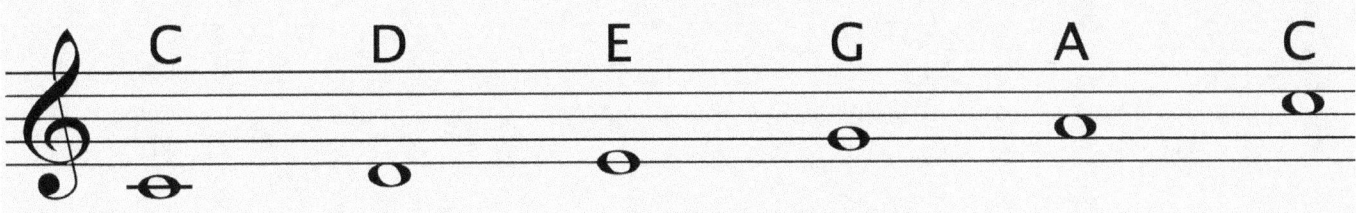

Figure 1.13. Major Pentatonic in C.

Figure 1.14. Minor Pentatonic in C.

MODAL PITCH RESOURCES

In addition to the notes provided by major, minor, and blues scales, rock songs sometimes use other scales known as **modes**. We know that white-note scales beginning on C or A produce a major or minor scale. These are also termed "major modes" and "minor modes" and are occasionally given the Greek names Ionian and Aeolian, respectively. But what about the white-note scales that begin on other notes? Like those on C and A, the scales beginning on D, E, F, G, and B each have a specific pattern of whole and half steps and thus their own character and name. Two of these modes—starting on F and G—are essentially major scales with one altered scale degree. And two others—starting on D and E—are minor with one altered scale degree. To see where the whole and half steps fall in each of the modes, simply look at the piano keyboard.

A white-note scale built on F, which is called the Lydian mode, has the pattern W-W-W-H-W-W-H. If we transpose that pattern to start on C, we can easily compare the major and the Lydian scales. They are the same except for one note, the fourth scale degree, which is raised by a half step (see figures 1.15 and 1.16).

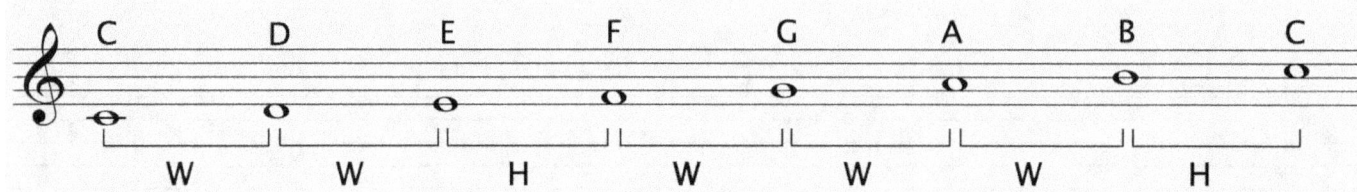

Figure 1.15. C Major.

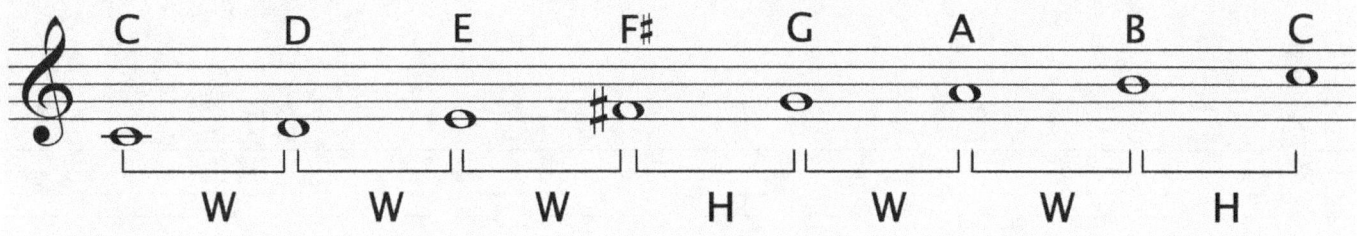

Figure 1.16. C Lydian.

Similarly, a white-note scale beginning on G produces the Mixolydian mode. The Mixolydian interval pattern is W–W–H–W–W–H–W, which is similar to a major scale but with a lowered seventh scale degree (see figure 1.17).

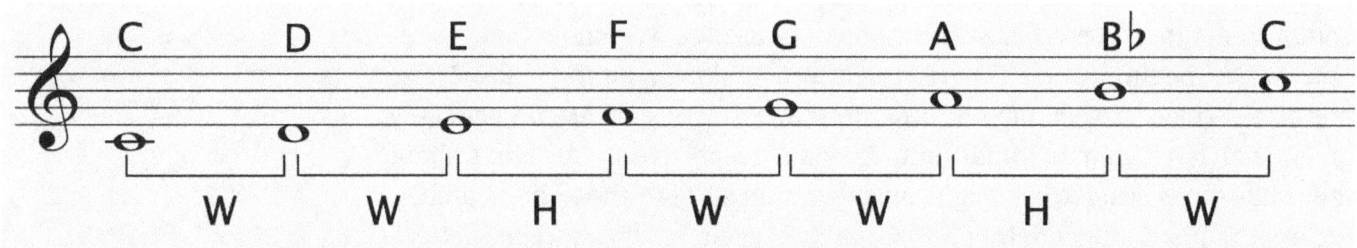

Figure 1.17. C Mixolydian.

Songs may have an exclusively modal feel. But often a song is basically in major or minor and occasionally borrows from a mode to create a particular effect. Because Lydian and Mixolydian modes sound so much like major scales, they may expand the pitch resources for a major mode song, offering a temporary raised fourth or flatted seventh scale tone. We can think of these as Lydian or Mixolydian inflections.

The Dorian and Phrygian modes sound similar to the minor mode, again with one note altered (see figures 1.18–1.20).

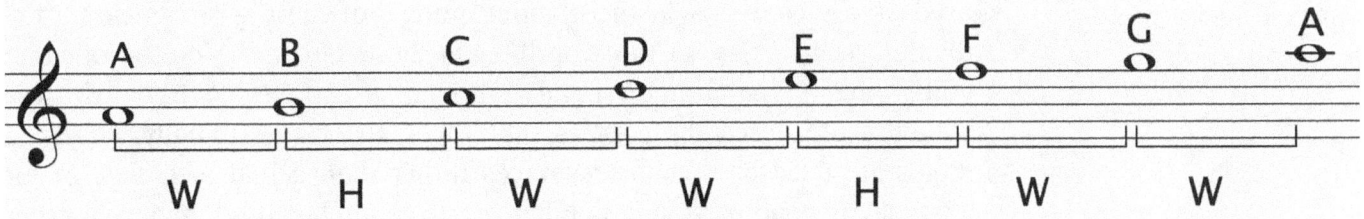

Figure 1.18. A Minor.

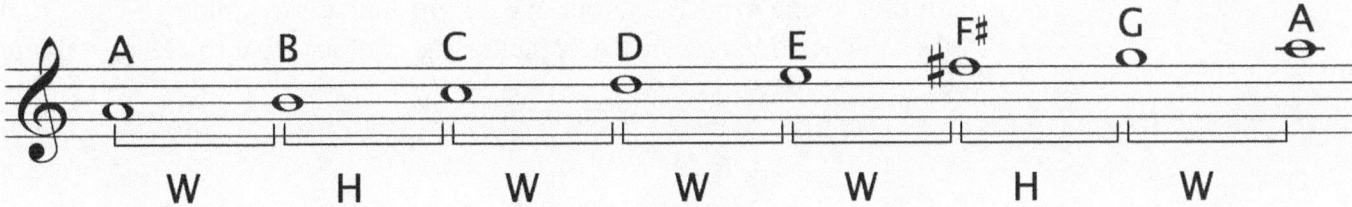

Figure 1.19. A Dorian.

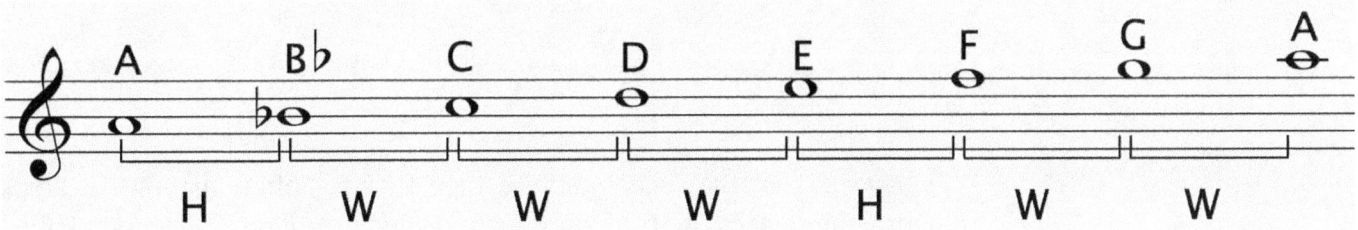

Figure 1.20. A Phrygian.

The last of the seven modes is the Locrian mode, built on the seventh scale degree. This mode is rarely used, and you will not encounter it among the tracks in this book. Notice, however, its unique quality. While every other mode has an interval of a *perfect* fifth (seven half steps) between scale degrees one and five, Locrian has a diminished fifth (six half steps). The tonal stability provided by the typical relationship between one and five in any key or mode is absent in the Locrian (see figure 1.21).

Figure 1.21. B Locrian.

MELODY

A **melody** is a sequence of notes sounded one at a time. A scale can be used as a melody, as in the opening phrase of the Christmas carol "Joy to the World" ("Joy to the world! / The Lord is come") or the opening guitar line in the Grateful Dead's "Friend of the Devil." Both of these melodies are descending scales that cover an octave. Usually, however, scales are used as melodic resources rather than actual melodies. If, for example, instead of simply playing the scale pitches in alphabetical order we invent our own sequence—let's say C–F–E–G–A–B–G—we are using the resources of the C scale to create our own melody. As a melody unfolds, it forms a line whose contour moves up and down among higher and lower pitches. Musical notation makes the contour easy to see (see figure 1.22).

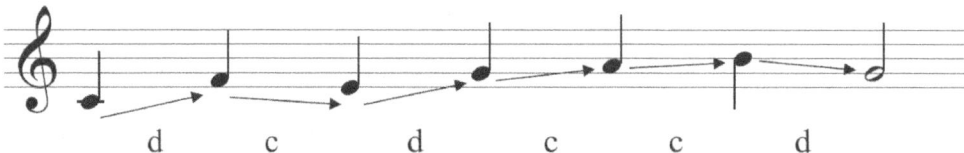

Figure 1.22. Melodic Contour.

Notice, too, that the intervals vary in size, often moving in steps but other times by a third or fourth. Melodic motion by step is called **conjunct motion**; motion by larger intervals is called **disjunct motion**. Effective melodies usually contain a mix of both kinds of motion. Conjunct motion gives the feeling of a smooth flow, while disjunct motion breaks the regularity and often provides a dramatic surprise.

Let's sing a familiar melody, "Happy Birthday." In addition to noticing the melodic direction and type of motion, notice the pacing. When we sing this tune, we all take a breath after "to you." The melodic fragment corresponding to the words "Happy birthday to you" is called a **phrase**. Though not a complete musical statement, a phrase represents a coherent musical thought. The pause in which we take a breath is the punctuation between phrases. Much like prose, where word phrases make sentences and sentences make paragraphs, musical statements string together shorter phrases into longer phrases and longer phrases into complete musical statements (see figure 1.23).

If the musical breath that marks phrase endings is analogous to a comma in prose, the ending of a larger musical segment, called a **cadence**,

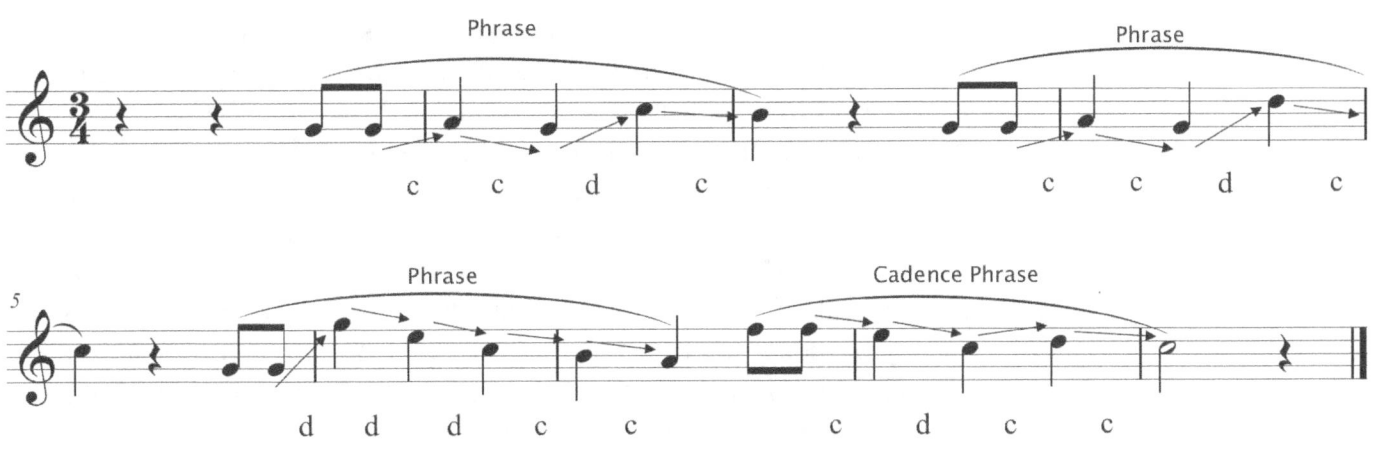

Figure 1.23. "Happy Birthday."

is similar to a period. A cadence marks the end of a complete musical statement and feels like a point of arrival. In "Happy Birthday," the end of the fourth phrase is the cadence. Notice, too, that the final note of the melody is C, the same as the scale the melody is based on. This is the primary note of the key. It serves as a kind of gravitational center, which is why we get a feeling of arrival and closure at the cadence. The primary pitch of any key (which is the pitch the scale begins and ends on) is called the tonic.

RHYTHM

It takes more than pitches to make the tune for "Happy Birthday." The song unfolds over time according to a specific **rhythm**. Just as we organize the frequency spectrum into discrete pitches, we can mark the passing of time with a steady **beat**. This establishes a **tempo** (speed) and a feeling of regularity. Accenting beats at regular intervals provides a further degree of organization, called **meter**. The groups of beats falling between **accents** are called **measures**, or **bars**. The first beat of each bar—the one with the accent—is the strongest. It is called the **downbeat**. Accents have an implied hierarchy. The downbeat of a four-beat measure is the strongest, the third beat is somewhat less strong, the second and fourth beats are the weakest, and any note occurring between the beats is weaker still. If the music places accents on weaker beats or between beats, these accents are referred to as **syncopation**.

Four-beat meter (4/4): | 1 2 3 4 | 1 2 3 4 | 1 2 3 4 |
Three-beat meter (3/4): | 1 2 3 | 1 2 3 | 1 2 3 |

Meter provides a foundation over which specific rhythms play out in terms of **attack** (when a note starts) and **duration** (how long it lasts). In "Happy Birthday," most attacks fall on beats but the syllable "-py" falls between beats two and three. So the two syllables "hap-" and "-py" both occur in the space of one beat. The duration of each is one half of a beat. The note durations for the syllables "birth-day to you" each last one full beat. The pause for breath at the end of each phrase is marked by one beat of **rest**. By convention, the notes of one-beat duration in "Happy Birthday" are called quarter notes; the ones of half-a-beat duration are called eighth notes. Following this logic, whole notes last four beats and half notes last two beats. Further subdividing the quarter-note beat produces triplets (three to the beat) and sixteenth notes (four to the beat).

Figure 1.24. Note Values.

GROOVE

Groove is a general rhythmic feel created by a repetitive rhythmic pattern. Listen to Fats Domino's "Blueberry Hill." When the singing starts, the piano plays a continuous string of notes grouped three to a beat. These beat **subdivisions** are called **triplets**. Although only the piano plays constant triplets, the feel of the groove permeates the track. Listen to how the bassline locks in with the piano even though it does not play every triplet. And although the saxophones play primarily notes of long duration rather than triplet subdivisions, when they do move melodically, they too line up with the triplet groove. We can hear this during the phrase "The wind in the willow played" (0:53).

The other common groove subdivision is the **duple** feel created by subdivisions of two (eighth notes) or four (sixteenth notes) attacks per beat. Although both two and four are duple subdivisions, they feel quite different. Listen to the opening guitar riff on Neil Young's "Heart of Gold." The first six strums are all eighth notes, announcing the song's underlying groove with which all the other parts align, most noticeably, the vocal melody.

Contrast this with the four-note subdivisions of the Sister Sledge track "He's the Greatest Dancer." Listen to the opening guitar riff playing constant sixteenth notes, with varying accents. This extra action between the beats gives the groove an urgent energy typical of funk music. Listen also to the accompanying rhythm guitar (right side in the stereo field) playing syncopations that line up with the underlying sixteenth-note groove.

Sometimes the groove is temporarily suspended, leaving space to highlight a voice or instrument or to punctuate the musical form. This technique is called **stop-time**. Listen to Little Richard's "Tutti Frutti." In the last four bars of each verse ("She rock to the east"; "She knows how to love me"), the band plays only a short downbeat on each bar, leaving the voice otherwise unaccompanied.

Rocking Rhythm

The essential rhythmic element of rock and roll is the **backbeat**. The backbeat rhythm places a strong accent, usually with the snare drum, on beats two and four, which are normally the weaker of the four beats in a 4/4 measure. Accenting two and four propels the music forward.

HARMONY

When any two or more pitches sound simultaneously, they produce **harmony**. Like scales, harmony involves patterns of pitch organization. Random note combinations will not give us attractive vocal harmonies such as those on the Everly Brothers' "All I Have to Do Is Dream" or the Beatles' "Nowhere Man." The notes must be arranged in specific ways to make pleasing sounds, which are called **consonances**. More than simply pleasing, however, consonances provide a sense of tonal stability. Some note combinations, by contrast, sound unsettled and in certain contexts, harsh. These are called **dissonances**. Both consonances and dissonances are important for creating musical interest.

The opening of the piano ditty "Chopsticks" is a good example of consonance and dissonance working together. The opening is a dissonant interval (a major second) repeated six times. It is followed by a consonant interval (a third). This musical gesture has a feeling of tension followed by resolution. As the dissonant interval repeats, it becomes slightly grating and we anticipate its move to a more pleasing sound. In creating this sense of anticipation, the dissonance drives the music forward. As we shall see, however, dissonance is not always a source of harmonic instability. It can also produce a range of rich harmonic colors.

When three or more pitches sound together, it produces a **chord**. The basic chords of songwriting are consonant three-note combinations called **triads**. The successive notes in a triad are separated by the interval of a third. So, a C triad has the pitches C–E–G, a G triad has the pitches G–B–D, and so forth. Chords are linked together in a harmonic sequence or **chord progression**, providing a sense both of forward motion and of shifting harmonic color.

Every note in a scale can be the basis, or **root**, of a triad. But because of the patterns of whole and half steps that make up a scale, triadic structures vary. Looking at the piano keyboard, count the half steps between the lower two notes of triads built on C and D. The third from C to E is made up of four half steps. The third from D to F is three half steps. The larger interval, a major third, is the basis of a major triad (see figure 1.25). The smaller one, a minor third, is the basis a minor triad (see figure 1.26). Like major and minor keys, major and minor triads have their own distinct feel.

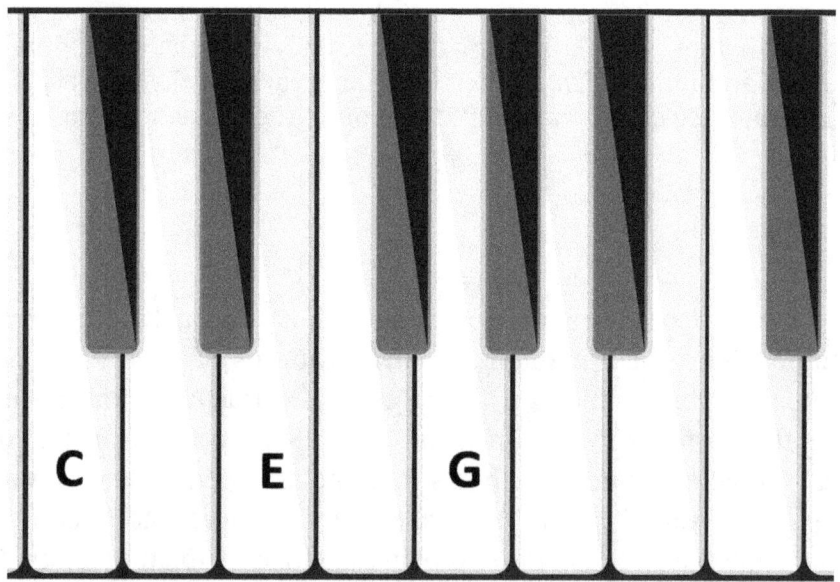

Figure 1.25. C Major Triad.

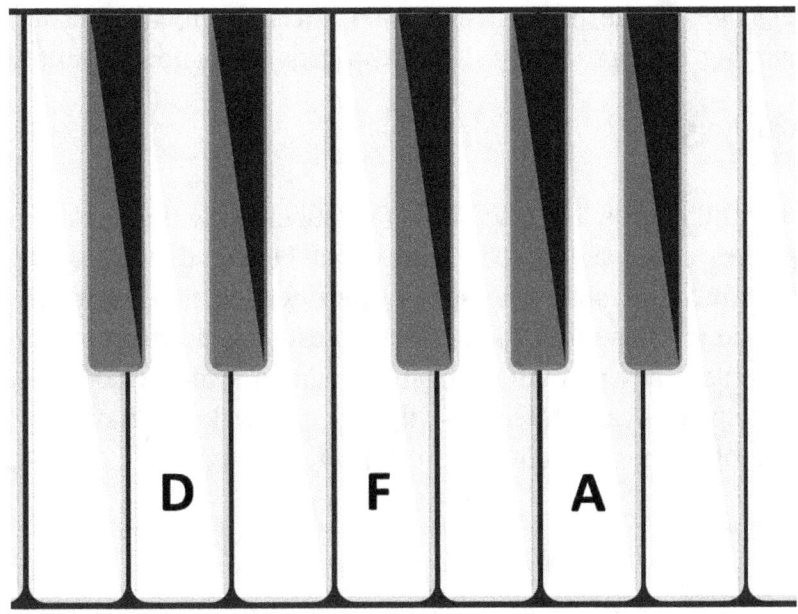

Minor 3rd + Major 3rd

Figure 1.26. D Minor Triad.

Chords are often named by a number corresponding to their root's position in the scale. Distinctions between major and minor chords are made with upper- and lowercase Roman numerals. In major keys, chords built on scale degrees one, four, and five are major (I, IV, V). Chords built on scale degrees two, three, and six are minor (ii, iii, vi). The outlier chord is the one built on scale degree seven, which is made up of two minor thirds. This type of chord is called **diminished** (vii°).

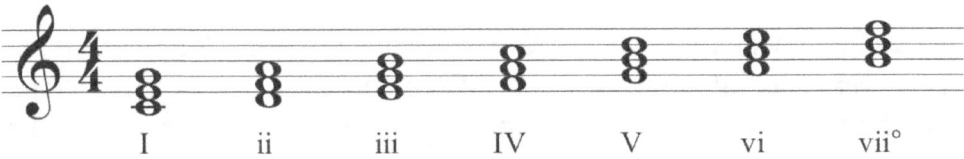

I   ii   iii   IV   V   vi   vii°

Figure 1.27. Triad Notation.

While triads are songwriters' fundamental harmonic building blocks, chords often contain more than three notes. In general, the extra notes result from stacking up more thirds. So, the triad C–E–G, for example, could gain a B and become C major 7 (B is a seventh away from C). But adding a B, or any other note, to the C triad will create a dissonance with one or more of its basic constituents. What effect this will have in the music depends, as always, on context. Dissonance will always provide a further color to the triad. It may also affect the tonal direction of the song, pushing it more strongly toward a cadence or toward another key.

CHROMATICISM

The scales and chords described thus far all belong within a circumscribed set of pitches called a **key**. The notes that belong to the key are called **diatonic**. But as we shall see, songs often employ notes that do not fall within the key. These non-diatonic notes are called **chromatic**. As their name suggests, they can add a dash of color to a melody or chord. They can also displace scale notes to establish a new key. Changing keys in the course of a song is called **modulation**.

FORM

Form is the structure of the musical narrative. It provides coherence and a sense of logic. The three key principles that govern all forms are repetition, variation, and contrast. Repetition is an exact restatement of a melody, rhythm, or harmonic pattern; variation is restatement but with some difference; contrast is a move into new territory. As we hear these strategies in action, we discern discrete sections within the larger piece. This sense of organization in the musical flow helps listeners make sense of the unfolding narrative. While there are innumerable ways of using the three formal principles to create a coherent design, there are several conventional patterns that are fundamental. Let's take a look at a few song forms that we will encounter often and see how they are shaped by repetition, variation, and contrast.

VERSE-CHORUS

In a **verse-chorus** form such as James Taylor's "Fire and Rain," the music of the verses is different from that of the choruses. We hear the verses and choruses as separate, contrasting sections, yet we understand that both are part of the same song. The way we make sense of the song depends in part on recognizing that the music of the verse and chorus alternate with each other so that the song's structure is based on both repetition and contrast.

When we include the song's lyrics, a more nuanced picture emerges. In each verse the music repeats but the lyrics are different. This technique is itself a common song form known as **strophic form**. Since the music for the verses repeats but the words do not, each verse represents a variation on the initial idea. Each chorus ("I've seen fire"), on the other hand, repeats both words and music. With all three structural principles at work, the song is a good illustration of the flexible and layered nature of form.

AABA

Another common song form is the **AABA** pattern. An initial idea (**A**) is presented and then essentially repeated, though usually with some variation, at least in the lyrics. Often, the two initial **A** sections make a single large section by varying their final cadences. The first **A** ends on a V chord, which preserves forward momentum, while the second **A** comes to rest on the tonic. The **B** section, also called the **bridge**, provides a contrast, followed by a return to **A**. The typical **AABA** form is thirty-two bars long, eight for each section. Frankie Lymon and the Teenagers' "Why Do Fools Fall in Love" is a good example.

Many rock songs, however, use the **AABA** design but alter the conventional proportions and length. The Beatles' "A Hard Day's Night" extends each **A** section to twelve bars but keeps the bridge at eight. The Five Satins' "In the Still of the Nite" adds an extra two bars to all but one of its **A** sections to make room for a repeated **refrain** (words that recur throughout the song). And the Shirelles' "Will You Love Me Tomorrow," while keeping equal proportions among the sections, elongates the entire form to sixty-four bars by doubling the length of each section.

BLUES

Although blues originated as a rural music whose design was largely created in the moment, in its urbanized form certain conventions emerged. The blues forms that we will encounter consist of twelve-bar choruses. (This usage of "chorus" is different from that of the verse-chorus form.) Each chorus follows a prescribed sequence of chords (I, IV, and V), which change at specific times in the twelve-bar pattern.

Twelve-Bar Blues Progression

Chords: ‖ I | I | I | I | IV | IV | I | I | V | IV | I | V ‖
Lyrics: | a | a | b |

Another convention of blues form applies to the structure of lyrics, which tend to follow an *aab* sequence, with the second line repeating the initial idea and the third line providing a comment or punch line. In Elvis Presley's "Hound Dog," for example, the first line is "You ain't nothin' but a hound dog." The second line repeats these words and the melody they are set to, but the chord changes to the IV. The last line, "You ain't never caught a rabbit," provides a punch line and a harmonic climax as it moves to the V chord.

A Pesky Term: *Chorus*

There are a few musical terms that can cause confusion because they may mean different things depending on context. No term has more meanings than "chorus," which may denote a large vocal ensemble, an element of musical form, or an electronic effect. Here are the uses of the term you will encounter in this book:

1. A section in a verse-chorus form that typically repeats words and music each time it occurs.
2. One iteration of an entire AABA form.
3. One iteration of a twelve-bar blues form.
4. An electronic effect.

(To eliminate at least a bit of confusion, a large vocal ensemble will be referred to as a "choir.")

Extensions of Form

Arrangements usually enhance the basic song form with added sections:

1. To kick things off, most **tracks** begin with an **introduction** (**intro**).
2. Choruses are often set up with a **pre-chorus** (Marvin Gaye, "I Heard It through the Grapevine").
3. After a chorus we often find a musical **interlude** before the beginning of the next verse (Miracles, "The Tracks of My Tears").
4. At the end of a blues chorus, a **turnaround** sets up the following chorus (Buddy Holly, "Peggy Sue").
5. A **vamp** is a kind of musical placeholder that repeats until the next large section begins (Byrds, "My Back Pages").
6. Somewhere in the course of the track, the singing usually stops to make way for an instrumental break, or simply a **break** (Shirelles, "Will You Love Me Tomorrow").
7. At the end of a track an added **coda** (Beach Boys, "God Only Knows"), a brief **outro** (Clash, "London Calling"), or an even briefer **tag** (Wanda Jackson, "I Gotta Know") often adds a finishing touch.

1.3. SONGS ON RECORD: ARRANGEMENT • STEREO • VOICE • LYRICS • SHAPING THE MIX

Songs are to records as a screenplay is to a film. They provide the essence of a narrative—its story, characters, emotional tone—but they are only starting points. They need to be fleshed out with actual sounds and enacted through musicians' performances. Like the props, actors, special effects, lighting, and camera work that bring a screenplay to life, songs are subject to treatments called **arrangements**. Arrangements indicate stylistic direction by specifying instrumentation, developing a rhythmic groove, and inventing musical parts to accompany the song. Arrangements expand the form by adding introductions, instrumental breaks, and the like. Rock arrangements also include the specific sounds and performances captured in the recording and then blended in the finished **mix**.

Let's listen to the arrangement for Paul Young's version of the Daryl Hall and John Oates song "Everytime You Go Away," a number-one hit from 1985 that clearly illustrates some of that era's common pop production techniques.

Before the song begins, the mood is set in the intro by sounds and rhythm. As the track opens, we hear a voice pleading "Don't leave me all alone," followed by the sound of a jet plane taking off. Both of these sounds reflect the song's central theme, and the voice's heavy **reverb** suggests that the protagonist inhabits the place left empty by the plane's departure. The plane sound is followed by an eruption of layered sound. As the eruption dies away, we hear individual sounds—**synthesizers**, bass, and drums. The synthesizer sounds are thick, evoking characteristics of brass and string instruments. The bass has a deep, rich quality. Many of its notes are doubled by the kick drum, intensifying the solidity of the groove. The snare drum gives a bright edge to what is otherwise a warm, blooming texture. At 0:40, we hear the faint sound of a strummed electric guitar. This very quiet sound alerts the careful listener to the track's deep background. At 0:56, an electric sitar plays a fragment of melody. It's a strange twanging sound supported by a very bright piano that doubles some of its notes. The piano is "behind" the electric sitar, just adding color. But in between the sitar phrases, the piano, now more to the right of the mix, plays a phrase of its own. Finally, at 1:20, the voice begins singing the song. The intro presents a set of sounds—timbres—that are unique to this track and define its sonic landscape.

Each timbre occupies a specific range of the frequency spectrum. The bass and kick drum fill out the low-end while the snare drum sits generally in the mid-range. The rattles of its wires, however, also provide a high-frequency element. The two synthesizers are low and high relative to each other, but both fill the mix's mid-range. The piano is in a high range with a bright, brittle sound. The sounds are arranged to complement one another, making a balanced image that fills out the frequency spectrum.

Notice, too, how timbres are combined and layered to create **textures**.

1. The "eruption" sound is multilayered; most of its individual sounds are indistinguishable.

2. The bass and kick drum work together in the low-end.

3. The two synths combine to form a complex string-brass sound covering much of the mid-range.

4. The sitar line is mixed with some piano sound to provide a bit of percussive edge.

In the bigger picture, the sections of the track have their own distinguishing textures. As we move from the intro into verse one, the texture thins out; other than bass and drums, the only instruments are two synths—one playing sustained chords (a **pad**) and the other, a harp-like sound. At the arrival of the pre-chorus at 1:39, the texture begins to thicken with the introduction of a distorted electric guitar. Then, at the chorus, we're back to a full-blown texture similar to the intro but with more continual piano and sitar activity and a group of backing singers. As the track progresses, the textural ebb and flow is part of the unfolding narrative.

Timbre on records is always influenced in some way by electronic processing. Beginning with the amplification of a microphone signal, each step in the recording-mixing process involves electronic mediation. Sometimes the electronic influence is disguised to render the sound as transparently as possible. But rock records and rock performances also use electronics to create special timbral effects. "Everytime You Go Away" has an array of electronically altered timbres. Listen to the distorted guitar at 1:39, the strange guitar sound at 1:48 produced by a digital chorusing effect, or the **echoes** on the snare and kick drums produced by digital delay. The rock recording palette includes not only any instrument imaginable but any timbre that strikes the artist's fancy.

A Rock Band's Typical Timbres

1. Guitars: acoustic, electric
2. Bass: guitar, keyboard
3. Drum set: kick, snare, hi-hat, toms, cymbals
4. Keyboards: piano, organ, synthesizer, **sampler**

STEREO

Until the late 1960s, the dominant mix format for pop records was **mono** (**monophonic**), which combines all sounds in a single speaker. Since the late 1960s, however, it has been standard practice to mix records in **stereo**. Stereophonic sound reproduction uses two audio channels—left and right—which is thought to create a more life-like sound as if the musicians were playing in the room for the listener. The **stereo image** creates the impression of a field or stage. All sounds are sent to the left and right channels in some proportion to occupy a specific position on the stage. A sound assigned equally to both channels will appear in the center of the stage, and a sound panned hard right or hard left will appear on only one side of the stage; the position of sounds panned partially to the left or right depends on how much of their signal is assigned to the left or right channel.

In the intro to "Everytime You Go Away," the drums and bass are in the middle. The two synthesizers are panned in a left–right balance. The electric guitar is on the right. The electric sitar is in the center with a bit of soft piano support mixed just to its left. The much louder piano phrase that answers the sitar is on the right with its reverb tailing off to the left. The placement of sounds and their movement in the stereo field amount to a kind of choreography, which, like the track's textural sequence and song form, is another element of its narrative design (see figure 1.28).

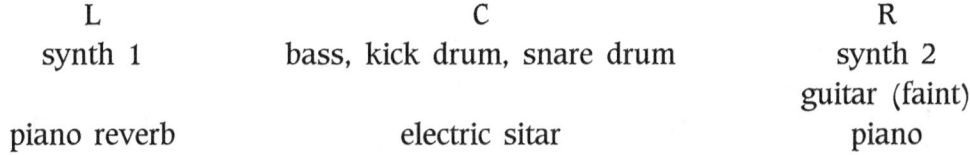

L	C	R
synth 1	bass, kick drum, snare drum	synth 2
		guitar (faint)
piano reverb	electric sitar	piano

Figure 1.28. "Everytime You Go Away": Stereo Configuration for Intro.

VOICE

Among all the sounds on a track, pride of place goes to the voice. The voice is usually placed at the center of the stereo field and all other sounds are arranged in a support role. Voices, of course, convey the song's lyrics and melody, the elements that stand out immediately to most listeners. They also present a character, both in their sound and in their performance style. Listeners are oriented immediately by certain vocal qualities they have heard before. Is it a light pop voice like Diana Ross's or a full, soulful one like Aretha Franklin's? Is it a clear, sweet voice like Paul Simon's or an intense wail like Robert Plant's? Does the singer perform in a straightforward manner like James Taylor or with stylized vocal tricks like Elvis Presley? In addition to the meaning of the lyrics, these performance qualities give listeners a sense of what the singer and the song are all about.

Paul Young's voice is high and fairly sweet but with a bit of the roughness we expect in a soul singer like Otis Redding. When white singers borrow vocal techniques and mannerisms from black soul singers, the style is often referred to as **blue-eyed soul**. (Other famous blue-eyed soul singers include Michael McDonald, George Michael, Amy Winehouse, and Adele.) In addition to the quality of his voice, Young projects the attitude of a soul singer with his free rhythmic phrasing, which seems like spontaneous reactions to the emotion of the moment. He also tends to end phrases with a **melisma** (several notes sung on a single syllable) and to interject nonverbal sounds. These are techniques of **improvisation**—music made up on the spot—which, again, heighten the sense that the singer is deeply in the moment. (Of course, these mannerisms can be memorized and repeated, but stylistically they indicate spontaneous expression.)

LYRICS

The lyrics to "Everytime You Go Away" express a feeling of loss and romantic longing. The verses explore aspects of the protagonist's state of mind while the chorus lyrics return to the central problem. The words provide a character and a story, which the singer enacts. Young sings with an earnestness, projecting a sense of yearning tinged with despair, all of which is suggested by the song's lyrics.

Songs about romantic relationships are standard pop fare. But song topics in rock expanded during the 1960s to include all sorts of other subjects. Drugs, sex, politics, war, history, spirituality, memory, and suicide have all been the subjects of hit songs. On the lighter side there is a song about a purple people eater, a wooly bully, an itsy bitsy teeny weenie yellow polka dot bikini, an octopus's garden, and walking like an Egyptian. Indeed, a rock song can be about anything or nothing at all. The Trashmen's "Surfin' Bird" and the Kingsmen's "Louie Louie" are paragons of rock nonsense. Both take existing songs and turn them into utter gibberish. The fact that they nonetheless serve as foundations for successful records is a good illustration of how rock songs work.

Because rock songs are heard primarily as records, the song, in a sense, *is* the record. Words, music, performance, and sound are inseparable. Because lyrics are only one part of this combination, their meaning is often suggestive rather than concrete. Whatever logical sense the words make, it is the sound of their enactment and the supporting arrangement that produces their ultimate meaning. In other words, the meaning of

"Surfin' Bird" can only really be inferred by listening to the record. Even a song whose lyrics are closer to poetry—Simon and Garfunkel's "America," say—imparts its full meaning through its overall sound.

SHAPING THE MIX

Record making is often likened to painting. As in the visual medium, sound colors are juxtaposed and layered to create expressive textures. The musical performances and sounds committed to tape are the materials with which engineers and producers fashion the finished work as they sit before the loudspeakers, which serve as a sounding "canvas."

Mixes have four basic dimensions that can be thought of as analogous to height, width, depth, and time. Height is equivalent to the frequency range, whether a sound is high or low. Width is the stereo field. Depth refers to a sound's relative prominence, whether it appears closer or further away from the listener. (This is partly a function of loudness, but there are other contributing factors, as we shall see.) And time refers to the unfolding musical form.

Consider the first verse and pre-chorus of "Everytime You Go Away" with these dimensions in mind. The verse is set up like this:

Frequency Range

High-end: Snare wires, voice (sibilance and "air").
Mid-range: Snare drum, synthesizers, voice (body).
Low-end: Kick drum, bass.

Notice that the voice and snare drum occupy more than one area of the frequency range. All sounds actually contain a broad range of constituent frequencies. The kick drum provides a wallop in the low-end but the sound of its beater hitting the drumhead also produces a click that may reach into the 8k Hz range, which is higher than the highest note on a piano. In the case of the snare drum, the snare wires are pitched considerably higher than the drumhead, so it has a presence in both the mid-range and the high-end. The voice, in addition to its mid-range body, produces high-frequency sibilant sounds (letters such as "s" and "t") as well as airy breath sounds that may reach above 10k Hz.

Stereo

The focus is on the center of the stereo field. The bass, kick, snare, harp-synth, and voice are all in the center. Only the pad-synth is panned off to the left and right.

Prominence

The track's depth has three receding planes:

1. Closest to the listener are the voice and snare drum.

2. Slightly behind are the bass, kick, and harp-synth.

3. In the back of the mix is the pad-synth, the softest sound

At the pre-chorus (1:39) the texture begins to change. A prominent distorted electric guitar sounds on the right of the stage, introducing an element of urgency mirroring the harmonic shift from a major to a minor key and the singer's anxious tone. Doubling the guitar on the downbeat is a piano on the left. At first the piano is less prominent than the guitar, but two bars later when it hits the downbeat again, it sounds louder, and we also notice some faint piano sound echoing on the right side of the stereo field. Finally, at 1:48, as the pre-chorus winds up to deliver the chorus, another electric guitar appears on the left with ear-grabbing loudness and distinctive electronic processing. These successive changes in texture, which mirror the song's form, are examples of the *time* element in mixing. The unfolding mix follows a similar kind of narrative logic to the song form.

STYLE

Rock on Record organizes records largely by genre—folk rock, hard rock, disco, and so forth. Each of these genres has a set of common characteristic features that add up to a recognizable **style**. To some extent every distinctive performer has a style of his or her own, but there are shared qualities that allow for broad categories. In 1960s soul music it is customary to hear a hoarse vocal quality among male singers: Think of Wilson Pickett, Otis Redding, or James Brown. Hard rock must have loud, distorted guitar sounds: Think of Led Zeppelin, Black Sabbath, AC/DC, or Metallica. Singer-songwriter music deals in intricate lyrics—Bob Dylan, Joni Mitchell, Neil Young, or James Taylor. Each of these generalizations is true because the artists and fans agree on a set of conventions that orient expectations and provide aesthetic pleasure. It was not surprising that when Jimi Hendrix convinced a club DJ to play Bob Dylan's recording of "Blowin' in the Wind"—whose arrangement consists entirely of voice, acoustic guitar, and harmonica—the dancers were not amused.

Style is defined by the configuration of elements such as timbre, vocal technique, rhythmic groove, melodic and harmonic language, and form. Most listeners sense style without consciously analyzing these elements, but the more aware we are of specific style features, the more we appreciate the ways that artists play with our expectations as they mix and match stylistic pieces to create original work. One reason the Beatles were at the forefront of rock through the 1960s was their continuing stylistic evolution. It was an intriguing surprise when they substituted a string quartet for their normal band lineup on "Yesterday" or introduced an Indian sitar on "Norwegian Wood." Likewise, when the Rolling Stones employed the classical music sound of The London Bach Choir for the intro of "You Can't Always Get What You Want," the stylistic departure invited fans on a novel musical adventure.

Style is a key factor in tracking audience response. Record firms and radio stations track activity in music markets according to broad style categories: rock, pop, country, R&B, and so forth. Charts map commercial activity in each genre, including retail, radio play, and digital downloads. When records sell in multiple markets, they are called crossover records. The crossover principle, however, is far more than a market phenomenon. As we shall see, the story of rock involves continual crossing of stylistic borders and the regular emergence of new stylistic fusions and hybrids.

2

NEW SOUNDS
Mainstream Pop

Before there was such a thing as rock and roll, big changes were already underway in American popular music, facilitated by a dramatic increase in the production and circulation of records. After World War II, record sales began to surge, with Columbia Records reporting an increase of 850 percent from 1945 to 1946 and all the other large companies showing profit gains of at least 100 percent in the same year.[1] The rapid rise in sales spurred increased record releases and record company start-ups across the country. Furthermore, as radio networks (which had provided most of the nation's programming in the form of live shows) turned their attention to the new medium of television, radio stations needed a source of programming and records filled the bill. As record making accelerated, studio culture evolved rapidly. Seeking to produce records that would stand out in the crowded marketplace, record producers pursued novel techniques that made records distinct from live performances. The relationship of the new wave of pop records to live pop performances was like that of movies to plays. Rather than simply capturing faithful snapshots of performances, studio teams worked like film crews to create musical dramas that existed only in the electronic realm.

The pop world of the 1930s and through World War II was dominated by the big dance bands and the swing style. Bands such as those led by Benny Goodman, Glenn Miller, and Duke Ellington were among the star outfits that filled dance halls and theaters around the country. In the big band scene, singers were adornments with relatively small parts to play in what was predominantly instrumental music. In the early 1940s, however, the band-singer relationship began to change, driven in particular by the surging popularity of Frank Sinatra. By the early postwar period, the situation had shifted 180 degrees. Songs were now the main attraction and singers were the biggest stars.

The language of songwriting, too, was in the midst of significant changes. Historically, America's song mill was Tin Pan Alley—not a place, literally speaking, but a term applied to the music publishing enterprise based in New York City. Popular songs of all sorts, including those for Broadway musicals and Hollywood films, were turned out by songwriters working daily at their craft. Tin Pan Alley shared a number of songwriting conventions, such as song topic, harmonic language, principles of melodic design, and musical form. For such songwriters as Irving Berlin, Cole Porter, and George and Ira Gershwin, the Tin Pan Alley style amounted to a musical language whose rhetoric they manipulated with consummate skill, creating what were considered to be classics of the pop song repertory—songs such as "Puttin' on the Ritz," "Night and Day," and "I Got Rhythm."

But many postwar pop hits fell into the **novelty** category, a catchall term referring to quirky ditties (e.g., "Too Fat Polka," "How Much Is That Doggie in the Window?") and songs that included elements of country, folk, or rhythm and blues stylings (e.g., "Tennessee Waltz," "Goodnight Irene," "A Little Bird Told Me"). Such tunes were considered inferior by Tin Pan Alley professionals, yet the public, especially the young, embraced them enthusiastically. Because these hits came out of the blue and were often the products of small, newly formed record firms (**indies**), they upset the music industry's conventional wisdom. And as they accumulated in the nation's pop consciousness, novelty songs broadened the stylistic range of the pop mainstream beyond the language of New York songwriters. As a *Billboard* commentary put it in 1961, "In a phrase: Tin Pan Alley is now the United States of America."[2]

The new approaches to record production were also considered a kind of novelty. Producers increasingly abandoned the conventions of swing style and big band instrumentation. One-off instrumental ensembles existing only for the duration of a recording session often provided arrangements devised for a single record. Or an unusual sound might become a new style feature in itself. For example, Rosemary Clooney's hit "Come On-A My House" featured a harpsichord, as did many of her subsequent up-tempo hits (e.g., "Mambo Italiano," "This Ole House"). This new focus was summed up by a somewhat baffled Bing Crosby: "Those who are now in charge of production at the various recording companies tell me that to awaken popular interest in a record they've got to produce a new 'sound': an unusual combination of instruments or voices which record buyers haven't heard before."³ In prior years, songs and performances were what sold records. Now, as Crosby observed, the key to pop success might be simply in a record's sound.

Style mixture was another way that producers created distinctive records. Elements such as rhythm, harmony, and instrumentation were lifted from particular styles and recombined as hybrid concoctions invented in recording studios. Stylistic authenticity became a moot issue as simple folk or folk-inspired songs took on lavish orchestral trappings and complex harmonies (as in Frankie Laine's "That Lucky Old Sun") and pop standards were treated to over-the-top arrangements and melodramatic performances (as in Peggy Lee's "Lover").

Finally, studio wizards captivated pop fans with what seemed like electronic magic. The manipulation of **reverb**, as on the indie million-seller "Peg O' My Heart" (1947), was a sonic thrill available nowhere in the natural acoustic world. Listeners were also fascinated by electronic echo. A record called "Mr. Echo," which featured the trick prominently, was a hit in three different versions in the summer of 1951. **Overdubbing**—adding to a performance after the fact—was perhaps the most mysterious technique of all, for it completely upended the idea of musical time. Because a musical event had always been defined by what took place during a specific period of time, overdubbing presented listeners with an impossible musical image. No one could sing multiple parts simultaneously in real time. But on Patti Page's "Tennessee Waltz," a 1950 megahit, the singer did just that.

While rock and roll would drive profound changes in popular music culture and record production during the latter half of the 1950s, the mainstream novelty pop that preceded it set in motion a volatile musical tide drifting ever further from the moorings of the swing era.

Production Tricks

Reverb, or ambience, is, in a sense, the sound of a room. It is the acoustic effect produced when a sound bounces off the surfaces in an enclosed space—a room, a concert hall, a studio. The innumerable and random sonic reflections bathe sounds in what producer Mitch Miller called a "sonic halo." Because reverb can influence the expressive character of sound, it is often manipulated to produce a particular effect.

Beginning with decisions about microphone placement, recording engineers shape a desired ambient image. (Microphones close to a source pick up more direct sound and thus less reverb; those placed further away pick up more of the room sound.) In addition to the sound of the recording space, reverb can be created and added to the sound electronically. Today this is usually done with digital reverb effects. There are also analog electronic devices for producing reverb with springs or metal plates.

The original technique for producing added reverb, however, involved the use of a second architectural space, a so-called echo chamber. An audio signal was sent to a speaker in the chamber where a microphone picked up the resulting reverb and sent it back to the mixing console to be combined with the original sound.

Echo is a repeat of a sound. The terms "echo" and "reverb" are often used interchangeably (as in echo chamber), but they are in fact different phenomena. Reverb is made of echoes, but the echoes are so numerous and random that they blend into a kind of acoustic cloud. Echoes produced in the studio are discrete copies of a sound that are created by an electronic recording (analog or digital). Echoes are clearly perceptible as sonic replicas even if they are faint (e.g., "hello, hello, hello, hello"). The effect has many uses and is a standard production device, as we shall see.

Overdubbing is a recording technique whereby performances are recorded in sequence rather than simultaneously. As a recorded performance plays, a live one is recorded "on top" of the previous one using a **multitrack** tape machine. This kind of music making was never possible before sound recording. Its defiance of the natural acoustic order fascinated listeners amazed at the sound of a person singing with herself, as Mary Ford did on her recordings with Les Paul. It began as a gimmick but would become common practice in rock record production.

Tape speed is the rate at which magnetic tape moves across the heads (erase, record, and playback) of a tape recorder. If a performance is recorded and played back at the same speed, the recording sounds like a replica of the performance. If, however, the playback speed is different from the record speed, elements such as pitch, tempo, and timbre change. A doubling of playback speed, for example, raises the pitch by one octave; halving the speed lowers the pitch by one octave. More modest speed variation has a less noticeable effect on pitch but can be a very effective timbral device.

2.1. "THAT LUCKY OLD SUN (JUST ROLLS AROUND HEAVEN ALL DAY)" (1949): FRANKIE LAINE

During a six-month period beginning in the fall of 1949, Frankie Laine enjoyed three number-one hits: "Mule Train," "The Cry of the Wild Goose," and "That Lucky Old Sun." All three were produced by Mitch Miller, who would become the most successful pop producer of the 1950s. Miller was an innovative producer always on the lookout for what he called "the sweet surprise," some kind of novel hook that would make the record stand out and catch the listener's ear. Whether manipulating musical style or electronic effects, Miller delighted in using what his critics called gimmicks to give each record some mark of distinction.

Frankie Laine was among a new breed of postwar pop singers who, though schooled in jazz singing, became famous with a more plainspoken, declamatory style. The hit repertory often consisted not of Tin Pan Alley material but of novelty songs. Laine also followed a new path to pop success: achieving overnight stardom thanks to scoring a hit record. Earlier stars developed successful show business careers through years of performances. Even once they were established enough to interest a record company, their records were considered secondary to their in-person and live radio performances. But the rapidly growing record market changed the formula. Now a complete unknown could become a coast-to-coast sensation on the strength of a single record.

"That Lucky Old Sun" is a good example of style mixture. The song has a folk-like quality in its melody and chord progression—simple and straightforward. The lyrics evoke a honky-tonk country music theme: an everyman protagonist musing on life's travails. They also have a spiritual aspect common in gospel music, a plea for transcendence of earthly worry and deliverance to a heavenly paradise. Laine enacts the everyman ethos with a full-chested, forthright performance that appears utterly sincere and authentic.

But though Laine's performance is stylistically consistent, the musical arrangement is another story. It begins with a spare accompaniment of guitar and bass appropriate to the style of the song. In verse two, however, a choir enters and then strings, woodwinds, and brass—an entire orchestra. The guitar's simple diatonic triads are overlaid with the choir's fancy chromatic harmony. Before long, what began as a straightforward folk-country presentation sounds more like a sentimental Hollywood film score.

In addition to its eclectic harmony and instrumentation, the arrangement stretches the song's form well beyond folksong conventions. In its original form, the song consists of a series of verses (each ending with a refrain) and a bridge—an easy-to-follow design. But after the track's second verse, the arrangement adds a transitional interlude that is extremely unfolk-like. Beginning with the line "right from the dawning," the choir introduces a brief chromatic flourish that sounds jarring in this context.

The form appears to get back on track when Laine comes back in with the line "weary, so weary." But rather than a new verse, this turns out to be a continuation of the interlude. Laine's phrase is followed with one from the strings and woodwinds that leads to the true beginning of verse three. In a final piece of misdirection, however, the verse begins not with Laine but with the choir. This tricky twelve-bar interlude is heard only once. It serves to break up the regularity of the form and to underscore that the track belongs to its own stylistic universe.

Listening Guide

"That Lucky Old Sun (Just Rolls around Heaven All Day)" (Haven Gillespie, Beasley Smith), Mercury (mono)
Recorded in New York City, June 1949
Frankie Laine (voice), Harry Geller Orchestra
Arranger: Harry Geller
Producer: Mitch Miller
Charts: Popular Records: Best Sellers in Stores #1
Key: D, F
Meter: 2/4

Time	Section	Lyric Cue	Listen For
0:00	**Intro** (4)		Guitar and bass play a country groove, a so-called two-step, with accents on every other beat.
0:06	**Verse 1** (16)	"Up in the morning"	Voice, guitar, and bass in a spare folk style.
0:18	Refrain	"But that lucky old sun"	
0:30	**Verse 2** (16)	"Show me that river"	Choir enters, adds chromatic harmony.
			Style begins to morph.
0:42	Refrain	"Like that lucky old sun"	Choir out.
0:51	**Interlude** (12)	"Right from the dawning"	Choir takes the lead.
			First bar overlaps last bar of previous section, like an interruption.
0:57		"Nothing but slaving"	Groove stops; increased harmonic richness in choir.
1:05		"Weary so weary"	"False" entrance; Laine seems to begin a new verse. Strings and woodwinds add yet another style layer.
1:10	**Verse 3** (16)	"Up in the morning"	Lyrics repeat **verse 1**; choir sings first line.
1:15		"Work like a devil"	Laine takes over, accompanied by oboe.
1:19			Brass flourish.
1:22	Refrain	"But that lucky old sun"	Texture is pared back to guitar, bass, and choir.
1:34	**Verse 4** (16)	"Fuss with my woman"	Woodwinds featured, especially oboe.
1:46	Refrain	"While that lucky old sun"	Choir sings lyrics, answered by violins.
1:59	**Bridge** (16)	"Good Lord above"	Violins play countermelody.
2:11		"Send down that cloud"	Voice becomes increasingly impassioned.
			Soprano voice takes over countermelody.
2:18		"Lift me to paradise"	Choir and orchestra join in crescendo; modulation to new key.
2:25	**Verse 5** (16)	"Show me that river"	New key (F).
			Lyrics repeat **verse 2**.
			Choir/string texture continues.
			Melodic and harmonic variation add to heightened emotion.
2:38	Refrain	"Like that lucky old sun"	Groove stops for dramatic finish.
			Vocal cadence is followed with a brass flourish.

2.2. "LOVER" (1952): PEGGY LEE

On a series of hits from Capitol Records during the 1940s, Peggy Lee established herself as a star among pop-jazz singers of the day. She was an adventurous performer willing to take on diverse repertory and meld styles to create her distinctive interpretations. Her career would eventually include such hits as the country-flavored "Riders in the Sky," the bluesy "Fever," and, in 1969, the half-spoken, existential cabaret number "Is That All There Is?" Her recording of "Lover" is one of the most unusual million-sellers of the early 1950s, blending chromatic orchestral textures with a busy Latin percussion section to accompany a melodramatic vocal persona bordering on delirium. The record prompted her colleague, Ella Mae Morse, herself a fine jazz singer, to comment, "I thought she must be kidding. I kept waiting for Mel Blanc [the voice of Bugs Bunny, Daffy Duck, and other cartoon characters] to come in and start purring like a cat or quacking like a duck."[4] Morse's gibe echoed a general dismay among many in the music industry establishment over the broad popularity of such melodramatic musical displays.

Inspired by a scene in a film, Lee came up with the general idea for a dramatic musical arrangement that would mirror a character's increasing emotional agitation. She wanted to impart the restlessness created by the sound of horses accelerating to a fast gallop, as seen and heard in the film. Seeking a song that might lend itself to this treatment, she settled on "Lover," written by Broadway songwriters Richard Rodgers and Lorenz Hart for the film *Love Me Tonight* (1932). The song has an unusual, even quirky, chromatic melody and chord progression, both of which descend in a series of five half steps. In its original form, "Lover" is a waltz (a 3/4 meter), and to make it fit the galloping hooves image, the meter had to be changed to 4/4. But Lee was drawn to the song for its sense of the musically exotic and its lyrics, which suited the character she sought to portray: a woman driven by passion to abandon all restraint.

Capitol Records was unwilling to record Lee's version of "Lover" because it already had a novelty version of the song in its catalog—one by Les Paul that he had made himself by overdubbing multiple guitar parts. Decca producer Milt Gabler, who had heard Lee's rendition in her nightclub show, managed to woo her to Decca with a promise that "Lover" would be a top priority. Gabler was a master producer with an ear for striking musical gestures. He produced records of all kinds in several eras of pop music, from the '30s through the '60s, including sides for Louis Jordan, one of R&B's greatest stars of the 1940s, and Bill Haley and His Comets, rock and roll's first international stars. "Over the decades," said fellow producer Jerry Wexler, "he truly understood the natural art of bending and blending genres."[5] In the early '50s, Gabler's eclectic sense was exactly in tune with the times.

Gabler assigned the arranging job to Gordon Jenkins, who had emerged as Decca's star arranger with a number of hit collaborations with the Weavers, Louis Armstrong, and the Andrews Sisters. Jenkins's arrangements were in the manner of a film score, always aiming to create a dramatic effect with expressive flourishes from orchestra and chorus.

For "Lover," he translated Lee's idea into music by using a series of rising stepwise modulations to build intensity, accompanied by a busy Latin percussion section. The song's form is a conventional thirty-two-bar AABA, which the arrangement repeats three times, changing key with each repetition. (Each of these thirty-two-bar units is called a chorus, in yet another usage of the term.) As the key rises from F to G to A♭, so does Lee's voice, which serves to heighten her character's emotional intensity.

Following this general plan, Jenkins creates a musical dialogue between singer and orchestra whereby vocal phrases are answered by instrumental ones that mirror the singer's emotional state. Lee's first chorus is fairly straightforward, though rhythmically out of sync with the orchestra. She sounds as though she is in her own world, perhaps recalling the remnants of the original waltz.

With each of the succeeding two choruses, her performance takes on more vocal mannerisms: slides, swoops, melismas, repeated words. As the track progresses, listen to the way Lee sings the word "lover" at the beginning of each A section. Her performance of that word alone, becoming wilder as the track progresses, maps the character's changing mood. The lyrics repeat with each chorus, so the focus is on Lee's evolving interpretation. Apparently beset by a rising, desperate desire, the protagonist seems to be gradually losing control of her emotions. The track's increasing urgency reaches a climax in the final B and A sections. The following coda finds the protagonist spent, murmuring a woozy "surrender" as the orchestra sweeps her away. She lets out one final cry of "Lover!" before succumbing.

Jenkins sets a turbulent scene as the track opens with a tense, rushing violin figure, joined by brash-sounding trumpets, a slapped bass, and a Latin percussion section that included such instruments as congas, bongos, and shakers. The track's general sense of delirium is enhanced by its overall sound. The recording was made at Decca's Pythian Temple studio in Manhattan, a large space in which the sounds of orchestra and percussion swim in a reverberant fog.

Listening Guide

"Lover" (Richard Rodgers, Lorenz Hart), Decca (mono)
Recorded at the Pythian Temple, New York City, May 1952
Peggy Lee (voice), Gordon Jenkins (orchestra arranger and conductor)
Producer: Milt Gabler
Chart: Popular Records: Best Sellers in Stores #3
Key: F, G, A♭
Meter: 4/4

Time	Section	Lyric Cue	Listen For
0:00	Intro (6)		Rushing violins set tense atmosphere.
0:03			Trumpets, slapped bass, percussion.
	First Chorus		
0:10	A (8)	"Lover when you're near"	Voice is out of sync with orchestra.
			Descending chromatic figures in high (primarily flutes) and low (primarily cellos) registers.
			High-register line is **staccato**; low-register line is **legato**.
			Agitated, reverberant percussion texture.
0:22			Rush of violins punctuates the section.
0:23	A (8)	"Lover it's immoral"	Violins play a series of "sighing" chords.
0:34			Full orchestra transition.
0:36	B (8)	"I say the devil is in you"	Key change.
			More stable harmony.
			Violins and cellos in **counterpoint** with voice.
0:49	A (8)	"Lover please be tender"	Back to tonic key (F).
			Similar texture to first **A**.
	Second Chorus		
1:02	A (8)	"Lover when you're near"	Key changes to G.
			Vocal phrasing is freer.
			Thinner orchestra texture focuses more attention on voice.
1:16	A (8)	"Lover it's immoral"	Descending cello line returns.
1:25			"Falling" violin line.
1:30	B (8)	"I say the devil is in you"	Key change; more stable harmony.
			New rhythmic figure in brass.
1:42	A (8)	"Lover please be tender"	Back to tonic key (G).
			Pizzicato violins play chromatic descent.
	Third Chorus		
1:55	A (8)	"Lover when you're near"	Key changes to A♭.
			Male voices sing chromatic descent.
			Meandering string lines in background.
2:08	A (8)	"Lover it's immoral"	Texture continues.
2:19			Brassy transition.

Time	Section	Lyric Cue	Listen For
2:21	B (8)	"I say the devil is in you"	Key change; more stable harmony; bolder brass texture.
2:34	A (8)	"Lover please be tender"	Back to tonic ($A^\flat$).
			Protagonist's climactic moment.
			"Lover" is elongated with an exaggerated melisma while the following lyrics are compressed into one breathless phrase.
			Orchestra, too, reaches dramatic climax with quick march-like figure, which transitions into **coda** texture.
2:48	Coda (10+)	"Surrender"	Violins and cellos play descending glissandi (a reference to the high- and low-register descending figures from first A section).
			Protagonist repeats "surrender" as if in a rapture, her sliding pitches and out-of-time rhythm add a touch of surrealism.
			Nervous trumpet figure holds the rhythmic tension as the voice seems to melt away.
3:05		"Lover!"	Stop.
			One final cry from voice and brass; final timpani roll.

2.3. "VAYA CON DIOS" (1953): LES PAUL AND MARY FORD

Les Paul was already a well-established electric guitarist with a reputation for electronic trickery when he teamed up with and eventually married singer and rhythm guitarist Mary Ford. The duo became one of the most successful acts of the early 1950s. Although he was the resident guitar virtuoso in both the Fred Waring and Bing Crosby bands in the 1930s and 1940s, Paul had been working alone since coming up with the "new sound," novel recordings that relied on overdubbing, echo, and tape speed effects. His own hit version of "Lover" (1948) is an instrumental consisting of eight guitar parts, all of which he played. When Paul and Ford began working together, she, too, became adept at overdubbing, singing along with herself in both harmony and counterpoint. Recording together in their home studio, Paul and Ford turned out numerous hit records containing the sounds of multiple guitars and voices. But no matter how rich the texture, the "band" consisted only of the two of them and a tape recorder.

Paul was a new kind of pop musician. He blended the tasks of performer and arranger with those of inventor and recording engineer. From childhood, music and electronics were his twin passions, which he brought together in one innovation after another. Before the advent of tape, he built his own disc-based recording machines, bouncing sound from one disc to another as he added overdubs. He built his own electric guitar, and his ideas went into the making of the Gibson Les Paul, which would become a signature rock guitar used by such players as Jimmy Page (Led Zeppelin) and Pete Townsend (the Who). When Paul was introduced to tape recording in the late 1940s, he devised modifications to allow for overdubbing on a single machine. In 1957 he took delivery of the first eight-track tape recorder. His would remain one of the few in existence until the recording industry finally embraced eight-track in the late 1960s.

Paul's technical innovations were extensions of his musical imagination, transforming what many considered gimmicks into musical resources. Mindful, for example, that recording and playing back at different speeds changed pitch and timbre, he manipulated tape speed to expand his arranger's palette while working with a single guitar. Recording a line at 15 inches per second (ips) and playing it back at 7 1/2 ips, he dropped the guitar's pitch by an octave, effectively turning it into a bass. The opposite technique raised the pitch beyond the guitar's normal range and created a new sound color. Paul was also fond of using tape to create echo effects, which he used in various ways to enhance a recording's texture. And, of course, the overdubbing that he and Ford raised to an art form allowed them to build recordings like a painter working at a canvas. Their pioneering work would become standard practice in the rock era.

"Vaya con Dios" was the duo's biggest seller, claiming the number-one chart position for eleven weeks in 1953. Like "That Lucky Old Sun," it has a folk feel—simple and plainspoken. Ford's performance is plaintive yet restrained. Her only overdubbing is a harmony part highlighting the song's repeated admonition—"Vaya con Dios"—which she delivers with a combination of hopeful plea and fatalistic resignation. The guitar arrangement, on the other hand, has several parts.

1. A simple rhythmic accompaniment provides the waltz-like feel.

2. A low-register line serves as a bass.

3. A lead part plays the song's melody in the intro and instrumental break and supplies harmony for the vocal melody during the verses.

4. Ornamental flourishes provide textural enhancements and a running dialogue with the voice.

The song is a farewell to a lover, bidding them to go with God. The refrain has two phrases, which repeat the song's title but with different music. In Ford's performance, each phrase also has a slightly different emotional tone. She accomplishes this effect by giving each phrase a different vocal character. In the first phrase—"Vaya con Dios my darling"—the song's main melody is taken by the higher voice of the two-voice harmony. In this phrase, which begins on the song's highest note, the upper tonic (E), Ford's performance seems to suggest a plea that her beloved take care. In the second phrase—"Vaya con Dios my love"—which descends back into the lower register, the main melody switches to the lower voice. The tone and character of this voice is more reserved, imparting a sense of resignation.

Paul mirrors this phrase contrast in the guitar arrangement. In the intro the guitar plays the vocal melody from the chorus using two distinct sounds. The first phrase is played in a high register with a subtle echo effect that disappears into the background of the mix. The second phrase is played in the low register without echo. Similarly, in the instrumental break the guitar plays the vocal melody from the verse, which is also in two phrases. For the first phrase, Paul uses a plucked **tremolo** effect (not to be confused with electronic tremolo, which is produced by rapid changes in amplitude), while the second phrase drops the tremolo in favor of simple vibrato (an expressive effect produced by rapid, minute pitch changes). By aligning his arrangement with the song's phrase structure, Paul tightens the connection among the track's various elements.

The song's form is AABA, with each section doubled from the standard eight to sixteen bars. The refrain takes up the second half of each A section. Because the refrain takes up eight bars, it might be heard as a section in its own right, a chorus in a verse-chorus form. But there is a clue that points to the AABA. Notice how the vocal melody in the refrain of A1 ends on scale degree three, while A2 ends on the tonic. A1 feels like it is leaving things open, as if to continue, which it does. A2, on the other hand, brings a sense of closure. Everything else about the melodies of A1 and A2 is the same, but this difference in their endings links the two to form one sixteen-bar section.

Listening Guide

"**Vaya con Dios**" (Larry Russell, Inez James, Buddy Pepper), Capitol Records (mono)
Recorded in the Paul/Ford home in Mahwah, New Jersey, 1953
Mary Ford (voice), Les Paul (guitar)
Producer and engineer: Les Paul
Charts: Best Popular Records: Best Sellers in Stores #1
Key: E
Meter: 3/4

Time	Section	Lyric Cue	Listen For
0:00	Intro (8)		Guitar plays vocal **refrain** melody (in two-part harmony).
			The first guitar phrase (high register) has a subtle echo effect; second phrase (low register) is dry.
			Three other guitar parts: bass, rhythm, ornamental responses.
			Voices fill background texture with two-part harmony ("ooh").
0:15	A1 (8)	"Now the hacienda's dark"	Voice is doubled by guitar playing in harmony.
			Ornamental guitar part answers each vocal phrase.
			Bass and rhythm continue as in **intro**.
0:30	Refrain (8)	"Vaya con Dios"	Vocal overdub replaces guitar harmony.
			Two phrases contrast in register and emotional tone.
			Phrase 1: High voice sings main melody.
			Phrase 2: Low voice sings main melody.
			Ends on scale degree 3 (G#).
0:45	A2 (8)	"Now the village"	Similar to **A1**, with different guitar ornamentation.
1:00	Refrain (8)	"Vaya con Dios"	Similar to previous **refrain**.
			Ends on 1 (E).
1:14	Bridge (8+8)	"Wherever you may be"	Voice sings without guitar doubling. Restrained guitar responses.
1:44	A3 (8)	"Now the dawn"	Similar to **A2**, with different guitar ornamentation.
1:59	Refrain (8)	"Vaya con Dios"	Similar to previous **refrain**.
			Ends on 1 (E).
2:14	Break (8)		Guitar plays vocal melody from **A** (in two-part harmony).
			First phrase played with plucked tremolo; second phrase played with vibrato.
			Voices fill background texture with two-part harmony ("ooh").
2:29	Refrain (8)	"Vaya con Dios"	Similar to previous **refrain**.
			Ends on 1 (E).
2:41			Guitar tag.

NOTES

1. Joe Carlton, "Columbia Profits Jumped 850% in 1946, Industry Dough Swirls for Majors," *Billboard*, March 29, 1947, 16.
2. "An Editorial," *Billboard*, January 30, 1961, 13.
3. Bing Crosby and Pete Martin, *Call Me Lucky: Bing Crosby's Own Story* (New York: Da Capo Press, 2001), 142–43.
4. Ella Mae Morse, "Terrible Thing Is Happening to Singers!" Everybody Shouts, *Down Beat*, 19 November 19, 1952, 2.
5. Jerry Wexler and David Ritz, *Rhythm and the Blues: A Life in American Music* (New York: Knopf, 1993), 63.

FURTHER READING

Laine, Frankie, and Joseph F. Laredo. *That Lucky Old Son: The Autobiography of Frankie Laine.* Ventura, CA: Pathfinder, 1993.
Lee, Peggy. *Miss Peggy Lee: An Autobiography.* New York: Donald I. Fine, 1989.
Paul, Les, and Michael Cochran. *Les Paul: In His Own Words.* York, PA: Gemstone Publishing, 2005.
Zak, Albin. *I Don't Sound Like Nobody: Remaking Music in 1950s America.* Ann Arbor: University of Michigan Press, 2010.

FURTHER LISTENING

Eddy Arnold, "The Cattle Call" (RCA Victor, 1955)
Tony Bennett, "Cold, Cold Heart" (Columbia, 1951)
Rosemary Clooney, "Mambo Italiano" (Columbia, 1954)
Tennessee Ernie Ford, "Sixteen Tons" (Capitol, 1955)
Dean Martin, "Memories Are Made of This" (Capitol, 1955)
Patti Page, "Tennessee Waltz" (Mercury, 1950)
Johnnie Ray, "Cry" (Okeh, 1951)
Jane Turzy, "Good Morning, Mr. Echo" (Decca, 1951)
Weavers, "Wimoweh" (Decca, 1951)

3

RHYTHM AND BLUES FOR THE KIDS
Doo Wop

In the early 1950s, an increasing number of records crossed over from the rhythm and blues (R&B) to the pop charts. It was a sign that black pop music was growing in popularity among white listeners and, in turn, selling to a much larger market. But it also signaled a new direction in R&B itself. Many of the crossover records were made by groups of young African American men with little or no experience as professional entertainers. They sang unaccompanied on street corners and tenement stoops, in school yards and subway stations, improvising their harmonies and developing their sound through trial and error. The music would become known as doo wop, a youthful music unlike the urban blues that typified grown-up R&B at the time. This was music for kids, and American kids of all races and ethnicities responded.

In addition to the doo wop groups, there were important new soloists who emerged mid-decade and began to have crossover success—figures like Fats Domino, Chuck Berry, LaVern Baker, and Little Richard. These stars, too, purveyed a new flavor of R&B. Each performer had his or her own style, but the common link was the departure from urban blues. Fats Domino brought a sweet and easy New Orleans feel to original material such as "Ain't That a Shame," as well as older pop hits such as "Blueberry Hill" and "Blue Monday." LaVern Baker hit the pop charts in 1955 with the novelty song "Tweedle Dee." Chuck Berry was a prolific songwriter, mixing country and R&B elements with lyrics that spoke to teenagers' everyday experience. Little Richard transformed the blues into a manic torrent of rock and roll energy that thrilled kids even as it terrified their parents. Together, the vocal groups and the new generation of soloists presented the country, and soon the world, with a new flavor of rhythm and blues that demanded a new name: rock and roll.

The growth in record sales following World War II spawned innumerable small record companies across the United States. These companies were referred to as independents, or indies, because they operated outside the distribution networks of major labels like Columbia, RCA Victor, and Decca. The indies formed a kind of parallel universe to the majors, which was reflected not only in their small size and relatively small production and marketing budgets but in the repertory they recorded. The majors had the vast mainstream pop market largely to themselves and so were initially less interested in the much smaller R&B market. The indies seized the opportunity to service R&B fans, who turned out to be more numerous than anyone had imagined. Hustling for every dollar, indie record companies went far off the beaten show-business path looking for talent that the majors had no idea even existed.

R&B crossovers also brought a distinctive **lo-fi** sound to the pop mainstream. The indies, usually working on a shoestring budget, often recorded in non-studio locations (e.g., a backyard garage for the Penguins' "Earth Angel," a church basement for the Five Satins' "In the Still of the Nite") using primitive equipment and untrained recording engineers. The results sounded much rougher than the records produced by big companies. The sound could be distorted, poorly balanced, and generally ragged. But as the records spun over and over on juke boxes, record players, and radio, their sound seeped into public consciousness. The raw sound came to appear as an element of expressive style, a legitimate new possibility for what music might sound like. In fact, the roughness of the records was heard by young fans as a sign of energy and vitality.

As was now common in the music business, commercially successful groups were launched via records from complete obscurity to overnight, if usually ephemeral, stardom. A great many doo wop groups were one-hit wonders, but their sheer numbers made the genre a powerful force in the music business and the nation's changing pop soundscape. Record scouts haunted neighborhoods to find the raw vocal talent, which they took into studios and paired with experienced session musicians. The result was often a fascinating musical mismatch, naive exuberance meeting worldly experience. The combination made for a clash in rhythmic feel between the instrumentalists' tendency toward nuanced swing and the singers' simpler on-the-beat orientation. On such records as the Crows' "Gee," the Chords' "Sh-Boom," and Frankie Lymon and the Teenagers' "Why Do Fools Fall in Love," we hear a fusion of different musical sensibilities. Although these different approaches to rhythmic feel are essentially contradictory, when combined on a recording they form a unique blend whose tension is part of the track's charm and freshness.

3.1. "IT'S TOO SOON TO KNOW" (1948)

THE ORIOLES

In 1948 the R&B charts were fluid, producing more than twice as many number-one hits as in each of the previous three years. The stylistic range of these records included pop-jazz (Dinah Washington, "Am I Asking Too Much"), Caribbean-tinged jump blues (Louis Jordan, "Run Joe"), boogie-woogie (Amos Milburn, "Chicken Shack Boogie"), and something new—a rough, amateur emulation of the male vocal group sound typified by the Ink Spots. The record "It's Too Soon to Know" crossed over to the pop charts and rose higher (number thirteen) than any other R&B record that year, bringing the performers, a group called the Orioles, into the national spotlight. The sound was raw, lacking the polish of the Ink Spots' performances and the refined production standards of their record company (Decca). In fact, The Orioles record was made on a shoestring and distributed by a company specializing in gospel music and Yiddish comedy. It was a telling sign of the topsy-turvy times that from such an unlikely source came the year's biggest crossover hit.

The Orioles were five young men from Baltimore, Maryland, fronted by lead singer Sonny Til. They met at Baltimore's Avenue Cafe while performing individually on the club's amateur nights. In the spring of 1948, they traveled to New York City to appear on the popular radio show *Arthur Godfrey's Talent Scouts*, a contest format judged by audience response, much like *American Idol*. The group did not win but generated so many favorable telephone calls that Godfrey, a popular radio host, had them back twice more to perform, which effectively launched their career. Within months they had signed a record deal and were in a New York City studio for their first professional recording session, which yielded, among other tracks, "It's Too Soon to Know."

The song, a slow ballad, is performed in a crooner style, accompanied by vocal harmony and a minimal instrumental ensemble of guitar and bass. In concept, it is not unlike The Ink Spots' 1946 hit "The Gypsy," which likewise features a seductive lead voice accompanied by vocal harmony and a small instrumental group. Both records also include a change of vocalist in their respective bridge sections. Despite the similarities, however, the two tracks come across quite differently. The Ink

Spots' track has a polished refinement that's lacking with the Orioles. The instruments sound clear and well balanced. The lead vocal is precise and controlled, and the vocal harmonies are smooth and subtle. By contrast, the Orioles' track opens with a slightly ragged guitar followed by Sonny Til's slightly ragged voice, a streetcorner croon with the idiosyncratic diction to match. The second lead voice, that of baritone George Nelson, is husky and even less polished. The instruments are in the far background. The vocal harmonies lack the older group's seamless blend, and the intonation is at times wobbly.

The track's success signaled that audiences were listening for more than sophisticated musical execution. A 1951 review of an Orioles show in New York City summed up the situation. The group was "just about as unmusical and sloppy an act as has been seen hereabouts," the reviewer wrote. Yet the group's "poor man's Ink Spots routine nevertheless seemed to win the audience."[1] In a music business accustomed to professional standards in everything from songwriting to record production, "It's Too Soon to Know" was a warning shot, isolated at the time but prefiguring radical changes to come.

"It's Too Soon to Know" was written by Deborah Chessler, a young woman who worked as a salesclerk but had designs on show business. In addition to writing songs, she managed the Orioles, overseeing their career development. "She made it possible for the Orioles to become whatever we became," recalled Til.[2] Like the singers, Chessler was an amateur. She could neither write music down nor play an instrument. She dreamed up songs, wrote down the lyrics, and sang the melody to herself until she could remember it. What she lacked in professional skill, however, she made up in musical imagination.

The song entwines music and lyrics to a unified dramatic purpose. The lyrics express hopeful longing tempered with fearful uncertainty, an ambivalent combination that Chessler reflects both in the song's melody and in its phrase structure. In the first phrase, listen to the melodic pitches on the words "believe her" and "tells me so." These notes (B and C$^\sharp$) are not part of the underlying tonic chord of D major. They are dissonances that help to evoke the protagonist's uncertainty. They give a feeling of floating freely above the harmonic foundation as the protagonist poses his unanswerable questions. There are many such melodic dissonances scattered through the song.

The phrase structure is an interesting twist on Tin Pan Alley conventional song form. Instead of AABA, we get A, A2, A3 (i.e., a series of variations). The first two A sections form two similar yet contrasting twelve-bar segments (instead of the conventional eight), resulting in a continuous twenty-four-bar section.

The first A repeats a four-bar harmonic phrase focused on the tonic (ii | V | I | I), followed by a move to the IV chord in measure nine (0:38). After the relatively static harmony of the first two phrases, the IV provides a sense of contrast and movement toward a cadence as the lyrics move from question to declaration. The melody moves higher, as if to a climactic moment.

The move to cadence, however, is short-circuited. Instead, the music starts over, restating the song's opening phrase and initiating the A2 section (0:54). What sounds like it might have been aiming for a conventional sixteen-bar section composed of two parallel eight-bar phrases turns out to be still developing toward an as yet unpredictable outcome. This uncertainty mirrors the protagonist's expression of apprehension.

The ii | V | I | I phrase occurs only once this time around (0:54–1:09), and then we move again to the IV chord. Now the climax follows through, confirmed by the melody rising to its highest pitch on the word "die" (F♯), followed by a non-diatonic E major chord (1:21). To use this chord in the tonic key of D major requires changing the G♮ that occurs normally in D major to a G♯, which adds intensity to the climactic moment. The following chord is E minor (which restores the G♮), producing a major-minor juxtaposition that also reflects the protagonist's sense of ambivalence.

The last phrase of A2 (phrase six) finally delivers the delayed cadence as the music settles down with an arrival on the tonic in both melody and harmony. Because the two A segments are more complementary than parallel, this twenty-four-bar section sounds like a single, seamless expressive line.

Harmonic Phrases (4 Bars Each)
A
1. ii | V | I | I
2. ii | V | I | I
3. IV | IV | I | I

A2
4. ii | V | I | I
5. IV | IV | I | II (E major)
6. ii (E minor) | V | I | turnaround

The Ink Spots' record changes voice at the bridge, from tenor to baritone. The far less conventional "It's Too Soon to Know" has no bridge, but the record takes a similar approach to timbral contrast, switching to baritone George Nelson at the start of the A3 section. He sings phrases one and two (from A), and then, as the tenor resumes the lead, the music moves to phrase five (from A2). In combining elements of the A and A2 sections, A3 produces yet another variation on the song's phrase structure. Once again, phrase five provides a climax, this time with the beat suspended, allowing Til space for an impassioned melisma on the word "die."

Listening Guide

"It's Too Soon to Know" (Deborah Chessler), Jubilee Records (mono)
Recorded in New York City, July 1948
Sonny Til (lead voice), George Nelson (second lead voice), Alex Sharp (voice), Johnny Reed (bass and voice), Tommy Gaither (guitar and voice)
Producer: Sid de May
Charts: Popular Records: Best Sellers in Stores #13, Best Selling Retail Race Records #1
Key: D
Meter: 4/4

Time	Section	Lyric Cue	Listen For
0:00	Intro		Solo electric guitar plays in tempo rubato.
0:06	A (12)	"Does she love me"	Phrase 1: Lead voice begins with rubato upbeat, stressing the word "love" with a hoarse pitch bend.
			Bass plays chord roots on beats 1 and 3.
			Backing voices sing sustained harmonies.
0:15		"Believe her . . . tells me so"	Melodic dissonances.
0:23		"Is she fooling"	Phrase 2: Similar to phrase 1.
0:38		"A one-sided love"	Phrase 3: Move to IV chord.
0:54	A2 (12)	"If she don't love me"	Phrase 4: Repeat phrase 1 melody.
1:09		"Though I'll cry"	Phrase 5: Move to IV chord.
1:17			Melodic peak on the word "die."
1:21			E major chord.
1:24		"Is it so"	Phrase 6: Cadence and turnaround.
1:40	A3 (10+stop time)	"Does she love me"	Change to baritone lead voice (phrases 1 and 2).
2:11		"Though I'll cry"	Change to tenor voice (phrase 5).
2:15			Stop-time; melisma on "die."
			Rubato to end.

3.2. "WHY DO FOOLS FALL IN LOVE" (1956)

FRANKIE LYMON AND THE TEENAGERS

Frankie Lymon and the Teenagers were one of hundreds of vocal groups in the New York City area, but they quickly rose to the top of the heap. The lead singer, thirteen-year-old Frankie Lymon, had a remarkable high tenor voice, a gift for showmanship, and a charismatic presence. His adoring fans felt intuitively that he was one of them, yet special, touched by an extraordinary gift. The Teenagers were discovered by Richard Barrett, a member of another New York group, the Valentines. Barrett also worked as an A&R operative for George Goldner, one of New York's most successful independent label owners and producers. Goldner was an important figure in rock and roll, producing The Crows' crossover doo wop hit "Gee" in 1954 and The Chantels' prototypical girl group hit "Maybe" in 1958. In between came The Teenagers with a string of hit records, as well as television and film appearances.

Barrett convinced Goldner to audition the group, then calling themselves The Premiers, in the fall of 1955. Goldner already had vocal groups on his labels and was at first lukewarm about hearing another one. His interest, however, perked up when he met the group. Even by contemporary standards the boys were remarkably young, ranging in age from thirteen to fifteen years old, with a fresh sound and an image teenagers would clearly identify with. One of their songs, at the time called "Why Do Birds Sing So Gay," was particularly impressive. Lymon, however, was not the lead singer. When Goldner decided to record the group he insisted on two changes: Frankie, with his high, boy's voice, was to take the lead, and the song would be renamed "Why Do Fools Fall in Love." He paired the group with session musician and sax player Jimmy Wright and Wright's band and took them to Bell Sound Studios in Manhattan. Wright suggested one further change: To further capitalize on their youthful image, he advised the group to change its name to The Teenagers.

"Why Do Fools Fall in Love" is set in a thirty-two-bar AABA form typical of older Tin Pan Alley songs. It displays its rock and roll innocence, however, in its limited harmonic vocabulary. During the A sections, a two-bar chord sequence—the doo wop staple I–vi–ii–V—is simply repeated over and over, each chord lasting two beats. The contrasting B section, or bridge, is also minimal in its harmonic content but creates an interesting shift in momentum. Each chord in the bridge lasts eight beats instead of two, as in the A sections. In effect, the harmony acts as a rhythmic device. Changing the harmonic rhythm can change the pace of a track without changing its tempo or groove.

A ‖: I vi | ii V :‖ 4 times
B ‖ IV |IV | I | I | IV | IV | V | V ‖

> ### Doo Wop Harmony and Harmonic Rhythm
>
> The I–vi–IV (or ii)–V chord progression is a doo wop staple. It appears in many of the genre's biggest hits. The pacing (harmonic rhythm) is always regular, with chords changing every bar or every half bar. For contrast, doo wop songs often provide a break from this harmonic loop, shifting in the song's bridge to a different chord progression and slowing the pace of the chord changes.

The lyrics pose a series of questions expressing a surprisingly worldly, adult sentiment, as Frankie Laine noted when he introduced the Teenagers on his television show, which was the Teenagers' first nationwide television appearance. "What does a thirteen-year-old boy know about love?" he asked his young namesake. "Well Mr. Laine, I have been falling in love since I was only five," said Frankie with a dreamy expression, following the script flawlessly. Then, with a sly smile, he said, "But I've been a fool about it since I was eleven."[3] Lymon's charm and precocious show business sophistication came across loud and clear.

The track begins with bass vocalist Sherman Garnes setting the scene. He sings the chord roots of the doo wop progression in nonsense syllables typical of doo wop accompaniments. His two-bar intro is punctuated by a loud snare crack on the fourth beat of the bar, a rock and roll fundamental. The rest of the intro orients the listener to the sound of the group's vocal blend, concluding with an announcement of the song's title highlighted in stop-time.

As the track proceeds, Frankie's voice is clearly the focal point in the mix. But listen to the textural filigree behind him. The other voices create a contrapuntal accompaniment to the lead, while the saxophone plays lightly swinging **riffs** (short, repeated musical figures), all of which is anchored by the solid snare backbeats and the bass accents on beats one and three.

The bridge, in addition to changing the chord progression and harmonic rhythm, creates a textural contrast. Shifting accompaniment to sustained notes, the background voices simplify the texture. The bridge ends, like the intro, with two bars of stop-time rhythm. The stop-time effect serves both to punctuate the arrangement and to relaunch the background filigree of the following A section. It also highlights a key moment in the song where Frankie reveals "that fool is me."

Jimmy Wright was a hard-swinging R&B sax player and his band was composed of experienced musicians. The combination of mature musicians and neophyte singers led to a creative mismatch of musical styles. While the vocal sections have a heavy orientation toward beats one and three (especially noticeable in the bass part), in the instrumental break the rhythm section shifts to a more complex swing feel overlaid with syncopated guitar riffs accompanying the rhythmically fluid saxophone solo. The saxophone's lustiness also contrasts sharply with the naive charm of the vocal. Furthermore, the solo invokes a strong blues feel that is lacking in the vocal sections. It sounds as if the record shifts not only rhythmic but also stylistic gears as it moves into the sax solo and then back to the voices. The record, then, is a combination of contrasting musical sensibilities electronically fused to form a single, eclectic musical statement.

Much of the group's mass appeal lay in Lymon's projection of boyish innocence. The world would learn later that the facade hid a reality of turmoil in Lymon's upbringing. After the Teenagers' eighteen-month run of success ended, Frankie would sink into a life of drug addiction, dying of a heroin overdose in 1968 at the age of twenty-five. But the records endured, and Frankie's influence would be acknowledged with affectionate gratitude by such future stars as Ronnie Spector, Smokey Robinson, and Brian Wilson.

Listening Guide

"Why Do Fools Fall in Love" (Jimmy Merchant, Herman Santiago), Gee 1002 (mono)
Recorded at Bell Sound Studios, New York City, December 1955
Frankie Lymon (lead voice), Jimmy Merchant, Herman Santiago, Joe Negroni, Sherman Garnes (voice), Jimmy Wright (tenor saxophone), Jimmy Shirley (guitar), Al Hall (bass), Gene Brooks (drums)
Producer: George Goldner
Charts: Popular Records: Best Sellers in Stores #6, R&B Records: Best Sellers in Stores #1
Key: F
Meter: 4/4

Time	Section	Lyric Cue	Listen For
0:00	**Intro** (2+8)	Doo wop syllables	Bass voice sings a two-bar figure outlining typical doo wop chord sequence.
0:04		"Ooh wah"	Bass, drums, and voices enter with Frankie's voice out in front.
			Groove emphasizes the on-beats.
0:12		"Why do fools"	Stop-time.
0:14	**A** (8)	"Why do birds sing"	Lead voice sings lyrics while accompanying voices sing rhythmic doo wop syllables.
			Bass and snare keep the rhythm focused on the beats.
			Sax riffs in the background.
0:26	**A** (8)	"Why does the rain"	Same texture.
0:36	**B** (8)	"Love is a losing game"	Backing voices switch to sustained notes and legato lines.
			Chord sequence changes; harmonic rhythm slows.
0:45		"For that fool"	Stop-time.
0:47	**A** (8)	"Tell me why"	Lymon pleads "why" through the entire section.
			Prominent sax riff sets up solo.
0:58	**Break** (16)		Groove shifts to swing.
			Bass changes to steady "walking" rhythm.
			Guitar riffs.
			Swinging saxophone solo is filled with blues inflections (bent notes, slurs).
			Harmonic progression is suspended.
1:20	**A** (8)	"Why do birds sing"	Arrangement follows previous **AABA**.
1:31	**A** (8)	"Why does the rain"	
1:42	**B** (8)	"Why does my heart"	Different lyrics from first bridge.
1:53	**A** (8)	"Tell me why"	
2:04	**Outro** (8)	"Why do fools"	New material for concluding phrase.

3.3. "IN THE STILL OF THE NITE" (1956)

THE FIVE SATINS

The Five Satins were formed by lead singer Fred Parris in New Haven, Connecticut. At nineteen, Parris was already a doo wop veteran, having cut several sides with his group the Scarlets while still a high school student. After graduation and induction into the Army, he often returned to New Haven from his posting in Philadelphia to rehearse and then record with the Five Satins. During one of his visits, the group (reduced to four voices on this session) was joined by a group of musicians in the basement of the Parish Hall of Saint Bernadette Church in New Haven to record "In the Still of the Nite," which Parris is reported to have written while on guard duty. The recording was supervised by Marty Kugell and his partner Tom Sokira, local teenagers who had started their own record label, Standord. Their only significant asset was a recording rig, which, since they lacked studio access, they carried from place to place. In addition to Saint Bernadette, they also recorded at the local VFW hall.

The early 1950s saw a mania for what was called **hi-fi** sound. The idea was to create recordings and sound reproduction equipment that gave listeners the truest possible representation of live music making. Rather than hearing records as sound worlds unto themselves, hi-fi enthusiasts sought an electronic illusion of natural acoustic sound. Hi-fi, however, was the province of major record labels. It required top-quality recording equipment, recording studios, and professional engineers to achieve the desired result. Indie labels worked in an altogether different universe. Equipment was limited; studios were often primitive or, as in the case of "In the Still of the Nite," nonexistent; and the recordings were often made by amateurs. Thus, "In the Still of the Nite" sounds nothing like a well-balanced recording of natural musical sound. It is more like a piece of obscure, willfully lo-fi sonic surrealism. Its sonic strangeness, however, is precisely what gives the record its unique, expressive aura.

The track, like many other doo wop hits, moves at a moderately slow ballad tempo, fitting its theme of amorous longing ("Before the light / Hold me again") mingled with a nostalgic backward glance ("I remember that night in May"). It begins with one pass through a standard doo wop chord sequence sung to doo wop syllables, each chord lasting a full bar. After this intro, the form follows a modified AABA structure. As was often the case with the amateur songwriters of the day, however, this would-be conventional form goes a bit sideways. The first A section has only four bars (instead of the normal eight) and the second and third A sections each have six. The bridge, on the other hand, sticks to the eight-bar standard. Altogether, the form, which would normally be thirty-two bars, comes in at twenty-eight.

But the song has an even more basic fundamental pattern. Aside from the bridge, the form boils down to a series of four-bar phrases. The two-bar extensions on the A sections are simply turnarounds that provide a brief respite from the doo wop chord progression and a place for the backing singers' refrain. Whenever the lead voice is singing in the A sections—and during the saxophone solo—the phrasing is always tied to the four-bar doo wop loop.

From the outset, the mix sets a strange mood. The loudest part of the vocal harmony is the middle voice, obscuring the other voices with a two-note part that persists throughout the track. The minimalism of the part strips the harmonic flow to its barest form and eventually proves hypnotic in its effect. Meanwhile, the instruments are submerged in murkiness; the only clear timbre is that of the deep snare drum. The piano is difficult to hear at first and the reason becomes clear at the break: it is lost in a reverberant fog, as though emanating from a different sonic dimension than the rest of the instruments. The overall texture is tinged with a hazy distortion, giving the track a dreamlike quality. And the oddly proportioned mix makes the background difficult to hear distinctly, creating a sense of mysterious depth.

Lo-fi ballads (other famous ones include the Orioles' "It's Too Soon to Know," the Penguins' "Earth Angel," and the Drifters' "There Goes My Baby") were part of the doo wop ethos. Instead of a liability, the rough sounds seemed to add to the appeal for young fans. They gave the records a grittiness and an emotional poignancy. They also distinguished the records markedly from their major label hi-fi counterparts. For teenagers, lo-fi records had the advantage of being far too primitive for grown-up tastes, making them immediately recognizable as music for a new generation. Lo-fi sounds changed the pop soundscape permanently as rock and roll seemed to acquire a sense of its own history almost overnight. By the end of the decade, these hit singles were reissued on compilation albums, collections of tracks that were already referred to as "oldies." "In the Still of the Nite" was among the tracks on the first such album, *Oldies but Goodies* (1959), compiled by Los Angeles DJ Art Laboe. Although the Five Satins' record had a limited initial chart run, it went on to sell millions of copies in the coming years.

Listening Guide

"In the Still of the Nite" (Fred Parris), Standord, later Ember (mono)

Recorded at Saint Bernadette Parish Hall, New Haven, Connecticut, February 1956

Fred Parris (lead voice), Al Denby, Jim Freeman, Ed Martin (voice), Vinny Mazzetta (saxophone), Curlee Glover (piano), Doug Murray (bass), Bobby Mapp (drums)

Producers and engineers: Marty Kugell and Tom Sokira

Charts: Popular Records: Best Sellers in Stores #24, R&B Records: Best Sellers in Stores #4

Key: G♭

Meter: 4/4

Time	Section	Lyric Cue	Listen For
0:00	**Intro** (4 bars)	Doo wop syllables	Doo wop chord sequence.
			Middle voice is the most prominent.
			Prominent snare backbeat.
			Murky instrumental texture.
			Piano plays triplets typical of early rock and roll ballads.
0:14	**A** (4 bars)	"In the still of the nite"	Lead voice enters.
			Intro texture continues.
0:27	**A** (4+2 bars)	"'Cause I love"	
0:40		"In the still of the nite"	2-bar turnaround.
			Backing voices sing refrain.
0:47	**B** (8 bars)	"I remember"	Backing voices repeat "I remember"; middle voice remains the most prominent of the backing voices.
1:07		"To keep"	Stop-time.
			Reverberant piano sound suggests a separate sonic dimension.
			Snare fill doubles lead voice melisma on the word "love."
1:13	**A** (4+2 bars)	"Well before the light"	Backing voices return to doo wop syllables.
1:27		2-bar turnaround.	Backing voices sing refrain.
1:33	**Break** (4+4+2)		Sax solo loosely follows bass voice phrasing, sometimes doubling the bass melody.
			Doo wop chord sequence continues.
			New doo wop syllables.
2:00			Turnaround.

Time	Section	Lyric Cue	Listen For
2:07	A (4+2 bars)	"So before the light"	Lead voice returns; backing voices return to previous syllables.
2:24		"In the still"	Last bar is stretched for expressive effect.
2:30	Outro (fade)		Lead voice sings falsetto over fade.

NOTES

1. Hal Webman, "Night Club Vaude Reviews: Strand, New York," *Billboard*, May 12, 1951, 38.
2. Marv Goldberg, "The Orioles—Part 1: The Early Jubilee Years 1949–1951," Marv Goldberg's R&B Notebooks, 2009, http://www.uncamarvy.com/Orioles/orioles1.html.
3. Frankie Lymon and the Teenagers, "Why Do Fools Fall in Love," YouTube video, 0:47, January 19, 2006, https://www.youtube.com/watch?v=q96ylFiQK_I.

FURTHER READING

Goldberg, Marv. Marv Goldberg's R&B Notebooks. http://www.uncamarvy.com/marvart.html.
Gribin, Anthony, and Matthew Schiff. *Doo Wop: The Forgotten Third of Rock 'N Roll*. Iola, WI: Krause, 1992.
Groia, Phillip. *They All Sang on the Corner: New York City's Rhythm and Blues Vocal Groups of the 1950s*. Setauket, NY: Edmund, 1974.

FURTHER LISTENING

Chords, "Sh-Boom" (Cat, 1954)
Crests, "Sixteen Candles" (Coed, 1958)
Crows, "Gee" (Rama, 1953)
Dominoes, "Sixty Minute Man" (Federal, 1951)
Flamingos, "I Only Have Eyes for You" (End, 1958)
Heartbeats, "A Thousand Miles Away" (Hull 1956)
Imperials, "Tears on My Pillow" (End, 1958)
Penguins, "Earth Angel" (Dootone, 1954)
Spaniels, "Goodnight Sweetheart, Goodnight" (Vee-Jay, 1954)
Willows, "Church Bells May Ring" (Melba, 1956)

4

ROCKING COUNTRY
Rockabilly

Country music increased its presence on the mainstream pop charts throughout the 1940s with such crossover hits as Al Dexter's "Pistol Packin' Mama" and Bob Wills's "New San Antonio Rose," both of which were also covered by Bing Crosby, the reigning king of pop. By the 1950s, country music itself was showing signs of influence from both pop and R&B. Records such as Eddy Arnold's "The Cattle Call" and Tennessee Ernie Ford's "Sixteen Tons" did away with traditional country instrumentation to offer country-pop hybrids with orchestral arrangements. Some younger musicians, on the other hand, incorporated the big beat and rollicking tempo of such R&B records as Wynonie Harris's "Good Rockin' Tonight" and Jackie Brenston's "Rocket 88." This style was named variously "hillbilly bop," "western and bop," "non-Nashville country," and eventually "rockabilly" (combining "rock and roll" and "hillbilly," as country music was often called). Its early stars included Bill Haley and His Comets, Carl Perkins, Gene Vincent, and Elvis Presley. By the end of the decade, they would be joined by the likes of Buddy Holly, Eddie Cochran, Ricky Nelson, and three very young women: Wanda Jackson and Janis Martin, who were making records while still in high school, and Brenda Lee, who was thirteen when she had her first rockabilly hit, "One Step at a Time" (1957).

Early records that showed signs of country-R&B fusion include Sidney Louis "Hardrock" Gunter's "Birmingham Bounce" (1950), Bill Haley and the Saddlemen's "Rock the Joint" (1952), and Autry Inman's "That's All Right" (1953), the same Arthur Crudup song Presley would record a year later. But the most prolific purveyor of mid-1950s rockabilly—though he did not care for the term, preferring simply "rock and roll"—was not a musician but a record producer: Sam Phillips. In his studio in Memphis, Phillips produced records by Elvis Presley, Carl Perkins, Jerry Lee Lewis, and Johnny Cash, among others, and released them on his Sun Records label.

Phillips's recording sessions were freewheeling explorations. Without regard for the studio clock that ruled sessions in big-city studios (where sessions were usually limited to a union-mandated three hours), he pushed musicians to reach beyond their comfort zones. "Sam . . . knew what he wanted out of me," remembered blues singer and pianist Rosco Gordon, "so he would keep me there until he got that out of me."[1] Phillips sought, as he put it, to "draw out a person's innate, possibly unknown talents," however long it took.[2]

Like the performers he favored, Phillips's recording techniques were unrefined. Both in music making and sound engineering, he was more concerned with spirit than accuracy. His goal was to create records with personalities all their own. He was not interested simply in capturing clean, competent performances. He was after untamed musical expression, which he shaped electronically at his mixing console. It was not only what musicians played that mattered to Phillips but what they left behind—what they left in the record's grooves. Memphis rockabilly was a fusion of human and electronic energy, born not on a stage but in the studio of Phillips's Memphis Recording Service (Sun Studio's original name).

The rockabilly strain of rock and roll complemented doo wop in the emerging universe of postwar youth music. Like doo wop, rockabilly records emerged from the margins of the music business. It was a mixture of styles. The musicians were young and usually burst on the scene virtually overnight via hit recordings. As the doo wop vocal groups brought a fresh brand of R&B to the nascent idiom of rock and roll, so too young rockabilly performers reimagined country music. The country elements of rockabilly included a southern diction style and a guitar-centered instrumental texture. From R&B, the musicians took a rhythmic urgency—evident in the relentless syncopation and driving slapped bass—and an unrestrained vocal style. The mixture electrified young audiences eager for musical adventure.

4.1. "CRAZY MAN, CRAZY" (1953)

BILL HALEY AND HIS COMETS

Bill Haley, a champion yodeler, worked hard to become a star country singer. With his groups the Four Aces of Western Swing and then the

Saddlemen, he played the country circuit around Philadelphia. He also hosted a country music radio show. But while their early records featured country material, the Saddlemen also covered such R&B songs as "Rocket 88" and "Rock the Joint" to offer a bit of novelty. In 1952 they recorded Haley's Hank Williams–inspired weeper "Icy Heart," on which he pinned his hopes of appearing in the *Grand Ole Opry* in Nashville. The record's B side was a rockabilly version of "Rock the Joint," which had been a hit for R&B bandleader Jimmy Preston. The public's unexpected response to the record changed the group's career trajectory and musical identity. "Icy Heart" went nowhere, but "Rock the Joint" was a hit. Suddenly, the group was riding a wave they hadn't even known existed, propelled by teenagers hungry for novel sounds. "I had never in years thought that this would happen," Haley said. "Here I was with the sideburns, cowboy boots and almost ten years of promoting myself as a country and western singer. What was I going to do?"[3]

What the group did was change its name to Bill Haley and His Comets and continue to develop a sound that would influence young fans around the world, including the first generation of musicians to grow up on rock and roll. In 1955 the band became international stars with the megahit "(We're Gonna) Rock Around the Clock," which was released on Decca and appeared in the film *Blackboard Jungle*. But the record that brought the group to the attention of major label executives in the first place was "Crazy Man, Crazy," a 1953 release on the independent Essex label that reached number twelve on the pop chart.

The track is a transition between the band's country records and the rock and roll that was to come. It is a good example of the kind of hybrid that was emerging among early '50s country musicians who incorporated R&B elements into their sound. While the track features steel guitar—an unmistakable marker of country style—the driving rhythmic momentum, the loud snare accents, and the black slang of the lyrics all point to an R&B influence. The way the drums are used also indicates a transitional style. Instead of functioning as the track's rhythmic backbone with steady backbeat accents, the drummer mostly plays ornamental flourishes, leaving the bass to drive the groove. The snare backbeat appears only during the "Go, go, go everybody" chant and the instrumental break. The reason the bass, rather than the drums, keeps the beat is that the band, like most country bands of the day, had played for years without a drummer. The addition of studio drummer Billy Gussak was an ornamental overlay.

The song's form is an interesting derivation of blues form. Recall that the conventional twelve-bar blues has three four-bar phrases, each associated with specific chord changes (see chapter 1). "Crazy Man, Crazy" takes this structure apart, turning it into a verse-chorus arrangement while preserving its harmonic sequence. The first blues phrase, expanded from four to eight bars, serves as the verse ("When I go out"; "They play it soft"). The second and third blues phrases serve as the song's chorus ("Crazy man, crazy"). Further, there are actually two kinds of verses. They share the same bassline, but their vocal melodies differ significantly, as do their textures. In verse A, Haley sings a swinging melody with rhyming couplet lyrics, accompanied by syncopated **comping** (rhythmic chordal accompaniment) from guitar and steel guitar. Verse B drops the lead vocal for a group chant ("Go, go, go everybody"), with the word "go" landing squarely on the strong beats (one and three). The guitar and steel guitar drop out, but the drums become more active, answering the chant with accented backbeats.

Listening Guide

"Crazy Man, Crazy" (Bill Haley), Essex Records (mono)
Recorded at Coastal Studios, New York City, April 1953
Bill Haley (voice, guitar), Marshall Lytle (bass), Billy Williamson (steel guitar), Johnny Grande (piano), Art Ryerson (lead guitar), Billy Gussak (drums)
Producer: Dave Miller
Charts: Popular Records: Best Sellers in Stores #12
Key: B♭
Meter 4/4

Time	Section	Lyric Cue	Listen For
0:00	Intro (4)		Snare drum rolls and rimshots followed by guitar/steel guitar "growl," grabbing listeners' attention.
0:06	Chorus (8)	"Crazy man, crazy"	Slapped walking bass drives the groove.
			Snare drum plays ornamental accents. Piano comps in background.
			Guitar and steel guitar riffs answer vocal phrases.
			Chord changes are equivalent to phrases 2 and 3 of a blues progression.
0:17	Chorus (8)	"Crazy man, crazy"	Repeat
0:28	Verse A (8)	"When I go out"	Guitar and steel guitar comp.
			Snare drum dialogue with voice.
			Prolonged tonic harmony is equivalent to first phrase of a blues progression.
0:40	Chorus (8)	"Crazy man, crazy"	Chorus texture.

continued on next page

Time	Section	Lyric Cue	Listen For
0:51	Verse B (8)	"Go, go, go everybody"	Solo voice replaced by group vocal riff. Guitar and steel guitar out. Snare drum switches to steady backbeat accents. Ends with shouts of revelry.
1:03 1:14	Break (8+8)		Two choruses. Steady backbeat on snare. Guitar solo (8). Steel guitar solo (8).
1:26	Chorus (8)	"Crazy man, crazy"	Chorus texture.
1:38	Chorus (8)	"Crazy man, crazy"	Repeat.
1:49	Verse A (8)	"They play it soft"	Verse A texture.
2:01	Chorus (8)	"Crazy man, crazy"	Chorus texture.
2:12	Verse B (8+)	"Go, go, go everybody"	Verse B texture. Ends with raucous party sounds punctuated by guitar and steel guitar rhythmic stabs and glissandi.

4.2. "BLUE MOON OF KENTUCKY" (1954)

ELVIS PRESLEY

In the summer of 1954, Elvis Presley, a nineteen-year-old truck driver, recorded a version of Arthur Crudup's "That's All Right," an R&B song first released in 1948. It was Presley's first commercial release. He had been dropping in on Sam Phillips's Memphis Recording Service studio for about a year, hoping to get noticed by the producer. Phillips had finally decided to make a record with the kid, just to see if he had anything different to offer. The song chosen for the session, which included guitarist Scotty Moore and bassist Bill Black, was a country ballad, Leon Payne's "I Love You Because." The recording, however, was not meeting Phillips's expectations. He wasn't sure exactly what he was after, but he knew he wanted something new, even unprecedented. Presley was a raw talent, an amateur like so many other young rockers, and Phillips was following a hunch. But so far, nothing was happening.

During a break, the group began playing "That's All Right," just fooling around, burning off nervous energy. In the studio's control room

Phillips's ears perked up. He had heard Presley sing pop, country, and gospel songs but was surprised the young man was familiar with this R&B song, let alone that he could pull off such a fresh rendition. The performance merged a country and an R&B feel but belonged to neither of those idioms. In its youthful energy and innocence, the performance had an originality about it, which, Phillips now realized, was precisely what he had been looking for. The rest of the session was spent shaping and capturing a performance of "That's All Right."

The recording, which was to be released on Phillips's Sun label, was a success when played on Memphis DJ Dewey Phillips's (no relation to Sam) *Red Hot and Blue* radio show. The switchboard lit up with calls from enthusiastic listeners and Dewey had Presley in for an on-air interview. Because listeners had a hard time discerning whether the singer was white or black (which would have helped identify this idiosyncratic new style), Dewey cleverly identified Presley's race by asking him which high school he had gone to. In segregated Memphis, everyone knew that Presley's answer, Humes High, meant that he was white, which tipped listeners to the significance of the stylistic fusion.

There remained a problem, however: the record could not be released. There was no B side. And with the A side having emerged more or less out of the blue, a musical accident, it was clear to no one where to go with this sound. "There was nothing like a direction," recalled Scotty Moore. "There was just a certain . . . feel."[4] Following little more than intuition, the team eventually decided to record a version of Bill Monroe's bluegrass song "Blue Moon of Kentucky."

Again, the style was very different from the original. Presley's version stresses rhythmic vitality above all else. It dispenses with Monroe's mid-tempo waltz and dives straight in to a quick 2/4 romp with an introduction that alerts listeners that this is not bluegrass. The rhythmic energy is immediately apparent in the slapped bass and acoustic guitar texture. The voice, too, is charged with rhythmic urgency as Presley rushes ahead of the beat, changing his vocal timbre as though inhabiting multiple characters. He also dispenses with the "untrue" / "blue" rhyme of the original song. Instead, he ends each eight-bar A section with the same line ("gone and left me blue"). Diminishing the meaning of the lyrics, Presley de-emphasizes words in favor of his stylized vocal performance. In true rock and roll fashion, he tells the story primarily through sound.

As was customary for country records—and Presley, fitting no other established category, was at first identified as a country artist—there are no drums. Instead, Phillips pushes the percussive clacking of the slapped bass to the front of the mix, especially during the guitar solos. He also added a **slapback echo** effect to the voice that created further rhythmic chatter. Slapback echo, which would come to be identified as a key style feature of rockabilly music, was a purely electronic contrivance. It was created by sending an audio signal to two tape recorders at once and then feeding the signal from the second tape recorder back to the first to be combined with the original signal. Because of the space between record and playback heads on the tape recorder, the signal sent between the two recorders arrived a split second later than the original, resulting in an echo. The loudness of the echo could be controlled at the mixing console, where Phillips mixed the track as the performers played. Along with his controls for guitar, bass, and voice was one for echo, the electronic member of the band.

Presley's first record set a pattern that was followed by most of his subsequent Sun releases: one side an R&B song, the other a country song. Neither, however, was really R&B or country. As each record acknowledged its sources, it absorbed and transformed them into something else: rock and roll.

Walking Bass and Boogie-Woogie

The basic groove for "Blue Moon of Kentucky" is a country two-step, a firm duple feel, which the bass emphasizes by playing chord roots on each downbeat. In Scotty Moore's guitar solos, however, the groove picks up momentum. The change of feel is caused by the bass doubling up its attacks to play steady eighth notes, which gives the music a "walking" sensation. The bass notes outline **broken chords** (chord tones played one at a time) characteristic of the **boogie-woogie** style. Boogie-woogie is a piano-based blues genre that rock and roll musicians often adapted to their own needs, often dispensing with the harmonic structure of the blues. What always remains is the broken-chord texture and the sense of rhythmic momentum.

Listening Guide

"Blue Moon of Kentucky" (Bill Monroe), Sun Records (mono)
Recorded at the Memphis Recording Service (Sun Studio), Memphis, July 1954
Elvis Presley (voice, acoustic guitar), Scotty Moore (electric guitar), Bill Black (bass)
Producer and engineer: Sam Phillips
Charts: #1 Country and Western (C&W) Territorial Best Sellers, Memphis
Key: A
Meter: 2/4

Time	Section	Lyric Cue	Listen For
0:00	Intro (16)	"Blue moon"	Presley sings in a husky, declamatory style. Slapped bass/acoustic guitar/electric guitar texture. Bass plays two-step groove. Slapback echo on voice.
0:18	A (8)	"I said blue moon of Kentucky"	Voice stays in declamatory mode but occasionally hints at a lighter timbre. Slapback echo on voice is louder. Ends on V.
0:26	A (8)	"I said blue moon"	Texture continues, lyrics repeat. Ends on I.
0:35	B (8)	"Well it was on one moonlight night"	Vocal timbre changes to a lighter, pleading tone.
0:44	A (8)	"Blue moon of Kentucky"	Voice transitions back to husky sound.
0:52	Break 1 (16)		Groove changes. Bass becomes more active, plays boogie-woogie figure. Guitar solo composed of rhythmic fragments.
1:10	A (8)	"Well I said blue moon of Kentucky"	Like previous A sections but with continued variations in vocal timbre.
1:18	A (8)	"I said blue moon"	
1:27	Break 2 (16)		Similar to **break 1**.
1:44	B (8)	"Well it was on one moonlight night"	Lighter vocal timbre.
1:52	A (8)	"I said blue moon of Kentucky"	Finishes in husky voice.

4.3. "I GOTTA KNOW" (1956)

WANDA JACKSON

Born in Oklahoma in 1937, Wanda Jackson began singing and playing at an early age. She performed country and western on the radio as a teenager and was signed to Decca at sixteen. After graduating from high school, Jackson joined the *Ozark Jubilee* country music television show. She appeared in concert with such country stars as Faron Young and Porter Wagoner. But in 1955 she also found herself on tour with Elvis Presley, who was still classified as some sort of country singer. The two became friends and he encouraged her to try a more rocking style, which she could see was driving his young fans wild with enthusiasm. She was afraid, however, of losing her country audience and was unsure of her own ability to pull it off. In fact, Jackson's was already a sassy, fresh style, evident on such records as "Lovin' Country Style" and "You Can't Have My Love." In 1956 she moved from Decca to Capitol Records, which was looking feverishly for its own young rockers. The stage was set for Jackson to rock and roll.

Her producer at Capitol was Ken Nelson, head of the company's country division, who was committed to catching the rock and roll wave sweeping the industry. He produced Gene Vincent and His Blue Caps' "Be-Bop-A-Lula" just a month before "I Gotta Know," which was cut at Jackson's first Capitol session. It was a tentative step. The record's A side, "Half as Good a Girl," was straight country, as were the other two sides recorded at the session: "Cryin' thru the Night" and "Step by Step." But "I Gotta Know" marked the beginning of a long run of Jackson's rockabilly recordings that by the early '60s included "Fujiyama Mama," "Mean, Mean Man," "Let's Have a Party," and the proto-psychedelic "Funnel of Love," as well as hard rocking covers of records such as Little Richard's "Long Tall Sally," Clyde McPhatter's "Money Honey," Elvis Presley's "Hard Headed Woman," and Jerry Lee Lewis's "Whole Lotta Shakin' Goin' On."

"I Gotta Know" is a play on the contrast between homespun country and newfangled rockabilly. The track begins with a slow country waltz featuring fiddle and steel guitar. After a single phrase of perfectly idiomatic country flavor, the beat stops and Jackson belts out "Well!" Apparently, the force of her exclamation shocks the musicians into an entirely different musical sphere because when the music picks up again it has shifted into a quicker tempo and left the waltz for a twelve-bar blues in 4/4. The fiddle drops out, and the instrumental texture features a strong backbeat with slapback echo and rockabilly-style licks on electric guitar. Jackson sings in a clipped, rhythmic delivery reminiscent of Presley, especially in her hiccupped "I gotta know" lines. The vocal melody is just a four-note riff repeated again and again.

This up-tempo section turns out to be the verse of a verse-chorus form. After the third "I gotta know," Jackson and the band slide back into the waltz. Jackson downshifts to a languid drawl accompanied by weepy steel guitar. The vocal melody switches from rhythmic riffing to legato lyricism. Her diction and vocal mannerisms seem exaggerated for effect, mirroring the contrast in the musical arrangement. As she changes the mood, her character slips from rock-and-roll modern to country traditional. The verses are all aggressive in attitude, both in her singing style and in the lyrics chiding a boyfriend more interested in dancing than romancing. The choruses melt into an old-fashioned plea for marriage—the "real thing."

Listening Guide

"I Gotta Know" (Thelma Blackmon), Capitol Records (mono)
Recorded at Capitol Studios, Hollywood, June 1956
Wanda Jackson (voice), Joe Maphis (lead guitar), Buck Owens (rhythm guitar), Jelly Sanders (fiddle), Ralph Mooney (steel guitar), studio musicians (bass, drums)
Producer: Ken Nelson
Charts: C&W Best Sellers in Stores #15
Key: D
Meter: 3/4, 4/4

Time	Section	Lyric Cue	Listen For
0:00	Intro		Instrumental version of chorus. Country waltz (3/4) featuring fiddle and steel guitar.
0:09		"Well!"	Waltz stops.
0:10	**Verse 1** (12)	"I thought that you"	Tempo picks up; meter changes to 4/4.
			Voice sings in clipped rhythmic riffs.
			12-bar blues form.
			Lead guitar plays rockabilly-style licks.
			Strong backbeat.
			Slapback echo on snare and rhythm guitar.
			Fiddle and steel guitar out.
0:21		"I gotta know"	Stop-time; voice invokes Presley with stylized hiccups.
0:27	**Chorus** (4)	"If our love's the real thing"	Country waltz.
			Vocal melody and style emphasize the shift to country.
			Fiddle and steel guitar featured.
0:35	"Yeah!"		Signals return to rock and roll.
0:36	**Verse 2** (12)	"We rocked and rolled"	Back to 4/4.
			Guitar licks become more prominent; otherwise similar to **verse 1**.

continued on next page

Time	Section	Lyric Cue	Listen For
0:52	Chorus (4)	"If our love's the real thing"	Country waltz.
1:00			Snare fill signals return to rock and roll.
1:03	Break (12+12)		Two verses of guitar solo.
			First verse features rockabilly licks.
1:18			Second verse uses two-string technique.
1:33	Verse 3 (12)	"Well I thought that you"	Rockabilly.
1:49	Chorus (4 bars)	"If our love's the real thing"	Country.
1:58	Verse 4 (12)	"When you're on that floor"	Rockabilly.
2:15	Chorus (4+tag)	"If our love's the real thing"	Country.

NOTES

1. Quoted in John Floyd, *Sun Records: An Oral History* (New York: Avon Books, 1998), 117.
2. Quoted in Greil Marcus, *Mystery Train: Images of America in Rock 'n' Roll Music* (New York: E. P. Dutton, 1976), 168.
3. Quoted in John Swenson, *Bill Haley: The Daddy of Rock and Roll* (New York: Stein and Day, 1982), 37.
4. Quoted in Peter Guralnick, *Last Train to Memphis: The Rise of Elvis Presley* (Boston: Little Brown, 1994), 103.

FURTHER READING

Escott, Colin, with Martin Hawkins. *Good Rockin' Tonight: Sun Records and the Birth of Rock 'n' Roll.* New York: St. Martin's Press, 1991.

Garbutt, Bob. *Rockabilly Queens: The Careers and Recordings of Wanda Jackson, Janis Martin, Brenda Lee.* Toronto: Ducktail Press, 1979.

Morrison, Craig. *Go Cat, Go!: Rockabilly Music and Its Makers.* Urbana: University of Illinois Press, 1996.

Tosches, Nick. *Country: The Twisted Roots of Rock 'n' Roll.* New York: Da Capo Press, 1996.

FURTHER LISTENING

Johnny Cash, "So Doggone Lonesome" (Sun, 1955)
Sanford Clark, "The Fool" (Dot, 1956)
Eddie Cochran, "Summertime Blues" (Liberty, 1958)
Buddy Holly and the Crickets, "That'll Be the Day" (Brunswick, 1957)

Brenda Lee, "One Step at a Time" (Decca, 1957)
Janis Martin, "Will You, Willyum" (RCA Victor, 1956)
Ricky Nelson, "Believe What You Say" (Imperial, 1958)
Carl Perkins, "Blue Suede Shoes" (Sun, 1955)
Billy Lee Riley and His Little Green Men, "Red Hot" (Sun, 1957)
Gene Vincent and His Blue Caps, "Be-Bop-A-Lula" (Capitol, 1956)

5

LO-FI RAVE-UP
Recasting the Blues, Reinventing Song

The year 1955 was when rock and roll staked out a consistent presence on the pop charts. Alongside mainstream pop hits from Frank Sinatra ("Learnin' the Blues"), Joan Weber ("Let Me Go Lover"), and Dean Martin ("Memories Are Made of This"), brash new sounds elbowed their way into the top ten. Records like Bill Haley and His Comets' "(We're Gonna) Rock around the Clock," Chuck Berry's "Maybellene," Fats Domino's "Ain't That a Shame," and Little Richard's "Tutti Frutti" served notice that a boisterous new music was now selling millions of records.

This chapter focuses on four early rock and roll stars and four tracks that typify key features of the new style: driving rhythm, rambunctious performances, and a noisy lo-fi sound. Three of the tracks feature the electric guitar, which would become the new music's iconic instrument. The artists and producers seem unconcerned with the polished craftsmanship that typified major label pop productions. In their animated, stylized performances and rough sonic textures, these tracks exemplify a new aesthetic principle in record production: for rock and roll, what mattered most was not pleasant listening but vivid character.

Rock and roll musicians borrowed freely from other idioms, combining style features at will. All of the tracks in this chapter use elements of the twelve-bar blues form. None, however, has the authentic blues feeling of older rural (e.g., Son House, Robert Johnson) or more contemporary electrified blues (e.g., Muddy Waters, Elmore James). As with all their sources, rock and roll musicians appropriated blues elements without regard for convention or tradition and used them for their own purposes. Buddy Holly's "Peggy Sue" and Elvis Presley's "Hound Dog" use the blues chord progression as a vehicle for adolescent expressions of romantic desire and pent-up energy, respectively. Chuck Berry's "Rock and Roll Music" and Little Richard's "Tutti Frutti" use the blues form as one part of a larger verse-chorus structure. As in so many early rock and roll songs—such as Presley's "Jailhouse Rock," Danny and the Juniors' "At the Hop," Jerry Lee Lewis's "Great Balls of Fire," and Carl Perkins's "Blues Suede Shoes"—the blues is simply a resource employed in the production of a pop record.

As we have seen, the rough sounds of indie records were usually the result of limitations such as primitive studios and bare-bones equipment. But as rock and roll expanded the public's listening habits, lo-fi sound became not merely acceptable but desirable. It imparted the raucous, rebellious attitude that many teenagers came to expect from their musical idols. It was also a mark of distinction, distancing rock and roll records from the slicker sounds of mainstream pop. The irony, of course, is that almost overnight these rough, rowdy sounds themselves became part of the new mainstream.

Along with the new sounds came new ideas about songwriting. Rock and roll songs were routinely dismissed by music industry veterans as inept and amateurish, and from a Tin Pan Alley perspective, this was true. The Great American Songbook's musical and lyric sophistication was rarely found in rock and roll songs. This criticism, however, failed to grasp the fact that songs and records were becoming inextricably linked. "Song" and "record" became synonymous in the public mind, so the traditional elements of a song—its melody, chords, and lyrics—represented only part of the project. Songs were starting points for records, much as a screenplay is for a film. "The thing to remember," said Jerry Leiber, cowriter of "Hound Dog," "is you're not writing a song but a record."[1] In its finished form, a rock and roll song conveyed far more than its music and lyrics.

The fusion of song, performance, and sound on records took the place of the song sheet as the industry's primary medium of commerce and public engagement. Fans identified specific renderings of songs as the authentic versions, a notion few would have imagined in earlier years. "In the old days," remembered Tin Pan Alley songwriter Johnny Green ("I Cover the Waterfront," "Out of Nowhere"), "the impetus for making a successful popular song came first from the composer and lyricist. Nowadays, it's the performing artist who makes or breaks a song and who is the initiator of all activity."[2] Indeed, songwriters often wrote songs with a particular voice in mind.

In 1955, rock and roll was an amorphous concept. Was it a new kind of music or simply a marketing term for R&B, describing the crossover success of records assumed to appeal primarily to African American audiences? No one knew for sure. In the early 1950s, the popular and influential DJ Alan Freed referred to his radio show *The Moon Dog House*, aired on Cleveland station WJW, as a "Moondog rock and roll party."[3] The show consisted largely of R&B records, and he admitted later that in using the term "rock and roll" he had no intention of identifying a new music. He simply wanted a catchy name attached to his show. But amid the uncertainty, both in the music industry and in the culture at large, a new musical idiom was in fact taking shape. The tracks presented in this chapter are not R&B. Like doo wop and rockabilly, they represent a new musical hybrid whose combination of features set them apart from grown-up R&B, giving teenagers—both black and white—a music all their own.

5.1. "TUTTI FRUTTI" (1955)

LITTLE RICHARD

Little Richard (Richard Penniman) was among rock and roll's first wave of spectacular performers. He brought a wild-eyed intensity to his stage shows and film appearances, exhilarating his young fans and confirming for mainstream America that rock and roll was a rowdy and, many thought, potentially dangerous art form. Richard was able to translate his manic energy onto vinyl, establishing in the process a core rock and roll principle: Rock and roll records, at their best, are possessed of an animated presence that projects from loudspeakers with irresistible force.

"Tutti Frutti" was recorded in New Orleans in the late summer of 1955 for Art Rupe's Los Angeles–based Specialty label. Like Presley's "That's All Right," the record was something of a fluke. After two days of recording, producer Robert "Bumps" Blackwell had eight tracks finished, none of which he thought to be hit material. But then, during a break in recording and with little studio time remaining, he heard Richard playing a bawdy song he performed in southern night clubs. The lyrics were too raw for radio airplay, but the performance had a fire unlike anything Richard had yet recorded. Blackwell, aware that in 1955 "people were buying feel," thought this burst of frenetic energy was just the thing to appeal to the growing youth market.[4] He had local songwriter Dorothy LaBostrie write a new set of lyrics, and in short order the track was completed.

The song's lyrics are minimal, often nonsensical. If "Tutti Frutti" had been sold primarily as a piece of sheet music, as in earlier times, it would have offered little appeal. But in rock and roll terms—as a screenplay for a record—it provided an effective vehicle for Richard's performance. When we hear him singing the song's lyrics in his high-spirited, raspy rant, their minimalism seems beside the point. His performance imparts a meaning that words alone never could. Indeed, as he launches into the song with a string of nonsense syllables, we understand that the singer's untamed state is simply too wild for words.

The song form is a hybrid mixture of structural elements. From one perspective the track presents a series of nine twelve-bar blues choruses. But there is also a verse-chorus form at work (note the two meanings of the term "chorus" here). The verses are the three blues choruses that impart the story ("Got a gal named Sue," etc.). The "Tutti frutti" refrain serves as the chorus. The choruses follow the typical twelve-bar blues chord sequence, while the verses veer away from the conventional form in their concluding four-bar stop-time phrases ("She rock to the east," etc.). These four bars would normally provide the blues chorus's concluding harmonic cadences, but instead they stay on the I chord as Little Richard winds up to launch into the next "Tutti frutti" refrain.

Note how the track differentiates verse and chorus by varying the length of the stop-time phrases: two bars in the choruses ("A wop bop a loo mop") and four bars in the verses ("She rock to the east"). Also, all choruses except the last one end "A wop bop a loo mop, a lop *bomp bomp*." The final chorus changes "*bomp*" to "*boom*." The shorter syllable on the first three choruses drives the turnaround seamlessly into the pickup for the next verse ("bomp bomp / Got a gal . . ."). Only when the song is over does Little Richard sing an emphatic "boom" to put an appropriate punctuation mark on the headlong gallop.

The session musicians are New Orleans regulars known as the Studio Band. They play in an energetic shuffle style characteristic of New Orleans R&B, a loosely swinging, infectious groove that captures the city's "let the good times roll" ethos. Richard's piano, however, works at cross purposes to the rest of the band. Unlike the band's swing-triplet orientation, his right hand pounds out insistent eighth notes. As the drummer Earl Palmer commented years later, "On 'Tutti Frutti' you can hear me playing a shuffle. Listening to it now, it's easy to hear I should have been playing that rock beat."[5] Several prominent examples of the shuffle rhythm vs. Richards' pounding eighth notes are noted in the Listening Guide.

The triplet feel characteristic of so many 1950s rock and roll records would eventually give way to duple subdivisions, which would become rock's rhythmic foundation. Little Richard's eighth-note eruptions offer a telling glimpse of the music's future. This significant detail, however, was another result of happenstance. Huey Smith, playing in the same

New Orleans style as the rest of the Studio Band, had played piano on the other tracks recorded at the session, while Richard concentrated on his vocals. Blackwell switched to Little Richard on the piano only because time was short and Richard already knew the song.

The record was made at Cosimo Matassa's J&M Studio, the first of several he owned and operated in New Orleans. He started it in 1945 in a back room of his record shop with only the barest equipment inventory and no prior training in electronics or music. But his instinctive ability to capture the energy of the performances, coupled with the fact that his was the first and for many years the only recording studio in New Orleans, eventually brought record labels from far and wide to record their artists at J&M. Besides Little Richard, Matassa's recordings include those of Fats Domino, Lloyd Price, Shirley and Lee, Clarence "Frogman" Henry, and Dave Bartholomew, in short, a who's who of New Orleans R&B musicians.

Listening Guide

"Tutti Frutti" (Richard Penniman, Dorothy LaBostrie), Specialty Records (mono)
Recorded at J&M Studio, New Orleans, September 1955
Little Richard (voice, piano), Justin Adams (guitar), Lee Allen (tenor saxophone), Alvin "Red" Tyler (baritone saxophone), Frank Fields (bass), Earl Palmer (drums)
Producer: Robert "Bumps" Blackwell
Engineer: Cosimo Matassa
Charts: Popular Records: Best Sellers in Stores #17, R&B Records: Best Sellers in Stores #2
Key: F
Meter: 4/4

Time	Section	Lyric Cue	Listen For
0:00	**Intro** (2)	"Wop bop a loo mop"	Little Richard sets a high-energy, manic tone.
0:03	**Chorus** (12)	"Tutti frutti"	12-bar blues.
			New Orleans shuffle is especially noticeable in the snare drum flourishes that accompany the saxophone riffs.
0:16		"Wop bop a loo mop"	Stop-time.

Time	Section	Lyric Cue	Listen For
0:18	**Verse 1** (8+4)	"Got a gal named Sue"	Eight bars of blues progression.
0:29		"She rocks to the east"	Stop-time; omits the V–IV–I harmonic climax of the choruses.
0:34	**Chorus** (12)	"Tutti frutti"	12-bar blues.
0:49	**Verse 2** (8+4)	"Got a gal named Daisy"	Similar to verse 1.
1:05	**Chorus** (12)	"Tutti frutti"	12-bar blues.
1:13			Piano eighth notes cut across the shuffle groove.
1:20	**Break** (12)		Saxophone solo over 12-bar blues.
1:24			Piano eighth notes.
1:35	**Chorus** (12)	"Tutti frutti"	12-bar blues.
1:51	**Verse 2 Repeat** (8+4)	"Got a gal named Daisy"	Similar to previous verses.
2:07	**Chorus** (12)	"Tutti frutti"	12-bar blues.
2:15			Piano eighth notes.
2:20		"A wop bop a loo mop a lop bam boom!"	Emphatic a cappella ending.

5.2. "HOUND DOG" (1956)

ELVIS PRESLEY

Elvis Presley's version of "Hound Dog" offers compelling proof that rock and roll was a new kind of musical sound. Having moved from Sun Records to RCA Victor, Presley was now recording for one of the oldest record firms in the world, and one with a long history of technological innovation and a commitment to high fidelity. The record was produced in a first-class New York studio with excellent equipment and acoustics and an experienced engineer. Yet it sounds like a crude, proto-punk outburst, a challenge to the standards of hi-fi propriety. A baffled reviewer for the British music publication *Melody Maker* wrote at the time, "My interest in Presley's 'Hound Dog' does not lie simply in the fact that I don't like it. The point about the whole thing is that, by all and any standards, it is a thoroughly bad record."[6] Clearly, however, "bad" and "good" were in the midst of a thorough redefinition.

This was not an early developmental phase for Presley; the record's A side, "Don't Be Cruel," is a polished pop production. Nor was the record a lackluster effort; it took thirty-one takes before Presley was satisfied. The record was a manifesto, its blunt impact an exuberant declaration that a willfully raucous sound was now a legitimate musical choice. Audiences agreed: "Hound Dog," like it's A side, hit number one on all three charts—pop, country, and R&B.

"Hound Dog" is also a good example of how rock and roll performers reinterpreted adult R&B as teenagers' music. Written by Jerry Leiber and Mike Stoller, the song had been a top R&B hit in 1953 in a version by Willie Mae "Big Mama" Thornton, who delivered its double entendres with a sly musical and sexual authority. On her original recording, the offending hound dog is "snooping" around her door. "You can wag your tail," she sings, "but I ain't gonna feed you no more." During the guitar solo, she gleefully growls "Now wag your tail," leaving no doubt what kind of dog she's talking about.

By contrast, like many rock and roll covers of R&B songs, Presley's version (borrowed from one by Freddie Bell and the Bellboys) "cleans up" the words for teenybopper consumption. This dog's offense, as we hear repeatedly, is that it has "never caught a rabbit." Although Presley's performance may be erotically charged, the words—reduced to two stanzas repeated over and over—make little sense. In place of the original's suggestive metaphors, these lyrics seem aimed literally at a loud, lazy pooch.

The musical arrangement, too, is fairly peculiar. The instrumental responses to the voice, nuanced on Thornton's recording, are reduced to jagged, noisy fragments from the guitar and a yammering set of snare triplets at the end of each verse. Across its eight choruses of twelve-bar blues, the music sounds like a juvenile eruption of pent up energy. The adult response to Presley's version was typified in his television appearance on *The Steve Allen Show* soon after "Hound Dog" was released. Allen set Presley up for ridicule, inducing the young star to sing the song to an actual basset hound while dressed in a tuxedo.

The track begins—is launched, really—with a half-growled, half-shouted one-bar **pickup** (notes occurring prior to the downbeat). When the band drops in on the downbeat, the texture is dominated by loud, bright snare backbeats and poorly coordinated hand claps. The electric guitar plays rhythm (doubled by a barely audible piano part) while the bass plays an arpeggio pattern. The texture is remarkably sparse for such a powerful blast of sound. Presley's highly charged vocal performance and the track's pounding backbeat provide the bulk of the record's energy.

Scotty Moore's guitar part provides the only real action in the track's instrumental mid-range. During the vocal choruses Moore plays a murky low-register rhythm part interrupted by a two-bar break, which he fills with a two-note response to the voice. In his two guitar solos he tilts toward the manic as backing voices, sounding woefully out of place, intone the blues harmonies in glee club style. The solos are cumulative in the sense that the second one takes the eccentricity of the first to a new level, careening along on the verge of imminent breakdown (a display Moore himself later described as "ancient psychedelia"). With its primitive guitar playing, its sloppy handclap rhythm, and its trashy sounding snare (something like pounding on the lid of a metal garbage can), the track appears to be not the result of a well-financed production effort but the spontaneous eruption of a street band.

It is remarkable that such a raw sounding track required so many takes. Although Steve Sholes supervised the recording session, Presley was in charge of production. (Sholes, a country music veteran with no real idea of what Presley was up to, was happy to let his new star follow his instincts.) With five top-forty hits in six months (two of which went to number one), Presley had gained enough clout with his new record company to break the typical three-hour session limit. He ran his sessions in the way he had learned from Sam Phillips—experimenting, reaching, doing whatever it took to breathe life into the record. With "Hound Dog" he was clearly seeking something that only the recording process could crystallize.

Listening Guide

"Hound Dog" (Jerry Leiber, Mike Stoller), RCA Victor (mono)
Recorded at RCA Studio A, New York City, July 1956
Elvis Presley (voice), the Jordanaires (backing singers), Scotty Moore (guitar), Gordon Stoker (piano), Bill Black (bass), D. J. Fontana (drums)
Producer: Steve Sholes
Engineer: Ernie Ulrich
Charts: Popular Records: Best Sellers in Stores #1, R&B Records: Best Sellers in Stores #1, C&W Records: Best Sellers in Stores #1
Key: C
Meter: 4/4

Time	Section	Lyric Cue	Listen For
0:0	**Chorus 1** (12)	"You ain't nothing but a hound dog"	Solo voice pickup. Phrase 1: Guitar strums in low register.

continued on next page

Time	Section	Lyric Cue	Listen For
0:07		"You ain't nothing but a hound dog"	Bass plays arpeggio figure loosely doubled by handclaps. Loud, bright snare. Phrase 2: Guitar drops strumming, plays two-note response to voice.
0:12		"You ain't never caught a rabbit"	Phrase 3: Same texture as phrase 1.
0:15			Snare triplets followed by voice pickup.
0:18	Chorus 2 (12)	"They said you was high class"	Texture as in chorus 1.
0:34	Chorus 3 (12)	"You ain't nothing but a hound dog"	Texture as in chorus 1.
0:50	Chorus 4 (12)		Guitar solo 1. Sustained vocal harmony. Handclaps switch from syncopation to doubling snare backbeat.
1:06	Chorus 5 (12)	"They said you was high class"	Texture as in chorus 1.
1:22	Chorus 6 (12)		Guitar solo 2. Texture as in chorus 4.
1:38	Chorus 7 (12)	"They said you was high class"	Texture as in chorus 1.
1:54	Chorus 8 (12)	"You ain't nothing but a hound dog"	Texture as in chorus 1.

5.3. "PEGGY SUE" (1957)

BUDDY HOLLY

Buddy Holly was among the wave of rockabilly musicians who followed Elvis Presley on to the national stage. Holly died in February of 1959 at the age of twenty-three, but in his short career as a rock and roll star, beginning with his 1957 hit "That'll Be the Day," he managed to create a body of work that would influence generations of rock fans, including the Beatles and the Rolling Stones. Born and raised in Lubbock, Texas, Holly merged his country roots with a big beat and a strident electric guitar—"western and bop" he called it early on. But he was also a fan of mainstream pop, whose influence is clearly felt in one of Holly's finest recordings, "True Love Ways." Like many early rock and roll musicians (Chuck Berry, Carl Perkins, Roy Orbison), Holly was a songwriter as well as performer. The stylistic diversity of his musicianship was mirrored in his songwriting, which ranged from the tender softness of "Words of Love" to the driving rhythm of "Not Fade Away" to the rockabilly "That'll Be the Day."

Holly made most of his recordings far from the pop capitals of Los Angeles, Nashville, and New York. Along with his band the Crickets, he traveled to Clovis, New Mexico, a small town not far from Lubbock, to record at a studio owned by Norman Petty, a recording engineer, producer, and leader of the Norman Petty Trio, a lounge-pop group. Here again there was no time limit on recording sessions. Petty ran a live-in operation with his wife and musical collaborator Vi. Musicians could work for days on end in an environment that welcomed experimentation. The resulting records often featured unusual timbres and sound processing techniques. On Holly's "Everyday," for example, we hear the sound of a celesta and percussion provided by hands drumming on knees. On "Not Fade Away" we hear the drum part played on cardboard boxes. "Well All Right" features a texture that combines acoustic guitar and a percussion part consisting of nothing but the bell of a cymbal. And on "Words of Love" Holly overdubs his voice and guitar parts.

Proving once again that rock and roll records are about much more than their songs, "Peggy Sue" achieves its distinctive quality primarily through Holly's stylized vocal performance, a propulsive rhythmic texture, and an unusual use of reverb. The song's content is minimal: just four short stanzas worth of lyrics in a twelve-bar blues form, each with many repetitions of a girl's name and each ending with the refrain "I love you Peggy Sue." The protagonist clearly adores Peggy Sue, but his obsessive insistence, his assertion "I feel blue," and the curious chord substitution in the third and sixth choruses (to the ♭VI chord) seem to imply some kind of trouble. What appears on the surface a bubblegum teenybopper blues also harbors a sense of adolescent uncertainty and vulnerability.

Holly's voice is by turns husky and airy, similar to Presley's multiple-voice approach though different in sound. He slips back and forth, stitching the two sounds into a single character. The quasi baby talk character of the higher voice produces an overtly stylized effect, but the husky voice can also veer in this direction, as we hear in the track's final phrase.

The rhythmic strumming of the guitar dominates the chordal part of the arrangement. Its propulsive effect is heightened by a layered rhythmic texture in which the bass plays quarter notes, the guitar plays eighth notes, and the drums play sixteenth notes. The relentless duple feel creates a momentum that sweeps through the track. Even the guitar solo is caught up in the flow. Instead of melody, the solo is all about rhythm and a very aggressive sound. Listen, too, for the layering in the rhythm guitar texture. A faint high-register part—clearly audible only in the intro—adds a little high-end brightness to an otherwise thick, mid-range sound.

The reverb on the drums is deliberately idiosyncratic. The mic signal is sent to an echo chamber, but instead of blending the reverb with the dry drum sound to create a single composite image, the reverb (wet) drums and the dry drums are treated as separate "instruments" in the track's arrangement. The effect is similar to a zoom lens, the wet drums receding into the distance and the dry ones rushing to the front of the mix. In the intro the effect is switched on and off every two beats. When the voice enters in chorus one, the drums remain in reverb mode. For all we know at this point, the alternating reverb trick was just an attention-grabbing kickoff.

But at the turnaround following chorus one, the dry drums suddenly return, only to fade back to reverb when the voice begins chorus two. Now the listener is aware that these contrasting drum images are likely to switch places at any time, and sure enough the wet and dry drums continue to alternate, as indicated in the Listening Guide. The curious technique seems to have some intentional purpose, something thematic, like the development of a musical idea. The dry drum sound only appears when Holly is not singing, so there is some sort of pattern. But why the reverb is treated this way is left to the listener's imagination. Likely, the move is simply a token of the recording team's creative whimsy, something to delight and intrigue the listener's ear.

Listening Guide

"Peggy Sue" (Buddy Holly), Coral (mono)
Recorded at Norman Petty Studios, Clovis, New Mexico, June 1957
Buddy Holly (guitar, vocal), Niki Sullivan (guitar), Joe B. Mauldin (bass), Jerry Allison (drums)
Producer and engineer: Norman Petty
Charts: Popular Records: Best Sellers in Stores #3, R&B Records: Best Sellers in Stores #2
Key: A
Meter: 4/4

Time	Section	Lyric Cue	Listen For
0:00	Intro (2)		Drum sound alternates wet and dry sounds every two beats, coinciding with the chord changes.
			Rhythmic layers:
			Bass: quarter notes
			Guitar: eighth notes
			Drums: sixteenth notes
0:06	Chorus 1 (12)	"If you knew"	Rhythmic ornamentation in voice ("Pe-heh-gy Su-u-ue").
			Wet drum sound.
0:23			Turnaround: dry drum sound.
0:26	Chorus 2 (2)	"Peggy Sue"	Voice hints at baby talk ("yearns for you").
			Wet drum sound.
0:37			Brief interjection of dry drum sound between vocal phrases.
0:42			Turnaround: dry drum sound.
0:45	Chorus 3 (12)	"Peggy Sue"	Husky voice.
			Wet drum sound.
0:49			Chord substitution ($\flat$VI).
0:56			Brief interjection of dry drum sound between vocal phrases.
1:02			Turnaround: dry drum sound.
1:04	Chorus 4 (12)	"I love you"	Baby talk vocal.
			Wet drum sound.
1:21			Turnaround: dry drum sound.
1:24	Chorus 5 (12)		Guitar solo forgoes melody, opting instead for a blast of noise consisting of chords and rhythm.
			Dry drum sound.
1:43	Chorus 6 (12)	"Peggy Sue"	Husky voice.
			Wet drum sound.
1:46			Chord substitution ($\flat$VI).
1:53			Brief interjection of dry drum sound between vocal phrases.
1:59			Turnaround: dry drum sound.
2:02	Chorus 7 (12)	"I love you"	Wet drum sound.
2:22			4-bar extension; husky voice dips into low range.

5.4. "ROCK AND ROLL MUSIC" (1957)

CHUCK BERRY

Chuck Berry was the most prolific hitmaker among early rock and roll songwriters, with nine top-forty hits in the 1950s. His records exemplify the new approaches to blues and to songwriting discussed in this chapter, as well as the eclectic style mixture characteristic of the new music. Most of his hits employ some kind of blues variant in their musical form, but they do not sound like idiomatic blues. They are laced with melodic and rhythmic ideas borrowed from pop and country styles, and their lyrics often evoke teenage life ("School Day") and youthful iconoclasm ("Roll Over Beethoven"), not exactly blues topics.

"Rock and Roll Music" takes the form of a musicology/sociology lesson told in words and music. Aware of his professorial role, Berry wrote of the song in his autobiography: "I was heavy into rock 'n' roll even then and had to create something that hit the spot without question. I wanted the lyrics to define every aspect of its being and so worded it to do so."[7] The record is both a celebration and an elucidation of rock and roll.

The song is a good example of Berry's skill at writing clever lyrics. He has "no kick against modern jazz," he sings, "unless they try to play it too darn fast." This reference is a swipe at the virtuosic bebop style, which had indeed split off from more popular jazz styles. Through a seriousness akin to classical music ("sounds just like a symphony"), bebop lost its popular appeal ("the beauty of the melody") and became a music for connoisseurs. Rock and roll, by contrast, is the music from "across the tracks," the low-down side of town, where an R&B band led by a "wailing sax" rocks with the force of a "hurricane." In a reference to the country side of rock and roll, Berry tells us that it's also the music of southern country folk. At their "jamboree," drinking their own "home brew from a wooden cup," they go to dancing and get "all shook up" (this last image is a reference to Elvis Presley's recent hit "All Shook Up").

The message of the lyrics is echoed in the music as Berry sets up a contrast between verses and choruses. In each verse, the harmonic progression and rhythmic texture have a light, syncopated pop feel. The choruses, on the other hand, are in twelve-bar blues form (with an added two-bar tag on "if you want to dance with me"). As the lyrics bring us back to "rock and roll music" in each chorus, Berry emphasizes the point using the blues as a symbol of the music's essence. The choruses also feature a steady, driving eighth-note rhythm on guitar, another rock and roll essential in Berry's tutorial.

Even the eighth-note guitar strums that kick off the track make this point. Berry invented some of the most quoted guitar riffs in rock and roll, introducing such tracks as "Carol," "Roll Over Beethoven," and "Johnny B. Goode" with memorable guitar hooks. But "Rock and Roll Music" strips the opening guitar riff of melodic content, offering only an unadorned announcement, in its repeated eighth notes, of the bedrock new rhythm of rock and roll.

Berry also uses the chorus lyrics to remind us that rock and roll has "a backbeat, you can't lose it." Indeed, the snare backbeat anchors the groove through most of the track. In another instance of interlacing verbal and musical meaning, however, the backbeat drops out in verse four. As Berry invokes Latin genres in the lyrics (tango, mambo, conga), the groove shifts accordingly.

Further adding to the track's insistent rhythmic drive is the echo effect on guitar, voice, and snare, which is timed roughly to a sixteenth note. Mixed in the background, this further duple subdivision adds an edge to a rhythmic texture already tense with rhythmic contradiction. As in Little Richard's "Tutti Frutti," we hear different grooves clash against one another as the piano roams freely, out of sync with the guitar's steady eighth notes. Once again, words and music connect when Berry, at the end of verse four, sings "keep rocking that piano" and the piano falls in line with a quick set of straight eighth notes.

Listening Guide

"Rock and Roll Music" (Chuck Berry), Chess Records (mono)
Recorded at Chess Studios, Chicago, May 1957
Chuck Berry (voice, guitar), Lafayette Leake (piano), Willie Dixon (bass),
    Fred Below (drums)
Producers: Leonard and Phil Chess
Charts: Popular Records: Best Sellers in Stores #8, R&B Records: Best
    Sellers in Stores #6
Key: E♭
Meter: 4/4

Time	Section	Lyric Cue	Listen For
0:00	Chorus (12+2)	"Just let me hear"	Voice and guitar set the groove with an eighth-note pickup.
			Echo effect on voice, guitar, and snare drum adds a sixteenth-note subdivision to the background.
			Piano plays free rhythm, tugging against the guitar's steady strumming.
			12-bar blues chord sequence elongated by repeating the finial phrase.

continued on next page

Time	Section	Lyric Cue	Listen For
0:22	**Verse 1** (8)	"I have no kick"	Rhythmic texture shifts to syncopated and slightly swinging.
			Chord sequence changes from blues to pop.
0:34	**Chorus** (12+2)	"That's why I go for that"	**Chorus** texture.
0:54	**Verse 2** (8)	"I took my love"	**Verse** texture.
1:06	**Chorus** (12+2)	"That's why I go for that"	**Chorus** texture.
1:26	**Verse 3** (8)	"Way down south"	**Verse** texture.
1:38	**Chorus** (12+2)	"And started playing"	**Chorus** texture.
1:58	**Verse 4** (8)	"Don't care to hear"	Snare drum out; groove shifts to Latin feel.
2:08		"So I can hear"	Piano hammers out eighth notes doubling voice pickup in shifting back to rock groove.
2:10	**Chorus** (12+2)		**Chorus** texture.

NOTES

1. Quoted in "Tin Pan Alley: Jailhouse Rock," *Time*, April 20, 1959, 48.
2. Quoted in "Songwriter Johnny Green Likens R&B to Tarragon," *Down Beat*, September 19, 1956, 44.
3. John A. Jackson, *Big Beat: Alan Freed and the Early Years of Rock and Roll* (New York: Schirmer Books, 1991), 82.
4. Quoted in Charles White, *The Life and Times of Little Richard: The Quasar of Rock* (New York: Da Capo Press, 1994), 43.
5. Quoted in Tony Scherman, *Backbeat: Earl Palmer's Story* (Washington DC: Smithsonian Institution Press, 1999), 90–91.
6. Cited in Laurie Henshaw, "Rock-'n'-Roll Swamps '56 Music Scene," *Melody Maker*, December 15, 1956), 21.
7. Chuck Berry, *Chuck Berry: The Autobiography* (New York: Harmony Books, 1987), 154.

FURTHER READING

Altschuler, Glenn C. *All Shook Up: How Rock 'N' Roll Changed America.* New York: Oxford University Press, 2003.

Berry, Chuck. *Chuck Berry: The Autobiography.* New York: Harmony Books, 1987.

Guralnick, Peter. *Last Train to Memphis: The Rise of Elvis Presley.* Boston: Little, Brown, 1994.

Norman, Philip. *Rave On: The Biography of Buddy Holly.* New York: Simon and Schuster, 1996.

White, Charles. *The Life and Times of Little Richard: The Quasar of Rock.* New York: Da Capo, 1994.

FURTHER LISTENING

Toni Fisher, "The Big Hurt" (Signet, 1959)
Bobby Freeman, "Do You Want to Dance" (Josie, 1958)
Dale Hawkins, "Susie Q" (Checker, 1957)
Screamin' Jay Hawkins, "I Put a Spell on You" (Okeh, 1956)
Clarence "Frogman" Henry, "Ain't Got No Home" (Argo, 1956)
Jerry Lee Lewis, "Great Ball of Fire" (Sun, 1957)
Mickey and Sylvia, "Love Is Strange" (Groove, 1956)
Silhouettes, "Get a Job" (Ember, 1957)
Ritchie Valens, "Come On, Let's Go" (Del-Fi, 1958)
Link Wray and His Ray Men, "Rumble" (Cadence, 1958)

6

R&B WITH STRINGS
Sweet Soul

The crossover momentum established by doo wop groups was sustained by African American performers working in diverse styles as R&B developed in several new directions through the late 1950s and early 1960s. All brought a black sound and feel to the pop mainstream but, as with the vocal groups, their styles were different from the postwar urban blues performers, with a lighter touch that appealed to young audiences. Because the church was the first musical training ground for nearly all young black singers, traces of gospel were never far away. But the raw emotion of gospel was toned down and smoothed out, and what remained was a deeply expressive type of pop singing.

The styles presented in this chapter range from the New Orleans shuffle of Fats Domino to the pop crooning of Sam Cooke and the neo–doo wop of the Drifters. They are sufficiently different to resist grouping into any single genre, but they share some important similarities. In contrast to many blues records, for instance, the tracks in this chapter feature sweet voices, lyrical tunes, laid back grooves, and, in the Drifters and Sam Cooke selections, instruments more commonly found in major-label pop productions—strings, brass, and timpani. None of the songs has a blues form or feel. Although the artists are black, their records routinely crossed over from the R&B to the pop charts. Lew Chudd, the owner of Imperial Records, Fats Domino's label, put his finger on the nature of the phenomenon, pointing to the influence of the record-buying public in determining the evolving content of the pop charts. "When an artist sells 1,000,000 or more records," he said, "he's a pop artist, regardless of the type of material he's using."[1]

As fans voted with their cash and radio requests, old assumptions about the connections between musical styles, ethnicity, and markets fell apart. Moreover, black performers' pop success bred further style changes, which would become conspicuously evident in the Motown records of the 1960s.

6.1. "BLUEBERRY HILL" (1956)

FATS DOMINO

Fats Domino was a giant during the first decade of rock and roll, charting sixty-three R&B hits. His crossover history illustrates an interesting aspect of rock and roll's development. Before 1955, Domino had seventeen R&B hits, of which only three made a showing in the pop charts. After his 1955 top-ten hit "Ain't That a Shame" all but three of his further forty-six R&B chart hits went pop as well. Not only did he become a rock and roll star, but he was one of the era's top selling artists. Yet on the way to widespread popularity, Domino did not change his style, a sweet, Creole-tinged voice accompanied by a laid-back brand of New Orleans swing. Rather, the emerging rock and roll audience came to embrace what he was already doing. No one invented rock and roll. The idiom was born of a democratic process whereby fans voted with their record purchases, jukebox selections, and radio station requests. At a certain point the fans decided that Fats Domino's music was another flavor of rock and roll.

The triplets that characterized so much early rock and roll are well represented on "Blueberry Hill." The piano begins with a melody played in triplets and then, switching to chords, continues the rhythm in the right hand throughout the track, all the while doubled by the ride cymbal. The guitar and bass join the piano left hand in a boogie-woogie bassline that moves along with the triplet groove. The texture is a classic Fats Domino sound. In 1956 *Billboard* reported, with only slight exaggeration, that it was Domino "who many credit with starting that whole business of triplets" in rock and roll.[2]

Contrast is provided by the increased harmonic movement in the B section (thanks to a couple of chromatic chords), as well as producer Dave Bartholomew's saxophone arrangement. The saxophones switch from sustained chords in the A sections to legato melodic lines in the B, or bridge, sections. These lines drag the beat slightly, which, along with the similarly lazy snare backbeat, is characteristic New Orleans R&B style—a musical evocation of the New Orleans nickname, the Big Easy. This rhythmic effect of slightly delaying the beat contributes to the track's relaxed feel.

The musicians on the session are New Orleans players, members of Domino's touring band. But unlike so many other Domino sides, "Blueberry Hill" was recorded not in New Orleans but Los Angeles, where he was performing and where his record company Imperial was based. The session did not result in a usable take. The "performance" on the record was actually assembled through tape splicing by engineer Bunny Robyn, who copied part of the first B section and added it to the second one. "Don't put that thing out," Bartholomew insisted to label owner Lew Chudd. "It's no damn good." But it was too late. The young fans had already embraced it. "From now on, cut nothin' but no-good records," Chudd instructed Bartholomew. "We just sold three million."[3]

"Blueberry Hill" is a song from an earlier pop era, originally recorded by the cowboy singer Gene Autry and then in hit versions by Glenn Miller's big band (1940) and Louis Armstrong (1949, with an arrangement by Gordon Jenkins). It was Armstrong's version that led Domino to record the song. It was not unusual for rock and roll performers to use older pop material. For instance, in 1954, while still at Sun Records, Elvis Presley crooned versions of pop standards "Blue Moon" and "Harbor Lights"; in 1958 Little Richard recorded "By the Light of the Silvery Moon" (a song from 1910); and in 1956 the Platters topped the charts with "My Prayer," which had been a hit for the Ink Spots in 1939. The first generation of rock and roll stars grew up listening to and often idolizing older pop, country, and R&B performers. While the young stars wrote some of their own material, they also mined the trove of America's popular music legacy. In his sweet-voiced, soulful New Orleans version of "Blueberry Hill," Domino claimed the song for the rock and roll generation.

Listening Guide

"Blueberry Hill" (Al Lewis, Larry Stock, Vincent Rose), Imperial Records (mono)
Recorded at Master Recorders in Hollywood, June 1956
Antoine "Fats" Domino (voice, piano), Buddy Hagans, Wendell Duconge, Eddie Silvers (saxophones), Lawrence Guyton (bass), Walter Nelson (guitar), Cornelius Coleman (drums)
Producer: Dave Bartholomew
Engineer: Bunny Robyn
Charts: Popular Records: Best Sellers in Stores #2, R&B Records: Best Sellers in Stores #1
Key: B; Meter: 4/4

Time	Section	Lyric Cue	Listen For
0:00	Intro (4)		Boogie-woogie pattern played by piano left hand, guitar, and bass.
			Bright snare backbeat.
0:12	A (8)	"I found my thrill"	**Intro** texture continues.
			Piano triplets in right hand.
			Saxophones play sustained chords.
0:33	A (8)	"The moon stood still"	Texture continues.
0:53	B (8)	"The wind in the willow"	Saxophones play melodic answers to vocal phrases.
			Increased harmonic movement.
			Boogie-woogie pattern suspended.
1:14	A (8)	"Though we're apart"	Similar to previous **A**.
1:35	B (8)	"The wind in the willow"	Similar to previous **B**.
			The phrase "but all of those vows you made" is a spliced copy.
1:56	A (8)	"Though we're apart"	Similar to previous **A**.

6.2. "THERE GOES MY BABY" (1959)

THE DRIFTERS

The Drifters were formed in 1953 as a showcase for lead singer Clyde McPhatter. They shot to stardom with top R&B hits such as "Money Honey" and "Honey Love." After McPhatter left the group for a solo career, the Drifters carried on with other lead singers, notably Johnny Moore. But by 1958, amid a series of personnel problems and flagging record sales, manager George Treadwell, who owned the Drifters name, fired all the group's members. In their place he enlisted a New York City group known as the Crowns (formerly the Five Crowns), who changed their name and immediately began touring in fulfillment of the Drifters' outstanding contracts. The Crowns had scuffled along in the New York doo wop scene since 1952 with little success. Now, suddenly, they donned the mantle of a group they had previously looked up to as superstars. As they performed the Drifters' material over the next many months, they grew into the group's aura, setting the stage for a resurgence that would produce sixteen top-forty hits.

Atlantic Records producer and executive Jerry Wexler assigned Jerry Leiber and Mike Stoller to produce the first recording for the new Drifters. Leiber and Stoller were hot songwriters and record producers working on a series of hits for another Atlantic group, the Coasters, and Wexler hoped the pair might do the same for the Drifters. The song chosen was "There Goes My Baby," written by the group's lead singer, Ben E. King (formerly Ben E. Nelson). It is an unusual song in that it has almost no rhymes. It is a free-form cry of loss and heartbreak sung over a four-bar chord sequence that repeats without variation, keeping the spotlight fully on the protagonist's emotional performance.

What Leiber and Stoller came up with was radical. "Whenever I heard it on the radio," Stoller recalled, "I kept thinking I was getting two different stations on the same wavelength."[4] Wexler denounced it as "dog meat."[5] Ahmet Ertegun, the label president, shared the assessment but offered words of encouragement. "You can't hit a home run every time," he said, and no doubt their next attempt would be better.[6] But the pair believed in the record and convinced Ertegun to have ace Atlantic engineer Tom Dowd remix the track and release it. Dowd's remix may have improved things, but what remained was still obscure, a mix of oddly matched musical bits and pieces floating in a textural soup. Yet contrary to expectations, the record quickly soared to the top of the charts, confirming once again that the rock and roll audience rewarded records that broke the mold.

The track is striking, first of all, for what is missing: no drum set, no guitar, no saxophone, no piano. The only characteristic rock and roll instrument is the bass. Accompanying the familiar doo wop–style vocal textures (following the standard doo wop I–vi–IV–V progression), we hear strings, a timpani, and a vast, murky reverb. The low-end is an indistinct blur because the timpani (a pitched drum) never changes its pitch. As the bass moves through the chord changes, the repeated timpani note clashes with the bass notes and creates a masking effect. The timpani part was added on a whim simply because the drum happened to be in the studio. The drummer, however, was not a timpani player and did not know how to operate the pedal that changes the drum's pitch.

Meanwhile, the violins play bare melodies without chordal support. The groove is a plodding rhythm played by bass, timpani, and shaker (very faintly). The overall soundscape is strange, the texture both minimal and thick at the same time, a counterpoint of contrasting timbres juxtaposed in the imaginary space suggested by the reverb.

"There Goes My Baby" is often touted incorrectly as a "first" in rock and roll for its use of strings. Pointing out the strings on previous recordings, however, *Billboard* noted in early 1957 "how elegant some R&B records are these days."[7] The Dominoes used strings on a trio of

1957 hits: "Star Dust," "St. Therese of the Roses," and "Deep Purple." The Platters used strings on their 1958 number-one hit "Twilight Time." Later that year, at his last recording session, Buddy Holly's "True Love Ways" was set to a lovely string arrangement.

"There Goes My Baby" is distinctive, however, in how the strings are used. Strings in pop usually add a warm luster to a track's texture, drawing things together in a smooth blend of sound. And, indeed, the rock and roll tracks that had previously featured strings used them in this way, in effect invoking the adult easy listening style. But on the Drifters' track, the string texture is stark. Instead of a full complement of strings to fill out the frequency spectrum with full harmonies, there is only a group of violins, joined occasionally by a lone cello, playing unison melodies. Sounding nothing like easy listening, the string parts instead add an agitated feel to the track.

Furthermore, strings usually induced rock and roll singers to croon seductively like traditional pop ballad singers. Ben E. King, however, sings with an expressive animation more reminiscent of gospel music. In short, whereas strings were normally used as a smoothing influence, on "There Goes My Baby" they are one more edgy element in an overall edgy soundscape.

Mike Stoller's quip about hearing the track as if it were two radio stations superimposed describes a perception of both sound and style. The mix's balance and reverb give a surreal sonic impression, almost as if the performance is happening in different places simultaneously. Stylistically, the faintly Latin groove, the string melodies (which to Stoller bore a Russian classical music influence), the fervent lead vocal, and the doo wop backing make for a collage of associations. Taken together, song, arrangement, and recording add up to two minutes of rock and roll exotica.

Latin Rhythm in Rock and Roll

Latin rhythms had an important influence on rock and roll. Some of the biggest early hits to feature a Latin feel were those produced by Leiber and Stoller. They identified their Latin-influenced rhythms as derivatives of the Brazilian *baião*, but they were referring only to the bass drum pattern (see figure 6.1). Note that the symbol connecting the eighth note to the following quarter note (a **tie**) extends the duration of the eighth note.

Figure 6.1. Baião Rhythm.

The Latin feel in rock and roll is actually more general, borrowing rhythmic elements from rumba and tango as well. Among the many variants,

> the consistent feature is an accent on the "and" of the second beat (the eighth-note subdivision) usually played by the bass, bass drum, or both and often further emphasized in a higher register by another instrument. Some notable examples include the Drifters' "Save the Last Dance for Me," Ben E. King's "Stand by Me," the Marvellettes' "Please Mr. Postman," the Crystals' "Then He Kissed Me," Ray Charles's "Unchain My Heart," and Chuck Jackson's "I Don't Want to Cry."

Listening Guide

"There Goes My Baby" (Benjamin Nelson, Lover Patterson, George Treadwell), Atlantic Records (mono)
Recorded in New York City, March 1959
Ben E. King (lead voice), Charlie Thomas, Doc Green, Elsbeary Hobbs (voice), studio musicians (violins, cello, timpani, bass)
Arranger: Stanley Applebaum
Producers: Jerry Leiber, Mike Stoller
Engineer: Tom Dowd
Charts: Hot 100 #2, Hot R&B Sides #1
Key: A
Meter: 4/4

Time	Section	Lyric Cue	Listen For
0:00	Intro (4)	"Bom bom"	Doo wop vocal riff, prominent bass voice.
			Bass and timpani play Latin rhythm.
			"Big" reverb.
0:13			Strings rush upward toward **verse** downbeat.
0:15	Verse 1 (4)	"There goes my baby"	Backing voices out.
			Violins play legato descending sequence.
0:30	Verse 2 (4)	"I broke her heart"	Backing voices repeat riff from **intro** buried deep in reverb.
			Violins repeat descending sequence.
0:44	Verse 3 (4)	"There goes my baby"	Backing voices sing lyrics.
			Lead voice answers with wordless responses.
			Violins out; pizzicato cello in low register.
0:59	Verse 4 (4)	"I want to know if she"	Violins and cello play *marcato* figure in octaves.
			Backing voices out.
1:14	Verse 5 (4)	"I wonder why she"	Strings repeat *marcato* figure, adding a higher octave.
			Backing voices sing sustained harmony.

Time	Section	Lyric Cue	Listen For
1:29	Verse 6 (4)	"I just want to tell her"	Violins play descending sequence. Backing voices out.
1:44	Verse 7 (4)	"Where is my baby"	Backing voices sing riff from **intro**. Violins play descending sequence.
1:59	Verse 8 (4 bars to fade)	"There goes my baby"	Backing voices sing lyrics. Lead voice answers with wordless responses. Violins play descending sequence.

6.3. "A CHANGE IS GONNA COME" (1963)

SAM COOKE

Sam Cooke had thirty-two top-forty pop hits between 1957 and 1965, captivating audiences with his expressive tenor voice, good looks, and charismatic presence. Cooke was an established gospel star, lead singer for the Soul Stirrers, when he decided to turn to pop in 1956. Within a year he had a number-one pop hit with his song "You Send Me." In winning over pop audiences, Cooke tamed some of the raspy exuberance of his gospel style, but the fervent spirit remained. No matter how light the fare he offers up in such songs as "Twistin' the Night Away" or "Good Times," his soulful delivery gives his performances an expressive depth. His love songs, such as "Cupid" and "Bring It on Home to Me," have a heartfelt honesty that transcends pop artifice. It was not terribly surprising, then, that in the midst of the racial turmoil of the early 1960s he was moved to write and record an unusually serious pop song called "A Change Is Gonna Come." In Bob Dylan's "Blowin' in the Wind," which had become both a pop hit and an anthem of the civil rights movement, Cooke saw the public's growing acceptance for pop music that spoke to social issues. He wanted to lend his voice to the cause and in the process expand his artistic identity.

The song is both simple and eloquent. The simplicity of the chord changes and the strophic form gives it the feel of a folk song, something timeless and enduring. Yet despite its limited harmonic resources, the harmonic phrase structure is such that it underlines both the protagonist's suffering and his determination. The first four bars of each verse move from major to minor, from the tonic B♭ to the vi chord G minor. Here, in his characteristic ornamented vocal style, Cooke presents images of hardship—"It's been too hard living"; "there been times when I thought I couldn't last for long." The refrain that follows, which initially leads more strongly to the minor, ends up back in the major mode as it answers each hardship with a refrain of dogged faith: "I know a change is gonna come." The song's lyrics, enhanced by the harmony, and Cooke's performance convey an implacable resolve to keep putting one foot in front of the other. The sentiment was deeply personal. Even as a top-tier star, when he toured in the South, Cooke suffered the same indignities of racial segregation and discrimination as any other black American at the time.

The track's musical arrangement is akin to a film score. It heightens the emotional drama and mirrors the song's narrative with the orchestral sound of strings, brass, and timpani. The mix enhances the sumptuous effect of the instrumental forces by spreading them out on the stereo stage, enfolding the voice, which remains in the center. (This is the first stereo track we have studied. Several aspects of the stereo arrangement are noted in the Listening Guide.) Cooke's longtime arranger René Hall created a setting that sounds by turns prayerful, ominous, and triumphant, varying the texture with each verse to develop a musical story line. The track's dramatic sweep attracted filmmaker Spike Lee, who used it in his film *Malcolm X* (1992). The song's topic and the era of its release fit the film's historical context, but the arrangement gives it an especially resonant cinematic aspect as well. Lee uses the entire track as the underscore building to the film's climactic scene.

The track's intro sets the atmosphere with a mini-overture that introduces the orchestra and sets the stereo stage with instruments panned across the stereo field. Verse one is accompanied by a stately brass choir. The sustained chords are soft and warm, leaving enough textural space to hear an intriguing sonic detail. Listen to how the snare drum, which is panned to the right in the mix, seems to cast a "shadow" across the stereo stage as its reverb appears on the left. Verse two surrounds the voice with string melodies, which subside to sustained harmonies in the refrain. Verse three is full-textured, with string melodies and a new, punchy rhythmic figure in the brass. At the refrain, the sound is pared back to sustained brass chords similar to verse one. Through most of the refrain sections, a French horn melody lends a mournful air, playing its own tune separate from the other instruments.

The bridge brings a contrasting section, which culminates with the protagonist's lowest moment as he humbly reaches out for compassion, only to find himself once more on his knees. The strings murmur with restless tremolos (rapid back-and-forth bowing) as the French horn continues playing its lonely song in the background. At the climactic point (2:20, "Back down on my knees") the harmony moves to a nondiatonic chord, which propels the music forward to a strong arrival on the track's only V chord, highlighting the moment unmistakably. Verse four is dominated initially by the brass rhythm from verse three, resolutely mirroring the protagonist's resolve to "carry on." The final refrain brings the warmth of sustained string chords to end the track with a sense of hopeful benediction.

What Is 12/8 Time?

The meter 12/8 is a four-beat meter. It is called a **compound meter** because each beat is regularly subdivided into three instead of two. As we know, 4/4 is also a four-beat meter but its subdivisions are normally duple (this is called **simple meter**). The difference comes down to feel. Compound meters have an underlying sense of a lilt. In "A Change Is Gonna Come" we hear it when the bass plays notes between the beats while moving from one chord to another. We also hear it in the brass rhythm of verse three and the pickup figure in the bridge. Other common compound meters are 6/8 and 9/8.

Listening Guide

"**A Change Is Gonna Come**" (Sam Cooke), RCA Victor (stereo)
Recorded at RCA Studio, Hollywood, January 1964
Sam Cooke (voice), William Kurasch, Arnold Belnick, Ralph Schaeffer, Jack Pepper, Irving Lipschultz, Alexander Neiman, Sidney Sharp, Darrel Terwilliger, Leonard Malarsky, Israel Baker, Tibor Zelig (violin), Harry Hyams (viola), Emmet Sargeant (cello), Clifton White, Bobby Womack, René Hall, Norman Bartold (guitar), Harold Battiste (piano), William Hinshaw (French horn), John Ewing, David Wells, Louis Blackburn (trombone), Chuck Badie (bass), Earl Palmer (drums), Emil Radocchia (timpani)
Arranger and conductor: René Hall
Producers: Sam Cooke, Hugo Peretti, Luigi Creatore
Engineer: Dave Hassinger
Charts: Hot 100 #31, Hot R&B Singles #9
Key: B♭
Meter: 4/4 for **intro**, then 12/8

Time	Section	Lyric Cue	Listen For
0:00	Intro (3)		Violins (L), viola, and cello (R) frame the stereo field with descending melodies.
0:06			Brass enter.
0:08			Timpani.
0:11			French horn melodic tag (L).

continued on next page

Time	Section	Lyric Cue	Listen For
0:16	**Verse 1** (4+4)	"I was born"	Voice (C).
			Brass choir (L+R) plays sustained chords.
			Snare drum (R) reverb casts a reverb "shadow" (L).
		"Ever since"	Ends on G minor.
0:32	Refrain	"It's been a long"	Back to B♭ harmony.
0:38			Stronger move to G minor intensifies title lyrics.
0:45		"Oh yes it will"	Ends on B♭ major.
			French horn tag.
0:49	**Verse 2** (4+4)	"It's been too hard"	String melodies (L+R) play counterpoint to voice.
			Brass choir continues sustained chords.
1:05	Refrain	"It's been a long"	Strings join brass in sustained-chord texture.
1:22	**Verse 3** (4+4)	"I go to the movie"	Brass plays rhythmic figure.
			Strings play sporadic phrases.
1:39	Refrain	"It's been a long"	Brass texture as in **verse 1**; strings out.
1:55	**Bridge** (8)	"Then I go to my"	Brass pickup.
			Tremolo strings.
			French horn answers vocal phrases.
2:03			Timpani echoes pickup figure.
2:20			Brass and timpani pickup leads to climactic chord change (V), highlighted by timpani roll and downward rushing strings.
2:29	**Verse 4** (4+4)	"There's been times"	Brass rhythmic figure from **verse 3**.
			French horn melody.
2:45	Refrain	"It's been a long"	Strings play sustained chords.
3:03	Tag		Full ensemble holds final chord.

NOTES

1. Mike Kaplan, "New Definition of a Pop," *Variety*, March 27, 1957, 51.
2. Bill Simon, "Rhythm-Blues Notes," *Billboard*, May 5, 1956, 51.
3. Quoted in Jeff Hannusch, *I Hear You Knockin': The Sound of New Orleans Rhythm and Blues* (Ville Platte, LA: Swallow Publications, 1985), 102.
4. Quoted in Charlie Gillett, *Making Tracks: The Story of Atlantic Records* (London: Souvenir Press, 1974), 162.
5. Jerry Wexler and David Ritz, *Rhythm and the Blues: A Life in American Music* (New York: Knopf, 1993), 136.
6. Quoted in Jerry Leiber and Mike Stoller with David Ritz, *Hound Dog: The Leiber and Stoller Autobiography* (New York: Simon and Schuster, 2010), 160.
7. Gary Kramer, "On the Beat," *Billboard*, March 2, 1957, 61.

FURTHER READING

Coleman, Rick. *Blue Monday: Fats Domino and the Lost Dawn of Rock 'n' Roll.* Cambridge, MA: Da Capo Press, 2007.

Guralnick, Peter. *Dream Boogie: The Triumph of Sam Cooke.* New York: Little Brown, 2005.

Leiber, Jerry, Mike Stoller, and David Ritz. *Hound Dog: The Leiber and Stoller Autobiography.* New York: Simon and Schuster, 2010.

FURTHER LISTENING

Maxine Brown, "All in My Mind" (Nomar, 1961)
Jerry Butler, "He Will Break Your Heart" (Vee-Jay, 1960)
Ray Charles, "I Can't Stop Loving You" (ABC-Paramount, 1962)
Chuck Jackson, "Any Day Now (My Wild Beautiful Bird)" (Wand, 1962)
Gladys Knight and the Pips, "Every Beat of My Heart" (Vee-Jay, 1961)
Johnny Mathis, "Chances Are" (Columbia, 1957)
Clyde McPhatter, "A Lover's Question" (Atlantic, 1958)
Dionne Warwick, "Don't Make Me Over" (Scepter, 1963)
Jackie Wilson, "Lonely Teardrops" (Brunswick, 1958)

7

EASY LISTENING AND SLOW DANCING
Rockaballad

Early press accounts stressed rock and roll's "big beat." A typical description in a 1956 *Time* magazine article reads as follows:

> Characteristics: an unrelenting, socking syncopation that sounds like a bull whip; a choleric saxophone honking mating-call sounds; an electric guitar turned up so loud that its sound shatters and splits; a vocal group that shudders and exercises violently to the beat while roughly chanting either a near-nonsense phrase or a moronic lyric in hillbilly idiom. . . . Only the obsessive beat pounds through, stimulating the crowd to such rhythmical movements as clapping in tempo and jumping and dancing in the aisles. Sometimes the place vibrates with the beat of music and stamping feet.[1]

But rock and roll was more varied than its critics acknowledged, balancing raucousness with a softer side. From the beginning, tender ballads were popular with teenagers attracted by the sentimental romanticism and nostalgia of the lyrics, as well the opportunity for the close contact of slow dancing. The point was crystallized when, a few months after he released "Hound Dog," Elvis Presley had another number-one hit with "Love Me Tender," a record reminiscent of crooners past. Presley, however, was simply following an established trend. In 1955, the Platters landed two soft pop records at the top of charts ("Only You" and "The

Great Pretender"). Moreover, many of the earliest doo wop hits were ballads, including the Orioles' "It's Too Soon to Know" (1948), the Ravens' "Count Every Star" (1949), and the Moonglows' "Sincerely" (1952). By 1957, a new term, "rockaballad," was coined to describe records that blended elements of traditional pop with rock and roll. In 1958, *Billboard* reported that rockaballads were "one of the most recorded types of pop tunes." Many such records claimed the number-one chart position that year, including Presley's "Don't," the Platters' "Twilight Time," the Everly Brothers' "All I Have to Do Is Dream," and the Teddy Bears' "To Know Him Is to Love Him."

Typical rockaballad features include a lyrical melody, a romantic topic (often wistful), and muted arrangements. In contrast to up-tempo rock and roll, the singer's diction is clear and deliberate, and the emotional tone is intimate. In other words, although this is clearly young people's music, it has many of the trappings of adult easy listening. The record's overall sonic texture is calculated for a specific effect: to make the listener feel a close, personal connection with the sounds wafting from the radio or record player. In the soft warmth of such tracks as Buddy Holly's "True Love Ways" or the Fleetwoods' "Come Softly to Me," teenagers felt their own romantic fantasies and aspirations expressed by the stars they admired. Rockaballads, then, represent the third large area of rock and roll appropriation. Just as R&B and country sources were absorbed and synthesized, mainstream pop, too, received its own rock and roll makeover.

7.1. "ONLY YOU (AND YOU ALONE)" (1955)

THE PLATTERS

The Platters emerged from the lively Los Angeles vocal group scene centered in high schools of the city's Watts neighborhood and amateur night contests at Club Alabam. The group was assembled and managed by show business veteran Buck Ram, who also managed the Penguins ("Earth Angel"). He put lead singer Tony Williams, a New Jersey transplant who had come to his attention through the amateur contests, together with three Los Angeles natives: Herbert Reed, Alex Hodge, and David Lynch. In an unusual move for the time, he also included a young woman, Zola Taylor, to complement the men's voices. Ram, who was also a songwriter, was one of the few music industry pros who found a way to blend traditional pop with the new sounds of rock and roll. He coached the group for several months before recording. With smoothly blended backing voices and a stunning lead, the resulting sound was smooth and sophisticated, more like the Platters' pop elders, the Ink Spots, than the rough-and-ready streetcorner doo wop of their peers.

The Platters first recorded "Only You" in 1954 for Syd Nathan's Federal label (an indie), but the result was poor and the record was not released. Ram was convinced that the song had hit potential, and when he secured a deal with a major label, Mercury, he insisted on rerecording it. His instincts were proven correct when the record not only claimed the number one spot on the R&B chart but also crossed over to pop, rising to number five. The group's next single, "The Great Pretender," another Ram composition, came out five months later and rose to number one on both charts. The Platters would go on to score twenty top-forty hits over the next six years, establishing their refined neo-traditional pop balladry as a key element of rock and roll.

The mainstream pop aspects of "Only You" are easily apparent. The song uses a Tin Pan Alley–style harmonic language, which provides the necessary chromatic notes to lead smoothly from the tonic key of $E^\flat$ briefly to C minor to $A^\flat$ and back again. Tony Williams's rendition of the song's elegant melody is masterful, emotive yet polished. The backing voices are blended smoothly, and the instrumental accompaniment is subtle. The record's sound has the major-label sheen characteristic of Mercury's mainstream pop products. In short, in a crowd of lo-fi amateur vocal group records, "Only You" made a strong case for a broader conception of rock and roll's potential.

At the same time, the record shows off its rock and roll intentions from the outset with a pronounced triplet figure led by a slightly distorted electric guitar. The gruffness of the guitar sets up an effective contrast with Williams's silky entrance. The band settles into an accompaniment that features several requisite rock and roll elements. The piano plays a pulsing triplet figure throughout. The bass, doubled by saxophone, plays a slow broken chord pattern reminiscent of boogie-woogie but adapted to fit the more elaborate chord changes. And the snare drum emphasizes the backbeat.

Although Williams's sweet voice and strong technique are reminiscent of mainstream pop singers, his mannerisms are more flamboyant. His opening phrase presents the vocal theme that will permeate the track. It begins with a pickup sung in confident, powerful tones ("on-ly") leading to a sweet falsetto note ("you") that he holds through the measure with a dreamy wistfulness. Williams plays on this contrast of vocal timbres throughout the track, sweeping effortlessly from strong declamation to vulnerable intimacy in the course of a single phrase. He also uses idiosyncratic diction, along with hiccups and hesitations, to heighten the sense of romantic transport.

Easy Listening and Slow Dancing

The song's thirty-two-bar structure is a type of binary form (A–B), each section composed of sixteen bars. The A section ends with a cadence to the V chord. The B section is identical to the A for its first eight bars but veers away in the second eight and cadences on I.

The sixteen bars of each section are divided into two eight-bar segments with differing harmonic rhythm. For the first eight bars the harmonic rhythm moves at a deliberate pace, with each chord sustained for two full bars. As the second eight-bar segment begins, the pace increases to one and then two chords per bar.

A Section Harmonic Rhythm (* indicates chromatically altered chord)
Segment 1: | $E^\flat$ | $E^\flat$ | G^* | G^* | C minor | C minor | $E^\flat 7^*$ | $E^\flat 7^*$ |
Segment 2: | $A^\flat$ | $B^\flat$ | $E^\flat$ G^* | C minor C major* | F^* | F^* | $B^\flat$ | $B^\flat$ |

As chords change more rapidly, they likewise change the feel of the song's flow. The harmonic effect underlines a quickening sense of excitement in the singer's delivery and a change in the texture of the backing voices. This shaping of the harmonic rhythm along with the liberal use of chromaticism in the chord progression are clear evidence of Ram's experience with older pop styles. Such collaborations between seasoned pros and rock and roll's fresh-faced amateurs ensured that the skills and sounds of pop tradition would be as much a part of rock and roll as boogie-woogie and honking saxophones.

Listening Guide

"Only You (And You Alone)" (Buck Ram), Mercury Records (mono)
Recorded in Los Angeles, April 1955
Tony Williams (lead voice), David Lynch, Herbert Reed, Paul Robi, Zola Taylor (voice), studio musicians (piano, saxophone, bass, drums)
Producer: Buck Ram
Charts: Popular Records: Best Sellers in Stores #5, R&B Records: Best Sellers in Stores #1
Key: $E^\flat$
Meter: 4/4

Time	Section	Lyric Cue	Listen For
0:00	Intro (2)		Guitar, piano, bass texture.
			Guitar introduces triplet figure with a gruff, distorted timbre.

continued on next page

Time	Section	Lyric Cue	Listen For
0:06	A (8+8)	"Only you"	Lead voice's sweet timbre and smooth style contrast with **intro** sound.
			Backing voices, singing "ooh," hold each chord for 2 bars.
			Piano triplets.
			Bass and saxophone play a slow boogie-woogie pattern.
			Snare plays light backbeat accents with brushes.
0:30		"Only you"	Backing voices change to "ah" and become louder as the harmonic rhythm picks up momentum.
0:48			Section cadences on V chord.
0:51		"Uh-only . . ."	Pause highlights stylized vocal gesture.
0:54	B (8+8)	". . . you"	Music is identical to **A** for first 8 bars.
1:18		"When you hold"	Begin second 8 bars with varied chord progression and melody; harmonic rhythm quickens.
1:36		"Only you"	Ends with cadence on tonic.
1:39		"Uh-uh-only . . ."	Pause highlights stylized vocal gesture.
1:42	B (8+8)	". . . you"	Varied melody in the lead voice; otherwise a repeat of first **B** until stop-time ending.

7.2. "ALL I HAVE TO DO IS DREAM" (1958)

THE EVERLY BROTHERS

Don and Phil Everly began singing together as children. Their parents Ike and Margaret were country musicians, and the boys grew up with both music and show business. They began appearing with their parents on *The Everly Family Show*, a radio program broadcast on station KMA in Shenandoah, Iowa, when the boys were eight and six. In the summers the family toured the country music circuit. By the time the brothers began recording, in their late teens, they had developed a vocal blend as clear and fresh as a mountain stream. Their voices rang out in two-part harmony from an impressive string of hit records. This kind of harmonizing had a long history in country music, including other popular brother acts such as the Delmore Brothers and the Louvin Brothers. But with a softened twang and the rocking guitar rhythm of such tracks as "Wake Up Little Susie" and "Bird Dog," the Everlys established such harmonizing as a fixture of rock and roll as well.

The Everly Brothers influenced such 1960s duos as Peter and Gordon, Chad and Jeremy, and Simon and Garfunkel. The sound was expanded to three-part harmonies by such groups as the Beatles and the Byrds. In contrast to doo wop singing, with its clear distinction between lead and accompaniment, the Everlys' style of harmonizing treats the voices as equal participants in a composite sound. Both are at equal volume and both sing all the lyrics in the same rhythm. With Don taking the lower part and Phil on the upper, only their notes are different. This technique proved equally effective in up-tempo numbers and in slow ballads. At a fast pace, the ringing vocal sound infuses the records with sparkling energy. Slowed down, the effect can be mesmerizing.

"All I Have to Do Is Dream" was written by Boudleaux Bryant, who was already a successful country songwriter when he met the Everlys in 1956 soon after they came to Nashville. Usually collaborating with his wife, Felice, Bryant had written songs that were recorded not only by country singers but also by pop singers such as Frankie Laine and Tony Bennett. The Bryants contributed the Everlys' first two hits, "Bye Bye Love" and "Wake Up Little Susie," and would write several more.

In "All I Have to Do Is Dream," Bryant blends Tin Pan Alley and doo wop conventions: a thirty-two-bar AABA form and a repeating I–vi–IV–V chord progression (two chords per bar). Yet while the chord sequence (which repeats throughout the A section) is unchanging, the melody has a definite feeling of progression. The A sections are made up of four phrases, each two bars in length. The first two phrases are melodically identical. Both are relatively static, using only three notes. The third phrase adds three new notes to expand the melodic range in both upper and lower directions. The fourth provides a sense of arrival, delivering the word "dream" in a lyrical, legato melisma. The fourth phrase is also a repeated refrain—a kind of mini-chorus—at the end of each A section. It stands out from the other lyrics not only in its repetition throughout the track but in its departure from the regular rhyme scheme.

The song's B section performs the conventional task of providing contrast. It moves to a different chord progression and slower harmonic rhythm, one chord per bar instead of two. The phrases are twice as long as those in the A sections, four bars each instead of two. Even with the longer phrases, however, the rhymes flow more quickly within the phrase ("mine"; "wine"; "anytime"). These changes provide a clear sense of a shift in pacing, as though the track is drawing a long sigh.

The track's arrangement focuses on atmosphere rather than narrative. The intro begins with a single strum on an electric guitar whose amplifier is set to a quick tremolo, an electronic effect created by oscillations in amplifier volume (different from the string tremolo on "A Change Is Gonna Come"). Before any voices are heard, this signature timbre provides the listener a stylistic clue: this may be a Nashville record, but it's rock and roll, not country. The brothers enter with the "dream" refrain sung in seductive voices. The tremolo guitar continues in accompaniment, joined by a second electric guitar without tremolo playing simple lines in its low register, reinforcing the bass part. The lightly accented backbeat is hypnotic as it ticks away throughout the track, uninterrupted by drum fills. Liner notes indicate the presence of acoustic guitars and piano, but they are barely audible. In fact, aside from the tremolo guitar and the dry backbeat snare, the overall instrumental texture is a hazy blend of sounds, which suits the song's mood and the brothers' performance. The texture set in the intro continues through the track without change. Once cast, the dream-spell remains unbroken.

Listening Guide

"All I Have to Do Is Dream" (Boudleaux Bryant), Cadence Records (mono)
Recorded at RCA Victor Studios, Nashville, March 1958
Don Everly (voice, guitar), Phil Everly (voice, guitar), Chet Atkins (electric guitar), Hank Garland (electric guitar), Ray Edenton (guitar), Floyd Cramer (piano), Roy Huskey (bass), Buddy Harman (drums)
Producer: Archie Bleyer
Engineer: Bill Porter
Charts: Popular Records: Best Sellers in Stores #1, R&B Records: Best Sellers in Stores #1, C&W Records: Best Sellers in Stores #1
Key: E
Meter: 4/4

Time	Section	Lyric Cue	Listen For
0:00	Intro (4)		Electric guitar chord with tremolo.
0:03		"Dream"	Voices in harmony.
			Texture: low-register guitar line, tremolo guitar, acoustic guitars, piano, bass, drums.
			I–vi–IV–V chord progression.

Time	Section	Lyric Cue	Listen For
0:12	A1 (8)	"When I"	Phrase 1: 2 bars.
0:16		"When I"	Phrase 2: 2 bars.
0:21		"Whenever I"	Phrase 3: 2 bars.
0:26		"Dream"	Phrase 4: 2 bars.
0:30	A2 (8)	"When I feel blue"	Phrase 1: 2 bars.
		"And I need you"	Phrase 2: 2 bars
		"Whenever I"	Phrase 3: 2 bars
		"Dream"	Phrase 4: 2 bars; chord progression suspended; cadence to tonic.
0:49	B (4+4)	"I can make you mine"	New chord progression, slower harmonic rhythm. Longer phrases, but compressed rhyme scheme.
1:07	A3 (8)	"I need you so"	Follows the phrase structure of A2.
1:30	B (8)	"I can make you mine"	Similar to previous B.
1:49	A4 (8+fade)	"I need you so"	Same lyrics as A3 but no cadence to tonic.

7.3. "CRYING" (1961)

ROY ORBISON

Dubbed "the Caruso of rock," Roy Orbison was one of rock and roll's most distinctive voices and original songwriters. (The Everly Brothers recorded Orbison's "Claudette" for the B side of "All I Have to Do Is Dream.") In 1960 he seemed to burst onto the charts out of nowhere with his number-two pop hit "Only the Lonely." With its polished production (which included a choir and a string section) and stunning vocal performance, the record stood out among its rock and roll peers—its sound was "curiously timeless and placeless," as one writer put it. Yet although "Only the Lonely" seemed a bolt from the blue, Orbison had been recording since 1955. Like Buddy Holly, he was a West Texan and some of his earliest recordings were made at Norman Petty's studio in Clovis. In 1956 he had a modest hit for Sam Phillips's Sun Records with the up-tempo rockabilly record "Ooby Dooby."

Like the Everly Brothers, Orbison grew up with country music, but he was also a fan of major-label pop (including Mitch Miller productions). Gradually he developed a unique stylistic blend of dramatic pop ballad and honky-tonk heartbreak. "Only the Lonely" was the first the public heard of what was by then a full-blown conception, which would produce such future hits as "In Dreams," "Running Scared," and "Crying." Each record has a unique, prose-like musical form that builds to a peak climax, taking advantage of Orbison's wide vocal range. Each has instrumentation that mixes electric guitars and drums with strings and light pop backing voices. Each uses unusual phrase lengths that give the melodies a sinuous quality.

Orbison's song forms and track arrangements employ the basic principles of repetition and variation, but each unfolds according to its own particular narrative. So although "Crying" is nominally a verse-chorus design, it diverges from convention in several ways. The first six bars of each verse have the same music. But at the downbeat of the seventh bar the music stops, and from this point the melodies of each verse differ significantly. In verse one, Orbison drops into his lower register with a three-bar phrase leading into the first chorus. Verse two, by contrast, is followed by a rising melodic line and a four-bar phrase, heightening and prolonging the protagonist's expression of desperation.

The choruses are similar, though an octave apart in register and with different arrangement details. They are both twelve bars in length, broken into three four-bar subsections.

CHORUS SUBSECTIONS

1. Delivers the song's hook with a melisma on the word "crying."

2. Lyrics explain the reason for the singer's anguish.

3. "Crying" repeated four times over four different chords.

Only the second of these sections differs from one chorus to the next, largely as a matter of accommodating different lyrics. A more significant change occurs in the extension that follows each chorus. Each has altogether different music, lyrics, and phrase lengths, and each serves a different dramatic purpose. The first ("It's hard to understand") is a ruminative reflection, a sort of pause before we continue on to the next verse. The second ("I'm crying") is an all-out climax.

The arrangement for "Crying" is a good example of how Orbison's tracks often integrate various elements to create a sweeping dramatic effect. (The arranger for the session is uncredited. Some Orbison tracks used string and vocal arrangements by Anita Kerr or Jim Hall, whereas other arrangements were invented by Orbison himself. Unfamiliar with music notation, he sang the parts to bassist Bob Moore who wrote them down for the musicians to play and sing.) Three ideas in particular shape the arrangement's flow: (1) a rhythmic motive somewhat reminiscent of the Spanish **bolero** rhythm (see figure 7.1), which is reinterpreted here (see figure 7.2); (2) variation in the relative textural consistency from one section to the next; and (3) the composition of the stereo field. (These are detailed in the Listening Guide.) In addition to the song's large-scale divisions of verse and chorus, the arrangement uses these three ideas to delineate smaller subsections, which are synchronized with the song's phrase structure in support of the dramatic narrative.

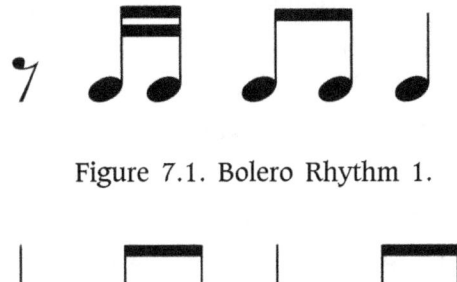

Figure 7.1. Bolero Rhythm 1.

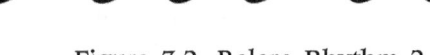

Figure 7.2. Bolero Rhythm 2.

In the chorus one, for example, the first two subsections use the same instrumental texture. They flow together seamlessly. But in the third subsection the instrumentation thins out, exposing the protagonist's vulnerability. In chorus two, on the other hand, each subsection differs in a marked, almost schizophrenic way. The first presents a kind of preclimax, with voice and strings rising into the high register and the bolero rhythm becoming more insistent, played in unison by most of the instruments. The second subsection steps back from the climax. The strings and bolero drop out and the voice comes down from its previous heights. The third subsection starts a buildup to the song's true climax as all instruments play the bolero rhythm in unison, driving Orbison implacably through his final ascent to a desperate finish.

Listening Guide

"Crying" (Roy Orbison, Joe Melson), Monument Records (stereo)
Recorded at RCA Studio Nashville, June 1961
Roy Orbison (voice), Harold Ray Bradley (guitar), Boudleaux Bryant (guitar), Scotty Moore (electric guitar), Floyd Cramer (piano), Charlie McCoy (vibraphone), Bob Moore (bass), Buddy Harman (drums), studio musicians (strings), studio musicians (choir)

Producer: Fred Foster
Engineer: Bill Porter
Charts: Hot 100 #2
Key: D
Meter: 4/4

Time	Section	Lyric Cue	Listen For
0:00	**Intro** (2)		Bolero-type rhythm played on muffled drum (C); reverb panned R creates a "shadow."
			Two acoustic guitars (C+L) reinforce bolero rhythm; guitar reverb (R).
			Soft cymbal strikes on downbeats provide high-end contrast to mid-range guitar/drum texture.
			(Note: The right side of the stereo field remains empty except for the snare-and-acoustic guitar "shadow" until the string entrance at 0:16.)
0:06	**Verse 1** (11)	"I was alright"	Voice (C) is full bodied, with a prominent reverb tailing toward the mix's background. Quasi-conversational tone is underscored by static harmony.
			Drum figure shifts 2 beats later.
			Muted electric guitar (L) doubles bass (C) (guitar timbre complements muted drum).
			Acoustic guitars move to background.
			Vibraphone (L) plays 1 chord per bar.
0:16		"I saw you"	Low-register strings (R).
			Harmony begins to change.
			Drum replaced by hi-hat (R).
0:20		"Stop"	Music stops, then voice continues in low register.
0:33	**Chorus 1** (12)		
	Subsection 1 (4)	"Crying"	Sung softly with introspective mood.
			Strings are joined on right side by backing voices.
0:42	Subsection 2 (4)	"And you"	First phrase, strings out.
0:47		"standing"	Second phrase, strings in, voices out.
0:52	Subsection 3 (4)	"Crying"	Vibraphone tremolo.
			Strings out.
1:02	**Extension** (6)	"It's hard to understand"	Strings re-enter.
1:14			Drum re-enters with bolero rhythm (C).

Time	Section	Lyric Cue	Listen For
1:17	Verse 2 (12)	"I thought"	Strings (R) and vibraphone (L) take up bolero rhythm.
1:27		"I love you"	Backing voices in (R).
1:32		"But darling"	Stop; voice continues in upper register, building toward the **chorus.**
			Strings mirror the move to the upper register.
			Strings, drum, and vibraphone suspend bolero rhythm.
1:46	**Chorus 2** (12) Subsection 1	"Crying"	Preclimax: vocal melody, sung partially falsetto, is one octave higher than **chorus** 1. Strings in high register.
			All guitars, bass, vibraphone, and drum play bolero variant in unison.
1:56	Subsection 2	"Yes now"	Retreat from climax: bolero suspended; strings out.
2:06	Subsection 3	"I'll be crying"	Begin buildup to final climax; bolero variant played in unison by all instruments.
2:17	**Climax** (10)	"I'm crying"	Kick drum joins the rest in rhythmic unison; full texture and full frequency range; loudest point; strained voice depicts protagonist at the edge of control.

NOTE

1. "Yeh-Heh-Heh-Hes, Baby," *Time*, June 18, 1956, 54.

FURTHER READING

Amburn, Ellis. *Dark Star: The Roy Orbison Story.* New York: Carol, 1990.
White, Roger. *Walk Right Back: The Story of the Everly Brothers.* London: Plexus, 1984.

FURTHER LISTENING

Johnny Ace, "Pledging My Love" (Duke, 1954)
Fleetwoods, "Come Softly to Me" (Dolphin, 1959)
Connie Francis, "Who's Sorry Now?" (MGM, 1958)
Buddy Holly, "True Love Ways" (Coral, 1958)
Elvis Presley, "Love Me Tender" (RCA Victor, 1956)

Teddy Bears, "To Know Him Is to Love Him" (Dore, 1958)
Tune Weavers, "Happy, Happy Birthday Baby" (Checker, 1957)
Ritchie Valens, "Donna" (Del-Fi, 1958)
Little Willie John, "You're a Sweetheart" (King, 1958)

8

BRILL BUILDING POP
Girl Groups

Women were fixtures on the pop charts in the 1940s and through the first half of the 1950s. The Andrews Sisters, Patti Page, Mary Ford, and the singer's singer Ella Fitzgerald were just a few of the many female stars who brought their craft, artistry, and glamour to the pop scene. The first wave of rockers, however, were mostly young men. During the initial "floodtide of rock and roll," *Billboard* reported, "the popularity of girl singers was at a nadir."[1] But in 1957, the situation began to change with the Bobbettes' hit "Mr. Lee" and then, the following year, the Chantels' "Maybe" and Connie Francis's "Who's Sorry Now" and "Stupid Cupid." By 1961 women's voices, both solo and in so-called girl groups, once again dotted the pop soundscape.

The Shirelles' "Will You Love Me Tomorrow" (1960) was the first number-one record by a girl group and it was followed by dozens more girl group hits over the next few years. The Shirelles themselves produced another ten top-forty hits in the early 1960s. The girl group trend began in New York but quickly spread across the country, notably to Detroit and Los Angeles, where Berry Gordy's Motown and Phil Spector's Philles Records turned out many girl group classics. Although the first girl groups were black and all female, the genre soon expanded to include white groups such as the Shangri-Las, the Angels, and the Paris Sisters, as well mixed-gender groups such as Ruby and the Romantics, the Essex, and the Orlons. Along with a new generation of female soloists (Lesley Gore, Mary Wells, Tina Turner) and songwriters (Carole King, Ellie Greenwich, Cynthia Weil), and even a prominent label owner (Florence Greenberg), the girl group trend infused rock and roll with a fresh sound and sensibility.

The girl group sound is essentially female doo wop. The groups were usually amateur a cappella outfits that producers paired with studio musicians. The records, however, do not display the kinds of stylistic mismatches found in earlier doo wop. Rock and roll had been around long enough that many of the songwriters, arrangers, musicians, and producers were themselves members of the generation that grew up with the music. They had, by now, a firmer sense of the rock and roll language.

The production process for girl groups resembled the professional practices of an earlier pop era, where division of labor was the norm. Following Tin Pan Alley practice, songwriters provided the songs and performers made the records. And many of the most successful songwriters worked in and around Broadway's famous Brill Building, which was for years home to Tin Pan Alley songwriters and publishers.

One of the most successful neo-Brill companies was Aldon Music, a publishing firm owned by partners Don Kirshner, a music industry novice, and Al Nevins, a longtime pro. Though Kirshner himself was unskilled musically, he had a gift for recognizing talent. In quick succession he signed young songwriting teams who would turn out some of the era's most durable hits, writers such as Carole King and Gerry Goffin, Cynthia Weil and Barry Mann, and Neil Sedaka and Howie Greenberg. In a scene reminiscent of an earlier time, the songwriters went to work each day in cubicles, each furnished with an upright piano.

The big difference was that in addition to simply writing the songs Kirshner demanded that the writers also record demo tapes. By now, the standard method of pitching material to prospective performers took the form of recordings rather than live song pluggers. Kirshner said that he wanted his writers "to learn to produce," and they did, sometimes blurring the distinction between songwriter and producer. Goffin and King recorded a demo of their song "Locomotion," for example, sung by their fifteen-year-old babysitter Eva Boyd (Little Eva). Kirshner liked what he heard and decided to release the demo to debut his newly formed Dimension label. It rose to number one on both the pop and R&B charts in 1962.

Many of the Brill Building girl group records combined diverse cultural experiences and sensibilities. Most of the writers were Jewish kids; most of the performers were black kids. Each inhabited different parts of the city and their lives rarely intersected. Listening to rock and roll on DJ Alan Freed's radio show on WINS, which was at the center of teenage life in New York City, Carole King was aware that the records by black performers represented "another culture that really we were not close to." But, she recalled, "We became close to it through the music."[2] Though neither group knew much of one another's social sphere, rock and roll provided a common cultural space in which the two interacted.

The Aldon songwriters were part of a scene that also included the teams of Doc Pomus and Mort Shuman, Ellie Greenwich and Jeff Barry, and Burt Bacharach and Hal David. Reigning as elder statesmen, though only in their mid-twenties, were Jerry Leiber and Mike Stoller, who had written hit songs throughout the 1950s for both R&B (e.g., Big Mama Thornton, Wilbert Harrison) and rock and roll performers (e.g., Elvis Presley, the Coasters). The other writers idolized Leiber and Stoller, according to Aldon songwriter Barry Mann. Collaborating with them, said Cynthia Weil, Mann's writing partner, "was like going to songwriters' school."[3] To Carole King, "they were really trailblazers."[4]

In addition to their songwriting prowess, Leiber and Stoller were in the vanguard of a new industry trend: the rise of independent producers. In the past, record producers at large companies had worked as salaried employees. But increasingly in the early 1960s, many producers were developing their own projects, eventually selling or leasing the recordings to a record company or in some cases starting labels of their own. Having written the song, it was a natural next step to turn it into a recording. In the new way of things, many songwriters turned their songs into sound as a matter of course.

In the wake of the Shirelles' success, the flood of groups populating the charts of the early '60s included the Chiffons, the Cookies, the Exciters, the Jaynetts, the Marvelettes, Martha and the Vandellas, the Crystals, Little Eva, the Dixie Cups, the Jelly Beans, and the Murmaids. Some had many hits, some only one. But together, the sound of girl groups—which included bits of Latin music, Broadway, R&B, and even classical music—added a new flavor and a new dimension to the developing rock and roll language.

8.1. "WILL YOU LOVE ME TOMORROW" (1960)

THE SHIRELLES

The Shirelles were a group of young women from Passaic, New Jersey—Shirley Owens, Doris Cole, Addie "Micki" Harris, and Beverly Lee—who attended Passaic High School. They came to the attention of a classmate's mother, Florence Greenberg, a housewife "anxious," she said, "to get out of the house." Fascinated with the music business, Greenberg had taken to hanging around the Brill Building in Manhattan, learning the ropes and meeting industry types. She started a record label called Tiara for which she convinced the Shirelles to record their self-penned song "I Met Him on a Sunday" in 1958. The record aroused enough attention around

New York for the group to land a contract with Decca, but their next two single releases failed to chart. Decca dropped the group and Greenberg signed them to her new company, Scepter.

Greenberg was a first-rate record promoter but realized that production was not her forte ("I couldn't carry a tune," she claimed). She enlisted a partner in Luther Dixon, a successful songwriter and studio hand who cowrote and produced the 1959 Crests hit "Sixteen Candles." Greenberg ran the company; he produced the records. His first production for the Shirelles was a song he cowrote with lead singer Shirley Owens, "Tonight's the Night," which, in 1960, became the group's first top-forty hit. On the strength of that success, Scepter moved to 1650 Broadway, a building near the Brill where Don Kirshner had set up offices for Aldon Music. Through Kirshner, Dixon found the song that would be the Shirelles' follow-up single, "Will You Love Me Tomorrow" by Gerry Goffin and Carole King. In mood and topic, the song was a natural successor to "Tonight's the Night."

In its lyrical melody, its use of harmonic color, and its AABA form, the song is a youthful evocation of the Tin Pan Alley tradition, and its string arrangement alludes, at least in instrumentation, to an older pop style. But the track's sound is clearly rock and roll—more naive exuberance than polished craft. As in "There Goes My Baby" (see chapter 6), the groove is based on a Latin-style rhythm, which is played by the bass (see figure 8.1).

Figure 8.1. "Will You Love Me Tomorrow" Bassline Rhythm.

This foundation is overlaid with rhythmic figures for cellos, backing vocals, and percussion, creating an animated texture. Especially noticeable is the snare drum's double hit on beat two, which accents the bass's syncopation. This snare rhythm, sometimes referred to as Merseybeat, is common on both girl group and surf tracks. One scholar of girl group music, who calls this the "heartbeat rhythm," notes an affinity with the clapping that accompanies many schoolgirl games.[5]

Carole King, nineteen at the time, was the primary musical contributor to the Goffin–King partnership. To Dixon's surprise, she insisted on writing the track's string arrangement, her first. The resulting arrangement has the charm of a prom dress, an adolescent's first stab at adult finery. King's string writing effectively reflects the song's theme of innocence mixed with coming-of-age anxiety and desire.

King also shows us how harmony can heighten the effect of a song's words, framing the central question ("Will you love me tomorrow?") with a harmonic surprise. Notice how the third line of each A section ("Tonight the light," "Can I believe," "So tell me now") seems to raise the protagonist's sense of urgency. This is accomplished by using a chord outside the tonic scale, which serves to intensify the harmonic motion.

The song's key is C. The foreign chord is E major (normally in a C scale, the chord built on E would be E minor).

C scale: C, D, E, F, G, A, B
E chord: E–G#–B

Changing the G to G# strengthens the move to the next chord, which is minor. This brief move beyond the safe confines of the major-mode tonic key to a strong arrival in the minor mode stresses the protagonist's underlying uncertainty—a good example of the dramatic effect chords can have.

One of the track's key expressive elements is Shirley Owens's performance, which conveys strength in the face of uncertainty. The song presents a dreadful question, encapsulating a universal fear. As the song's young protagonist weighs the question against the stirrings of her passion, there is a distinct potential for melodrama. But Owens's delivery remains straightforward, unaffected, and clear-eyed. She leaves the drama to the violins. Although she would "like to know" that her boy's love is one she "can be sure of," she seems to know that no assurance carries a guarantee. There are only questions. She asks: Is it a lasting treasure? A moment's pleasure? Can she believe the magic? Will the spell be broken? Yet despite her doubts, all she asks for is a simple, single-word answer to her closing question: "Will you still love me tomorrow?"

Listening Guide

"Will You Love Me Tomorrow" (Gerry Goffin, Carole King), Scepter Records (mono)
Recorded at Bell Sound Studios, New York City, October 1960
Shirley Owens (lead voice), Doris Cole, Addie "Micki" Harris, Beverly Lee (voice), studio musicians (guitar, bass, drums, strings, percussion)
Arranger: Carole King
Producer: Luther Dixon
Charts: Hot 100 #1, Hot R&B Sides #2
Key: C
Meter: 4/4

Time	Section	Lyric Cue	Listen For
0:00	Intro (4)		Latin groove in bass.
			"Heartbeat" rhythm on snare.
			Sixteenth-note figure in cellos.
			Single electric guitar strum on downbeat of every other bar.
0:08	A (16)	"Tonight you're mine"	Lyrics describe a situation.
0:21		"Tonight the light"	Harmonic intensifier (E major).
			Backing voices enter singing long notes.
			Cellos switch to long notes.
0:28	Refrain	"But will you"	All voices sing lyrics.
			Violins enter.
0:35	A (16)	"Is this a lasting"	Lyrics shift to questioning.
			Cellos return to rhythmic figure.
			Backing voices sing rhythmic figure.
			Violins answer lead vocal phrases.
0:49		"Can I believe"	Harmonic intensifier (E major).
			Backing voices switch to long notes.
			Cellos switch to long notes.
0:56	Refrain	"Will you still"	All voices sing lyrics.
1:03	B (16)	"Tonight with words"	Pizzicato cellos join bass groove.
			Violins become more active.
			Backing voices out.
			Mid-range texture thins.
1:25		"When the night"	Backing voices sing call-and-response with lead voice.
1:32	A (16)	"I'd like to know"	Lyrics demand an answer.
			Texture as in previous A.
1:46		"So tell me now"	Harmonic intensifier.
1:53	Refrain	"Will you still"	
2:00	A (First Half, 8)		Instrumental break features violin melody.
2:14	A (Second Half, 8)	"So tell me now"	Begins with harmonic intensifier.
			Texture as in previous A sections.
2:21	Refrain	"Will you still"	Repeat to fade.

8.2. "BE MY BABY" (1963)

THE RONETTES

The Ronettes were a trio—sisters Veronica (Ronnie) and Estelle Bennett and their cousin Nedra Talley—from New York City's Washington Heights neighborhood. In 1959, while still in their teens, they won an Amateur Night contest at Harlem's Apollo Theater harmonizing as the Darling Sisters. Later, they worked as dancers at the Peppermint Lounge and in shows produced by DJ Murray the K at Brooklyn's Fox Theater during the twist dance craze of the early '60s. They were signed by Colpix Records in 1961, going by the name Ronnie and the Relatives. Their Colpix releases failed to chart, but in 1963 they began singing backup for Darlene Love and Bob B. Soxx and the Blue Jeans on records produced by Phil Spector, an innovative young producer with keen commercial instincts. They had finally found their show business home. Within months, they had their own debut single on Spector's Philles label with "Be My Baby," the record that would make them international stars.

Spector cowrote "Be My Baby" with Ellie Greenwich and Jeff Barry, another of the New York husband-and-wife songwriting teams that produced so many girl group hits (other Greenwich-Barry songs include "Da Doo Ron Ron," "Chapel of Love," and "Then He Kissed Me"). The song is in verse-chorus form. Each verse has sixteen bars, which are divided into two distinct halves. The first is diatonic and harmonically stable, while the second is propelled by a series of chromatically altered chords. Every chord in the second half of the verse except the last contains a chromatic note, which turns the chord from minor to major and upsets the diatonic order. Creating this sense of harmonic agitation heightens the sense of forward motion as the song drives toward its chorus.

Verse-Chord Progression
First 8 bars: ‖: E | E | F# minor | B :‖
Second 8 bars: | G# | G# | C# | C# | F# | F# | B | B |
E Scale: E, F#, G#, A, B, C#, D#, E

The G# chord adds B#, C# chord adds E#, and F# chord adds A#. Each of these three major chords would normally be minor in the tonic key of E.

The eight-bar chorus settles into the standard doo wop chord progression, I–vi–IV–V (two bars for each chord), but with an interesting use of melodic dissonance. The chorus hook, sung by the backing singers, accents the pitch D# repeatedly over the E, C# minor, and A chords ("be *my*, be my *ba*-by"). In relation to the underlying chord roots, the

D♯ makes dissonant intervals of a seventh (over E), a ninth (over C♯), and an **augmented** fourth (over A). This melody is derived from that of the first half of the verse, where the lyrics express a desperate plea for love ("The night we met I knew I needed you so"), and its dissonant flavor in the chorus lends a bittersweet tone even as the groove picks up momentum. Although the D♯ presents different colors as it changes from seventh to ninth to augmented fourth, its relentless dissonance leaves a sense of uncertainty about the protagonist's romantic prospects.

"Be My Baby" Chorus

Melody	D♯ (7th)	D♯ (9th)	D♯ (aug. 4th)
Lyrics	"my," "ba-"	"one," "ba-"	"my," "ba-"
Harmony	E	C♯ minor	A

By 1963, Phil Spector, then only twenty-two, owned a successful record label and had become rock and roll's most visible record producer. He had developed a signature production style—the so-called wall of sound—that he used on all the recordings made by the various groups signed to his label. Arrangements varied, but all of Spector's tracks produced a similar effect, a thick textural mass in which few individual sounds could be made out clearly. The point, rather, was to create a unique sound grander than the sum of its parts, a sound, as Spector put it, "that no one can copy or 'cover.' "[6]

The basic ingredients of the wall of sound are thick musical arrangements and copious reverb. Gold Star Studios, Spector's production home, was small relative to the musical forces he routinely called for: multiple bass players, drummers, and guitar and keyboard players, all playing at once. (Spector regularly employed members of a group of studio musicians known informally as the Wrecking Crew.) The room filled with blended sound and each instrument's microphone inevitably picked up the sounds of other instruments as well (often referred to as microphone "bleed").

When the mic signals were fed to the recording console, they could be routed both to a tape recorder and to Gold Star's famous echo chamber. The chamber, designed and built by studio co-owner Dave Gold, contained a loudspeaker and a microphone. As sound from the speaker echoed off the lacquered walls, floor, and ceiling, it was captured by the microphone and returned to the recording console to be mixed with the studio sound, producing a composite sonic image that blurred the individual instruments. It might take hours or days to get the mix Spector was after, with the musicians playing the song again and again. Once he was happy with the sonic texture, the recording usually required only one take. Vocals and strings were added as overdubs.

Typical of Spector productions, which he called "little symphonies for the kids," "Be My Baby" has a textural ebb and flow that is a combination of musical arrangement and mix. The track begins with a solo drum set (with handclaps doubling the snare) bathed in cavernous reverb. The reverb is so prominent that it seems to be not merely the drums' ambience but a character in its own right. This striking sonic image takes on a thematic quality all its own as it returns to the spotlight late in the track (2:07).

Throughout the verse, the groove is restrained, with backbeat accents limited to the fourth beat. The first vocal entrance presents the song's protagonist as a lone voice amid a pulsing rhythmic texture. In the second eight bars—as the harmonic motion picks up—backing voices and low-register saxophone reinforce the accompaniment with sustained notes. In the bar before the chorus, the tension of the restrained groove is released with an exuberant drum fill, and as the chorus begins the track flows freely. The snare and handclaps now double up their backbeat accents and light percussion adds a sixteenth-note rhythmic layer. The backing voices take the main melody while Ronnie sings melodic fragments in a call-and-response vocal arrangement.

The second verse returns to the sparser groove but has a thicker texture than the first. The saxophone and backing voices are in from the beginning, and the voices add a new melodic fragment answering Ronnie's phrases. They sing the first half of the verse on the syllable "ooh," a restrained sound fitting the simple harmonic setting. In the second half, as the chromatic notes begin to drive the harmonic motion, the voices open up on the syllable "ah," which makes the push to the second chorus all the more compelling.

The second chorus again releases the tension of the verse but now adds in a layer of strings. These may have been playing during the verse, submerged in the haze, but it's difficult to tell. In any case, we now hear them clearly, though faintly. As yet, they only hint at the lead role they will assume in the upcoming instrumental break. In terms of the mix, the string part in the second chorus provides a textural transition to the break. Such textural moves are ongoing in the track. At times subtle, at others bold, they repay the careful listener with the impression of an aural kaleidoscope bathing the ear in swirling, ever-changing colors.

Listening Guide

"Be My Baby" (Ellie Greenwich, Jeff Barry, Phil Spector), Philles Records (mono)
Recorded at Gold Star Studios, Los Angeles, July 1963

Ronnie Spector (voice), Estelle Bennett, Nedra Talley (nominal voices; replaced by studio singers including Cher), Wrecking Crew, studio musicians (strings)
Arranger: Jack Nitzsche
Producer: Phil Spector
Engineer: Larry Levine
Charts: Hot 100 #2, Hot R&B Singles #4
Key: E
Meter: 4/4

Time	Section	Lyric Cue	Listen For
0:00	Intro (4)		Drums introduce groove with exaggerated reverb.
			Backbeat falls on beat 4 only.
0:04			The rest of the instruments enter, blending with the drum reverb to create a hazy texture pulsing with eighth notes. Castanets and handclaps sharpen the backbeat accents.
0:08	Verse 1 (8+8)	"The night we met"	Voice stands out in relief against the textural haze.
0:23		"So won't you"	Begin sequence of chromatic chords. Texture thickens with low saxophone notes and backing voices ("ooh").
0:35			Groove releases with drum fill.
0:37	Chorus 1 (8)	"Be my, be my baby"	Momentum increases as backbeat doubles up (accents on beats 2 and 4).
			Backing voices sing main melody. Persistent melodic dissonance.
			Lead voice and backing voices sing call-and-response.
0:52	Verse 2 (8+8)	"I'll make you happy"	Backing voices sing new part on "ooh."
1:07		"Oh since the day"	Begin sequence of chromatic chords. Backing voices open up ("ah").
1:20			Drum fill.
1:22	Chorus 2 (8)	"Be my, be my baby"	Similar to **chorus 1**, with strings.
1:37	Break (8)		Texture as in **verse 2**.
			Strings play first 2 phrases of lead vocal melody.
1:52	Chorus (8)	"Be my, be my baby"	Similar to **chorus 2**.
2:07	Intro Reprise (2)		Drums and reverb solo.
2:11	Chorus (8 + fade)	"Be my, be my baby"	Similar to **chorus 2**.

8.3. "REMEMBER (WALKING IN THE SAND)" (1964)

THE SHANGRI-LAS

The Shangri-Las were two sets of sisters, Mary and Betty Weiss and Marge and MaryAnn Ganser. All attended Andrew Jackson High School in Queens, New York. Ranging in age from fifteen to seventeen when they signed with Leiber and Stoller's Red Bird Records, the group projected an image of youthful, streetwise rebellion. Their most successful records were produced by a studio maverick named George "Shadow" Morton, who claimed that "Remember" was not only the first record he had ever produced but the first song he had ever written and, in fact, the first time he had anything to do with the music business. The strange demo he made with the Shangri-Las got both the group and the producer signed to Red Bird. This collaboration among amateur singers, songwriter, and producer launched a partnership that—with some help from Ellie Greenwich and Jeff Barry—yielded some of the era's most deliciously peculiar records.

The Shangri-Las were "tough girls," said Greenwich. "They had an attitude *before* they made it."[7] Their song lyrics bore out the group's outsider image. The boyfriend that shows up in Shangri-Las songs like "Give Him a Great Big Kiss," "Out in the Streets," and "Leader of the Pack" (all produced by Morton) wears his hair "a little too long"; he has "dirty fingernails" and "dirty old black boots." He is a romantic misfit, "always looking like he's got the blues," a guy parents consider to be "from the wrong side of town," his deepest feelings understood only by the special girl who recognizes he is "bad but he's not evil." Mary Weiss, the youngest member, sang lead on most of the hit recordings. She poured her heart into enactments of teenage alienation and longing. "I had enough pain in me at the time," she told an interviewer, "to pull off anything and get into it and sound believable."[8] The melodramas she starred in combined music, spoken word, and sound effects, creating what Jeff Barry called "a movie for the ear."

"Remember" consists primarily of two large sections. The A section is based on a looping chord progression that repeats three times, accompanying the protagonist's tale of abandonment and heartbreak. Aside from piano, bass, and drums, the instrumentation is impossible to make out clearly. What is clear is the effect created by concentrating timbres in the track's low-end, where piano and bass both play a descending line, producing a dark, remote texture to match the protagonist's state of mind. The piano timbre is a distinctive, lo-fi rumble. Its ominous sound is a fitting match for the minor-mode chord progression. The only textural variation in the first A section is the alternating "ooh" and "ah" in the backing voices.

Before the B section begins, the groove comes to a stop with the protagonist repeating to herself "Oh no, oh no," isolated and vulnerable. At the end of this two-bar break, the backing voices intone a half-whispered "Remember," which the protagonist answers with memories of the time before her "baby went away." As she remembers "walking hand in hand" along the beach, seagull sounds permeate the track. Otherwise the texture is spare, leaving the protagonist largely alone with her thoughts. The lead melody becomes static, hovering around the tonic. Harmony, too, is restricted to the tonic. The percussion resumes at a quicker tempo but not with drums, only finger snaps and handclaps—sounds of the street or the beach. The lyrics build anticipation, leading to a mildly erotic climax ("Softly we'd meet with our lips") that slows the tempo back down and leads to the second A section.

The track rushes to its conclusion as the final A section is truncated to eight bars of rising desperation. Pitifully, Weiss asks what she will do with her life now that she's given it to her faithless lover, while the other Shangri-Las sing out in full voice, both sympathetic and angry at their sister's fate. Omitting the vocal break, the track moves straight into the B section, which fades, along with the memories, amid the seagull cries.

Listening Guide

"Remember (Walking in the Sand)" (George Morton), Red Bird Records (mono)
Recorded at Mira Sound, New York City, July 1964
Mary Weiss (lead voice), Betty Weiss, Marge Ganser, MaryAnn Ganser (voice), studio musicians (piano, bass, drums)
Producers: George Morton; demo reworked by Jeff Barry, Artie Ripp
Engineer: Brooks Arthur
Chart: Hot 100 #5, Hot R&B Singles #5
Key: D minor
Meter 12/8

Time	Section	Lyric Cue	Listen For
0:00	A (4+4+4) Harmonic Phrase 1	"Seems like the other"	Impassioned lead vocal. Murky, distant texture of piano, bass, and drums. Backing voices alternate "ooh" and "aah" in successive bars.

Time	Section	Lyric Cue	Listen For
0:16	Harmonic Phrase 2	"It's been two years"	
0:31	Harmonic Phrase 3	"He said that we were"	
0:45	Break (2)	"Oh no"	Rhythmic flow is interrupted; voice is exposed.
0:53	B (16)	"Remember"	Faster tempo.
			Sparse texture: handclaps, finger snaps, bass, sounds of seagulls and surf.
			Backing voices (doubled by bass and piano) sing "remember" once every 2 bars.
			Lead voice answers with fragments of memory.
			Melody hovers around tonic.
1:18			Original tempo and texture return.
			Harmony moves to V setting up return to **A**.
1:22	A (8)	"Whatever happened"	Only two harmonic phrases.
			Backing voices sing "ah" throughout in full voice.
1:51	B (13 to fade)	"Remember"	Similar to previous **B**; fade.

NOTES

1. Ren Grevatt, "Gal Singers Make the 'Sick' Scene," *Billboard*, February 27, 1961, 5.
2. Morgan Neville, *Hitmakers: The Teens Who Stole Pop Music*, DVD (Peter Jones Productions, 1999).
3. Quoted in Ken Emerson, *Always Magic in the Air: The Bomp and Brilliance of the Brill Building Era* (New York: Viking, 2005), 137–38.
4. Neville, *Hitmakers*.
5. Jacqueline Warwick, *Girl Groups, Girl Culture: Popular Music and Identity in the 1960s* (New York: Routledge, 2007), 35.
6. Alan Betrock, *Girl Groups: The Story of a Sound* (New York: Delilah Books, 1982), 24.
7. Quoted in Emerson, *Always Magic in the Air*, 228.
8. Quoted in Emerson, 227.

FURTHER READING

Betrock, Alan. *Girl Groups: The Story of a Sound*. New York: Delilah Books, 1983.
Emerson, Ken. *Always Magic in the Air: The Bomp and Brilliance of the Brill Building Era.* New York: Viking 2005.

Ribowsky, Mark. *He's a Rebel: Phil Spector: Rock 'n' Roll's Legendary Producer.* New York: E. P. Dutton, 1989.

Warwick, Jacqueline. *Girl Groups, Girl Culture: Popular Music and Identity in the 1960s.* New York: Routledge, 2007.

FURTHER LISTENING

Angels, "My Boyfriend's Back" (Smash, 1963)
Chantels, "Maybe" (End, 1958)
Chiffons, "One Fine Day" (Laurie, 1963)
Crystals, "Then He Kissed Me" (Philles, 1963)
Exciters, "Tell Him" (United Artists, 1962)
Leslie Gore, "It's My Party" (Mercury, 1963)
Jaynetts, "Sally, Go 'Round the Roses" (Tuff, 1963)
Little Eva, "The Loco-Motion" (Dimension, 1962)
Marvelettes, "Please Mr. Postman" (Tamla, 1961)
Kathy Young and the Innocents, "A Thousand Stars" (Indigo, 1960)

9

AFFIRMING A NEW POP TRADITION
The Beatles

They called it Beatlemania, the apparent affliction that drove young fans crazy at the mere mention of the word *Beatles*. With catchy songs, spirited performances, and ringing vocal harmonies, Beatles records were the stuff of rhapsody. An actual sighting of the group's members caused near-riots. The Beatles—John Lennon, Paul McCartney, George Harrison, and Ringo Starr—hailing from the northern English seaport of Liverpool, burst into the global limelight with amazing speed, attracting fans of all ages and musical persuasions. When they came to America for the first time, in February 1964, an estimated 73 million viewers tuned in to see their performance on *The Ed Sullivan Show*. Beatlemania was, as one writer put it, a "shared sentiment that spread convulsively, . . . finally embracing virtually everyone in the world."[1]

By 1963, the Beatles had become well established throughout the United Kingdom and many parts of Europe, but America was slower to be seduced. It was a rarity for foreign pop stars to make an impression with the American public, and even the Beatles' American record company was skeptical about the prospect. As John Lennon put it, making it in America "was just something you could never do."[2] Capitol Records, the US partner to the Beatles' UK label EMI, declined to release even Beatles records that had already hit big in England (e.g., "Please Please Me," "She Loves You"). These records were instead licensed to US indie labels Vee-Jay and Swan. Only when Ed Sullivan booked the band on his show was the Beatles' manager, Brian Epstein, able to convince Capitol to release the band's records, six of which went to number one in 1964.

The Beatles brought America more than a fresh new sound and an appealing personal charm. Landing in New York only months after the assassination of President John F. Kennedy, the Beatles brought to a saddened nation a celebration of its own music. The Beatles performed and recorded songs by Chuck Berry, Little Richard, Carl Perkins, and Buddy Holly. They covered such Motown artists as the Miracles and Barrett Strong and girl groups such as the Marvelettes, Shirelles, Cookies, and Donays. Their performances captured the spirit not only of the songs but also of the original recordings. (Compare, for instance, their recording of Buddy Holly's "Words of Love" or Little Richard's "Long Tall Sally" with the originals.) The covers blended seamlessly with the Beatles' original material, an implied affirmation that this eclectic range of songs flowed from a single musical tradition. What many in the music industry thought was the aimless musical meandering of amateurs through the course of the 1950s was now shown, by the example of pop music's new superstars, to have been the birth of a new pop idiom.

Having hit with such force, the Beatles worked fast. They recorded and toured at a furious pace, assuming that like most pop stars they would have a brief time in the sun. From 1963 to 1966, they released two fourteen-song albums each year (except for *A Hard Day's Night*, which has thirteen), as well as singles and EPs of other material. The music evolved quickly. They moved from the pure pop of "She Loves You" to the existential "Nowhere Man" in a scant two years. Their sound palette expanded to include string quartet, sitar, orchestra, and a range of electronic treatments. They defied pop's conventional boundaries with their mid-1960s albums *Rubber Soul* and *Revolver*. Their next album, *Sgt. Pepper's Lonely Hearts Club Band,* was among the decade's high cultural watermarks. A *Village Voice* review called it "the most ambitious and most successful record album ever issued, and the most significant artistic event of 1967."[3] *Time* magazine ran a Beatles cover story that cast the group as "messengers from beyond rock 'n' roll." *Sgt. Pepper's*, the article claimed, provided convincing evidence that the Beatles were "leading an evolution in which the best of current post-rock sounds are becoming something that pop music has never been before: an art form."[4]

The Beatles were signed to the EMI subsidiary Parlophone by George Martin after being turned down by other record companies in London. Martin, who was a classically trained musician, would produce most of the Beatles' records. His collaboration with the band was exceptionally close. In addition to running the control room, he advised on repertory, played piano in the studio, wrote arrangements, and, as the music grew more experimental, helped realize the band's intuitive creativity by solving technical and musical problems beyond their grasp. Together, the Beatles and Martin, often credited as the "fifth Beatle," blazed a path of continuous innovation throughout the decade.

The Beatles commanded the 1960s pop universe, which also meant they commanded a bully pulpit among the youth. In addition to inspiring the formation of hundreds of rock bands, they influenced young people's views of what it meant to be a young person. With public comments on fashion, politics, religion, sex, drugs, meditation, Indian music, and more, the Beatles spoke for and to a generation for whom music was a force for change and a crucial element of identity.

9.1. "A HARD DAY'S NIGHT" (1964)

In the summer of 1964, the Beatles starred in a feature film, *A Hard Day's Night*, which was accompanied by an album of the same name, the first to include only the group's original songs. Unlike the string of corny B movies Elvis Presley appeared in, *A Hard Day's Night* was hip. Depicting "an exaggerated day in the life of the Beatles," as director Richard Lester put it, the film is filled with clever ad-libs and scenes of the band exhilarating in their band-ness, transcending the mundane pressures of stardom as they tumble through the day.[5] Audiences were swept along with the apparently carefree, nonconformist spirits of the coolest band in the world, playing the coolest music in the world and acting, well, cool. The film and its music offered a template for rock and roll as the music moved decisively toward the future. According to the Beatles' example, rock and roll bands wrote their own songs and played their own instruments; a band's primary lineup consisted of guitar, bass, and drums; all band members sang and their records rang with harmony; and as far as a generation's potential, the sky was the limit. In Lester's words, "The Beatles told everybody, 'You can do anything you damn well like.' "[6]

The title track is a good example of Lennon's and McCartney's songwriting skills (primarily Lennon in this case). It manages to effortlessly blend major, minor, and Mixolydian modes; chromaticism; and a brief blues inflection into an infectious pop song. The A sections are mostly major, and the B section mostly minor. The modal feeling comes from the flatted VII chord (F) in the third and seventh bars of the A sections ("I've been *working*" "should be *sleeping*"). The chromaticism is in Lennon's and McCartney's vocal parts in bars eight to ten of the A sections ("But *when I* get *home to* you," "find *the* things *that you* do"). And the trace of blues is felt in Lennon's flatted third on "feel *al*-right." The way it all fits together seamlessly is a perfect example of the band's mastery of rock's fusion principle.

> ## A Mixed Harmonic Palette
>
> "A Hard Day's Night" is in G major but uses several notes not in the G scale.
>
> 1. The flatted VII chord (F) is borrowed from the Mixolydian mode.
>
> 2. The chromatic notes (D♯, E♯, G♯) occur in the two-part vocal harmony as passing tones (i.e., notes that move between chord tones).
>
> 3. The blue note is B♭, the flatted third in G.

The song's form follows an AABA structure but not the conventional 8+8+8+8 proportions. Instead, each A section is extended to twelve bars. The first eight consist of two musically identical four-bar phrases (each containing the Mixolydian F chord). The four-bar extension that follows serves as a cadence phrase (containing the chromatic and blue notes). Although the A section is not a twelve-bar blues, it is structurally similar to the lyrics of a blues chorus. Both follow an *aab* pattern.

The contrasting B section sticks to the normal eight-bar length. It moves the harmony further afield, introducing minor chord sonorities that change the track's mood. Another point of contrast is the shift in lead vocal from Lennon to McCartney. Again, however, the switch is seamless.

Whoever sings the lead, the voice is double tracked via overdub, a standard Beatles device for creating a sense of aural excitement. Double tracking requires singing the song twice. Since it is impossible to synchronize the two performances perfectly, the inevitable pitch and timing discrepancies create a "thicker" vocal sound that projects from the loudspeakers with assertive force.

Another doubling (this one requiring no overdubbing) that produces a distinctive sound is the combination of piano and electric twelve-string guitar that plays the melody in the instrumental break. Not only is this a composite timbre made from the sounds of two instruments, but it also has an electronically induced timbral effect created by doubling the speed of the original recording. In effect, the recording team created an instrument never heard before. Like the intro chord and the twelve-string arpeggios in the outro, the instrumental break provides "A Hard Day's Night" with a unique signature sound.

The intro chord—speaking of cool—is one of the most famous introductions in all popular music, kicking off the track (which also opens the album and the film) with its ringing call to pop fans everywhere. The chord is remarkable in several respects.

1. It makes a dramatically short introduction.
2. Its pitches produce a mildly dissonant clang (D, F, A, C, F, G, A), a cheeky token of rebellion.
3. Its sound—a mixture of guitar, piano, and bass blended into a single sonic impression—is a hook unto itself.

The instrument that provides the high-end ring is the electric twelve-string. Harrison plays it throughout the track, but you can hear it most clearly on the brief outro. The sound of the twelve-string was one of the influences that rippled from *A Hard Day's Night*. Roger McGuinn, for one, seized on it immediately as the foundational sound for his new band the Byrds.

Note: Although most Beatles records were released in mono and stereo versions, the mono mixes got the most attention because mono was the dominant radio broadcast format until the rise of FM in the late '60s. In 1968, stereo mixes took on a new importance with the tracks for *The Beatles* (White Album), and by *Abbey Road*, stereo was the exclusive format. Accordingly, the Listening Guides for "A Hard Day's Night," "Nowhere Man," and "Eleanor Rigby" refer to the mono versions.

Listening Guide

"A Hard Day's Night" (John Lennon, Paul McCartney), Parlophone Records (mono). Also appears on the album *A Hard Day's Night*.
Recorded at EMI Studio Two, London, April 1964
John Lennon (guitar, voice), Paul McCartney (bass, voice), George Harrison (guitar), Ringo Starr (drums, percussion), George Martin (piano)
Producer: George Martin
Engineer: Norman Smith
Charts: Hot 100 #1, Top LP's #1
Key: G
Meter: 4/4

Time	Section	Lyric Cue	Listen For
0:00	Intro		Dissonant chord: piano, bass, electric 12-string guitar.
0:04	A (4+4+4)	"It's been a hard"	Lennon's lead vocal double tracked.
			Guitars (electric and acoustic)/bass/drums texture augmented with bongos.
0:07		"working"	F chord (Mixolydian inflection).
0:10		"It's been a hard"	Phrase 2

continued on next page

Time	Section	Lyric Cue	Listen For
0:14		"sleeping"	F chord.
0:17		"when I get"	Phrase 3, chromatic passing tones in voices.
0:21		"feel"	Blue note (B♭).
0:24	A (4+4+4)	"You know I work"	Similar to previous A.
0:45	B (8)	"When I'm home"	McCartney takes the lead.
			Key changes briefly to minor.
			Cowbell adds rhythmic drive.
0:59	A (4+4+4)	"It's been a hard"	Similar to previous A.
1:20	A (4+4+4)		Instrumental break for first 8 bars.
			Electric guitar and piano play melody in unison; half-speed recording creates a unique timbre.
1:34		"So why on earth"	Voices return for cadence phrase.
1:41	B (8)	"When I'm home"	Similar to previous B.
1:55	A (4+4+4)	"It's been a hard"	Similar to previous A.
2:16	Extension	"You know I feel"	
2:22	**Outro** (fade)		Electric 12-string arpeggios (F chord).

9.2. "NOWHERE MAN" (1965)

The album *Rubber Soul*, on which "Nowhere Man" appears, was the Beatles' sixth album release in less than three years. It marked the beginning of a new phase in the band's career. "We finally took over the studio," said Lennon. "We were more precise about making the album." McCartney recalled that "the direction was moving away from the poppy stuff," and into "more psychedelic or surreal" territory. George Martin remembered *Rubber Soul* as a particularly ambitious undertaking. "For the first time," he said, "we began to think of albums as art on their own, as complete entities."[7] The primary vehicle of rock and roll expression and commerce had always been the single. Albums were simply collections of singles. Now, however, the Beatles began to think in terms of a larger canvas—the album as a coherent artwork.

"Nowhere Man" begins a cappella, shining a spotlight on the voices and the words, which are a marked departure from what Lennon referred to as his and McCartney's "I love you and you love me" songs. Themes of isolation ("sitting in his nowhere land"), self-absorption ("just sees what he wants to see"), and aimlessness ("knows not where he's going to") run through the song's A sections, leavened by a plea for optimism in the B sections ("the world is at your command," "don't worry," someone will "lend you a hand"). Aside from the first A, which is treated like an introduction, each A section is followed by a B section. The song moves according to a cycle that moves repeatedly in and out of the nowhere man's shadowy world.

Two timbral elements are especially distinctive. First to appear is the tight three-part vocal harmony (each voice double tracked). Having captured listeners with its striking a cappella entrance, the three-voice texture continues through the A sections. The sound contrasts with that of the B sections where Lennon sings the lyrics by himself (still double tracked), while McCartney and Harrison switch to a syllabic accompaniment ("ah la la la").

The track's other signature sound is that of the bright electric guitars playing in unison with an exaggerated high-end boost. (These guitars end each A section with a two-bar response and take the lead in the instrumental break.) Their overly bright timbre provides a counterpoise to the warmer texture of acoustic guitar, drums, and bass. This guitar sound is an example of the Beatles' growing interest in record production and their growing clout with the record company. EMI was an old firm and its engineers were trained according to traditional recording precepts. But the Beatles wanted to push the envelope, seeking new sounds and new directions in record making. As Paul McCartney explained it,

> We were always forcing them into things they didn't want to do. "Nowhere Man" was one. I remember we wanted very treble-y guitars, which they are, they're among the most treble-y guitars I've ever heard on record. The engineer said "All right, I'll put full treble on it" and we said "That's not enough" and he said "But that's all I've got, I've only got one pot [tone controller] and that's it!" and we replied "Well, put that through another lot of faders and we'll put full treble up on that. And if that's not enough we'll go through another lot of faders and . . ." so we were always doing that, forcing them. . . . We were always pushing ahead: *"louder, further, longer, more, different."*[8]

Listening Guide

"Nowhere Man" (John Lennon, Paul McCartney) Parlophone Records (mono). Also appears on the album *Rubber Soul*.
Recorded at EMI Studio Two, London, October 1965

John Lennon (voice, guitar), Paul McCartney (voice, bass), George Harrison (voice, guitar), Ringo Starr (drums)
Producer: George Martin
Engineer: Norman Smith
Charts: Hot 100 #3, Top LP's #1
Key: E
Meter: 4/4

Time	Section	Lyric Cue	Listen For
0:00	A (8)	"He's a real"	A cappella voices, Lennon (the middle voice) has the lead.
0:08		"Making all his"	Acoustic guitar, bass, drums (warm texture).
0:14			"Treble-y" electric guitars (bright texture).
			Bass plays running eighth note line.
0:16	A (8)	"Doesn't have a"	Warm texture.
0:28			Treble-y guitar response.
0:32	B (8)	"Nowhere man"	McCartney and Harrison switch to vocal syllables ("ah la la la").
0:48	Break (8)		Follows A section chord progression.
			Treble-y guitars play melody.
1:04	A (8)	"He's as blind"	Similar to previous A.
1:19	B (8)	"Nowhere man"	Similar to previous B.
1:35	A (8)	"Doesn't have a"	Similar to previous A.
1:50	B (8)	"Nowhere man"	Similar to previous B.
2:06	A (8)	"He's a real"	Similar previous A.
2:22	Coda (8)	"Making all his"	Repeat final phrase twice; last time high harmony voice (McCartney) sings one octave higher.

9.3. "ELEANOR RIGBY" (1966)

During their middle period, the Beatles steadily expanded their timbral palette. George Martin was called on increasingly to provide arrangements, augmenting the band's guitar/bass/drums foundation. Likewise, through George Harrison's interest in Indian classical music, the sounds of sitar, tamboura, and tablas turned up on Beatles tracks. The first recording to stand out as a dramatic stylistic departure was McCartney's "Yesterday," from the album *Help!* (1965). McCartney is the only Beatle on the track, singing and playing acoustic guitar, joined by a classical string quartet (two violins, viola, and cello) playing an arrangement written by George Martin. The track would become a rock classic, but at the time the group was "a little embarrassed about it," as McCartney remembered later.[9] The sound certainly did not fit the band's self-image as hard-edged rockers. They buried it on the album as the next-to-last track. Only after DJs began playing "Yesterday" on their own was it released as a single and then only in the US. (The Beatles' influence was such that within six months, the band that was supposedly their antithesis, the Rolling Stones, would also employ a string quartet for their recording of "As Tears Go By.")

"Eleanor Rigby" appears on the album *Revolver*, a record whose instrumentation, electronic processing, and arrangements pushed further into unexplored pop territory. The track brings back the string quartet idea, but now there is no tentativeness or apology. In fact, the arrangement (again by Martin) uses a double string quartet (four violins, two violas, two cellos) and does away with guitar, bass, and drums completely. Although the song had the group's input, it was primarily a McCartney composition. Like Lennon's "Nowhere Man," "Eleanor Rigby" demonstrates a turn to song topics rarely before explored in pop music. Both men were by now feeling the influence of Bob Dylan, who had shown that serious songs and pop hits were not mutually exclusive.

The strings on "Eleanor Rigby" have a particular sound that, along with the arrangement's incisive rhythm, gives them a trenchant rock feel. Geoff Emerick had by now taken over from Norman Smith as chief engineer on Beatles sessions and he had a number of ideas about recording that ran counter to EMI dogma. As the Beatles moved further in an experimental direction, they now had an equally adventurous engineer. In the case of "Eleanor Rigby," Emerick broke with classical recording convention by placing microphones very close to the instruments. The string players thought it annoyingly inept, but Emerick knew what he was doing. His mic placement produced an aggressive sound, which intensified the bleak atmosphere surrounding the song's sad characters.

Revolver also saw the introduction of a new studio technology developed by EMI technician Ken Townsend. Beatles records had always featured double-tracked vocals, which involved considerable effort. Townsend came up with a method for automatic double tracking (**ADT**), which allows the voice to be doubled electronically, producing a similar effect. The process involves echo, but unlike the standard tape echo effects, ADT uses such a short delay time that the echo is not perceptible as a separate sound. It simply enhances the source sound. On "Eleanor

Rigby" you can hear the effect used on McCartney's voice to create a contrast between verse and chorus. In the verses, which are dry, McCartney's voice has an intimate quality, as though confiding in the listener. At the chorus, the ADT kicks in, thickening the voice and changing its unadorned personal tone to a fuller choral effect. This change mirrors the lyric shift from a focus on individuals to a more generalized image of "all the lonely people."

"Eleanor Rigby" is in E minor but makes effective use of the Dorian mode, which raises the sixth scale degree to C♯.

E minor scale: E, F♯, G, A, B, C, D
E Dorian scale: E, F♯, G, A, B, C♯, D

This pitch is used to provide a Dorian flavor to the melody. It has no influence on the chords. In the phrase "picks up the rice in the church," for example, "in" and "church" are both sung on C♯. But when the chord progression moves to VI in bars four and nine of each verse, the chord is the normal C. The half step tension between the C♯ and C♮ adds to the song's haunting quality. (The C♯ also appears in the descending chromatic string line in the choruses.)

Noteworthy, too, is the phrase structure in the verse, which falls into a five-bar pattern that further divides into 4+1. The first four bars describe an image and the next bar a provides a comment or question. So, in verse one, for example, the first four bars describe Eleanor Rigby picking up rice in a church, followed by the one-bar comment "lives in a dream." This description/comment dualism is heightened by the C♯/C♮ contrast. The Dorian inflection always occurs in the four-bar description segment, while the C♮ is the featured melodic pitch in the comment phrase.

The song's lyrics are an evocation of isolation and loneliness. The first verse introduces the title character cleaning up a church. In only a few words the song sketches a portrait of a woman perpetually waiting. In the second verse, we meet the church's priest, Father Mackenzie, equally alone and detached. Since both characters occupy the church, they are literally alone together. The final verse depicts Eleanor Rigby's funeral attended only by Father Mackenzie, suggesting a paradoxical solidarity amid alienation. The choruses zoom out from the close focus on the song's characters to a broader rumination on "all the lonely people." The questions posed in the chorus—"Where do they all come from?" and "Where do they all belong?"—expand the song's thematic reach from character study to existential contemplation.

New Sonic Images

Revolver uses a broad palette of sounds and textures that set it apart from contemporary records as well as the Beatles' own previous work. In addition to the strings and ADT on "Eleanor Rigby," listen to these examples of the Beatles' 1966 sonic vocabulary.

Reverse-tape electric guitar on "I'm Only Sleeping"
Indian sitar and tabla on "Love You To"
Sound effects on "Yellow Submarine"
Clavichord and French horn on "For No One"
Brass on "Got to Get You into My Life"
Lennon's vocal on "Tomorrow Never Knows" processed with a Leslie rotating speaker (intended as an electronic effect for organ)
Tape loops on "Tomorrow Never Knows"

Listening Guide

"Eleanor Rigby" (John Lennon, Paul McCartney), Parlophone Records (mono). Also appears on *Revolver*.
Recorded at EMI Studios Two and Three, London, April–June 1966
Paul McCartney, John Lennon, George Harrison (voice), Tony Gilbert, Sidney Sax, John Sharpe, Jurgen Hess (violin), Stephen Shingles, John Underwood (viola), Derek Simpson, Norman Jones (cello)
Producer, George Martin
Engineer: Geoff Emerick
Charts: Hot 100 #11, Top LP's #1
Key: E minor
Meter: 4/4

Time	Section	Lyric Cue	Listen For
0:00	Intro (8)	"Ah, look at all"	Group vocals.
			Violins answer vocal phrases.
			Strings play incisive rhythm, accenting every beat.
			Cello fragments end on accented offbeats.
0:14	Verse 1 (5+5)	"Eleanor Rigby"	Solo voice, dry.
			Strings play quarter notes.
			Dorian inflection (C♯) on "in" and "church."
0:21		"Lives in a"	C♮ on "dream" replaces Dorian with minor.
0:23		"Waits at the"	Violins switch to eighth notes.
			Dorian ("that" and "keeps").
0:30		"Who is it for"	Minor ("for").

continued on next page

Time	Section	Lyric Cue	Listen For
0:31	**Chorus 1** (8)	"All the lonely"	ADT on voice.
			Descending chromatic violin line includes both $C^\sharp$ and $C^\natural$.
0:45	**Verse 2** (5+5)	"Father Mackenzie"	Similar to previous **verse**.
0:51		"Look at him"	New cello line.
0:55			New violin line.
1:03	**Chorus 2** (8)	"All the lonely"	Similar to previous **c**horus.
1:17	**Interlude** (8)	"Ah, look at all"	Repeat **intro**.
1:31	**Verse 3** (5+5)	"Eleanor Rigby"	Strings play eighth notes.
			New violin line.
1:40		"Father Mackenzie"	Strings switch to quarter notes.
			New cello line doubles voice.
1:49	**Chorus 3** (9)	"All the lonely"	Similar to previous **c**horus.
			Intro melody (sung by McCartney with rotating speaker timbral effect) superimposed on primary melody.

9.4. "WHILE MY GUITAR GENTLY WEEPS" (1968)

"While My Guitar Gently Weeps" was written by George Harrison, the youngest Beatle and the last of the group's three songwriters to take up writing. With several years' head start, Lennon and McCartney had established themselves as the group's primary songwriters, with Harrison contributing only two songs to the band's first five albums. As he gained experience, however, Harrison's songs, while still far outnumbered, became essential to the Beatles' catalog. He would contribute two iconic Beatles songs—"Something," and "Here Comes the Sun"—to the band's final album, *Abbey Road*.

"While My Guitar Gently Weeps" is one of the standout tracks on *The Beatles*, which would become known as the White Album because of its plain white cover. The album, the band's ninth, is a sprawling two-LP set that takes listeners on a musical and sonic journey filled with surprising twists and turns. Over the course of twenty-two tracks, the album moves from high-energy rock to intimate ballad, from social critique to willful nonsense, from pristine sounds to harsh distortion. The tracks flow one into another as though the whole thing were meant to be heard as a continuous work. With the release of their groundbreaking *Sgt. Pepper's Lonely Hearts Club Band*, the Beatles had left no doubt that the studio was their artistic home. Making the White Album, even as they endured serious difficulties in their relationships with one another, the band spent nearly five months working long hours in the studio, laying down hundreds of takes and finishing with a marathon twenty-four-hour session.

"While My Guitar Gently Weeps" evolved slowly over the course of many takes in sessions scattered from late July to early September. The Beatles were by now wealthy enough to not worry about the expense of studio time. Instead of working out arrangements and rehearsing before they came to the studio, they used the studio as a venue for composing, "writing" their ideas to tape in a trial-and-error process. After several failed attempts to capture the song's plaintive mood, the group finally got a basic track of bass, drums, and guitars that satisfied Harrison. In an extremely unusual gesture, he then asked Eric Clapton to overdub a lead guitar part. Up to that point, other rock musicians had not played on Beatles records and Clapton was initially hesitant. Finally, he agreed to sit in and with a single take recorded one of rock's iconic, though at the time uncredited, guitar solos.

Clapton was keen to make the part sound idiomatic, something appropriate for a Beatles record rather than for his own band, Cream. The solution was to treat his guitar part with ADT, which was not simply an echo-delay technique but potentially a timbral one as well. The motor on the tape machine producing the echo was fitted with a variable-speed oscillator, which controlled the motor's speed. The oscillator, in turn, was controlled by a knob, which could be manipulated to change the tape speed on the fly. Since tape speed determines the time between a source sound and its echo, changing speed means changing the nature of the effect in real time. Sweeping back and forth within a particular time range—between, say, twenty and thirty-five milliseconds—produces the slightly psychedelic (or weeping) effect we hear on the guitar. The effect is also featured on the organ part.

The song's sixteen-bar A sections are composed of two nearly identical eight-bar harmonic phrases (only the penultimate chord in each phrase is different). Each harmonic phrase is further divided into two four-bar vocal phrases, which mirrors the protagonist's halting narrative. Phrases one and three offer an observation ("I look at you all"; "I look at the floor"); phrases two and four respond with "my guitar gently weeps." The tempo as articulated by the acoustic guitar is not particularly slow, yet the track trudges along heavily due in part to the half-time drum groove. This deliberate pacing is underscored by the bassline, which plays a heavy downbeat in each bar.

The lyrics, too, contribute to the feeling of slow unfolding because rhymes are spaced relatively far apart. The word at the end of phrase one ("sleeping"), for instance, waits until the end of phrase three for its rhyme ("weeping"). So, although the vocal phrases are four bars long, the rhymes are eight bars apart, separated by the repeated line "While my guitar gently weeps." As this constant refrain draws out the rhyme scheme, it adds to the track's overall sense of troubled hesitancy.

Although the B section is structured similarly to the A section in its eight-bar harmonic phrases, in other respects it provides a contrast. The texture is fuller, the instrumental parts more active. Also, the eight-bar segments are not subdivided into 4+4. Instead of offering a fragmentary observation (four bars) followed by the refrain (four bars), as in the A section, the voice now expresses a more complete thought that unfolds over the full eight-bar phrase even as a series of internal rhymes quickens the flow of ideas (e.g., "told/fold," "controlled/sold," "diverted/perverted").

The bridge also brings a sudden key change from A minor to A major. This does little, however, to brighten the song's mournful tone. Five bars of each eight-bar phrase are colored by minor chord harmonies, and the ADT-treated organ adds a wobbly pitch effect that destabilizes the track's tuning. The organ's woozy effect amplifies the protagonist's expression of uncertainty ("I don't know how"; "I don't know why").

Clapton's guitar, which plays throughout the track and is the featured character in the instrumental break and coda, is nearly equal to the voice in its dramatic role. Using extensive string bends and vibrato, Clapton plays a crying blues, aptly personifying the song's central symbol, the weeping guitar. In the extended coda, played over the chords of the A section, Clapton's guitar soars with a magnificence transcending the cries of pain in Harrison's moaning voice, thus epitomizing the psychic purpose of the blues.

Listening Guide

"While My Guitar Gently Weeps" (George Harrison) Apple Records (stereo). Appears on the album *The Beatles*.
Recorded at EMI Studio Two, London, September 1968
George Harrison (voice, guitar), Eric Clapton (lead guitar), John Lennon (guitar), Paul McCartney (voice, bass, organ), Ringo Starr (drums, percussion)
Producer: George Harrison
Engineer: Ken Scott
Charts: Top LP's #1
Key: A minor
Meter: 4/4

Time	Section	Lyric Cue	Listen For
0:00	Intro (8)		Stereo field: piano (L), acoustic guitar (C), bass, drums (R).
			Same chord sequence as **A**.
0:14			Electric guitar (with ADT) entrance (L).
0:16	**A** (8+8)	"I look at you all"	First harmonic phrase.
			Harrison sings alone.
			Bass emphasizes downbeats.
0:34		"I look at the floor"	Second harmonic phrase.
			McCartney adds vocal harmony in first 4 bars.
0:50	**B** (8+8)	"I don't know why"	First harmonic phrase.
			Shift from A minor to A major.
			Organ treated with ADT (L).
			Bass more active.
1:07		"I don't know how"	Second harmonic phrase.
1:24	**A** (8+8)	"I look at the world"	Similar texture to previous **A**.
			Vocal harmony in first 4 bars.
			Organ out.
1:41		"With every mistake"	Vocal harmony in first 4 bars.
1:57	**Break** (16)		Guitar solo.
			Same chord sequence as **A**.
			Organ in.
2:30	**B** (8+8)	"I don't know how"	Similar texture to previous **B**, add tambourine (R).
2:47		"I don't know how"	
3:04	**A** (8+8)	"I look at you all"	Similar texture to previous **A**; organ and tambourine out.
3:20		"I look at you all"	Organ (L) in.
3:37	**Coda** (32 bars to fade)		Guitar solos over **A** section chords, answered by moaning voice.

9.5. "SUN KING"/"MEAN MR. MUSTARD"/ "POLYTHENE PAM"/"SHE CAME IN THROUGH THE BATHROOM WINDOW" (1969)

The White Album was released in November 1968, and despite serious tensions within the group, the Beatles were back recording by the following January. McCartney had the idea that the band should "get back" to its roots, and although his attempts to restart the Beatles' performing career ultimately failed, the project did take them back to a more stripped-down recording process. The songs for the album, which was to be called *Get Back*, were recorded over the course of ten days in sessions described by Harrison as "the low of all time" and by Lennon as "hell . . . the most miserable sessions on earth."[10] The project was a testament to their perseverance and professionalism, but the band members were deeply unhappy and feeling that perhaps the end was near. The project culminated in the final live Beatles performance on the roof of their Apple offices in London. It was the first time the group had performed in public since 1967, and it caused quite a stir in the street below until the police shut it down. In the end, however, *Get Back* was judged unfit for release. The album was set aside until the spring of 1970, when it was released as *Let It Be* after a reworking at the hands of Phil Spector.

In the summer of 1969, the Beatles, sensing that it might be their last project together, decided to make an album they could be proud of. The record would be called *Abbey Road*, which is where the EMI recording studios are located and where the Beatles had spent so much of their creative lives during the 1960s. McCartney approached George Martin, who had given up on the splintered group. Martin agreed to produce on the condition that they work with the concerted effort that had characterized their best recordings. All three primary songwriters came through with excellent material and Ringo Starr, historically a marginal contributor in the songwriting department, brought in the best of his Beatles efforts: "Octopus's Garden." The group returned to the layered arrangements and recording techniques of the records prior to *Get Back* and, perhaps most important, everyone cooperated in the project of creative collaboration. "Before the *Abbey Road* sessions," said McCartney, "it was like we should put down the boxing gloves and try and just get it together and really make a very special album. . . . I think it was in a way the feeling that it might be our last, so let's just show them what we can do."[11]

It was clear from the quasi concept album *Sgt. Pepper's Lonely Hearts Club Band*, and the linked songs on the White Album, that the group and their producer were thinking in larger terms than individual pop songs. It was decided that *Abbey Road* would include an extended medley of Lennon and McCartney song bits stitched together to form a cohesive whole. Extended album pieces exploring a particular theme were becoming popular in late-1960s rock. In 1968, the Kinks released *The Kinks Are the Village Green Preservation Society*, a nostalgic collection of songs about small-town English life. In the same year, the Small Faces' album, *Ogdens' Nut Gone Flake*, whose second side is dedicated to the character Happiness Stan, topped the UK album charts.

These albums, however, were collections of individual songs held together by a thematic narrative. The Beatles' *Abbey Road* medley, on the other hand, is a single piece created by linking song fragments. The songs only become finished as they are joined together and enfolded into a larger whole. There is no literal narrative to the piece. Instead, it takes listeners on a stream-of-consciousness journey that fascinates even as it mystifies. Listeners intuit meaning through suggestive lyrics, expressive performances, changing sonic colors, and the compelling flow of the musical arrangement.

The tracks conjoined to form the medley are "You Never Give Me Your Money," "Sun King," "Mean Mr. Mustard," "Polythene Pam," "She Came In through the Bathroom Window," "Golden Slumbers," "Carry That Weight," and "The End." The Listening Guide outlines a four-song excerpt beginning with "Sun King" and finishing with "She Came In through the Bathroom Window." The first three are by Lennon and the last by McCartney. "Sun King" and "Mean Mr. Mustard" were recorded as a single track, as were "Polythene Pam" and "She Came In through the Bathroom Window." As with other songs in the medley, they were then spliced together.

"Sun King" is an evocation of whispering drowsiness painted in rich three-part vocal harmonies. The lyrics are minimal and ultimately—when they switch to a random mix of Italian, Spanish, Portuguese, and English—nonsensical. Yet Lennon's performance is convincing in its dreamy intimacy, his message communicated more by sounds than words. The song structure is in two parts, A and B, one in the key of E and one in C. Transitions between the two keys are sudden, creating an abrupt harmonic surprise. The A section makes dynamic use of panning. At the outset the drums and guitar one move across the stereo field from left to right. When a second guitar enters with its hypnotic arpeggio figure, it wanders back and forth in a series of three phrases, finally taking up a fixed position on the left side (opposite guitar one) for the B section.

"Sun King" segues via drum fill into "Mean Mr. Mustard," a brief character sketch of an odd man who "sleeps in the park" and "always shouts out something obscene" when his sister Pam "takes him out to look at the Queen." Much like an actor assuming a role, Lennon changes his vocal style to embody the new character. The tempo increases and the rhythmic texture becomes more insistent, with a piano part playing steady eighth notes and a guitar doubling the snare backbeat. As if to emphasize the character's quirkiness, the vocal melody is phrased in a series of three-beat fragments that cut across the four-beat meter. Also, the bass switches from the lush, warm sound we hear on "Sun King" to the biting tone of fuzz distortion.

"Mustard" is interrupted by a second character sketch, "Polythene Pam," which further increases the tempo and overall energy. Again, Lennon changes character, now assuming the Scouse accent of his childhood home, Liverpool. Aside from presenting a pair of unconventional characters, the two songs are vaguely linked by the possibility that Mustard's sister Pam may be the Polythene one. As "Polythene Pam" transitions smoothly into "She Came In through the Bathroom Window," we get another possible character connection: the unidentified "she" may again be Pam. We do not know, nor does it really matter. It's enough that we sense at some level a rightness about the narrative flow.

Some of the musical connections, on the other hand, are quite tangible. For example, the primary key in the first three songs is E, while the last song is in A, a fifth lower. Any two notes separated by a fifth have a special sort of relationship, which can define a key harmonically just as clearly as a scale does melodically. The fifth scale degree—in this case, E in the key of A—is called the **dominant**. A chord built on the dominant scale degree feels as though it wants to push forward to reach the tonic (scale degree one) and thus achieve a sense of closure. The dominant is the strongest chord to precede the tonic at cadences, producing a clear sense of arrival. Since E is the dominant of A, there is a sense in this *Abbey Road* excerpt of preparing in the first three songs (as the tempo and energy build) for an arrival at a destination key in song four. The descending bassline from E (E, D, C#, B, A) that segues from "Polythene Pam" (song three) to "Bathroom Window" (song four) emphasizes the feeling of coming in for a landing.

Also, the tempo changes from "Mustard" to "Pam" to "Bathroom Window" are rhythmically linked. At the end of "Mustard" ("dirty old man") the beat shifts from quarter note to dotted quarter, which "Pam" then uses as the new half-note, effectively increasing the original tempo by 50 percent. "Window" cuts the new tempo in half by changing the half note to a quarter note.

Rhythmically Determined Tempo Changes
"Mr. Mustard" dotted quarter note = "Polythene Pam" half note
= "Bathroom Window" quarter note

"Bathroom Window" has some further rhythmic tricks. The first line of verse one ("She came in through") falls in the arrival bar for the descending bassline coming out of "Pam," serving as a pickup to the beginning of the verse. (In a sense, "Pam" ends and "Bathroom Window" begins in the same bar.) The verse groove and harmonic phrase start in the next bar. The pickup phrase is repeated in bars three ("protected") and five ("but now"). Then the steady pacing (a pickup in every other bar) is compressed as a shorter pickup phrase occurs in bar six and moves to a cadence. This ending feels sudden, like an interruption, the result of the verse's oddly proportioned seven-bar structure.

The chorus also begins with a pickup ("didn't anybody"). This one is simpler rhythmically, avoiding the many syncopations of the verse. But it, too, launches a series of vocal phrases that result in a seven-bar section (the last bar is extended to 6/4), creating a similar feeling of interruption. Notice how the shaping power of the pickup phrase in both verse and chorus is enhanced by the stop-time accompaniment. Whether moving into the verse or chorus, the groove is suspended each time, delineating the beginning of the new section. Though all of this may seem complicated, the performance belies my explanation. The phrasing flows effortlessly, a vivid example of McCartney's deceptively sophisticated melodic sense.

Abbey Road is the first Beatles album to be recorded entirely with eight-track tape machines. ("While My Guitar Gently Weeps" was the first Beatles eight-track recording.) The added tracks were an obvious boon to the layered arrangements, but the evolving technology, which also included a new console, also brought changes in the overall sound compared with earlier Beatles records. The console now used solid-state transistors instead of tubes. Engineer Geoff Emerick felt that tubes had a "punchier sound," while the transistors' sound was "softer and rounder." "It's subtle," he wrote in his memoir,

> but I'm convinced that the sound of that new console and tape machine overtly influenced the performances and the music on *Abbey Road*. With the luxury of eight tracks, each song was built up with layered overdubs, so the tonal quality of the backing track directly affected the sound we would craft for each overdub. Because the rhythm tracks were coming back off tape a little less forcefully [due to the solid-state technology], the overdubs . . . were performed with less attitude.[12]

Another first for a complete album of Beatles songs was the exclusive focus on stereo mixes. (The soundtrack album for *Yellow Submarine* was stereo-only, but half of it was orchestral music.) Although the band's stereo mixes became increasingly complex and interesting from *Rubber Soul* on, they remained relative afterthoughts until the White Album. Since most record buyers had mono players and AM radio—the primary pop format at the time—broadcast in mono, those were considered the primary mixes. The stereo mixes for the White Album received much more attention than previous ones, and the album's US release was stereo-only.

For *Abbey Road*, mono mixes were abandoned entirely (mono versions of the album that appeared in some markets were made from the stereo mixes). Although Phil Spector, who was by then a legendary producer, publicly advocated a "back to mono" movement, multichannel listening would remain the new normal.

Listening Guide

"Sun King"/"Mean Mr. Mustard"/"Polythene Pam"/"She Came In through the Bathroom Window" (John Lennon, Paul McCartney), Apple Records (stereo). Appears on the album *Abbey Road*.
Recorded at EMI studios Two and Three, London, July–August 1969
John Lennon (voice, guitar, piano), Paul McCartney (voice, bass), George Harrison (voice, guitar), Ringo Starr (drums), George Martin (organ)
Producer: George Martin
Engineers: Geoff Emerick and Phil McDonald
Charts: Top LP's #1

Time	Song/Section	Lyric Cue	Listen For
	"Sun King" Key: E; meter 4/4		
0:00	A (16+2)	Instrumental	Guitar 1, bass, drums enter (L); guitar and drums move (R).
0:15			Guitar 2 enters (R), wanders back and forth across the stereo field.
0:52			Rhythm stops; voices enter; harmony (F triad over G bass) signals key change.
0:59	B (16)	"Here comes"	C major.
			Three-part vocal harmony, Lennon on lead.
			Guitar 1 (R) doubles vocal melody; guitar 2 (L) strums chords.
1:18			Organ enters (R), doubled at 1:22 by guitar 1.
1:24		"Everybody's laughing"	Backing voices shift to syllables; lead vocal phrases answered by organ/guitar.
1:37		"Here comes"	Backing voices return to words.
1:50	A (12)	"Quando para"	Key changes back to E.
			Nonsense lyrics.
			Instrumental texture as in previous A.

Affirming a New Pop Tradition 149

Time	Song/Section	Lyric Cue	Listen For
	"Mean Mr. Mustard" Key E; meter 4/4		
0:00	Verse 1 (4+2+2+2+4)	"Mean Mr. Mustard"	Tempo increases.
			Stereo field: bass/piano/tambourine (L); lead voice (C); electric guitar/drums (R).
			Bass sound changes to fuzz distortion.
			Vocal melody phrased in 3-beat segments.
0:26	Refrain	"Such a mean"	Harmony voices (L, R).
0:35	Verse 2 (4+2+2+2+4)	"His sister Pam"	Harmony voices continue.
0:59	Refrain	"Such a dirty"	Meter changes to 12/8, beat shifts to dotted quarter (50 percent slower).
	"Polythene Pam" Key E; Meter 4/4		
0:00	Intro (4)		Tempo doubles, half-note roughly equal to previous dotted quarter.
			Call-and-response between guitars.
			Stereo field: acoustic guitar, bass, drums (C); electric guitar (R).
			Note how the third acoustic guitar chord shoots to the left of the mix.
0:06	Verse 1 (8+2)	"Well you should see"	Lennon assumes Scouse accent.
			Eighth-note drum groove fills mid-range with toms.
0:17	Refrain	"Yeah, yeah, yeah"	
0:20	Interlude (4)		Similar to **intro**, without the quick stereo pan on acoustic guitar.
0:26	Verse 2 (8+2)	"Get a dose"	Similar to **verse 1**.
0:37	Refrain	"Yeah, yeah, yeah"	
0:40	Interlude (4)		Similar to previous **interlude**.
0:46	Coda (22 Bars)		Electric guitar (R) takes extended solo.
	"She Came In through the Bathroom Window" Key A; Meter 4/4		

continued on next page

Time	Song/Section	Lyric Cue	Listen For
0:00	**Transition** (4+1)	"Listen to that, Mal"	Descending bass and electric guitar line coming out of previous track.
		"Oh, look out!"	
0:06		"She came in through"	Tempo cut in half.
			McCartney takes lead vocal with pickup phrase.
0:09	**Verse 1** (7)		Groove begins.
			Backing voices (L).
			Guitar responses: acoustic (L); electric (R).
0:26		"Didn't anybody"	Pickup phrase; stop-time.
0:29	**Chorus** (7, Last Bar is 6/4)		Lyrics sung in harmony (C).
0:49		"She said she'd"	Pickup phrase; stop-time.
0:51	**Verse 2** (7)		Similar to **verse 1**.
			Backing voices out.
			Added drums (L).
1:10		"And so I quit"	Pickup phrase; stop-time.
1:12	**Verse 3** (7)		Backing voices (L) as in **verse 1**.
1:30		"Didn't anybody"	Pickup phrase; stop-time.
1:33	**Chorus** (7)		Similar to **previous chorus**.

NOTES

1. James Miller, *Flowers in the Dustbin: The Rise of Rock and Roll 1947–1977* (New York: Fireside, 1999), 206.
2. Quoted in The Beatles, *The Beatles Anthology* (San Francisco: Chronicle Books, 2000), 115.
3. Tom Phillips, "Beatles' 'Sgt. Pepper': The Album as Art Form," *The Village Voice,* June 22, 1967, 15.
4. "The Messengers," *Time,* September 22, 1967, 60.
5. Quoted in Miller, *Flowers in the Dustbin,* 216.
6. Quoted in Miller, 217.
7. Quoted in Mark Lewisohn, *The Beatles Recording Sessions* (New York: Harmony Books, 1990), 69.
8. Quoted in Lewisohn, 13.
9. Quoted in The Beatles, *The Beatles Anthology,* 175.
10. Quoted in Lewisohn, *The Beatles Recording Sessions,* 165.
11. Quoted in Thomas Hauser, "Reflections on the Beatles in America," in *Reflections: Conversations, Essays, and Other Writings* (Fayetteville: University of Arkansas Press, 2014), 40.

12. Geoff Emerick and Howard Massey, *Here, There and Everywhere: My Life Recording the Music of the Beatles* (New York: Gotham Books, 2006), 277.

FURTHER READING

Emerick, Geoff, and Howard Massey. *Here, There and Everywhere: My Life Recording the Music of the Beatles.* New York: Gotham Books, 2006.
Lewisohn, Mark. *The Beatles Recording Sessions.* New York: Harmony Books, 1988.
Martin, George. *All You Need Is Ears.* New York: St. Martin's Press, 1979.
Ryan, Kevin, and Brian Kehew. *Recording the Beatles.* Houston: Curvebender, 2006.
Spitz, Bob. *The Beatles: The Biography.* New York: Little, Brown, 2005.

FURTHER LISTENING: THE POP SIDE OF THE BRITISH INVASION

Dave Clark Five, "Catch Us If You Can" (Epic, 1965)
Petula Clark, "Downtown" (Warner, 1965)
Gerry and the Pacemakers, "Don't Let the Sun Catch You Crying" (Laurie, 1964)
Herman's Hermits, "I'm into Something Good" (MGM, 1964)
Hollies, "Bus Stop" (Imperial, 1966)
Lulu, "To Sir with Love" (Epic, 1967)
Manfred Mann, "Do Wah Diddy Diddy" (Ascot, 1964)
Peter and Gordon, "A World Without Love" (Capitol, 1964)
Searchers, "Needles and Pins" (Kapp, 1964)
Tremeloes, "Here Comes My Baby" (Epic, 1967)

BEATLES ALBUMS: STANDARD REISSUE SERIES

Please Please Me (1963)
With the Beatles (1963)
A Hard Day's Night (1964)
Beatles for Sale (1964)
Help! (1965)
Rubber Soul (1965)
Revolver (1966)
Sgt. Pepper's Lonely Hearts Club Band (1967)
Magical Mystery Tour (1967)
The Beatles (White Album) (1968)
Yellow Submarine (1969)
Abbey Road (1969)
Let It Be (1970)

10

LONDON BLUES
The Rolling Stones

If the Beatles spearheaded the British Invasion of the 1960s with a fresh reinvention of American rock and roll, the Rolling Stones came hard on their heels with a mix of American blues, R&B, and country. Taking their name from a song by bluesman Muddy Waters, the Stones—Mick Jagger, Keith Richards, Brian Jones, Bill Wyman, and Charlie Watts—came up in a different scene from the Beatles. Like fellow British Invasion groups the Kinks, the Yardbirds, and the Who, the Stones were based in London and their initial focus was R&B. Their public image, honed and exploited relentlessly by their manager Andrew Loog Oldham, conveyed a grimy picture of nihilist rebellion. Oldham fed the media such lines as, "Would you want your daughter to marry a Rolling Stone?" He orchestrated unruly incidents and invited the newspapers. "We went to the Grand Hotel in Bristol," recalled Keith Richards, "deliberately to get thrown out . . . because we were dressed incorrectly."[1] Since no band could compete with the Beatles at their own game, the idea was to highlight the Stones' differences. If the Beatles were charming, the Stones would simply be bad.

Despite the hyped contrast between the Beatles and the Stones, by the mid-1960s they were in fact fellow travelers, comrade rock stars in London's swinging pop scene. The Stones' second hit single was the Lennon and McCartney song "I Want to Be Your Man." Richards remembered that initially the Stones "saw no connection between us and the Beatles. We were playing the blues, they were singing pop songs dressed in suits."[2] But the Stones learned quickly that playing blues covers was not enough to punch a ticket to rock stardom. They needed hooks, and they needed to write them. Gradually Jagger and Richards became, like Lennon and McCartney, a solid songwriting team. In the end it was not their blues emulations but their original brand of pop songwriting that would propel the group to equal standing with the Beatles as the two bands came to epitomize 1960s rock.

Oldham is listed as producer on the first several Stones albums, but his role was more managerial than musical. He booked the studio time, which was sandwiched between tour dates; he pressed Jagger and Richards to begin writing original material; and, as a former publicist, he excelled at packaging and marketing the records and the band. To the extent that the first few years of Stones sessions were guided by any individual, it was Keith Richards, the band's lead guitarist and cochief songwriter. But what makes Rolling Stones records so unique is the evident collaboration and interaction of musical energy among the band members. In this sense the records are the result of a collective sensibility, which the Stones initially acknowledged by crediting some songs to the fictitious Nanker Phelge, a pseudonym for the band as a whole. Phil Spector and pianist and arranger Jack Nitzsche were also "around an awful lot," according to Richards. "Jack Nitzsche in particular," he said, "helped us enormously in a very unobtrusive way."[3]

In the summer of 1965, the Rolling Stones' had their first number-one hit in the US with "(I Can't Get No) Satisfaction." The record stood out among that year's top hits, most of which came from the sunnier side of the pop street. In addition to the Beatles and the Supremes, the year's top two hitmakers, the number-one records included the light British pop of Herman's Hermits, Freddie and the Dreamers, and the Dave Clark Five; folk rock by the Byrds and Sonny and Cher; Motown sound from the Temptations and Four Tops; and the effervescent pop of Petula Clark's "Downtown" and Gary Lewis and the Playboys' "This Diamond Ring." Nothing approached the gritty, nasty, snarling "Satisfaction." The Stones had managed to harness their raw, blues-influenced sound in a catchy, radio-friendly form, a feat they would repeat many times as they went on to create one of rock's richest discographies.

10.1. "PAINT IT BLACK" (1966)

Aftermath was the first Rolling Stones album to feature original material exclusively, and it was in that sense a coming of age for the band. The US version of the album opened with "Paint It Black." Although they were slower than Lennon and McCartney to develop as songwriters, Mick Jagger and Keith Richards had by now forged one of rock's great songwriting partnerships. Jagger tended to write the words, Richards the music, but, as with Lennon and McCartney, their roles were fluid, and either might contribute to any aspect of a song. Together they developed an original voice whose dark aura resonated with a broad, restless audience. "Paint It Black" is in the vein of other early Stones hits such as "Satisfaction," "19th Nervous Breakdown," "Under My Thumb," and "Get Off of My Cloud," all of which present an image of streetwise toughness. This was to be the Stones' central conceit. Even their ballads—"As Tears Go By," "Ruby Tuesday," "Lady Jane," or "Wild Horses," for example—infuse their musical sweetness with a Stones-like world weariness.

There is perhaps a faint suggestion of the Beatles' influence on "Paint It Black" in the use of an Indian sitar (which the Beatles first used on "Norwegian Wood" in 1965). But the use of exotic instruments was becoming common on Stones records thanks to the eclectic musical spirit of Brian Jones. In addition to playing the sitar part on "Paint It Black," he added various instrumental colors to other tracks on *Aftermath*: marimba on "Under My Thumb," dulcimer on "Lady Jane," and koto on "Take It or Leave It." As the Stones' career developed, Jones became increasingly mercurial, often failing to show up at recording sessions. Nevertheless, he contributed brilliant touches to the tracks. "Suddenly," Richards recalled, "he'd just walk in and lay some beautiful things down on a track, something that nobody'd even thought of."[4]

At their best, the Stones managed to capture a magnificent energy on their records. The playing and singing are rough and often sloppy. The sounds are raw, often distorted. But in the tradition of lo-fi rock and roll, the whole subsumes its parts. If the records have a general messiness to them, in the end it only adds to the sense of untamed musical force. Among the particular sources of energy on "Paint It Black" are (1) Charlie Watts's urgent drum groove, (2) a turbulent low-end reflecting the protagonist's obsession with all things black, (3) a hypnotic melodic line intoned like a chant, and (4) a sharp contrast between the song's A and B sections.

The chant melody is the first thing we hear, though at first it is in the form of an introductory guitar fragment. The line is answered rudely by a loud string of quarter notes on the high tom layered with eighth notes on the low tom ushering in the full band. The track's overall texture is thick in the low-end, creating a dark and murky sound befitting the lyrics. Bill Wyman adds bass pedals from a Hammond organ to augment his bass guitar part, and Charlie Watts omits the snare drum, shutting off the drums' high-end energy. When the vocal takes up the chant melody, it is doubled by both electric guitar and sitar, lending an exotic tinge to Jagger's haunting enunciation. His placid tone feels spooky in the midst of the driving rhythm parts.

This opening A section is followed by a fierce B section. The contrast is abrupt and dramatic. At the arrival of each B section, a crash cymbal opens up the track's high-end, supported by a switch from tom to snare. Watts drops the steady pulsing on the tom and moves into a furious backbeat groove. The voice changes to a defiant shouting tone. The electric guitar moves from melody to choppy rhythmic chords. The harmonic rhythm quickens. Although the track has a tense atmosphere throughout, the B sections project a heightened intensity. In effect the A section builds the tension that unleashes the B section's energy.

Harmonic Rhythm
A ‖: i | i | V | V :‖
B ‖ i VII | III VII | i | i | i VII | III VII | IV | V ‖

The lyrics have no repeated refrain. They move relentlessly through a continuous narrative of loss and bleakness, arriving at the coda in a breathless couple of minutes. The coda is quite long for its day, coming in at nearly one-and-a-half minutes. It is as if having arrived at the end so quickly, the track needs time to take stock of the protagonist's rush of emotion. A free-form jam ensues, which further develops elements of the track's texture. Notice the various rhythmic interjections from both acoustic and electric guitars, the powerful glissandi on the bass, the haunted humming of the chant melody, the texture's roiling turbulence, and Jagger's sudden eruptions riffing on the song's title. Although the entire coda takes place over the A section chord progression, its energy level remains that of the B section. In the end, elements of the track's two sections are fused in the coda's intense heat.

Note: During the 1960s most Rolling Stones singles were released in mono. When the tracks were released on albums, however, they were often in stereo versions. The Listening Guides refer to the mono single mixes for "Paint It Black," "Ruby Tuesday," and "Jumpin' Jack Flash" and stereo for "You Can't Always Get What You Want" and "Wild Horses."

Listening Guide

"Paint It Black" (Mick Jagger, Keith Richards), London Records (mono).
    Also appears on the album *Aftermath*.
Recorded at RCA Studios, Hollywood, March 1966
Mick Jagger (voice), Brian Jones (sitar), Keith Richards (guitars, voice),
    Bill Wyman (bass, organ bass), Charlie Watts (drums), Jack Nitzsche
    (piano)
Producer: Andrew Loog Oldham

Engineer: Dave Hassinger
Charts: Hot 100 #1, Top LP's #2
Key: E minor
Meter: 4/4

Time	Section	Lyric Cue	Listen For
0:00		**Intro**	Electric guitar plays chant fragment.
0:08			High tom accents quarter notes, low tom plays eighth notes.
0:11			Full band.
			Murky low-end: bass, bass pedals, toms.
0:15	A1 (8)	"I see a red door"	Voice takes up chant melody, doubled by electric guitar and sitar; hauntingly introspective vocal performance.
0:26	B1 (8)	"I see the girls"	Vocal character switches to defiant shout.
			Drums switch to backbeat groove with snare.
			Guitar switches from melody to rhythm chords.
			Harmonic rhythm increases.
0:39	A2 (8)	"I see a line of cars"	Similar to A1.
0:51	B2 (8)	"I see people turn"	Similar to B1.
1:03	A3 (8)	"I look inside"	Similar to A1.
1:14	B3 (8)	"Maybe then I'll"	Similar to B1.
1:27	A4 (8)	"No more will"	Drum and bass groove stops.
			Tight focus on melody.
			Tambourine and soft drum roll.
1:37			Intense drum interruption.
1:39	B4 (8)	"If I look hard enough"	Groove returns.
1:51	A5 (8)	"I see a red door"	Similar to A1.
2:04	B5 (8)	"I see the girls"	Similar to B1.
2:16	**Coda** (59 bars to fade)		A section chords repeat to end.
			Voice hums chant melody.
			Bass glissandi.
			Rhythmic interjections from acoustic and electric guitars.
			Dense, hyperactive texture.
2:39		"I want to see it"	Vocal improvisation on title lyrics.

10.2. "RUBY TUESDAY" (1967)

"Ruby Tuesday" appeared on the US release of the album *Between the Buttons*, which followed *Aftermath*. (Like "Paint It Black," the track was omitted from the album in the UK and released only as a single, backed with "Let's Spend the Night Together.") Recorded late in 1966, *Between the Buttons* was the Stones' deepest penetration yet into the pop sphere, expanding well beyond their roots to include a range of stylistic associations. As such, it reflects the changing face of rock during a year that saw other ambitious and groundbreaking projects such as the Beatles' *Revolver*, Bob Dylan's *Blonde on Blonde*, the Doors' *The Doors*, and the Beach Boys' *Pet Sounds*.

"Ruby Tuesday" is an example of the Stones' softer side. Written entirely by Richards, the song is a portrait of a free-spirited woman (former girlfriend Linda Keith, according to Richards). The lyrics invoke such recurring themes of mid-1960s youth culture as living in the moment and following one's dreams. The arrangement and mix were developed in a particularly close collaboration between Richards and Jones.

The track's central conceit is the stylistic and textural contrast between verse and chorus. The verse arrangement is vaguely classical sounding and essentially grooveless, using only piano, double bass, and recorder. (Again, Brian Jones provides the extra sounds; he plays both the piano and recorder.) The chorus answers with a rocking texture, adding in guitar, electric bass, and drums. Jagger, too, performs the contrast, singing the verses in a reserved way and then opening up in the choruses.

His enactment is supported by a difference in phrase structure between the two sections. The harmonic phrases of the sixteen-bar verse fall into a 4+4+2+2+4 AABBC pattern. The varying lengths of the A, B, and C phrases, together with the lack of any strong beat, produces a prose-like feel, which is underscored by the halting vocal melody. The chorus phrases follow a more regular 2+2+2+2 pattern, supporting the sing-along hook that helped to propel the record to the top of the charts in both the US and the UK.

Listening Guide

"Ruby Tuesday" (Mick Jagger, Keith Richards), London Records (mono).
    Also appears on *Between the Buttons*.
Recorded at Olympic Studios, London, November 1966
Mick Jagger (voice), Keith Richards (guitar, voice), Brian Jones (piano, recorder), Bill Wyman (double bass, electric bass), Charlie Watts (drums)

Producer: Andrew Loog Oldham
Engineer: Glyn Johns
Charts: Hot 100 #1, Top LP's #2
Key: C
Meter: 4/4

Time	Section	Lyric Cue	Listen For
0:00	**Verse 1** (16)		
	Phrase *a* (4)	"She would never"	Solo voice; prose-like vocal phrasing.
			Delicate instrumental texture: recorder, piano, double bass.
	a (4)	"Yesterday don't"	Harmony voice.
	b (2)	"While the sun"	Solo voice.
	b (2)	"Or in the darkest"	Harmony voice.
	c (4)	"She comes"	Solo voice.
0:37	**Chorus 1** (8)	"Goodbye Ruby"	Rocking groove: guitar, bass, drums.
			Lead voice sings more freely; harmony vocal throughout.
			Melodic phrasing changes from prose to sing-along (2+2+2+2).
0:55	**Verse 2** (16)	"Don't question"	Similar to **verse 1**.
1:33	**Chorus 2** (8)	"Goodbye Ruby"	Similar to **chorus 1**.
1:51	**Verse 3** (16)	"There's no time"	Similar to **verse 1**.
2:28	**Chorus 3** (8)	"Goodbye Ruby"	Similar to **chorus 1**.
2:47	**Chorus** (8)	"Goodbye Ruby"	Repeat.
3:05	**Coda** (4)		**Verse** texture.

10.3. "JUMPIN' JACK FLASH" (1968)

After parting ways with Andrew Loog Oldham, the Stones took a psychedelic side trip with the album *Her Satanic Majesty's Request*. Many felt that the record was a lackluster response to the Beatles' *Sgt. Pepper's* (though over the years the album has grown in popularity and acclaim). "We'd run out of gas," said Keith Richards. "That was a period where we could have foundered."[5] At a turning point and looking for a new direction, the band did a session with the American producer Jimmy Miller, just to get acquainted and to feel out the chemistry. Miller had produced records for such contemporary British bands as the Spencer Davis Group,

Traffic, and Blind Faith. A musician himself, he was well acquainted with American blues, the foundation from which the Stones had drifted in pursuit of pop success. Now the group was looking for a way forward by looking back to the influences that had first inspired them.

The all-day jam session yielded good results. The empathy between producer and musicians was evident in the recorded sound. It was apparent to Richards that Miller "was hearing the room, hearing the band."[6] Miller's sensitivity, the mark of a great record producer, led him to capture the essence of the Stones' interaction, their rough-and-tumble groove that set them apart from all others. He would remain with the group for the next five years, producing some of their finest work: *Beggar's Banquet*, *Let It Bleed*, *Sticky Fingers*, and *Exile on Main Street*.

On the first of these, *Beggar's Banquet*, the Stones showcased their affinity for blues and country sounds and made it clear that they were through with psychedelia. The album set a tone for the band's future work and fed the rising country-rock genre. But months before the album was released, the single "Jumpin' Jack Flash" had already signaled that the group was rocking in a new direction. It was the first of the Miller-produced tracks to be released, and though it was recorded during the same period as the *Beggar's Banquet* tracks, it appeared only as a single in both the UK and the US.

In many ways, "Jumpin' Jack Flash" is the quintessential Stones track. It begins with distorted acoustic guitar, alluding to the rough-sounding records the Stones grew up listening to. It contains a classic guitar riff, a nod to Stones hero Chuck Berry. It has harsh, cruel lyrics that bite even as they revel in a defiant sense of life. It has a drop-dead hook. Its pitch resources include blues notes (flatted third and seventh) even as its form adheres to the crisp structure of a pop song. And its groove is straight-to-the-point rock and roll.

To create the gritty, lo-fi acoustic guitar sound that opens the track, Richards recorded the part on a portable cassette deck, overdriving its small microphone to the point of distortion. This willful act of sonic subversion sets the tone for the entire track. The texture throughout is a knotted mass of murky sound from which a few broad gestures stand out. For example, in the intro we hear a three-chord guitar vamp over a distinctive bassline, followed by the famous guitar riff. Each of these gestures is succinct yet cuts a bold figure. In the midst of surrounding noise, they command attention.

"Jumpin' Jack Flash" offers a clinic in how to incorporate blues elements into rock. The blues notes that run through the track are the flatted third ($D^\flat$) and seventh ($A^\flat$) scale degrees. These are used both as melodic notes and as the roots of chords. In the three-chord guitar vamp, for instance, we hear A♭ as the root of the third chord (vamp: ‖: B♭ | E♭ A♭ :‖). Underneath the A♭, the bassline sounds the flatted third D♭.

The guitar riff uses A♭ repeatedly as a melodic note played over the tonic B♭ in the bass. As the riff continues to play through the verse, the feeling of the flatted seventh is pervasive. At the same time, the voice's persistent use of D♭ ensures that the track is saturated with a blues sonority. In the chorus, the blues notes again form the roots of chords, now built on both A♭ and D♭, preserving the track's blues flavor even as it delivers a pop-worthy hook (chorus: ‖: D♭ | A♭ | E♭ | B♭ :‖).

The song's lyrics are more evidence of the Stones' new direction. Like the music, the words hearken back to the band's earlier style but with a newfound vigor. Their hard edge is in a similar vein to other *Beggar's Banquet* songs such as "Sympathy for the Devil" and "Street Fighting Man." The protagonist is tough as nails. He responds to brutality by embracing it. He is an apt symbol for the Stones' turn away from psychedelia—an anti-hippie. In Mick Jagger's mind, "Flower power was just a load of crap, wasn't it? There was nothing about love, peace, and flowers on 'Jumpin' Jack Flash,' was there?"[7] His prideful assertion is easily read as a comment on the Stones' musical journey.

Listening Guide

"Jumpin' Jack Flash" (Mick Jagger, Keith Richards), London Records (mono)
Recorded at Olympic Studios, London, April 1968
Mick Jagger (voice), Keith Richards (guitars, bass, voice), Brian Jones (guitar), Bill Wyman (organ), Charlie Watts (drums)
Producer: Jimmy Miller
Engineer: Glyn Johns
Charts: Hot 100 #3
Key: B♭
Meter: 4/4

Time	Section	Lyric Cue	Listen For
0:00	Intro (9+4)		Distorted acoustic guitar vamp.
0:02			Electric guitar vamp.
0:06			Bass riff.
0:08			Drums.
0:16		"Watch it!"	Guitar riff.
			Bass stays on tonic.

Time	Section	Lyric Cue	Listen For
0:23	Verse 1 (8)	"I was born"	Guitar riff continues as accompaniment.
			Bass stays on tonic.
0:37	Chorus 1 (8+2)	"But it's alright now"	Bass moves, supporting chords.
			Chord progression (D♭–A♭–E♭–B♭) uses blues notes to create pop hook.
			Harmony voice.
			Added high-register guitar riff.
0:55	Riff (4)		Similar to **intro**.
1:02	Verse 2 (8)	"I was raised"	Similar to **verse 1**.
1:15	Chorus 2 (8+2)	"But it's alright now"	**Similar to chorus 1.**
1:33	Break (11)		Bass riff and vamp chords from **intro**.
			High- and low-register guitars riff over the chords.
			Maracas enliven high-end.
1:53	Riff (4)		Similar to **intro**.
1:59	Verse 3 (16)	"I was drowned"	Twice as many gritty images in this double-length verse.
2:27	Chorus 3 (8+2)	"But it's alright now"	Similar to **chorus 1**.
2:45	Coda (32 bars to fade)	"Jumpin' Jack Flash"	Based on chords of **intro** vamp.
			Voices chant title phrase.
2:52			Organ crescendo.
3:00			Jam to end features high-register guitar and organ.

10.4. "YOU CAN'T ALWAYS GET WHAT YOU WANT" (1969)

The Stones followed *Beggar's Banquet* with *Let It Bleed*, which continued to mine the territory of the previous record, melding blues and country in a way that was purely Rolling Stones. But *Let It Bleed* also added a distinctly modern twist to the traditional sounds of blues harmonica and slide guitar, country fiddle and mandolin. Extending the precedent of "Sympathy for the Devil" and "Jigsaw Puzzle," the longest tracks on *Beggar's Banquet*, the band recorded two tracks for *Let It Bleed* whose length and formal conception showed an ambitious scope. The opening and closing tracks on side two of the LP, "Midnight Rambler" and "You Can't Always Get What You Want" epitomize the Stones' skillful use of rustic roots material in crafting expansive and strikingly original tracks.

"You Can't Always Get What You Want" is a sweeping panorama of style, groove, and texture presented over a nearly static harmonic foundation that alternates stubbornly between C (I) and F (IV). It opens with an allusion to classical music with The London Bach Choir singing the song's first verse and chorus with formal diction and precise rhythmic articulation, both seemingly antithetical to the Stones' ethos. The lack of harmonic direction and the primitive vocal arrangement, however, are also antithetical to classical music. Clearly, we are embarking on some fantastical musical adventure where expectations should simply be set aside.

As the choir finishes, a lazily strumming acoustic guitar takes up the two-chord harmonic riff. The guitar is tuned to an open E chord (though with a capo on the eighth fret it sounds as C), which produces a different sonority than standard tuning. The guitar, which is panned to the right of the mix, is answered by a mournful French horn melody on the left. The horn, another classical music reference, performs a stylistic counterpoint to the country-folk guitar.

After the lengthy introduction—which lasts over a minute—Jagger repeats the first verse, now cast in a dramatically different style. He is accompanied only by the acoustic guitar, which continues strumming the same two chords. At the chorus, a shaker part begins to hint at a percussion groove. Finally, at the line "But if you try some time," a new chord is introduced. The texture suddenly thickens as keyboards fill the two sides of the stereo space—organ on the left and piano on the right. The keyboards are joined by a loose-jointed drum fill that delivers the chorus to its climax on the line "You get what you need," harmonized by a trio of women singing in a gospel-soul style, adding yet another stylistic layer.

The track's long-awaited groove—a syncopated rock shuffle played not by Watts but by Miller—is now in full swing after more than two minutes. In previous years, entire tracks weren't much longer than two minutes, but "You Can't Always Get What You Want" is just getting started. At the end of chorus one the texture is filled out with bass, percussion, and an electric guitar panned to the left, balancing the acoustic guitar. All of the textural elements have now been introduced. The rest of the track ebbs and flows with changes in rhythm and texture and an unfolding interplay of the stylistic layers suggested by the classical choir and the soulful women's voices.

The track has a certain mesmerizing quality due to the mantra-like harmonic stillness. It is easy in this drone-like harmonic atmosphere to add extra lines of lyrics, as happens in verse three. Even the crossing from verse to chorus is undifferentiated harmonically. As the voice moves to a more regular melody and repeated lyrics ("You can't always get"), and the texture thickens, the same two chords play on. This minimal harmonic activity makes the harmonic flourish at the chorus's climax sound, somehow majestic by contrast, even though it adds only one chord. The impact of this chord change to D is enhanced by the introduction of a non-diatonic note. The D major chord consists of D, F♯, and A. After so much F sonority in the repeating C–F loop, the F♯ displacement of F creates a brightening effect.

"You Can't Always Get What You Want" has one other harmonic flourish that also creates a sense of climax, this time for the track as a whole. In the instrumental break the music builds through a series of chords leading to G. The arrival of this very important structural harmony (the V chord, or dominant), its only occurrence in the track, is heightened by Jagger's scream (4:27). Along with its sheer dramatic effect, this climactic moment also ushers in a return of the choir, which will become an important element going forward.

The track culminates in a jam starting at 6:14 with the classical choir supplying the background vocals. This coda is shaped to give the track one final dramatic gesture. The choir is split into two sections (L and R) and at 6:30 the voices on the left begin to rise ever higher as they crescendo, reaching a peak at the seven-minute mark. At this point the rhythmic momentum takes a final uptick as the groove shifts to a steady backbeat rhythm, driving the track forward through the fade.

Perhaps the most novel effect on the track is the classical choir. It is unexpected, to say the least, and its contrast with Jagger's rough yelp and the women's gospel-style voices is an intriguing attention-getter. But the Stones are not content to leave it at novelty. The choir voices drop out for a while after kicking things off in the intro, but as detailed in the Listening Guide, they return in various textural guises as the one sonic element that, from start to finish, ties the sprawling track together. The choir's stylistic novelty also serves as part of the track's structural glue.

Listening Guide

"You Can't Always Get What You Want" (Mick Jagger, Keith Richards), London Records (stereo). Appears on the album *Let It Bleed*.
Recorded at Olympic Studios in London, November 1968
Mick Jagger (voice), Keith Richards (guitars), Jimmy Miller (drums), Bill Wyman (bass), Al Kooper (piano, organ, French horn), Rocky Dijon (percussion), Madeline Bell, Doris Troy, Nanette Workman (voice), The London Bach Choir (voice)
Producer: Jimmy Miller
Engineer: Glyn Johns

Charts: Top LP's #3
Key: C
Meter: 4/4

Time	Section	Lyric Cue	Listen For
0:00	**Intro** (16+8)		Choir sings first verse and chorus with formal diction and precise rhythmic articulation; harmonic accompaniment ("ah") repeats 2 chords throughout.
0:48			Choir fades, leaving acoustic guitar (R) strumming the same 2 chords; first bar has 6 beats.
0:54			French horn melody (L).
1:15	**Verse 1** (8)	"I saw her today"	Voice and guitar.
1:39	**Chorus 1** (12)	"You can't always"	Shaker begins steady groove (C).
1:56		"But if you try"	Organ (L), piano (R); chords change (D).
2:01		"You get what you"	Women's voices add harmony parts.
			Full groove: bass, drums, percussion (congas and shaker) (C); electric guitar (L).
2:13	**Verse 2** (8)	"I went down"	Leaner texture, keyboards out; electric guitar plays long notes highlighting chord changes.
2:35	**Chorus 2** (12)	"You can't always"	Thicker texture adds keyboards and women's voices; electric guitar switches to rhythm.
2:51		"But if you try"	Groove suspended; chord change; drums, percussion, women's voices out.
2:56		"You get what you"	Drums, percussion, women's voices return.
3:07	**Verse 3** (16)	"I went down"	Double-length verse. Texture as in **verse** 2 with added organ responses to vocal phrases.
3:29		"We decided that"	Piano chords on downbeats; organ switches to long notes; electric guitar becomes more active melodically.
3:50	**Chorus 3** (10)	"You can't always"	Similar to **chorus** 2 but 2 bars shorter.
4:17	**Break** (5)		Groove suspended; choir begins crescendo; harmonic progression builds to the track's only V chord.
4:30	**Chorus 4** (12)	"Aah"	Choir continues; Jagger out; otherwise similar to previous **chorus**.
4:45			Choir out.
4:50		"You get what you"	Jagger and women's voices return.
5:01	**Verse 1** (8)	"I saw her today"	Repeat **verse** 1 lyrics; texture as in **verse** 2 with added organ.
5:20			Piano entrance.

Time	Section	Lyric Cue	Listen For
5:22	**Chorus** (12)	"You can't always"	Similar to **chorus 2**; electric guitar more active melodically.
5:38		"But if you try"	Begin choir crescendo.
5:53	**Chorus** (12)	"You can't always"	Full chorus texture with both gospel-tinged women's voices and classical choir.
6:15	Coda	"Aah"	New melody in choir high voices (R); added percussion; jam texture.
6:30			Choir low voices begin rising line and crescendo (L).
7:01			Drums switch to steady backbeat groove.

10.5. "WILD HORSES" (1971)

"Wild Horses" is one of the Stones' country-rock tracks. We can hear evidence of the band's affinity for American country music as early as 1964 on the track "Some Things Just Stick in Your Mind" (unreleased until 1975). But beginning with *Beggar's Banquet,* the country strain became an essential ingredient in many Stones tracks, including "No Expectations," "Let It Bleed," and "Country Honk" (which was reworked into the hit single "Honky Tonk Women").

Many musicians speak about how recording locations influence the music being recorded. The Stones, who often recorded in American studios when they were on tour, had worked at Chess Studios in Chicago in 1964, recording songs like "Time Is on My Side" and "It's All Over Now" in the same space as many of their heroes: Muddy Waters, Howlin' Wolf, Chuck Berry. (They even employed the same engineer, Ron Malo.) Near the end of their fall tour in 1969 the band laid down several tracks at Muscle Shoals Sound Studio in Sheffield, Alabama, a hotbed of southern soul music. In just three days, they recorded three of the tracks that would appear on their *Sticky Fingers* LP: "Brown Sugar," "You Gotta Move," and "Wild Horses." Although they landed in rural Alabama largely by chance, the Stones could hardly have found a better place to tap into the atmosphere captured on "Wild Horses." Though little more than a shack, Muscle Shoals was, Richards recalled, the "perfect eight-track recording studio."[8] Away from the rock star glitter, the Stones spent three days channeling the rustic southern spirit that gives "Wild Horses" its loose country vibe.

The track begins with a guitar texture made from the sound of two acoustic guitars—a six-string and a twelve-string—and one electric. Each guitar has its own distinct stereo position (the twelve-string and electric are both on the right but to different degrees). Their diverse timbres create a blend that washes across the stereo field. The first sound we hear is the acoustic six-string guitar set up for so-called Nashville tuning, which replaces the bottom three strings with lighter strings tuned an octave higher than normal. The effect is a kind of timbral shimmer. Throughout the track, this six-string guitar moves from delicate filigree in the verses to a propulsive rhythm in the choruses, contributing to a general shift in the track's overall texture and momentum as it moves between the two sections.

The electric guitar serves as the lead instrument throughout the track, with a narrative pacing of its own. In verse one it provides a subtle complement to the six-string filigree. In chorus one it answers the vocal phrases (as in subsequent choruses). In the latter half of verse two, still answering the voice, it becomes more assertive. At the first instrumental break it commands full attention with a brief solo over a new chord progression. (Note that the bass and drums drop out here, further highlighting the guitar's central presence.) In verse three it remains prominent, answering the vocal phrases throughout. And in the second instrumental break it plays a longer solo, this time over the chord progression of the verse (and again without bass or drums). This narrative plan adds a layer of continuous unfolding on top of the song's pendular verse-chorus structure.

In addition to the country-folk-flavored guitars, the lead voice makes reference to a southern attitude. Jagger's parody of a southern accent is clearly inauthentic in its diction, yet, paradoxically, that is what makes it authentically rock. Rock musicians are not interested in idiomatic emulation. Rather, they appropriate whatever stylistic or cultural bits and pieces they sense will help them fashion and project a unique persona. Jagger is no more a country singer than a blues singer, but both country and blues fuel the core of the Rolling Stones' essential identity.

Listening Guide

"Wild Horses" (Mick Jagger, Keith Richards), Rolling Stones Records (stereo). Also appears on the album *Sticky Fingers*.
Recorded at Muscle Shoals Sound Studio, Sheffield, Alabama, December 1969
Mick Jagger (voice), Keith Richards (guitar, voice), Mick Taylor (guitar), Bill Wyman (bass), Charlie Watts (drums), Jim Dickinson (piano)
Producer: Jimmy Miller
Engineer: Jimmy Johnson
Charts: Hot 100 #28, Top LP's #1
Key: G
Meter: 4/4

Time	Section	Lyric Cue	Listen For
0:00	Intro (5)		Three-guitar texture:
			Acoustic guitar in Nashville tuning (L). Electric guitar (R).
			Acoustic 12-string guitar (R).
0:20	Verse 1 (8+8)	"Childhood living"	Voice (C).
			12-string continues rhythm; other guitars play filigree.
0:49		"Graceless lady"	Piano entrance (L).
1:17	Chorus 1 (8)	"Wild horses"	Bass (C) and drums (C).
			Harmony vocals.
			Acoustic 6-string returns to strumming. Electric guitar punctuates vocal phrases.
1:38		"Couldn't drag me"	Bass and drums out.
1:45	Verse 2 (8+8)	"I watched you"	Similar to **verse 1**, with piano.
2:12		"No sweeping exits"	Bass and drums in.
			More prominent electric guitar presence.
2:39	Chorus 2 (8)	"Wild horses"	Similar to **chorus 1**.
3:05	Break 1 (6)		Electric guitar solo.
			New chord progression.
			No bass or drums.
3:24	Verse 3 (8+8)	"I know I've dreamed"	Bass and drums in; otherwise similar to **verse 2**.
4:17	Chorus 3 (8)	"Wild horses"	Similar to **chorus 1**.
4:43	Break 2 (8)		Electric guitar solo.
			Same chords and similar texture to first 8 bars of **verse 2**.
			Again, no bass or drums.
5:08	Chorus (9)	"Wild horses"	Similar to **chorus 1**.
5:33			Cadence.

NOTES

1. Keith Richards, *Life* (New York: Little Brown, 2010), 168.
2. Quoted in Victor Bockris, *Keith Richards: The Biography* (New York: Poseidon Press, 1992), 57.
3. Quoted in Bockris, 78.
4. Quoted in Bockris, 99.
5. Richards, *Life*, 235.

6. Richards, 235.
7. Quoted in Bockris, *Keith Richards*, 144.
8. Richards, *Life*, 273.

FURTHER READING

Booth, Stanley. *The True Adventures of the Rolling Stones.* Chicago: Chicago Review Press, 2000.
Richards, Keith. *Life.* New York: Little, Brown, 2010.
Wyman, Bill. *Stone Alone: The Story of a Rock 'n' Roll Band.* New York: Viking, 1990.

FURTHER LISTENING: THE HEAVIER SIDE OF THE BRITISH INVASION

Animals, "The House of the Rising Sun" (MGM, 1964)
Jeff Beck Group, "I Ain't Superstitious" (Epic, 1968)
Spencer Davis Group, "I'm a Man" (United Artists, 1967)
Fleetwood Mac, "Stop Messin' Round" (Blue Horizon, 1968)
Kinks, "You Really Got Me" (Reprise, 1964)
Them, "Gloria" (Parrot, 1964)
Troggs, "Wild Thing" (Fontana, 1966)
Who, "My Generation" (Decca, 1965)
Yardbirds, "Shapes of Things" (Epic, 1966)

11

THE CALIFORNIA VIBE
The Beach Boys

The Beach Boys emerged from the surf and hot rod scene concentrated around Los Angeles. Their first single, "Surfin'," released on a small indie label in the fall of 1961, was a local hit and attracted enough national attention to land the group a contract with Capitol Records. The surf scene spawned dozens of groups, providing a soundtrack to the youth culture of Southern California and ultimately reaching an international audience. Many surf groups were purely instrumental outfits, such as Dick Dale and the Del-Tones ("Misirlou"), the Surfaris ("Wipe Out"), and the Chantays ("Pipeline"). Among the surf and hot rod groups that featured vocals were the Rip Chords ("Hey Little Cobra"), Ronny and the Daytonas ("G.T.O."), and Jan and Dean ("Surf City"). The Beach Boys were by far the most successful and the most musically accomplished of the surf groups, ultimately transcending the genre to become one of the best rock bands of the 1960s. They were among the few American pop musicians who held their own in the initial wave of the British Invasion.

The Beach Boys were a family affair: three brothers (Brian, Carl, and Dennis Wilson), a cousin (Mike Love), and a friend (Al Jardine). The Wilsons' father, Murry, was their manager. From the start, what set the group apart was their tight vocal harmonies, their blended vocal sound, and the original songs, arrangements, and production skill of group leader, Brian Wilson. The vocal arrangements mixed doo wop riffing with rich choral textures that reached high into the falsetto range. The rhythmic interplay among the voices was clean and precise. Yet while the Beach Boys could sound like a single integrated vocal organism, the voices retained their individuality, with various members taking turns at the lead.

Gifted both as a performer and composer, Brian Wilson had an exceptional ear and the benefit of some music theory training in high school. His grasp of music's inner workings allowed him not only to flesh out his intuitive musical ideas but also to articulate them for the other group members as well as the professional session players he employed in his increasingly complex productions. One of his early influences was the pop vocal group the Four Freshmen, who sang in tightly blended four-part harmony that included many complex chords and chord progressions. When Wilson was sixteen, he went to the office of the group's manager, Bill Wagner, and claiming he knew every vocal part of every Four Freshmen record, he insisted Wagner test him. Wagner chose a track he considered particularly difficult, "The Day Isn't Long Enough," and as he played the record four times in succession, Wilson sang each of the four parts note-perfect and precisely in tune.

The Beach Boys married the rich harmonies of older-style pop with the beat and instrumentation of rock and roll and wrote songs reflecting Southern California teenage life. In such songs as "Be True to Your School," "Fun, Fun, Fun," "Little Deuce Coupe," and "Surfin' Safari," they celebrated the optimism and sense of endless potential inherent in the veneer of the California dream. As the decade wore on, a darker side would emerge both in the culture and among the Beach Boys themselves, but in the first half of the 1960s their music defined an ethos of boundless youthful possibility.

Although the credits for early Beach Boys sessions listed Capitol A&R man Nick Venet as the producer, Brian was in charge of the recordings from the beginning. The first Capitol hits, "Surfin' Safari" and "409," were taken from a demo he had produced before the group even signed with the label. The records came quickly—ten albums in just over three years. By the third album, *Surfer Girl*, Wilson's ambition and ability were on full display both on ballads ("In My Room," "Surfer Moon") and up-tempo numbers ("Catch a Wave," "Little Deuce Coupe"). With double-tracked vocals, a rich instrumental palette (including harp and strings) complementing the guitars/bass/drums foundation, and liberal use of reverb, the tracks have a full, lustrous quality. Wilson had observed Phil Spector sessions and was impressed with the wall of sound approach. But the textural depth of Beach Boys records has a clarity about it unlike Spector's moody murkiness. Like Spector, Wilson liked to layer instruments until they lost their individual identity. And like Spector, he preferred mono mixes. But Wilson's layered sound remains clean and airy, infused with sunlight.

Although Wilson was the Beach Boys' musical leader, the group around him was exceptionally skilled. Mike Love was a frequent songwriting partner. The other members were adept instrumentalists and, of course, superb singers. Wilson's sophisticated vocal arrangements would have proven unworkable for most contemporary rock musicians. But for his fellow band members, with years of family harmonizing behind them, learning and producing the parts on demand was part of the natural order.

11.1. "I GET AROUND" (1964)

"I Get Around" was the Beach Boys' first number-one single, though they had been charting records for two years, including eight in the top forty. The record's B side, "Don't Worry Baby," was also a top-forty hit. The tracks were among a crop the Beach Boys produced in response to the Beatles' first American hits, which, as it happened, were released on the Beach Boys' label. Song topics like the beach and cars, which Capitol felt to be such sure bets that it initially showed no interest in releasing the Beatles' records, suddenly seemed less hip. "The Beatles invasion . . . eclipsed a lot of what we'd worked for," said Wilson. "We were very threatened by the whole thing."[1]

But if the Beatles' success was threatening, it also pushed Wilson to a series of creative peaks as he moved the group beyond their beach party image into more complex musical territory and varied song topics. The change in subject matter was gradual; the album on which "I Get Around" appeared, *All Summer Long*, also contains "Little Honda" and "The Girls on the Beach." "I Get Around" is itself stocked with buddies and cars and girls. But the chorus's urgent restlessness gives the song an unexpected emotional edge. And a few other songs on the album lean toward a more nuanced style of pop. "Wendy" sketches a sad portrait of heartbreak, and "All Summer Long" delves into bittersweet nostalgia. Moreover, even a song of the surfing life like "The Girls on the Beach" is treated to Wilson's increasingly complex harmonic style.

The central conceit for "I Get Around" is epitomized in its verse-chorus contrast. The vocal texture and the character of the lead voice in each section are markedly different, with the verses sung by the lone voice of Mike Love (double-tracked) and the choruses offering a full complement of group voices accompanying Wilson's falsetto lead. The textural and rhythmic settings of the instrumental arrangement follow a similar plan. The verse is sparse; the chorus features the full band. The verse's rhythmic accompaniment is a riff rather than a full groove; in the chorus, a flowing groove drives the pace. Finally, the harmonic progression in the verse is repetitive, bouncing continually between two chords. In the chorus, the harmonic momentum and variety moves into high gear.

The track's structure is surprisingly elaborate. It begins with a brief a cappella intro based on the chorus, followed by a full chorus. Next comes the expected verse, but less expected is the fact that there are two verses in a row separated by a brief two-bar interlude recalling the chorus texture. After these two verses, the full chorus returns, but now it is followed by a two-bar extension that modulates from the starting key of G to the new key of A as it transitions into the instrumental break. After the break, which features a surf-style guitar solo accompanied by doo wop–style vocalizing, the key changes again to A♭ where it remains for the rest of the track.

Verses three and four are similar to verses one and two (though in a different key). But chorus three is different from either of the preceding ones. Like chorus two it has an extension, but now the added material is three bars long. It makes a move to modulate—again like chorus two—but in the third bar it pulls back to A♭ just in time for the instruments to drop out for a repeat of the a cappella intro. The track finishes with a fading double chorus.

With a basic instrumental lineup and a time frame of just over two minutes, "I Get Around" is an impressive demonstration of how the Beach Boys' surf style could be distilled to a concentrated essence and employed in a relatively complex arrangement.

Listening Guide

"I Get Around" (Brian Wilson, Mike Love), Capitol Records (mono). Also appears on the album *All Summer Long*.
Recorded at Western Recorders, Hollywood, April 1964
Al Jardine (voice, guitar), Mike Love (voice), Brain Wilson (voice, bass, organ), Carl Wilson (voice, guitar), Dennis Wilson (voice, drums)
Producer: Brian Wilson
Engineer: Chuck Britz
Charts: Hot 100 #1, Top LP's #4
Key: G, A, A♭
Meter: 4/4

Time	Section	Lyric Cue	Listen For
0:00	**Intro** (4)	"'Round, 'round"	Bass glissando followed by a cappella **chorus** variant. Three vocal layers: Low voice. Harmony voices in rhythmic unison. High voice.
0:07	**Chorus 1** (8)	"I get around"	High voice (Brian Wilson) continues with lead melody in call-and-response with the other voices. Guitar/organ/bass/drums texture. Propulsive groove.

Time	Section	Lyric Cue	Listen For
0:20	Verse 1 (4)	"I'm getting bugged"	Lead voice changes (Mike Love).
			Sparse texture; groove out.
			Electric guitar and bass play rhythmic riff.
0:23		"I gotta find"	Handclaps and kick drum increase rhythmic activity.
0:27	Interlude (2)		Guitar melody; texture as in **chorus**.
0:30	Verse 2 (4)	"My buddies and me"	Similar to **verse 1** with added guitar doubling riff at higher octave.
0:37	Chorus 2 (8+2)	"I get around"	Similar to **chorus 1** with added 2-bar extension.
0:50	Transition	"I get around"	Modulates to new key (A).
0:53	Break (8)		Surf-type guitar solo accompanied by doo wop–style vocals.
1:04			Final chord pivots to new key.
1:06	Verse 3 (4)	"We always take"	Similar to **verse 1**; new key (A♭).
1:12	Interlude (2)		Similar to previous **interlude**.
1:16	Verse 4 (4)	"None of the guys"	Similar to **verse 2**.
1:22	Chorus 3 (8+3)	"I get around"	Similar to **chorus 2** with slightly different extension.
1:35	Extension	"I get around"	Three bars long; "false" modulation.
1:40	Intro (4)	"'Round, 'round"	Repeat **intro**.
1:47	Chorus (8)	"I get around"	Similar to **chorus 1**; no lyrics in high voice.
1:59	Chorus (8)	"I get around"	Fade.

11.2. "GOD ONLY KNOWS" (1966)

From the moment Capitol Records struck gold with the Beatles' "I Want to Hold Your Hand," Brian Wilson's competitive juices were fired. But it was *Rubber Soul* that really impressed him. At a time when rock albums typically contained some substandard "filler" material, *Rubber Soul* "was a whole album," he said, "with all good stuff."[2] He had been struggling to balance the commercial demands of the record company and some of his bandmates (Mike Love in particular) with his own artistic aspiration, and now he wanted the freedom to fully unleash his musical imagination. Proclaiming, "*Rubber Soul* is a complete statement, damn it, and I want to make a complete statement, too!"[3] he set out to produce his own album masterpiece. It would represent, he said, "the single-minded pursuit of a personal vision."[4] It would be called *Pet Sounds*.

In 1965 Wilson stopped touring with the group, devoting himself entirely to writing and producing. Evidence of his creative restlessness turned up on *The Beach Boys Today* (1965), which included such introspective songs and layered arrangements as "Please Let Me Wonder" and "She Knows Me Too Well." Despite its number-one single, "Help Me, Rhonda," the album raised some concern among record company executives, who urged Wilson to stick to what they saw as a surefire surf-hit formula. In truth, however, his work had rarely been formulaic. It had been developing all along, and now it moved into a realm where artistic commitment outweighed commercial concerns. He would work on *Pet Sounds* through the first half of 1966, using members of the Wrecking Crew and many other top Los Angeles studio musicians. Instrumentation included brass, woodwinds, strings, percussion, and keyboards.

"God Only Knows" leads off side two of the LP. It is one of the album's signature tracks, highlighted by Carl Wilson's sublime vocal and an opulent instrumental texture. The arrangement features two contrasting sonic characters. One is a staccato quarter-note pulse, a kind of "strum" made up of such percussive sounds as piano, harpsichord, and sleigh bells. The other sound blends such instruments as strings and accordion in blocks of sustained harmony. Each of these two textural elements is made up of many instruments layered to create unique timbral blends. This is Wilson's version of the wall of sound. Explaining his intention, he stated, "Rather than just say, 'That's a piano, that's a bass,' now we have . . . something else. Although it may be two or three instruments playing the same notes, it now sounds different."[5]

The lead vocal is touching in its bittersweet earnestness. Carl Wilson's pleading profession of undying love is utterly convincing. In deference to the intimate character of his vocal, the other voices are absent during his verses and choruses. But the track does feature two sections of beautiful vocal counterpoint. In the first of these—which employs three voices of individual character—each voice has its own syllables, attitude, and function. Voice one (listed in order of entrance) is high and airy, singing the syllable "uh" in long tones connected by glissando. Voice two has a similarly light character but sings a more rhythmic melody on the syllable "doo." Voice three, singing the syllables "bah pa pa," is also rhythmic but more strident, its earthy character contrasting with the angelic higher voices. The idea of contrasting long and short notes—as in the instrumental texture—remains in play here. Voices two and three follow the triplet groove of the bass and wood block, providing a rhythmic contrast to the sustained notes of voice one.

The second contrapuntal section is the track's coda. In this section we hear the chorus looped repeatedly through the fade. Voices one and two sing the chorus melody and lyrics in the form of a round, overlapping the beginning and end of their phrases. Voice three sings the lyrics set to a countermelody, recalling the French horn melody from the intro. The three parts swirl round and round as the instrumental texture, which thins out considerably at the beginning of the coda, grows fuller even as the track fades out of earshot.

"God Only Knows" makes effective use of chromaticism to intensify the lyrics' emotional impact. Chromatic notes also allow the track to slip effortlessly out of and back into the tonic key of E (scale: E, F♯, G♯, A, B, C♯, D♯). For example, the three-note instrumental fragment that leads into verses one and two (0:15, 0:39) contains a G♮, which makes the verse's first chord, D, sound momentarily like a potential new tonic. This impression is dispelled by the following chord, which reintroduces G♯. But because this chord still contains a D♮ (not the normal D♯), it suggests not the key of E but F♯ minor, and this is indeed the next chord. Finally, in the verse's fourth bar, we get the V chord (B) that identifies E as the tonic.

Verse-Chord Progression (First 4 Bars)
D/A | B minor 6 | F♯ minor | B/A (dominant of E)

This tonal ambiguity comes in handy in the transition from the chorus following the bridge to the last verse. The bridge is simply a verse sung without words. But the music is now in the key of A. The chorus following the bridge remains in that key. Because those first three chords we heard in verses one and two are all contained in the key of A, as the song moves into verse three it pivots seamlessly back into E as if by magic. Actually, this *is* the real-world magic of music's tonal system, of which Wilson was a master. Adding one further touch of harmonic intricacy, facilitating the song's tonal slipperiness, the bassline avoids most chord roots and never once plays the root of the tonic chord. This makes for a feeling of continuous harmonic suspension. The suspended effect resonates with the angelic vocals and the protagonist's repeated appeal to divine witness.

Listening Guide

"God Only Knows" (Brian Wilson, Tony Asher), Capitol Records (mono). Also appears on the album *Pet Sounds*.
Recorded at Western Recorders Studio 3 and Columbia Studio A, Los Angeles, March–April 1966
Carl Wilson (lead voice), Mike Love, Bruce Johnston, Brian Wilson (voice), Hal Blaine (drums), Jim Gordon (percussion), Carol Kaye (electric bass), Lyle Ritz (upright bass), Ray Pohlman (guitar), Don Randi

(piano), Larry Knechtel (organ), Carl Fortina (accordion), Frank Marocco (clarinet), Alan Robinson (French horn), Bill Green (flute), Leonard Hartman, Jim Horn, Jay Migliori (saxophones), Lenny Malarsky, Sidney Sharp, William Kurasch, Ralph Schaeffer (violins), Harry Hyams, Darrel Terwilliger (viola), Jesse Ehrlich (cello)

Producer: Brian Wilson
Engineer Chuck Britz
Charts: Hot 100 #39, Top LP's #10
Key: E
Meter 4/4

Time	Section	Lyric Cue	Listen For
0:00	Intro (8)		Two timbral-rhythmic characters:
			Short notes: quarter-note "strums" played by harpsichord, piano, etc.
			Long notes: sustained tones played by strings, accordion, etc.
			French horn melody.
0:08			Bass entrance.
0:15			Lead-in phrase.
0:17	Verse 1 (8)	"I may not always"	Carl Wilson vocal.
			Short-note texture; long notes out.
			Woodblocks and bass play triplet groove.
0:33	Chorus 1 (4)	"God only knows"	Continue **verse 1** texture.
0:39			Lead-in phrase (more instruments than before).
0:41	Verse 2 (8)	"If you should"	Short- and long-note textures together.
0:58	Chorus 2 (3)	"God only knows"	Continue **verse 2** texture.
1:04	Break (4)		Pulse stops; instruments in rhythmic unison; phrases punctuated with drum fills.
1:12	Bridge (8+3)		**Verse** music now in the key of A.
			Vocal counterpoint:
		"Huh"	Voice 1.
1:16		"Doo doo"	Voice 2.
1:18		"Bah pa"	Voice 3.
1:28	Bridge Chorus (3)	"God only knows"	Lead voice returns, still in A.
1:35	Verse 4 (8)	"If you should"	First three chords serve as pivot from A to E.
1:51	Chorus 4 (4)	"God only knows"	Continue **verse 4** texture

Time	Section	Lyric Cue	Listen For
1:59	**Coda** (24)	"God only knows"	Voice 1; "strum" texture drops out.
2:04		"God only knows"	Voice 2 overlaps voice 1; sings the same melody.
2:07			Begin drum fills.
2:08		"God only knows"	Voice 3 sings countermelody recalling French horn from **intro**.
2:17			Begin backbeat with sleigh bells/tambourine; fade.

11.3. "GOOD VIBRATIONS" (1966)

"Good Vibrations" was both the most ambitious and the most commercially successful track of the *Pet Sounds* period. It did not, however, appear on the album. Like some other pathbreaking tracks—the Beatles' "Strawberry Fields Forever"/"Penny Lane" from the *Sgt. Pepper's* period and "Jumpin' Jack Flash" from the Stones' *Beggar's Banquet* sessions—"Good Vibrations" was initially released only as a single. In its three-and-a-half minutes it embodies the scope of Brian's Wilson artistic ambition and showcases his acquired production skill. From start to finish, as Wilson experimented with various arrangements, recording and mixing consumed about ninety-four hours of studio time spread over nearly eight months and four recording studios. It cost approximately $50,000, which at the time was an unheard-of sum for a single. In assembling a series of recorded fragments (like the *Abbey Road* medley on a smaller scale), the track blends verse-chorus form with an elaborate multipart conception including several key and groove changes. In short, it exemplifies Wilson's notion that "a song can . . . have movements, in the same way as a classical concerto, only capsulized."[6] Although it does not reach the lengths of the Beatles' *Abbey Road* medley or the Stones' "You Can't Always Get What You Want," "Good Vibrations" nevertheless feels like a similarly broad canvas.

The track opens suddenly. Instead of an introduction to set up the song, the first sound we hear is Carl Wilson's sweet voice floating in as if on a breeze. He is joined by just two instruments, organ and electric bass, which create a surprisingly complex texture. The richness is due to both the instruments' sound and the parts Wilson wrote. The organ, bathed in heavy reverb, has a distorted quality and a changing timbre caused by a Leslie rotating speaker effect. Although the organ part is simply constant quarter notes, the rotating speaker creates its own rhythm, which is not timed to the quarter-note pulse. This creates the sense of a random rhythmic overlay. The bass part is played in a high register with a pick, creating a distinctive sound and emphasizing its melodic character. Its three-beat phrases add a further level of rhythmic ambiguity in their waltz-like whimsy. The second half of the verse introduces new timbral forces: woodwinds, a low bass part, percussion, and drums.

The verse hints at a triplet groove in the rhythmic subdivisions of the voice, high bass, and percussion. This is confirmed in the chorus when the track's full groove goes into motion. Along with the now-steady backbeat, a cello fuels the triplet-based momentum. (The use of cello in a predominantly rhythmic role is reminiscent of the arrangement for "Will You Love Me Tomorrow.")

The chorus also brings a change of the lead vocal character. Carl hands the lead off to Mike Love, who sings the same line ("I'm picking up . . . expectations") four times, each lasting four bars. After his first iteration, a layer of backing vocals joins in with a countermelody riff ("ooh bop bop") sung in three-part harmony. Four bars later, a second layer ("good, good, good") adds another countermelody, also in three-part harmony in the upper register.

After another verse and chorus—at the point where the track could easily begin a fade-out—the narrative moves from one surprise to another. A transition leads from chorus two to a completely new section of music ("I don't know where"), followed by a second transition and another new section ("Gotta keep those"). Here the voices fade, leaving only remnants of the instrumental texture. By now listeners have no idea what to expect. The changes are certainly imaginative, but the important principle of formal unity seems to be at risk. Suddenly, however, the voices burst forth with a loud "aah," like the sun breaking through clouds. A full-blown chorus fragment, all three vocal layers, brings us back to a familiar place, but only for a moment. This eight-bar fragment yields to a coda, which introduces yet more new music for the voices ("Na na na na"), followed by a brief, fading reminder of the chorus in an instrumental version.

The song moves through several tonal areas, illustrating once again the important role harmony and harmonic relationships played in Wilson's thinking. The verses are in E♭ minor; the choruses are in G♭ major. With the entrance of "Good, good, good," the key shifts up a whole step to A♭ and then, four bars later, up another whole step to B♭. So the chorus divides into four four-bar phrases pitched

1. "I'm picking up . . ." G♭
2. "Ooh bop bop . . ." G♭
3. "Good, good, good . . ." A♭
4. "Good, good, good . . ." B♭

The rising whole steps brighten the music and conveniently bring it to the V chord of E♭ minor (B♭), setting up a return to the verse.

The whole-step idea is also a thematic element that helps to structure the big picture. After the digressions that follow chorus two, the return of the chorus fragment (2:57) begins in B♭ and moves down by whole step to A♭ and then G♭. In the coda, the final section of vocal music ("Na na na na") starts in G♭ and once more works its way up in a series of repetitions to A♭ and B♭, dropping finally to A♭ for the fade-out.

As in "God Only Knows," many of the individual timbres on "Good Vibrations" are subsumed in the overall texture. But some colors stand out. We have already noted the organ and bass in the verse and the cello in the chorus. Another striking sound is the theremin, the electronic sound used in the chorus to evoke a sci-fi image of picking up cosmic vibrations. This idea of associating a timbre with a particular section of the track is also evident in the tack piano and jaw harp texture prominent in transition one and part two (1:41–2:14) and the "church" organ sound in transition two and part three (2:14–2:54). This sequence of changes in the track's sonic texture is yet another element of its narrative design.

Listening Guide

"Good Vibrations" (Brian Wilson, Mike Love), Capitol Records (mono)
Recorded at Gold Star, Sunset Sound, Western Recorders, and Columbia Studios, Los Angeles, February–September 1966
Carl Wilson (voice, bass guitar, percussion), Mike Love (voice), Bruce Johnston (voice), Al Jardine (voice), Brian Wilson (voice), Dennis Wilson (voice and organ), Carol Kaye (bass guitar), Ray Pohlman (bass guitar), Jimmy Bond (upright bass), Lyle Ritz (upright bass), Glen Campbell (guitar), Al de Lory (tack piano), Don Randi (harpsichord), Larry Knechtel (organ), Tommy Morgan (harmonica), Jesse Ehrlich (cello), Paul Tanner (theremin), Hal Blaine (drums, percussion), Jim Gordon (drums)
Producer: Brian Wilson
Engineer: Chuck Britz
Charts: Hot 100 #1
Key: Multiple, as detailed in Listening Guide
Meter: 4/4

Time	Section	Lyric Cue	Listen For
	Part 1		
0:00	Verse 1 (8+8)	"I, I love the colorful"	High voice (Carl Wilson); E♭ minor.
			Organ with Leslie, distortion, and reverb.
			High-register electric bass.
0:13			Low bass, woodwinds, percussion, drums.

Time	Section	Lyric Cue	Listen For
0:25	**Chorus 1** (16)	"I'm picking up"	Lead voice switches to Mike Love. Regular triplet groove driven by cello. Theremin sounds.
0:32		"Ooh bop bop"	Backing voices layer 1.
0:38		"Good, good"	Backing voices layer 2; shift to A♭.
0:44		"Good, good"	Shift to B♭; repeat previous phrase.
0:51	**Verse 2** (8+8)	"Close my eyes"	Similar to **verse 1**.
1:16	**Chorus 2** (16)	"I'm picking up"	Similar to **chorus 1**.
1:41	**Transition 1** (12)	". . . -tations"	Texture and groove change. Tack piano, jaw harp, harmonica, tambourine.
1:54		"Aah"	Voices enter.
2:01	**Part 2** (8)	"I don't know where"	New key: E♭. Voices sing descending lines.
2:14	**Transition 2** (4)		New key: F. Voices out; "church" organ. Pulse fades to background shaker part.
2:21	**Part 3** (24)	"Gotta keep"	Single-line vocal melody.
2:28			Pulse returns in bass; add harmony vocal and begin fading voices.
2:53		"Aah"	Voices return, cutoff leaves reverb sustaining.
2:57	**Chorus** (10)	"Good, good"	**Chorus** fragment; all 3 vocal parts in B♭.
3:04		"Good, good"	A♭
3:10			G♭; voices out.
3:13	**Coda** (13 to fade)	"Na na na na"	1 vocal line in G♭.
3:16		"Na na na na"	2 vocal lines in A♭.
3:20		"Na na na na"	3 vocal lines in B♭.
3:23		"Na na na na"	3 vocal lines in A♭.
3:27			Voices out; cello and theremin to fade.

NOTES

1. Quoted in Keith Badman, *The Beach Boys: The Definitive Diary of America's Greatest Band on Stage and in the Studio* (San Francisco: Backbeat Books, 2004), 52.
2. Quoted in Badman, 104.
3. Quoted in Timothy White, *The Nearest Faraway Place: Brian Wilson, the Beach Boys, and the Southern California Experience* (New York: Henry Holt, 1994), 252.

4. Brian Wilson with Todd Gold, *Wouldn't It Be Nice: My Own Story* (New York: Harper Collins, 1991), 140.

5. Quoted in David N. Howard, *Sonic Alchemy: Visionary Music Producers and Their Maverick Recordings* (Milwaukee, WI: Hal Leonard, 2004), 57.

6. Quoted in Charles Granata, *Wouldn't It Be Nice: Brian Wilson and the Making of the Beach Boys' Pet Sounds* (Chicago: Chicago Review Press, 2016), 38.

FURTHER READING

Badman, Keith. *The Beach Boys: The Definitive Diary of America's Greatest Band on Stage and in the Studio.* San Francisco: Backbeat Books, 2004.

Crowley, Kent. *Surf Beat: Rock 'n 'Roll's Forgotten Revolution.* New York: Backbeat Books, 2011.

White, Timothy. *The Nearest Faraway Place: Brian Wilson, the Beach Boys, and the Southern California Experience.* New York: Henry Holt, 1994.

Wilson, Brian, with Todd Gold, *Wouldn't It Be Nice: My Own Story.* New York: Harper Collins, 1991.

FURTHER LISTENING: SURF MUSIC

Chantays, "Pipeline" (Dot, 1963)
Dick Dale and the Del-Tones, "Misirlou" (Deltone, 1962)
Hondells, "Little Honda" (Mercury, 1964)
Jan and Dean, "Surf City" (Liberty, 1963)
Marketts, "Out of Limits" (Warner, 1963)
Rip Chords, "Hey Little Cobra" (Columbia, 1964)
Ronny and the Daytonas, "G.T.O." (Mala, 1964)
Surfaris, "Wipe Out" (Dot, 1963)
Trashmen, "Surfin' Bird" (Garrett, 1963)
Ventures, "Walk, Don't Run" (Dolton, 1960)

12

URBAN FOLK
Folk Rock

"Brave New Sound Sweeping Nation: Rock + Folk + Protest" announced a *Billboard* headline from late summer 1965. The accompanying article was evidence that a newly emerging rock genre had caused enough of a stir in the market to get the record industry's attention. As British groups laid claim to the US charts, American musicians, admittedly under a powerful Beatles influence, responded with a new musical hybrid that married elements from the urban folk genre with the instruments and beat of rock. A key musical ingredient was vocal harmony, a source of common ground between the two idioms. When folk musicians turned to rock, their harmonizing skills were put to good use in their new stylistic home. Groups such as the Mamas and the Papas, the Byrds, and the Grateful Dead, all with roots in the folk music scene, made vocal harmony a centerpiece of their sound.

The urban folk scene of the late '50s and early '60s was an outgrowth of a folk music revival with roots in the early decades of the twentieth century. Historically, the term "folk music" refers to everyday music making, with songs and tunes circulating in an oral tradition based on live music making. Typical instrumentation includes acoustic guitar, banjo, fiddle, mandolin, and stand-up bass. The folk traditions of the United States predate the commercial music industry that arose in the late nineteenth century, but in the early decades of the twentieth century, using both music notation and sound recording, song collectors began collecting folk songs. Music previously confined to specific regions of the country began circulating more widely in the form of sheet music and records. In the process, folk music gained a broad audience with figures such as Woody Guthrie and Leadbelly claiming national attention as rustic musical stars. And while the folk repertory included hundreds of traditional songs, folk performers also wrote new songs in folk styles.

The first true pop stars among folk performers were the members of the Weavers, a group that included Pete Seeger. From 1950 to 1954 the Weavers had a number of pop hits, including "Goodnight Irene" (which had been popularized in a version by Leadbelly) and Woody Guthrie's "So Long (It's Been Good to Know Ya)." The Weavers' commercial hits were folk-pop hybrids combining traditional folk instruments with orchestra and chorus. The records were produced in New York City by the well-known pop arranger and composer Gordon Jenkins and released on a major label (Decca). What had originated as a rural music was becoming urbanized. The trend continued with the 1958 pop success of the Kingston Trio, a San Francisco–based group with a straightforward folk instrumentation of two guitars and banjo. Their recording of the traditional song "Tom Dooley" sold several million copies. By the early 1960s, this new, urban folk music attracted young musicians across the country for whom pre-Beatles rock and roll had come to feel like teeny bopper fantasy. Many college campuses were folk music hotbeds with "coffee house" performance venues hospitable to acoustic music and thoughtful lyrics. But folk's vibrant nerve center was New York's Greenwich Village. Young stars such as Peter, Paul, and Mary; Joan Baez; and Bob Dylan became fixtures of this new folk scene, which began to produce significant pop hits such as Peter, Paul, and Mary's recording of Dylan's "Blowin' in the Wind."

Folk rock took many forms. Some tracks had a distinctly pop flavor, such as Sonny and Cher's "I Got You Babe," the Turtles' version of Dylan's "It Ain't Me Babe," and the Mamas and the Papas' "California Dreaming." Others aimed to bring social commentary to the top-forty. These included records such as Dion's "Abraham, Martin and John," Barry McGuire's "Eve of Destruction," and Buffalo Springfield's "For What It's Worth." Moreover, the genre's broad appeal soon gave it an international cast with the rise of stars such as Donovan (Scotland), the Seekers (Australia), and Fairport Convention (England).

What most set folk rock apart from other genres was its song lyrics. The traditional folk repertory included all sorts of topics (manual labor, murder, war, spiritual redemption) and characters (lumberjacks, miners, sailors, outlaws) rarely found in pop songs. The urban folk revival followed suit while adding a modern topical edge. Nowhere was the contrast between folk and rock of the early '60s more apparent than in the songs of Bob Dylan. While the Beatles sang "I Want to Hold Your Hand," Dylan was singing **protest songs** about racial discrimination ("Oxford Town"), war ("With God on Our Side"), and social justice ("The Lonesome Death of Hattie Carroll"). Yet by 1965 Dylan himself would be a rock star, his songs widely covered by rock musicians from the Byrds to Jimi Hendrix to Elvis Presley. As he demonstrated the commercial appeal of complex and varied song lyrics, Dylan effectively altered the conventional conception of a pop song.

Dylan and other wordsmiths such as Paul Simon and Joni Mitchell used metaphor and symbolic imagery, intricate rhyme schemes, and serious treatment of serious topics to write songs that were akin to poetry. Suddenly, rock and roll took on an unforeseen intellectual dimension. With any topic as fair game, songs weighed in on social and political events, as well as ongoing developments in the youth-driven counterculture. At the same time, the musical styles of both traditional and contemporary folk were combined with the timbres and rhythms of rock and brought into the creative sphere of the rock recording studio. And since folk rock was, after all, rock, it drifted far from its rustic roots and easily absorbed a host of varied stylistic influences.

12.1. "LIKE A ROLLING STONE" (1965)

BOB DYLAN

Bob Dylan took the New York folk scene by storm in 1961, soon after arriving from Minnesota where he was born and raised. Young, charismatic, and a gifted songwriter and performer, he won over the older "folkies" in Greenwich Village, which at the time was the center of the urban folk revival. Within the year he had a deal with Columbia Records and had recorded his first album. Two years after moving to New York, a *New York Times* critic wrote a glowing review of a Dylan concert at Town Hall. The songs combined "conversational folksay with a dash of Rimbaud's demonic imagery" as well as "social criticism." Dylan, the review continued, was "an incredibly gifted song writer . . . a young giant."[1] The folk music publication *Little Sandy* stated that Dylan was "certainly our finest contemporary folk song writer."[2]

Dylan changed the landscape of pop songwriting. No modern songwriter escaped his influence. He showed that it was possible to write complex lyrics about serious topics and still appeal to a broad public. He wrote songs of political protest, social commentary, and symbolist poetry. His song "Blowin' in the Wind" became an anthem of the civil rights movement. The version by Peter, Paul, and Mary reached number two on *Billboard*'s Hot 100. Dylan was on the stage at the Lincoln Memorial with Martin Luther King Jr. during the March on Washington for Jobs and Freedom in August 1963, when King gave his "I Have a Dream" speech. On that occasion Dylan sang "Only a Pawn in Their Game," which addressed the murder of civil rights worker Medgar Evers. Dylan appeared to his fans to be a heroic, if paradoxical, figure: a popular musician without commercial pretensions.

It was deeply unsettling, then, to many folk fans when he began to use electric guitars and drums on his recordings. Among folk purists, these were considered tokens of commercialism. There were rumblings when he included some electric guitar and bass on his *Bringing It All Back Home* album, released in the spring of 1965; outrage when he showed up at the Newport Folk Festival that summer with a rock band; and utter disillusionment when he released *Highway 61 Revisited* in September. Perhaps more disturbing still to many old fans was the fact that Dylan's electric sound won him so many new ones. *Highway 61* sold more copies than any of his previous albums, peaking at number three on *Billboard*'s Top LP's chart. The leading folk music publication, *Sing Out!*, lamented the loss of such a talent to the commercial clutches of the "American Success Machinery."[3] But Dylan, who had always been a rock and roll fan, created according to his own muse. In "going electric" he was simply fulfilling a personal artistic vision.

"Like a Rolling Stone" is the opening track of *Highway 61*, and it boldly states Dylan's intentions from its first sound. Start the recording and a snare drum cracks out a clarion pickup beat amplified with reverb that spills across the stereo soundstage. The first sound of the track, and the album as a whole, is the primal sound of rock and roll: the backbeat. At the same time, it pays little heed to prevailing rock conventions. As a six-minute track, it defies the time restrictions for radio airplay (stations played it anyway). And with Dylan's unique, non-pop vocal styling, poetic lyrics, and the cluttered complexity of instrumental textures, "Like a Rolling Stone" stakes out its own stylistic territory.

The song is filled with the profligate wordplay typical of Dylan's mid-1960s work. The playing has a loose, improvisatory feel, yet the song is tightly structured. The verses are twenty bars long, divided into three distinct segments of eight (*a*), eight (*b*), and four (*c*) bars. The *a* segment has two similar four-bar phrases. In each of these, the first two bars present a rush of words—often with internal rhymes tumbling over one another—followed by a two-bar breather. So in verse one we hear, "Once upon a time . . . so fine . . . a dime . . . your prime" followed simply by, "didn't you." And then, "People call . . . doll . . . fall . . . all" followed by "kiddin' you." The end-rhymes "didn't you" and "kiddin' you," set four bars apart, help tie the *a* segment together. The harmonic rhythm mirrors the pacing of the lyrics. The first two bars of each phrase contain four chords (one every two beats); the second two bars have only one.

The *b* segment of the verse, though also eight bars long, differs from the *a* in several ways. It introduces a new chord progression, melody, harmonic rhythm, and rhyme scheme. It is also phrased differently. While *a* is composed of a repeated four-bar phrase (4+4), the *b* phrases are just two bars long (2+2+2+2). Moreover, the first two of these shorter phrases contain different music from the second two. But if *b* is more active musically than *a*, it is less wordy, focusing on a single repeated rhyme ("about," "out," "loud," "proud").

The last segment of the verse, *c*, is four bars in length and functions as a pre-chorus, building anticipation. The V chord (G) is held for two bars as Dylan sustains the melody note, breaking finally into the chorus refrain "How does it *feel*?" as the musical energy drives the track into the chorus downbeat. The word sung to this long melody note always rhymes with "feel" ("meal," "deal," "steal," "conceal"), which provides a recurring rhyme that spans the length of the track.

The chorus releases the energy of the pre-chorus as it settles into a repeated two-bar harmonic loop. The lyrics focus on a single rhyme ("home," "unknown") aimed at the culmination of the hook phrase: "like a rolling *stone*." Subsequent choruses add other words, and an extra line, but all rhyme with "stone."

In addition to their verbal function (meaning, sound, rhythm), the song's rhymes affect both its pacing and structure. For example, the rapid internal rhymes that occur in the *a* segments of the verse cascade breathlessly, while the more deliberate and widely spaced *b* rhymes stretch out the pace. These rhymes are specific to the phrases in which they occur. On the level of long-range structure, the rhyming words for "feel" and for "stone" provide the song with recurrent rhymes that delineate its verse-chorus form.

The song's lyrics are dense with images and layers of metaphoric suggestion, which open up various possible meanings. While on the surface, the words are an admonishment directed at a fallen female character (a common Dylan character type), they can also be read more generally as a cautionary tale of hubris and the empty trappings of success and social acceptance. In this sense, the song could be about anyone; it could even be about Dylan himself. As one writer has put it, "Perhaps we can also recognize here (from our own experience) the voice of conscience, self-criticism, self-awareness."[4] The point is that the songwriter invites listeners to be part of the song's meaning as they interpret the song for themselves.

Listening Guide

"Like a Rolling Stone" (Bob Dylan), Columbia Records (stereo). Also appears on the album *Highway 61 Revisited.*
Recorded at Columbia Studio A, New York City, June 1965
Bob Dylan (voice, guitar, harmonica), Mike Bloomfield (lead guitar), Al Kooper (organ), Paul Griffin (piano), Joe Macho Jr. (bass), Bobby Gregg (drums), Bruce Langhorne (tambourine)
Producer: Tom Wilson
Engineer: Roy Halee
Charts: Hot 100 #2; Top LP's #3
Key: C
Meter: 4/4

Time	Section	Lyric Cue	Listen For
0:00	Intro (4)		Snare pickup (R).
			Band texture: piano (L), bass (L), voice (C), rhythm guitar (C), organ (R), lead guitar (R), drums (R), tambourine (R).
	Verse 1 (8+8+4)		3 parts (*a, b, c*), each with different rhyme scheme and harmonic rhythm.
0:11	*a* (4+4)	"Once upon a time . . . fine . . . dime"	Cascading lyrics, internal rhymes.
		". . . didn't you"	End rhyme.
		"People call . . . doll . . . fall"	Cascading lyrics, internal rhymes.
		". . . kiddin' you"	End rhyme.
0:31	*b* (2+2+2+2)	". . . laugh about"	Shorter phrases, single rhyme.
		". . . hanging out"	
		". . . talk so loud"	
		". . . seem so proud"	
0:51	*c* (4)	"About having to be . . ."	Pre-chorus.
		". . . *meal*/How does it *feel*?"	Refrain rhyme.
1:01	**Chorus 1** (10+3)	". . . without a home"	2-bar loop repeated 5 times, single rhyme.
		". . . complete unknown"	
		". . . rolling stone"	
1:26			3-bar extension continues chord progression with harmonica.

continued on next page

Time	Section	Lyric Cue	Listen For
1:34	Verse 2 (8+8+4)		Same structure as **verse 1**.
	a	"You've gone to . . ."	Cascading lyrics.
		". . . juiced in it"	End rhyme.
		"Nobody ever taught . . ."	Cascading lyrics.
		". . . used to it"	End rhyme.
	b	". . . compromise"	Shorter phrases, single rhyme.
		". . . realize"	
		". . . alibis"	
		". . . of his eyes"	
	c	"And say . . ."	Pre-chorus.
		". . . make a *deal*/How does it *feel*"	Refrain rhyme.
2:25	Chorus 2 (12+3)		Similar to **chorus 1** with an added line of lyrics.
2:55			Extension with harmonica.
3:02	Verse 3 (8+8+4)		Same structure as **verse 1**.
	a	"You never turned around . . . frowns . . . clowns"	Cascading lyrics, internal rhymes.
		". . . tricks for you"	End rhyme.
		"You never understood . . . good . . . should"	Cascading lyrics, internal rhymes.
		". . . kicks for you"	End rhyme.
	b	". . . diplomat"	Shorter phrases, single rhyme.
		". . . Siamese cat"	
		". . . discover that"	
		". . . where it's at"	
	c	"After he took . . ."	Pre-chorus.
		". . . he could *steal*/How does it *feel*"	Refrain rhyme.
3:53	Chorus 3 (12+3)		Similar to **chorus 2**.

Time	Section	Lyric Cue	Listen For
4:30	Verse 4 (8+8+4)		Same structure as **verse 1**.
	a	"Princess on the steeple . . . people/drinking . . . thinking"	Cascading lyrics, internal rhymes.
		". . . got it made"	End rhyme.
		"Exchanging all precious . . ."	Cascading lyrics.
		". . . pawn it babe"	End rhyme.
	b	". . . so amused"	Shorter phrases, single rhyme.
		". . . that he used"	
		". . . can't refuse"	
		". . . nothing to lose"	
	c	"You're invisible . . ."	Pre-chorus.
		". . . to *conceal*/How does it *feel*"	Refrain rhyme.
5:21	Chorus 4 (12+extension to fade)		Similar to **chorus 2**.

12.2. "MY BACK PAGES" (1967)

THE BYRDS

In 1964, three folk musicians—Jim (later called Roger) McGuinn, Gene Clark, and David Crosby—began singing together in Los Angeles. The rich blend of their voices became the foundation for the launch of a new pop genre. Emulating the Beatles, they complemented their vocal harmonies with the jangly sound of an electric twelve-string guitar (Jim McGuinn), electric bass (Chris Hillman), and drums (Michael Clarke). Their debut album *Mr. Tambourine Man* was released in the spring of 1965. By early summer its title track was at the top of the charts, the first folk-rock record to achieve such commercial success. "Mr. Tambourine Man" was one of four Dylan songs on the album, further evidence of his emergent appeal beyond the folk scene. The Byrds' version was streamlined for pop consumption. It contained only one verse (Dylan's acoustic version has four), two choruses, and a memorable electric twelve-string guitar riff—a mere two minutes of music before the track fades. But its commercial impact was stunning and its musical influence widespread. The combination of soft folk harmonies, loud rock band, and thoughtful lyrics produced not only a hit record but a template for a new sound that was dubbed, almost immediately, folk rock. It might as well have been called Byrds rock because it would forever be identified with their distinctive sound.

As the Byrds developed their stylistic blend, they wrote songs of their own—"Mr. Spaceman," "So You Want to Be a Rock 'n' Roll Star," "Eight Miles High"—but they also continued to record Dylan songs. In 1966, they recorded "My Back Pages," which had appeared on Dylan's *Another Side of Bob Dylan* in 1964. It was released both as a single and a track on their fourth album, *Younger Than Yesterday*. Although Gene Clark had left the band the year before, the Byrds' trademark vocal sound remained intact. Its most distinctive features were McGuinn's slightly edgy lead topped by Crosby's high harmony parts. Clark's voice filled and smoothed out the texture. This role was now taken by bassist Chris Hillman.

"My Back Pages" is a classic example of the Byrds' sound. It begins by setting up what was by then a familiar instrumental texture. Before any voice is heard, the record says, "Byrds." Two electric guitars repeat a scene-setting vamp, the all-important electric twelve-string claiming the greatest prominence. The twelve-string is panned left, while the other electric guitar provides a background presence on both sides of the stereo field. Next, bass and claves enter on the left followed by a fade-in from the drums on the right. At the verse downbeat an organ enters on the right. Once this texture is in place, it continues throughout the track, adding only a tambourine part during the guitar solo.

The center of the mix is reserved entirely for the voices and their substantial reverberant image. The only other sound to occupy this space is the twelve-string guitar solo. This mix configuration gives the voices plenty of room to breathe and establishes a strong vocal presence in the midst of a fairly loud band. The vocal arrangement follows a typical Byrds pattern: McGuinn's solo lead in the verses is followed by harmonized choruses. The sequence focuses the listener on McGuinn's unique, idiosyncratic voice and diction style even as it builds anticipation for the beautiful harmonies to come. In effect, no matter the song, the Byrds' vocal arrangements provide a natural hook.

The song form is verse-chorus, but the verse includes a segment that feels like a pre-chorus. Its twelve bars are configured such that the first eight bars fall into a 4+4 phrase structure. These two four-bar phrases are nearly identical musically and are further tied together by their end-rhymes (e.g., "traps," "maps"). They balance one another. The verse's final four-bar phrase, which sets up the chorus, begins on a different chord from the first two phrases and has no balancing phrase; it stands apart (e.g., "We'll meet on edges"). Further, its last word rhymes with the refrain line in the chorus (e.g., pre-chorus endings "brow," "somehow," "bow" rhyme with the refrain "younger than that now"). Thus, this last harmonic phrase in each verse is designed to underscore the refrain's arrival and to connect verses and choruses.

The song's lyrics are filled with symbolic imagery, but all support a central theme. At this point in his career, Dylan was transitioning to his electric style, which involved moving away from the songs of protest and social commentary and toward more personal expression. "My Back Pages" is an assessment of his previous position, which he expands into a more universal comment on the self-righteous certainty of youthful beliefs. The paradox repeated in each chorus, and which the Byrds mirror in the album's title, plays on a temporal contradiction: We somehow get younger as we age; we become "younger than yesterday." It is an elegant, pithy way to impart the idea that experience can lead to less certainty, greater acceptance, and a more flexible perspective on life.

Listening Guide

"My Back Pages" (Bob Dylan), Columbia Records (stereo). Also appears on the album *Younger than Yesterday*.
Recorded at Columbia Studios, Hollywood, December 1966
Jim McGuinn (voice, electric twelve-string guitar), David Crosby (voice, electric six-string guitar), Chris Hillman (voice, bass), Michael Clarke (drums)
Producer: Gary Usher
Charts: Hot 100 #30; Top LP's #24
Key: E
Meter: 4/4

Time	Section	Lyric Cue	Listen For
0:00	**Intro** (4)		Vamp: Electric 12-string (L) and electric 6-string (L and R).
0:04			Bass (L) and claves (L, reverb R).
0:06			Drums fade in (R).
0:08	**Verse 1** (8+4)	"Crimson flames"	McGuinn's lead vocal (C).
			Organ (R).
0:23		"We'll meet"	Pre-chorus.
0:31	**Chorus 1** (4+1)	"Ah but I"	Harmony voices (C).
0:41	**Verse 2** (8+4)	"Half-wracked"	Similar to **verse** 1.
0:56		"Romantic flanks"	Pre-chorus.
1:04	**Chorus 2** (4+1)	"Ah but I"	Similar to **chorus** 1.

continued on next page

Time	Section	Lyric Cue	Listen For
1:14	Verse 3 (8+4)	"In a soldier's"	Similar to **verse 1**.
1:30		"Sisters fled"	Pre-chorus.
1:37	Chorus 3 (4+1)	"Ah but I"	Similar to **chorus 1**.
1:47	Break (12)		Electric 12-string guitar solo (C) plays a variant of verse melody.
			Tambourine (L) adds a new rhythm.
2:10	Break Chorus (4+1)	"Ah but I"	Similar to **chorus 1**.
2:20	Verse 4 (8+4)	"My guard"	Similar to **verse 1**.
2:36		"Good and bad"	Pre-chorus.
2:44	Chorus 4 (4+fade)	"Ah but I"	Similar to **chorus 1**.
			Fade on **intro** vamp.

12.3. "AMERICA" (1968)

SIMON AND GARFUNKEL

Simon and Garfunkel became folk rockers by accident. They began singing together as teenagers and had a minor hit with a record called "Hey, Schoolgirl" while still in high school (going by the names Tom and Jerry). In the early 1960s, they turned to folk music and drifted into the Greenwich Village folk scene, adapting their Everly Brothers–influenced two-part harmonizing to the folk repertory and to Simon's folk-inspired songs. They were signed to Columbia Records in 1964 and released an acoustic album, *Wednesday Morning, 3 A.M.*, containing a few of Simon's songs and a mix of traditional and contemporary folk tunes, including Dylan's "The Times They Are A-Changin'."

The album sold poorly and the two went their separate ways. Simon left the US to perform solo in England. But one of the album's tracks, "The Sound of Silence," attracted enough attention that some radio stations began playing it in the summer of 1965. Columbia producer Tom Wilson, soon after producing Dylan's "Like a Rolling Stone," decided to overdub electric guitar, bass, and drums on the original acoustic track. The Byrds had already proven with "Mr. Tambourine Man" that electric folk could attract a mass audience and Wilson decided to take "The Sound of Silence" in the same direction, all without the knowledge of Simon and Garfunkel. The record entered the charts in the fall, and by New Year's Day 1966, it was number one, prompting the duo's rapid reunion. By the time Simon and Garfunkel realized they were folk rockers, it was already a fait accompli.

"America" appeared on Simon and Garfunkel's fourth album, *Bookends*, which includes "Mrs. Robinson," the number-one single that appeared in the film *The Graduate*. The album is a metaphoric examination of a society facing existential questions, as suggested in such song titles as "Save the Life of My Child" and "A Hazy Shade of Winter." Its textures blend acoustic sounds with some of the electronic effects of the contemporary psychedelic style. For example, "America" begins as a crossfade from the previous track, "Save the Life of My Child," whose buzzing Moog synthesizer bassline lingers across the fade. Then, amid a pure folk texture of humming voices accompanied by a strummed acoustic guitar a riff from a second guitar—its timbre altered by electronic processing—alerts us to a more complex sound world.

Complex, too, is the narrative of Simon's lyrics, exemplifying folk rock's poetic leanings. Juxtaposing ornate language ("We'll marry our fortunes together") with the everyday ("So we bought a pack of cigarettes"), Simon portrays different states of mind within the protagonist. An ordinary bus ride, reported in a matter-of-fact way, provides the setting for the protagonist's spiritual ruminations. His personal sense of emptiness and uncertainty is ultimately expanded to include America as a whole (symbolized by place names and "the cars on the New Jersey Turnpike"), its citizens constantly on the move in search of some elusive meaning.

The track's stereo mix comes together as a series of delicate brush strokes, building its texture gradually to the first climax at the end of verse two. The humming voices are panned so that the higher part appears in the center, the lower one doubled on the right and left. The main rhythm guitar is in the center and is joined first by another guitar treated with a rotating speaker-type timbral effect (R) and then a third, dry guitar (L). These three guitars provide the track's textural foundation. Gradually, drums, percussion, organ, and bass are introduced to the mix, each in their own stereo position. As the track progresses, listen for an intricate interweaving of timbres across the stereo field, creating a kind of dramatic underscore for the protagonist's musings.

The song's form is irregular, as are its phrase lengths. The prose-like unfolding of phrases reflects the protagonist's stream of consciousness expression. The four verses are presented in pairs and separated by an extended bridge. Verses one and two begin the same way but differ significantly after their opening phrases. Halfway through verse one, the protagonist switches to a conversational tone ("So we bought a pack of cigarettes"), while gentle chromaticism suggests a key change to E major. The music wanders gently toward the refrain line, "Look for America." By contrast, in the second half of verse two both the music and the singer remain focused and strongly directed toward the refrain with a decisive crescendo. Again, we move briefly to E major, but in a different way harmonically. Verses three and four are juxtaposed similarly. The four verses thus form two larger gestures, each punctuated by a climactic crescendo.

Two musical motives recur throughout the song, helping to delineate the musical structure in the midst of the song's irregular phrasing (see Listening Guide). The first (and most often repeated) is the descending line (motive *a*) we hear in the humming voices and guitar accompaniment in the intro and at the beginning of every verse. After the brief chromatic digression at the midway point of verses one and three, the motive is also used to return the song to the tonic, ending the verse as it began. The descending line also serves as a transition from the bridge back to verse three.

The second motive (*b*) is the whole-step harmonic move that appears in each section. In the verses the move is from E down to D at the refrain:

Verse 1: "walked *off*"
Verse 2: "look for A-*merica*"
Verse 3: "moon *rose*"
Verse 4: "look for A*merica*" three times

In the bridge, the whole-step move is initially from D down to C ("Laughing on the bus"). The music then moves twice from C back up to D (1:20–1:28). In each case, the whole step upsets the folky diatonicism, lending a tonal ambiguity to the song that resonates with the protagonist's unsettled state of mind.

The track reaches its ultimate climax with the last refrain, with its motive *b* repeated three times. This is the moment with the fullest instrumentation and loudest, most forceful performance from the musicians. Throughout the track, the first bar of each refrain is in 9/8 instead of the normal 6/8 meter, creating a phrase extension that sets off the word "America." Now this extension serves to further enhance the grandeur of the climax. Each time we hear "America," it is stretched out across the falling whole-step motive E–D. The sense of yearning is palpable. It is answered in the quiet coda with a wistful organ melody that leads the track's fade-out.

Listening Guide

"America" (Paul Simon), Columbia Records (stereo). Also appears on the album *Bookends*.
Recorded at Columbia Studios, New York City, February 1968

Paul Simon (guitar, voice), Art Garfunkel (voice), Larry Knechtel (organ),
   Joe Osborn (bass), Hal Blaine (drums), studio musician (saxophone),
   studio musician (strings)
Producers: Paul Simon, Art Garfunkel, Roy Halee
Engineer: Roy Halee
Charts: Top LP's #1
Key: D
Meter 6/8

Time	Section	Lyric Cue	Listen For
0:00	**Intro** (8)		Humming crossfades from previous track.
			Descending line (motive *a*) in low voice (R+L), high voice in harmony (C).
			Guitar (C), motive *a* with chords.
0:06			Guitar 2 with rotating speaker effect (R).
0:14			Guitar 3 dry (L), toms (R).
0:17	**Verse 1** (7+9)	"Let us be lovers"	Lead voice (C), doubled faintly (R).
			3-guitar texture continues (LCR).
			Motive *a* in guitar 3 (L); hi-hat (R).
0:25		"I've got some"	High harmony (L+R).
0:31		"So we bought"	Lyrics and melody change style; no voice doubling.
			Brief modulation to E major.
0:35			Kick drum (R).
0:39		"And walked off"	Refrain (motive *b*) returns to D major.
			Add extra beat (1 bar of 9/8).
			Lead voice doubled as before.
0:43		"America"	Motive *a* guitar.
0:46			Tom fill (R)
0:51	**Verse 2** (7+5)	"Kathy I said"	Similar to **verse 1**.
			Organ (R), bass (L).
			Drums begin groove.
1:05		"It took me four"	Crescendo to refrain; voices in unison.
			Brief modulation to E major but different from **verse 1**.
1:09		"I've come"	Refrain.
			Add extra beat (1 bar of 9/8).
1:12		"America"	Motive *b*, returns to D major.

continued on next page

Time	Section	Lyric Cue	Listen For
1:17	**Bridge** (14)	"Laughing on the bus"	Motive *b*; another whole step descent from D to C.
			No vocal harmony; full focus on protagonist.
			Organ (R) and bass (L) take prominent roles.
			Cymbals (R).
			Soprano saxophone (C) wanders freely, fades at end.
1:36		"a camera"	Motive *a* variant transitions back to **verse**.
1:44	**Verse 3** (7+9)	"Toss me a cigarette"	Similar to **verse 1** with bass; voice begins without doubling.
2:07		"Moon rose"	Refrain music, different lyrics.
			Add extra beat (1 bar of 9/8).
2:10		"open field"	Motive *a* guitar.
2:18	**Verse 4** (7+5)	"Kathy I'm lost"	Similar to **verse 2** with strings for fuller background texture.
2:36	(3)	"All come"	Refrain.
			Add extra beat (1 bar of 9/8).
2:40		"America"	Motive *b*.
2:43	(3)	"All come"	Add extra beat (1 bar of 9/8).
			Cymbal crashes (L).
2:47		"America"	Motive *b*.
2:50	(3)	"All come"	Add extra beat (1 bar of 9/8).
			New harmony line.
2:53		"America"	Motive *b*.
2:57	**Coda** (20 bars to fade)		Motive *a*; texture thins to guitars, bass, percussion, and new organ melody.

NOTES

1. Robert Shelton, "Bob Dylan Sings His Compositions: Folk Musician, 21, Displays Originality at Town Hall," *New York Times*, April 13, 1963, 11.
2. Quoted in Nat Hentoff, *The Freewheelin' Bob Dylan* liner notes, Columbia Records, 1963, 3.
3. Irwin Silber, "An Open Letter to Bob Dylan," *Sing Out!*, November 1964, 22.
4. Paul Williams, *Rock and Roll: The 100 Best Singles* (New York: Carroll & Graf, 1993), 89.

FURTHER READING

Dylan, Bob. *Chronicles, Volume One.* New York: Simon and Schuster, 2004.
Hilburn, Robert. *Paul Simon: The Life.* New York: Simon and Schuster, 2018.
Rogan, Johnny. *The Byrds: Timeless Flight Revisited: The Sequel.* London: Rogan House, 1997.
Sounes, Howard. *Down the Highway: The Life of Bob Dylan.* New York: Grove Press, 2001.
Unterberger, Richie. *Turn! Turn! Turn!: The '60s Folk-Rock Revolution.* San Francisco: Backbeat Books, 2002.

FURTHER LISTENING

Joan Baez, "The Night They Drove Old Dixie Down" (Vanguard, 1971)
Buffalo Springfield, "For What It's Worth" (Atco, 1966)
Crosby, Stills, and Nash, "Suite: Judy Blue Eyes" (Atlantic, 1969)
Donovan, "Catch the Wind" (Pye, 1965)
Arlo Guthrie, "Alice's Restaurant Massacree" (Reprise, 1967)
Richie Havens, "Maggie's Farm" (Verve, 1967)
Mamas and the Papas, "California Dreaming" (Dunhill, 1965)
Melanie, "Lay Down (Candles in the Rain)" (Buddha, 1970)
Traffic, "John Barleycorn Must Die" (Island, 1970)
Youngbloods, "Get Together" (RCA Victor, 1969)

13

BERRY GORDY'S EMPIRE
Motown

In 1959 Berry Gordy launched his first record label Tamla with Marv Johnson's "Come to Me" (distributed by United Artists). The record was a top-thirty hit and marked the beginning of what would grow to be a spectacularly successful entertainment complex. The enterprise, based in Detroit, was called Motown, and the music that poured forth from its writers, musicians, singers, and record producers penetrated deeply into the soundtrack and pop consciousness of the 1960s. The interactions and cooperative energies of this remarkable group of talented and ambitious people created what the company called "the sound of young America," a vital and unparalleled strain of 1960s music.

Gordy wanted all aspects of Motown controlled in-house: writing, arranging, recording, producing, distribution, marketing, publishing, and artist management. Taking his cue from the Brill-type operations in New York, Gordy developed a vertically integrated organization. The Motown headquarters, called Hitsville U.S.A., was spread among several houses on Detroit's West Grand Boulevard where a stable of songwriters, producers, engineers, star performers, and a regular group of studio musicians, dubbed the Funk Brothers, reported for work each day. The musicians not only contributed their playing abilities but often created the arrangements. A full-time choreographer (Cholly Atkins) provided the dance steps for Motown groups and a full-time finishing instructor (Maxine Powell) coached the young stars on how to dress and how to speak in public. Motown also had its own recording studios and tape library, as well as a staff of recording engineers under the direction of head engineer Lawrence Horn. The studios ran twenty-two hours a day, with the other two hours given over to the in-house staff of maintenance engineers. The "swinging company" even had a theme song, penned by Smokey Robinson. Its refrain referred to the "hard work" and "unity" at "Hitsville, U.S.A."[1]

Motown hummed with activity through the 1960s, releasing records by some of the era's most iconic stars: the Supremes, the Four Tops, Martha and the Vandellas, the Miracles, the Temptations, Stevie Wonder, Marvin Gaye, and Gladys Knight and the Pips, among many others. While all fell within a general Motown style, each artist contributed a unique voice and image. The writers and producers included Eddie and Brian Holland and Lamont Dozier (Holland-Dozier-Holland), Norman Whitfield, Smokey Robinson, Mickey Stevenson, and Gordy himself, each with a distinctive style. The company ran on the collective energies of its deep talent pool. It operated like a factory, along the lines of the Hollywood film studio system, turning out a steady stream of records. And for most Motown artists the aim and expectation was the same: mainstream pop success.

Motown was often contrasted with Stax, another indie label dedicated to black artists. Some criticism focused on the "whitening" effect of Motown's pop aspirations compared with Stax's more "authentic" connection to R&B and gospel roots. (An article about Motown that appeared in an early rock periodical, for instance, was titled "Motown: A Whiter Shade of Black.") But this argument relies too much on stereotype. There are more useful, less ideological distinctions to make between the two labels. Stax promoter and co-owner Al Bell pointed out one key difference: "Motown grew out of the urbanness of Detroit," he said, "a major metropolitan industrial kind of city. And its music was a reflection of that kind of lifestyle. The Stax sound was more rural America . . . and that lifestyle that you feel in the mid-South of this country."[2] This difference of cultural milieu is important. The polished veneer of sophistication long associated with mainstream pop (exemplified to perfection by Frank Sinatra) was associated with the urban centers of the music industry—New York and Los Angeles. Motown sought to emulate mainstream pop's cosmopolitan style and, in turn, its commercial viability. Berry Gordy—and Motown itself—was a product of Detroit's postwar black middle class, which aspired to the same opportunities white America had long enjoyed.

On the other hand, even with its pop trappings, Motown was still soul music. As children, Motown artists attended the same "school of music" as Stax artists: the black church. We can hear the spirit of gospel-tinged expression in the voices of the Temptations' David Ruffin ("Ain't Too Proud to Beg"), the Four Tops' Levi Stubbs ("Reach Out I'll Be There"), or Martha and the Vandellas' Martha Reeves ("Nowhere to Run"). Motown's play for mainstream success was not a denial of blackness but an expression of empowerment. Rather than a dilution of authentic black expression, it is easy to hear Motown records as an inclusive expansion of pop's stylistic palette that changed the course of the pop mainstream.

13.1. "STOP! IN THE NAME OF LOVE" (1965)

THE SUPREMES

The Supremes were three young women from Detroit: Diana Ross (lead), Mary Wilson, and Florence Ballard. They were the most successful of all the Motown groups in the 1960s, charting records throughout the decade, twelve of which reached number one. As Berry Gordy described them, "They were young, bright . . . very determined. They were captivating, they had energy, dynamism. And they had the sparkle of Diana Ross."[3] Signed to Motown in 1961 while still in their teens, they took the girl group sound to a new level of sophistication and commercial success. With six number-one singles in just over a year, beginning in the summer of 1964, the Supremes were second only to the Beatles in chart dominance even as the British Invasion was in full swing.

Although all three initially took turns singing lead, Diana Ross was the sole lead singer by the time they began to have hits. Her vocal style was pure pop, devoid of the gospel inflections of other female Motown artists such as Gladys Knight or Martha Reeves. Ballard's and Wilson's voices complemented Ross's with a somewhat fuller and earthier texture. (On "Stop! In the Name of Love," for example, listen to their parts "Baby, baby" and "Think it over" as they interact with the lead.) Ross's voice is light but versatile in character. She could be seductive ("Come See about Me"), warm ("Someday We'll Be Together"), pleading ("Baby Love"), and determined ("Love Child"). In "Stop! In the Name of Love" she plays the part of a desperate lover, betrayed yet pleading for reconciliation.

The song and production are by Holland-Dozier-Holland, who wrote and produced dozens of top-forty hits. Their style is among the most pop-inflected of all the Motown producers in its harmonic vocabulary and melodic conception, yet their approach encompasses a wide expressive range. Such hook-laden tracks as the Supremes' "You Can't Hurry Love" or the Four Tops' "I Can't Help Myself (Sugar Pie, Honey Bunch)" have an uncomplicated, buoyant effervescence. On the other hand, Martha and the Vandellas' "Nowhere to Run" or the Four Tops' "Bernadette" are urgent and emotionally charged. Brian Holland and Lamont Dozier wrote the music and produced the tracks, while Eddie Holland wrote the lyrics.

Typically, tracks were recorded in fully produced versions (lacking only vocals) before the lyrics were written.

Wasting no time getting to the hook, "Stop! In the Name of Love" begins with a phrase from the chorus. The track is instantly in full swing, with the full band playing and all of the voices belting the tune in unison. Set up by an organ glissando leading to a shouted "Stop!" this opening packs an arresting punch. The harmonic phrase is only four bars long, so as soon as it gets the listener's attention things settle down with an instruments-only version of a phrase that will recur throughout the track, linking verses and choruses. Its subsequent iterations will include the words "Think it over."

The verse is a sixteen-bar structure divided into four distinct phrases. The first phrase uses non-diatonic chords (v and VI) that reflect the protagonist's conflicted state of mind—a combination of love and hurt. The second phrase is straightforward, quickly restoring diatonic stability. The third begins as if to repeat phrase one but avoids the chromaticism except for a minor-mode inflection (iv) on its final chord at the words "alone and hurt." The fourth phrase is completely different from the preceding ones. The harmonic rhythm is suspended as Wilson and Ballard sing "Think it over," answered by Ross's pleading "After I've been good to you," all over the tonic chord. This is the linking phrase we heard in the intro.

This four-bar segment ends the verse and serves as a transition to the chorus. After the chorus, it returns as a transition to the following verse. Because it is repeated throughout the song, the phrase also takes on the role of a second refrain (in addition to the chorus). There is, however, one difference between the linking phrase following the verse and the one following the chorus. The verse phrase features call-and-response vocals; the chorus phrase is sung in unison.

The chorus is a dramatic foil to the verse. It is both simpler and bolder in its effect. The sudden shift from the major mode of the linking phrase to the minor chord on the chorus's downbeat heightens the exclamation "Stop!" The harmonic phrase structure is straightforward, just a single diatonic phrase repeated once with all voices singing in unison. In contrast to the strong rhymes of the verse, the chorus has no rhymes at all. Overcome with emotion, the protagonist abandons poetic convention for a cry from the heart.

The basic mix texture changes little throughout the track. Most of the mid-range harmonic space is filled by the organ. A vibraphone etches out a ringing high-end part. The snare drum hits most quarter-note pulses with other instruments accenting staccato backbeats, and the low-end is filled by not only bass and kick drum but also baritone saxophone. At times one instrument or another becomes a bit more prominent, but the track's narrative is carried primarily by the lead vocal character, the song form, and the interaction among the voices, which follows a particular pattern. In the introduction we hear the full-on power of the voices in unison. The verse begins with the lead voice on its own, highlighting the track's central character. The backing voices enter in the verse's second phrase with their soul-styled "Baby, baby," followed in the third phrase by a legato melody. In the fourth phrase, they sing call-and-response with the lead. Finally, in the chorus and interlude, all voices sing in unison once again.

Listening Guide

"Stop! In the Name of Love" (Lamont Dozier, Edward Holland, Brian Holland), Motown Records (mono)
Recorded at Hitsville U.S.A. Studio A, Detroit, January 1965
Diana Ross (lead voice), Florence Ballard, Mary Wilson, the Andantes (backing voices), Johnny Griffith (organ), Joe Messina (guitar), James Gitten (vibraphone), Mike Terry (baritone saxophone), James Jamerson (bass), Benny Benjamin (drums)
Producers: Eddie Holland, Lamont Dozier, Brian Holland
Charts: Hot 100 #1, Hot R&B Singles #2
Key: C
Meter: 4/4

Time	Section	Lyric Cue	Listen For
0:00	Intro (4+4)	"Stop!"	Organ glissando leads in to **chorus** hook. Voices in unison.
			Full instrumental texture.
0:10			Linking phrase, instruments only.
0:19	Verse 1 (16)	"Baby, baby"	Phrase 1: Lead voice alone.
			Non-diatonic chords in bars 3 and 4.
0:28		"I watch you"	Phrase 2: Backing voices enter ("Baby baby").
			Restores diatonic stability.
0:36		"But this time"	Phrase 3: Variation on phrase 1.
			Backing vocals sing legato descending line.
0:44		"Think it over"	Phrase 4: Linking phrase as in **intro**; call-and-response between backing singers and lead.
0:52	Chorus 1 (8+4)	"Stop!"	Like the first phrase of the **intro**; repeated once.
1:08		"Think it over"	Linking phrase; voices in unison.

Time	Section	Lyric Cue	Listen For
1:17	Verse 2 (16)	"I've known of your"	Similar to **verse 1**.
1:51	Chorus 2 (8+4)	"Stop!"	Similar to **chorus 1**.
2:07		"Think it over"	Linking phrase.
2:16	Verse 3 (12)	"I've tried so hard"	Similar to previous **verses**; no linking phrase.
2:32	Chorus (fade)	"Stop!"	After first phrase lead voice breaks out of the unison texture with "Baby think it over"; no linking phrase.

13.2. "THE TRACKS OF MY TEARS" (1965)

THE MIRACLES

The Miracles—Smokey Robinson (lead), Ronnie White, Claudette Rogers, and her cousin Bobby Rogers—were one of the many young neighborhood vocal groups in Detroit. They met Berry Gordy in 1957 when he was writing songs for Jackie Wilson and the idea of starting a record company had yet to take hold in his mind. From the start, however, Gordy was impressed with Robinson's voice, as well as his zeal for songwriting (skill would come with time). He began producing Miracles recordings, which were licensed to various labels.

Robinson, the only Motown artist to also become a company vice president, was instrumental not only in Motown's initial success but in its founding. When he saw how little income was generated by the Miracles' licensing deals with such companies as End and Chess, he suggested that Gordy start a label of his own. Once Tamla was up and running, the Miracles produced the company's first million-seller in 1961 with "Shop Around," cowritten by Robinson and Gordy. Robinson also wrote and produced the Motown label's first number-one pop hit, Mary Wells' "My Guy." He produced hits for the Temptations and several other Motown acts, as well as the Miracles (later renamed Smokey Robinson and the Miracles), who themselves would chart twenty-seven top-forty hits through 1971. As writer, performer, producer, and executive, Robinson was a unique figure at Motown and a central pillar of Gordy's entertainment empire.

Miracles hits include "You've Really Got a Hold on Me," "Going to a Go-Go," and "I Second That Emotion." The arrangements vary to suit the song, but whether lavish or lean, the distinctive core of the tracks was always Robinson's voice, the sweetest of Motown's male singers. On "The Tracks of My Tears" the voice's tenderness makes the heartbreak all the more palpable.

The track opens with a soft-focus multi-guitar texture followed by the fuller sound of bass, drums, tambourine, and backing singers. This warm, delicate intro sets a mood of vulnerability, reflecting the song's lyrics and the protagonist's state of mind. The intro texture continues into verse one as Robinson begins his confessional story in a confidential tone. With this intimate setting the singer invites listeners into what feels like a private place.

At the chorus, the track's texture becomes much thicker and never quite returns to the initial intimacy. As the chorus breaks into a cry of pain, brass, strings, and backing voices surge. The protagonist's anguish is emphasized with a triplet figure on the lines "*Look at my* face," "*Looks out of* place," and "*Ea-sy to* trace." These figures are doubled in rhythmic unison by the instruments. In fact, the orchestral texture extends the triplets past the end of the vocal phrases, driving the music each time to an arrival on the V chord.

In the brief interlude following the chorus, the protagonist cries out ("I need you") before moving on to verse two. The second verse begins with a texture similar to verse one, though a bit thicker and with some low-end reinforcement from the saxophone. The thicker texture is a residue left over from the previous chorus. This verse also introduces a new texture in its second phrase, as the backing voices repeat their intro parts, joined by a new violin line.

The bridge is the track's longest section and serves as the dramatic climax. It begins with a one-bar harmonic loop (taken from the interlude), over which Robinson and the Miracles trade phrases. The lyrics develop the song's contrast of inner feelings and outer appearances. When the Miracles sing "outside," Robinson answers that he is "masquerading." When they sing "inside," he admits his "hope is fading." After repeating the loop eight times, the harmonic rhythm is suspended as Robinson, the other Miracles, and all of the instruments repeat the triplet figure from the chorus insistently for two bars, driving home the song's central point ("My smile is my makeup"). The harmonic color in these bars is a shade of minor, the track's first and only minor-mode moment.

The climax is further heightened by its contrast with the song's prevailing harmonic rhythm, which has been unchanging up to this point. The harmonic resources for intro, verse, chorus, and interlude amount to only three chords, which always move on the "and" of the second beat of each measure, creating a clock-like regularity (see figure 13.1). The bridge's break in this rhythmic pattern seems to reflect the protagonist's own arrival at an emotional breaking point.

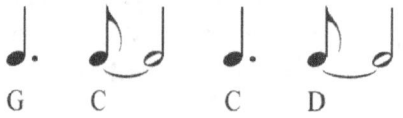

Figure 13.1. "The Tracks of My Tears": Harmonic Rhythm.

Listening Guide

"The Tracks of My Tears" (William Robinson, Warren Moore, Marvin Tarplin), Tamla Records (mono). Also appears on the album *Going to a Go-Go*.

Recorded at Hitsville U.S.A. Studio A, Detroit, May 1965

Smokey Robinson (lead voice), Claudette Robinson, Pete Moore, Ronnie White, Bobby Rogers (voice), Marv Tarplin (guitar), Funk Brothers (guitar, saxophone, bass, drums, percussion), and members of the Detroit Symphony (strings, brass)

Producer: Smokey Robinson

Charts: Hot 100 #16, Top Selling R&B Singles #2, Top LP's #8, Hot R&B LP's #1

Key: G

Meter 4/4

Time	Section	Lyric Cue	Listen For
0:00	Intro (8)		Multi-guitar texture.
0:10			Guitar phrase repeats, joined by bass, drums, tambourine, and backing vocals.
0:20	Verse 1 (8)	"People say"	Intimate vocal; **intro** texture continues; backing voices out.
0:40	Chorus (8)	"So take a good"	Full texture, includes brass, strings, saxophones, glockenspiel, backing voices; triplet figure.
1:00	Interlude (2)	"I need you"	Voices sing call-and-response.
1:05	Verse 2 (8)	"Since you left"	Fuller texture than **verse 1**.
1:15		"Although she may"	Backing voices repeat **intro** part; new violin part.
1:25	Chorus (8)	"So take a good"	Similar to previous **chorus**.
1:44	Interlude (3)	"I need you"	Similar to previous **interlude**.
1:49			1-bar stop
1:52	Bridge (11)	"Yeah"	1-bar harmonic loop as in **interlude**; call-and-response in voices.
2:11		"My smile is"	Climax: instruments and voices in unison; minor mode; suspended harmonic rhythm; extended triplet passage.
2:18	Chorus (8+8+fade)	"Baby take a good"	Double **chorus** to fade.

13.3. "I HEARD IT THROUGH THE GRAPEVINE" (1967)

MARVIN GAYE

Marvin Gaye, who hailed originally from Washington, DC, was signed to Motown in 1961. He had recently been a member of Harvey Fuqua's Moonglows vocal group and followed Fuqua to Detroit following the group's breakup. Hearing Gaye sing at the 1960 Motown Christmas party, Gordy was impressed with his moody, soulful style and signed him to the label. Gaye's rise to stardom, however, would be circuitous.

Gaye saw himself as a jazz-pop crooner of Tin Pan Alley–type material. "My dream," he said, "was to become Frank Sinatra. . . . He was the king I longed to be."[4] Gaye's first Motown album, *The Soulful Moods of Marvin Gaye*, included traditional pop fare by such songwriters as Irving Berlin, Cole Porter, and Rodgers and Hart. But the record, produced by Gordy himself, was a commercial failure, and gradually Gaye moved in a direction suggested by his childhood experience in a Pentecostal church called the House of God, where music was a thing not to be controlled but unleashed. After three failed singles, the soulful exuberance of Gaye's self-penned breakthrough hit "Stubborn Kind of Fellow" (1962) established the style that would make him one of Motown's biggest stars. He worked with the company's top producers—Holland-Dozier-Holland, Smokey Robinson, Norman Whitfield—charting seventeen top-forty pop singles through the 1960s. He collaborated on another ten top-forty hits with Kim Weston, Mary Wells, and Tammi Terrell. Motown tried stubbornly to establish Gaye as a modern Nat "King" Cole, releasing such albums as *Hello Broadway* and *A Tribute to the Great Nat "King" Cole*, but it was his pop-soul style that produced the hits. In the 1970s, Gaye himself moved into a producer's role, overseeing production on his classic albums, *What's Going On* (1971) and *Let's Get It On* (1973).

"I Heard It through the Grapevine" was written by Barrett Strong and Norman Whitfield, who also produced the record. Whitfield had worked with Gaye as early as 1963, cowriting the single "Pride and Joy." But Whitfield's real run of success began when he was assigned to produce records for the Temptations beginning in 1966. With such hits as "Ain't Too Proud to Beg," "(I Know) I'm Losing You," "Runaway Child, Running Wild," and "I Can't Get Next to You," he worked with the group to cultivate a funkier Motown sound (funkier, too, than the Temptations' previous work with Smokey Robinson as producer—e.g., "The Way You Do the Things You Do," "My Girl"). The style was cutting edge, often labeled "psychedelic soul." (Other contemporary psychedelic soul artists include Sly Stone and the Chambers Brothers.) Featuring intricate arrangements, emotional complexity, and often an aggressive rhythmic momentum, the style was an early incarnation of what would become known, aptly, as funk music.

"I Heard It through the Grapevine" was Gaye's first number-one hit and the biggest seller among several versions Whitfield produced, including one for the Miracles and one for Gladys Knight and the Pips. Remarkably, Gladys Knight's version was also a top hit, reaching number two on the pop chart nearly a year earlier than Gaye's. But although the song proved extremely popular and lucrative for the company, it initially had a hard time seeing the light of day. Gordy thought little of the song and refused to release the first "Grapevine" recording, the Miracles' version. Gaye's came next and again Gordy refused to release it. He finally relented with the Gladys Knight version and was happily surprised by its success. Still reluctant about Gaye's version, Gordy finally allowed it to be released, but only as an album track on *In the Groove*. Disc jockeys, playing the track from the album, received so many requests that they convinced the company to release it as a single. In the end, it sold more copies than any previous Motown record.

The record has an ominous quality, reflecting the protagonist's sense of impending loss. The introduction sets the scene: a chillingly subdued electric piano riff in the Dorian mode, a kick drum rhythm that sounds like a beating heart, a tambourine emulating a rattlesnake, and a French horn scream. One after another, each sound thickens the sense of apprehension. Gaye sings in a high, raspy voice that underscores the protagonist's fearful uncertainty. It was Whitfield's idea—resisted initially by Gaye—to pitch the song in such a high vocal register in order to intensify the sense of emotional urgency. The raw emotions Gaye imparts were reflections of his real-life marital difficulties. "I believed every word of the song," he said. "It *was* happening to me. The doubting, the friends whispering in my ear, the suspicions."[5]

The French horn crescendo to an octave leap—a gesture Gaye himself repeats with the words "some other *guy*" and "losing *you*"—is an especially spooky effect, like a sound of alarm. It is also a striking timbral signature. The horn returns in the brief instrumental break to reprise this timbral theme. The track's other prominent orchestral component is the violin arrangement, which varies from one section to the next. In the verse, the violins, in their low register, play melodic fragments that curl seductively around the vocal phrases. In the pre-chorus they move to a higher register and play a more sustained line. In the chorus they take a more incisive rhythmic role, joining the voice with a unison rhythm on the word "grapevine." Finally, in the interlude, violin tremolos keep the track on edge even as the protagonist takes a breather.

The rhythm track adds a murkiness to the texture by playing the backbeats on the toms, a darker sound than the snare. The backbeats are reinforced by sharp attacks on brass and guitar, which are mixed softly enough to add just a hint of edginess. The track's texture changes in the interludes. The rhythm section thins out as the toms stop playing, the kick returns to the heartbeat rhythm of the intro, and the groove percolates lightly in the congas. Meanwhile, that subdued piano riff momentarily cools the track's emotional heat until the next verse, when Gaye once again raises the temperature.

Listening Guide

"I Heard It through the Grapevine" (Norman Whitfield, Barrett Strong), Tamla Records (mono). Also appears on the album *In the Groove*.
Recorded at Hitsville U.S.A. Studio A, Detroit, April 1966
Marvin Gaye (voice), the Andantes: Jackie Hicks, Marlene Barrow, and Louvain Demps (backing voices), Funk Brothers (electric piano, guitar, bass, drums, brass, percussion), members of the Detroit Symphony Orchestra (French horn, violins)
Producer: Norman Whitfield
Charts: Hot 100 #1, Top 100 Soul Singles #1, Top LP's #63, Hot R&B LP's #2
Key: E♭ minor
Meter: 4/4

Time	Section	Lyric Cue	Listen For
0:00	**Intro** (10)		Successive entries: electric piano, kick drum/hi-hat, tambourine, brass/guitar, French horn, drum fill/bass.
			Piano plays signature Dorian riff; brass add harmonies to the riff.
0:21	**Verse 1** (8)	"I bet you're wondering"	Texture focuses on voice; violins "curl" around vocal phrases.
			Backbeat on toms is doubled by brass and guitar.
0:38	**Pre-Chorus** (4)	"It took me"	Backing voices enter.
			Sustained notes in violins.
0:46	**Chorus** (8)	"I heard it"	Rhythmic violin part sometimes doubles lead voice.
1:02	**Interlude** (4)		Piano riff and violin tremolo.
			Backing voices sing title lyrics.
			Thinner rhythm texture brings out congas.
1:10	**Verse 2** (8)	"I know a man"	Similar to **verse** 1.
1:26	**Pre-Chorus** (4)	"You could have"	Similar to **pre-chorus** 1.

Time	Section	Lyric Cue	Listen For
1:34	**Chorus** (8)	"I heard it"	Similar to **chorus** 1.
1:51	**Interlude** (4)		Similar texture to previous **interlude**.
1:59	**Break** (4)		Full rhythm texture as in **verse**. Violin and French horn featured.
2:07	**Verse 3** (8)	"People say believe"	Similar to **verse** 1.
2:23	**Pre-Chorus** (4)	"Do you plan"	Similar to **pre-chorus** 1.
2:31	**Chorus** (8)	"I heard it"	Similar to **chorus** 1.
2:47	**Coda** (fade)	"Yeah"	Based on **interlude**. Toms backbeat continues without brass/guitar doubling. Piano replaces riff with trill; riff remains in bass.

13.4. "SUPERSTITION" (1972)

STEVIE WONDER

Berry Gordy signed Stevie Wonder to Motown in 1961. Wonder was eleven years old. The following year he recorded the single "Fingertips," which would become Motown's second number-one hit. The record's cover trumpeted what seemed to be typical record company hype: Little Stevie Wonder the Twelve Year Old Genius. In this case, however, they were not exaggerating. Through the 1960s, Wonder would go on to record such hits as "Uptight," "I Was Made to Love Her," and "My Cherie Amour" within the Motown production system.

In the early, 1970s, however, Wonder took full artistic control. He began producing his own records, writing the songs and playing many of the instruments himself. In one of rock's great creative bursts, he turned out five remarkable albums in five years (*Music of My Mind, Talking Book, Innervisions, Fulfillingness' First Finale, Songs in the Key of Life*).

"Superstition" is from the album *Talking Book* (1972). It offers a textbook example of funk rhythm. Just as the rock and roll groove had shifted from triplets to straight eighth notes in the 1950s, funk, which emerged in the later 1960s, shifted the emphasis to sixteenth notes, peppering the rhythmic texture with syncopations. With each beat subdivided into four instead of two, funk arrangements sizzle with rhythmic electricity and complex rhythmic interplay.

The track's texture is built on a solid foundation of steady quarter notes played on the kick drum—the so-called four-on-the-flour groove—with snare hits on each backbeat. As the intro plays, only the hi-hat lightly tapping out the sixteenth-note subdivisions hints at what is about to happen. The hi-hat also clues us to a further rhythmic intricacy that underlies the track's overall feel. Notice how it has a slight swing feeling. This is not the kind of swing we have heard on tracks thus far, which works with eighth-note subdivisions. On "Superstition" the swing is at the level of the sixteenth note.

After four bars establishing this simple basic rhythm, an aggressively syncopated keyboard texture erupts filled with staccato accents. The components include the main riff (R), a subsidiary riff (L), and assorted "stabs" (i.e., short, accented chords). Wonder plays all of these in a series of overdubs using a Hohner Clavinet, a keyboard with a sharply percussive sound.

The keyboard parts are anchored by a Moog synthesizer bass part that doubles the kick drum rhythm. The Moog part repeats the tonic note $E^\flat$, supporting the Clavinet riffs, which all use an $E^\flat$ minor pentatonic pitch collection or blues scale ($E^\flat$, $G^\flat$, $A^\flat$, $B^\flat$, $D^\flat$). There are no chord changes until the refrain, which forms an extended concluding cadence for the verse and provides relief from the relentless pentatonic sonority.

After eight bars of the verse, another element is added to the mix: a horn riff played by trumpet and saxophone, which is doubled by the Moog bass. Like the Clavinet riff, this one is rhythmically animated, employing staccato accents and syncopations at the sixteenth-note level of subdivision. The riff also uses the minor pentatonic.

In the refrain the horns switch to major mode sonorities with a series of chords (V, VI, V, $^\flat$V, IV, V) that are played in long notes on beats one and three. After the cadence that marks the refrain's climax, a vamp brings back the intro/verse keyboard texture. But now we hear yet another element: a third horn part. This time it's a melody of sustained quarter notes, played mostly on the beat. In addition to the rhythmic contrast with the verse riff, this melody also differs in its pitch content. Its use of the note C marks it as Dorian instead of minor pentatonic.

The track ends with an extended coda, which introduces one last horn part playing sustained half notes. This melody also introduces another new pitch, the second scale degree F, which lands prominently on successive downbeats. Together, the track's four horn riffs, each associated with a particular section, offer both rhythmic and pitch variety over the repeating keyboard riff. In a sort of thematic recap, the coda includes three of the riffs played sequentially over the repeated keyboard texture (see Listening Guide). The coda also adds a nice stereo effect. Notice how riffs three and four occur first on the left side of the mix followed by a repeat on the right side. This new sensory effect makes a nice finishing touch to the mix.

Four Contrasting Horn Riffs Associated with the Track's Different Sections

Riff 1—Verse (syncopated line with staccato accents, minor pentatonic)

Riff 2—Refrain (sustained chords, V, VI, V, ♭V, IV, V)

Riff 3—Vamp (sustained line in quarter notes, Dorian)

Riff 4—Coda (sustained line in half notes with emphasis on second scale degree F)

Wonder's vocal performance on "Superstition" is charged with a soulful intensity that perfectly suits the song's lyrics and the track's hard funk vibe. It's worth noting that this is but one vocal character among a broad range in Wonder's repertory. To get a fuller sense of his expansive vocal expression, check out the sweetness of "My Cherie Amour," the ecstasy of "Isn't She Lovely," the rage of "Living for the City," and the vulnerability of "Love's in Need of Love Today."

Listening Guide

"Superstition" (Stevie Wonder), Tamla Records (stereo). Also appears on the album *Talking Book*.
Recorded at Electric Lady Studios, New York City, 1972
Stevie Wonder (voice, Hohner Clavinet, Moog bass, drums), Trevor Laurence (saxophone), Steve Madaio (trumpet)
Producer: Stevie Wonder
Engineers and synthesizer programmers: Robert Margouleff, Malcolm Cecil
Charts: Hot 100 #1, Best Selling Soul Singles #1, Top LP's #3, Best Selling Soul LP's #1
Key: E♭ minor
Meter: 4/4

Time	Section	Lyric Cue	Listen For
0:00	Intro (4+8)		Four bars of drums establish groove foundation.
			Multiple Clavinet parts:
			1. Main riff (R).
			2. Subsidiary riff (L).
			3. Intermittent chord stabs (L and R).

continued on next page

Time	Section	Lyric Cue	Listen For
0:30	**Verse 1** (8+8)	"Very superstitious"	Clavinet texture with vocal.
			Static harmony.
0:50			Horn riff 1 (syncopated with staccato accents).
1:09	**Refrain** (4)	"When you believe"	Harmony changes.
			Horn riff 2 (sustained chords).
1:18	**Vamp** (4)		Horn riff 3 (sustained quarter note melody).
1:28	**Verse 2** (8+8)	"Very superstitious"	Similar to **verse 1**.
2:06	**Refrain** (4)		Similar to **refrain 1**.
2:15	**Break** (12)		4 bars like **vamp** with horn riff 3.
2:24			4 bars like **refrain** with horn riff 2.
2:33			4 bars like **intro**, no horns.
2:43	**Verse 3** (8+8)	"Very superstitious"	Similar to previous **verses**.
3:21	**Refrain** (4)	"When you believe"	Similar to previous **refrains**.
3:30	**Coda**		4 bars—Riff 3 (L) repeated on R.
3:40			4 bars—Riff 4 (L) repeated on R.
3:49			4 bars—Riff 3 (L) repeated on R.
3:58			8 bars—Riff 1 (L) repeated three times on L and R.
4:16			4 bars—Riff 4 (L) repeated on R.
			Fade to following track.

NOTES

1. Berry Gordy, *To Be Loved: The Music, the Magic, the Memories of Motown* (New York: Warner Books, 1994), 169.

2. Quoted in Kwaku Person-Lynn, "Insider Perspectives on the American Afrikan Popular Music Industry and Black Radio," in *California Soul: Music of African Americans in the West,* ed. Jacqueline Cogdell DjeDje and Eddie S. Meadows (Berkeley: University of California Press, 1998), 187.

3. Quoted in J. Randy Taraborrelli, *Diana Ross: A Biography* (New York: Citadel Press, 2007), 42.

4. Quoted in David Ritz, *Divided Soul: The Life of Marvin Gaye* (New York: Da Capo Press, 2003), 29.

5. Quoted in Ritz, 122.

FURTHER READING

Early, Gerald. *One Nation Under a Groove: Motown and American Culture.* Ann Arbor: University of Michigan Press, 2004.

Flory, Andrew. *I Hear a Symphony: Motown and Crossover R&B*. Ann Arbor: University of Michigan Press, 2017.

George, Nelson. *Where Did Our Love Go?: The Rise and Fall of the Motown Sound*. Urbana: University of Illinois Press, 2007.

Gordy, Berry. *To Be Loved: The Music, the Magic, the Memories of Motown*. New York: Warner Books, 1994.

Smith, Suzanne E. *Dancing in the Street: Motown and the Cultural Politics of Detroit*. Cambridge, MA: Harvard University Press, 2001.

FURTHER LISTENING

Contours, "Do You Love Me" (Gordy, 1962)
Four Tops, "I Can't Help Myself (Sugar Pie, Honey Bunch)" (Motown, 1965)
Jacksons, "I Want You Back" (Motown, 1969)
Martha and the Vandellas, "Dancing in the Street" (Gordy, 1964)
David Ruffin, "My Whole World Ended (the Moment You Left Me)" (Motown, 1969)
Barrett Strong, "Money (That's What I Want)" (Anna, 1960)
Temptations, "I Can't Get Next to You" (Gordy, 1969)
Jr. Walker and the All Stars, "Shotgun" (Soul, 1965)
Mary Wells, "My Guy" (Motown, 1964)
Gladys Knight and the Pips, "I Heard It through the Grapevine" (Soul, 1967)

14

ROCK'S GOSPEL STRAIN
Southern Soul

Soul music grew out of the secularization of black gospel music. Many of the star soul singers began their careers with gospel groups: Sam Cooke with the Soul Stirrers, Wilson Pickett with the Violinaires, Solomon Burke with the Gospel Cavaliers, and James Brown with the Gospel Starlighters. For young black musicians, the church and its Sunday ritual filled with singing provided their earliest musical training. The soul repertory, too, was indebted to gospel. Ray Charles's 1954 hit "I've Got a Woman" was a rewrite of the gospel song "It Must Be Jesus," which had been recorded by the Southern Tones earlier that year. Don Covay's "Chain of Fools," covered in this chapter, was a rewrite of a gospel song called "Pains of Life."

The great gospel singer Mahalia Jackson called gospel "trial-and-tribulation music," and soul is likewise infused with a true-to-life feeling and fervent attitude. While doo wop was a new strain of R&B by and for kids, soul music brought gritty adult R&B to the pop mainstream. It took a while for the young audience to learn the appeal of such intense emotional expression. In the '50s, rock and roll was more concerned with thrilling restless teenagers. Ray Charles wrote in his autobiography that in the 1950s, "I never considered myself part of rock 'n' roll. . . . My stuff was more adult. It was more difficult for teenagers to relate to."[1] But as the first rock and roll generation began to mature, deeper R&B began to infiltrate the pop charts. Charles finally crossed over, in a big way, in 1959 with "What'd I Say." In the early '60s, thanks to singers such as Chuck Jackson, Solomon Burke, Jerry Butler, and Tina Turner, full-blooded passion became an increasingly familiar sound in the rock universe.

The roots of soul music are in the South. Even stars who grew up in the North were steeped in a southern musical culture brought to such cities as Detroit and Chicago by black people seeking better social and economic conditions. The quintessential soul labels, Stax and its subsidiary, Volt, were based in Memphis. The New York soul powerhouse, Atlantic Records, often recorded its artists in the South or imported southern musicians to New York, convinced that southern culture lent a unique earthiness to the music. Urban polish might diminish the effect. The instrumental timbres, the grooves, and the recorded textures have an expressive graininess that suits the raw, testifying quality of the vocals. As Stax studio guitarist Steve Cropper described it, the Stax sound "was a southern sound, a below-the-Bible-Belt sound. It was righteous and nasty. Which to our way of thinking was pretty close to life itself."[2]

Soul music's popularity grew rapidly. By 1967, it was a common flower in the Summer of Love's musical garden, growing alongside folk rock, psychedelic rock, and the year's most ambitious pop statement, the Beatles' *Sgt. Pepper's Lonely Hearts Club Band*. In style and sensibility, southern soul seems a world apart. The contrast was typified by Otis Redding and his band when they appeared at the Monterey Pop Festival wearing matching green suits amid a sea of psychedelic hippie regalia. Yet as the festival's appreciative audience made clear, rock's inclusive embrace knew few bounds in the 1960s. This down-to-earth music, as psychically potent as it was entertaining, enriched rock music with a heavy dose of intense, grown-up, and decidedly black expression.

14.1. "IN THE MIDNIGHT HOUR" (1965)

WILSON PICKETT

> Early one morning I ran out and hollered. My voice echoed down through the swamps and I thought, "Uh-oh. This is it."[3]
>
> —Wilson Pickett

Wilson Pickett was born in Alabama. As a teenager he moved to Detroit, where he joined his first group, a gospel outfit called the Violinaires. The group toured with such stars as the Soul Stirrers and the Swan Silvertones. He moved on to a secular vocal group, the Falcons, composed of other gospel alumni with whom he recorded "I Found a Love," a raw, funky track that reached number six on the R&B charts in 1962. With Pickett's hoarse, fervent shouting, the record was a blast of sanctified soul and a forecast of things to come. With that record still on the charts, Pickett recorded a solo demo, which he sent to Jerry Wexler at Atlantic, one of the oldest indie labels specializing in R&B. Wexler was impressed with both Wilson's voice and his songwriting ability and signed him to the label in 1964.

Wexler's production relationship with Pickett is an example of his role as a self-described "servant of the project." As he saw things, it was his job not to impose his will but "to enhance—meaning find the right song, the right arranger, the right band, the right studio—in short, do whatever it takes to get the best out of the artist."[4] Although it was clear to Wexler that Pickett "had that ability to transfer a slice of his soul to tape," as trumpeter Wayne Jackson put it, Pickett's first year at Atlantic produced no hits.[5] Part of the problem was that Wexler and Pickett had different ideas about suitable repertory. Finally, Wexler changed the subject and arranged for the two of them to get out of New York and take a trip to Memphis. He had a distribution arrangement with Stax, a Memphis label, and liked the sounds coming out of owner/engineer Jim Stewart's studio. The house band, Booker T. and the MG's, was terrific and Wexler loved the way they worked. Unlike the tightly scripted, three-hour New York sessions, these musicians had a loose way of working things out in the studio as **head arrangements**, taking their time. Their rapport, Wexler wrote in his memoir, "was as close as a classical string quartet's."[6] When the two arrived in Memphis, Wexler deposited Pickett in a hotel room with MG's guitarist and songwriter Steve Cropper. He left them with "a bottle of Jack Daniel's and the simple exhortation—'Write!'."[7] One of the songs they came up with was "In the Midnight Hour," which would become Pickett's first Atlantic hit.

For Wexler, it was the overall feel that made the MG's sound so infectious. "The feel was everything," he wrote.[8] "In the Midnight Hour" illustrates what he meant. The record is based on the feel of the groove, the feel of the sound, the feel of Pickett's vocal. As in most soul music, whose complexity lies in rhythmic interactions and vocal pyrotechnics, the feel comes through best when the song and arrangement are uncluttered. Accordingly, the track is based on a two-chord vamp on I and IV, which plays through the first eight bars of the verse. In the ninth bar (0:31 for verse one), the harmony finally moves to V and then IV before returning to the vamp. Each verse is built on this spare two-part structure.

Yet while the track's simple harmonic resources and musical form seem to indicate a predictable narrative, this is not the case. First of all, the straightforward plan leaves room for the dynamism and spontaneity of Pickett's performance. Also, the diatonic harmony is enriched with a persistent flatted seventh chord (D) that occurs in the intro, turnaround, and instrumental break. (The intro also uses the flatted third, G.) This chord injects a blues feeling into the harmonic texture that fits the arrangement's low-down quality and, of course, Pickett's bluesy performance.

Further, the horns provide a series of different textures that give each section a distinct flavor. After an introductory fanfare, the horns step back for the first half of verse one. In the second half they come in with sustained chords and then, when the vamp returns, they play a riff fragment. In verse two this fragment is developed as an accompaniment to the vocal. In the instrumental break the horns take the spotlight. In verse three they play a variation of the riff from verse two.

The track's groove was inspired by Wexler, a nonmusician but a man with sharp recording instincts. It occurred to him that a popular mid-1960s dance, the Jerk, in particular something about the dance's arm movements, might indicate to the band a rhythmic feel he sensed but could not convey in words. He left the control room and went into the studio where the band was working up the arrangement. He then began to dance his idea as the musicians, uncertain of what he was after, did their best to match his movements. In doing so, Cropper and drummer Al Jackson hit the backbeats with a deliberation that not only produced a heavy accent but also landed just after the beat, a few milliseconds late.

It was a eureka moment. The band agreed that the delayed backbeat feel gave the performance a unique rhythmic character. "It turned us on to a heck of a thing," Cropper recalled of what might have seemed a trivial change.[9] The MG's would use the technique again and again on subsequent records for various artists. Together with the track's rich low-end, the bass reinforced by baritone saxophone, the groove gives the record a signature foundation. And like the horn arrangement it changes in the course of the track, adding another element to the track's narrative form. Notice how the groove feels different in the instrumental break, where the snare part goes to steady quarter notes. Here, the snare plays squarely on the beats, changing the sense of flow. When the break ends and the voice returns, listen to how the groove shifts back to the feel created by the delayed backbeat.

Listening Guide

"**In the Midnight Hour**" (Wilson Pickett, Steve Cropper), Atlantic Records (mono). Also appears on the album *In the Midnight Hour*.
Recorded at Stax studio in Memphis, May 1965
Wilson Pickett (voice), Donald "Duck" Dunn (bass), Steve Cropper (guitar), Al Jackson Jr. (drums), Wayne Jackson (trumpet), Andrew Love and Charles "Packy" Axton (tenor saxophone), Floyd Newman (baritone saxophone)

Producers: Jerry Wexler, Jim Stewart
Engineer: Jim Stewart
Charts: Hot 100 #21, Top Selling R&B Singles #1, Top LP's #107, Top Selling R&B LP's #4
Key: E
Meter: 4/4

Time	Section	Lyric Cue	Listen For
0:00		Intro (4+2)	Measured drum roll; bluesy horn fanfare.
0:09			2-bar vamp; snare/guitar backbeat accents are slightly delayed; bass plays arpeggios reinforced with a pickup riff on the baritone saxophone.
0:13	Verse 1 (8+7)	"I'm gonna wait"	Vocal accompanied by vamp.
0:31		"I'm gonna take you"	Sustained horn chords.
0:39			Vamp with horn riff.
0:46	Turnaround (2)		♭VII chord (D).
0:50	Verse 2 (8+7)	"I'm gonna wait"	Vocal accompanied by vamp with added horn riffs.
1:07		"You're the only"	Sustained horn chords.
1:16			Vamp with horn riff.
1:23	Turnaround (2)		
1:27	Break (8)		Horns in unison; groove feel shifts slightly as snare plays straight time on every quarter note.
1:43	Verse 3 (19+ fade)	"I'm gonna wait"	Groove shifts again as delayed backbeat returns. Vamp plays throughout. Horn riffs are twice as frequent as in **verse 2**.

14.2. "CHAIN OF FOOLS" (1967)

ARETHA FRANKLIN

Aretha Franklin created the paradigm for the gospel-influenced female pop star, an example followed by such heirs as Whitney Houston and Mariah Carey. She seemed an overnight sensation when, in 1967, she began charting a string of hits that would win her eight consecutive Grammy Awards as best female R&B vocalist. But she was already an old hand in the industry and an old soul in life. "I might be just 26," she said, "but I'm an old woman in disguise, 26 goin' on 65."[10] Her voice conveyed a sense of truth-telling based on personal experience. It resonated far and wide—with black activists as well as white college kids. In 1968 Franklin was featured on a *Time* magazine cover. The accompanying article, which identified her by the title of her third Atlantic album, *Lady Soul*, spoke to her unmistakable authenticity: "She does not seem to be performing so much as bearing witness to a reality so simple and compelling that she could not possibly fake it."[11]

Franklin was recognized as a powerful singer even as a child performing in her father C. L. Franklin's church in Detroit and in his traveling revival show. (C. L. Franklin was born and raised in Mississippi, eventually settling into a Baptist ministry in Memphis, where Aretha was born.) By 1960, at age eighteen, Aretha Franklin had a Columbia Records contract and was singing a variety of material set to pop arrangements. Her expressive style was clearly miscast by the label's pop production department. As producers tried various approaches, Franklin sang with heart and a professional's commitment to craft. But while the emotional depth of her voice was never in question, Franklin's recordings met with little success. The setting was wrong. As John Hammond, the eminent record scout and producer who had signed her, saw the problem, "Columbia was a white company who misunderstood her genius."[12]

In 1967, when her Columbia contract expired, Jerry Wexler signed her to Atlantic. His first instinct was to get out of the way "to put Aretha back on piano and let the lady wail."[13] He wanted her to feel free to release the spirit he had heard in a recording made when she was fourteen, singing "Precious Lord" at her father's church. "The voice was not that of a child," he recalled, "but rather of an ecstatic hierophant."[14] Franklin had an apparent ability to give voice to every feeling in her deep well of emotional experience and Wexler wanted to capture it undiluted. At Atlantic she was "the central orchestrator of her own sound, the essential contributor and final arbiter of what fit or did not fit her musical persona."[15]

His next thought was that Franklin should record in the South. With Stax now reserving all studio time for its own artists, he decided on FAME Studio in Florence, Alabama, where the Muscle Shoals Rhythm Section was in residence. Wexler described the group as "that wonderful rhythm section of Alabama white boys who took a left turn at the blues."[16] The band worked in a similar way to the Stax musicians—loose, spontaneous, coming up with head arrangements on the spot and interacting as a single musical organism. The first record Franklin cut at FAME, "I Never Loved a Man (the Way I Love You)," became a top-ten pop hit and launched her on the path to stardom. "She started from zero . . . no one knew who she was," recalled Atlantic promoter Bob Rolontz. "That first record . . . in three months was a national treasure. She just exploded."[17] Thenceforth she would be universally known simply as Aretha.

As it happened, personal friction between Aretha's husband and studio owner Rick Hall made it impossible to return to FAME to cut any more tracks. Unwilling to lose the musical chemistry that produced the first record, Wexler brought the Muscle Shoals musicians to New York to record in Atlantic's studio, where "Chain of Fools" was cut. The song, written by Don Covay, is based on the gospel song "Pains of Life," recorded earlier in 1967 by E. Fair and the Sensational Gladys Davis Trio. The parallels include not only melodic similarity but also the chief rhyme. "Chain, chain, chain" is analogous to the original song's "Pain, pain, pain." The song has only one chord, yet its harmonic color is rich due to the proliferation of blues inflections. The major and minor versions of scale degree three alternate continually. Listen, for example, to the guitar intro. The first few notes are in C minor yet the final chord is C major. Similarly, Aretha begins "Chain, chain, chain" on E (major third above the tonic) but is joined on the last "chain" by the harmony voice singing E♭ (minor third). Along with the flatted fifth and the mixture of the major sixth and minor seventh scale degrees, as well as the microtonal vocal scoops, the track is awash in pitch complexities.

The track's groove is likewise a complex interplay of bass, drums, rhythm, and lead guitars. Like the Stax musicians, the band creates a signature communal groove that complements Aretha's performance. The lead guitar is a baritone, tuned a major third lower than a standard guitar. Its interaction with the bass fills the track's low-end with swampy atmosphere and balances the higher register of the voices. The snare drum part in the intro has a slight hiccup, which returns intermittently throughout the track. It involves moving the expected beat four accent an eighth note later, a funky bit of rhythmic trickiness to put things just slightly off balance. At the break, all instruments except the bass drum drop out, creating a space that Aretha fills with heightened emotional intensity.

The track opens with an introductory presentation of the song's chorus. The vocal arrangement is based on a call-and-response pattern between two sets of voices, which add not only pitch complexity but also rhythmic excitement and a sultry sexiness. The phrases (each two bars in length) are arranged as follows:

Phrase 1—Rising line with call-and-response imitation

Phrase 2—Falling line with call-and-response imitation

Phrase 3—Rising line answered by syncopated chords

Phrase 4—All voices in rhythmic unison for the "chain of fools" refrain

During the song's first verse the backing vocals drop out and Aretha plays a character obsessed with a faithless lover. Her bluesy wail is filled with vocal ornaments that give her performance a feeling of spontaneous expression, but it has a clear dramatic logic. The phrases follow a similar architecture to that of the chorus. Each is two bars in length, and they fall into pairs distinguished by register. The first and third phrases ("For five long years" and "But I found out") are higher in Aretha's range, while the second and fourth are lower. This arrangement is varied for verses three and four. The high register is emphasized in each of the first three phrases, moving lower only for the fourth phrase, which intensifies the emotional effect.

The instrumental arrangement frames Aretha's performance beautifully with its less-is-more conception. The baritone guitar answers her verse phrases with laconic coolness. And in the bridge, as Aretha raises the temperature, all instruments but the kick drum drop out, leaving a wide-open space for voices and handclaps. The backing voices remain cool, just lending support and a touch of syncopated swing. Meanwhile the lead vocal goes into a full-on blues wail, giving listeners a powerful shot of Lady Soul's truth telling.

Listening Guide

"**Chain of Fools**" (Don Covay). Atlantic Records (mono). Also appears on the album *Aretha: Lady Soul*.
Recorded at Atlantic Studios, New York City, June 1967
Aretha Franklin (voice and piano), Sweet Inspirations: Carolyn and Erma Franklin, Ellie Greenwich (backing voices), Jimmy Johnson (rhythm guitar), Joe South (baritone lead guitar), Spooner Oldham (electric piano), Tommy Cogbill (bass), Roger Hawkins (drums)
Producer: Jerry Wexler
Engineer: Tom Dowd
Chart: Hot 100, #2, Top Selling R&B Singles #1, Top LP's #2, Top Selling R&B LP's #1
Key: C blues
Meter: 4/4

Time	Section	Lyric Cue	Listen For
0:00	Intro		Baritone guitar riff, minor then major.
0:04	**Chorus** (8)	"Chain, chain, chain"	Phrase 1: Rising line; call-and-response imitation.
0:08			Phrase 2: Descending line; call-and-response imitation.
0:12			Phrase 3: Rising line answered by syncopated chords.
0:16		"Chain of fools"	Phrase 4: All voices in rhythmic unison.

continued on next page

Time	Section	Lyric Cue	Listen For
0:22	**Verse 1** (8)	"For five long years"	Each vocal phrase alternates between high and low registers. Guitars weave around vocal phrases.
0:38	**Verse 2** (8)	"You got me"	Similar to **verse 1**.
0:55	**Chorus 1** (4)	"Chain, chain, chain"	Phrases 1 and 4 only.
1:03	**Verse 3** (8)	"Every chain"	First three vocal phrases in high register; heightened emotional intensity.
1:19	**Bridge** (9½)	"You told me"	Pitched instruments out. Handclaps double kick drum on backbeats; strong beats omitted. Backing voices repeat syncopated chord.
1:39	**Chorus 2** (8)	"Chain, chain, chain"	Similar to **intro chorus**.
1:55	**Verse 4** (8)	"One of these mornings"	Similar to **verse 3**.
2:11	**Chorus 3** (16)	"Chain, chain, chain"	Double **chorus**.

14.3. "(SITTIN' ON) THE DOCK OF THE BAY" (1967)

OTIS REDDING

In the summer of 1967, at rock's psychedelic dawn, Otis Redding, along with his rhythm (Booker T. and the MG's) and horn sections (Mar-Keys), traveled to California to perform at the Monterey Pop Festival, an event showcasing a broad cross-section of contemporary sounds. The Who, the Byrds, the Mamas and the Papas, Jefferson Airplane, the Jimi Hendrix Experience, Big Brother and the Holding Company, Simon and Garfunkel, and Buffalo Springfield were among the performers at the three-day event. With bands representing genres from folk to blues to psychedelic to soul (not to mention some jazz and Indian music), the festival presented an opulent picture of rock's eclectic mosaic.

But most of the acts were white. Berry Gordy, for one, had declined to send any of Motown's acts to the festival, and Redding was one of only a handful of black artists to perform. As he watched the band warm up the audience before Redding came onstage, Jerry Wexler, who had convinced Redding's manager the gig would be a good opportunity, began to grow nervous about how Redding's style would be perceived by a crowd of mostly white kids tuned in to psychedelic and folk rock. The audience's enthusiastic reception showed that he needn't have worried.

Redding's success at Monterey was a declaration that amid the social and political upheavals of the time, rock music could be an inclusive cultural force.

During a follow-up trip to San Francisco for performances at the Fillmore Auditorium, Redding got the idea for "(Sittin' on) The Dock of the Bay," which he cowrote with Steve Cropper, who also produced the track. The record was something of a departure, and many at Stax, including label owner Jim Stewart, were wary. "Most people had doubts about it," recalled Redding's manager Phil Walden.[18] Perhaps it was too pop, too reserved, lacking the deep soul style Redding was famous for. But the singer was resolute. "I've got to change my style now. . . . I'm gonna be new."[19] Deeply impressed by the Beatles' *Sgt. Pepper's* album, and becoming more interested in multitrack recording and producing, he anticipated a new phase of his artistic evolution. He would not live to enjoy the fruits of his vision. He and many members of his touring band were killed in a plane crash soon after the recording was made (it had not yet been mixed). But in the winter of 1968 the record reached number one on the pop chart, his first to do so.

"Dock of the Bay" is one of Redding's many fine ballad recordings. Redding's are some of the most emotionally eloquent performances ever recorded, beginning with his first hit, "These Arms of Mine," and including such tracks as "Pain in My Heart," "That's How Strong My Love Is," I've Been Loving You Too Long," and "Try a Little Tenderness." Like his great influence, Little Richard, Redding could shout as if possessed with a testifying spirit. But he could also turn that intensity into intimate ballads laced with palpable vulnerability. On "Dock of the Bay" he takes a plaintive tone that connects listeners with the protagonist's deep sense of loneliness.

"Dock of the Bay" uses the signature Stax sounds that were by now fixtures in the pop soundscape thanks to hit records from Sam and Dave, Wilson Pickett, Eddie Floyd, Carla Thomas, and, of course, Redding himself, who was the company's commercial mainstay. The laid-back yet solid drum groove, the distinctive bassline, the spare electric guitar phrases, and the majestic horn arrangement are all characteristic.

The song has an unusual set of chord changes. Seven chords are used (G, A, B, C, D, E, F) and all are major. The tonic key is G, and since chords built on A, B, and E (ii, iii, and vi) are normally minor in this key, turning them into major chords requires non-diatonic pitches. F, the flatted seventh scale degree in G, also requires a non-diatonic note. Yet while the addition of four chromatic notes would seem to imply a sense of harmonic dynamism, the effect here is actually quite static. The two four-bar phrases in the verse are identical, each moving with chromatic passing tones in the bass and horn parts up from G to B and down from C to A. The vocal melody largely duplicates the chord roots, though it is ornamented with bluesy melismas. Like the ocean's waves and tides alluded to in lyrics and sound effects, the music rises only to fall back again.

The chorus is even more static. In a series of two-bar phrases the music repeatedly begins to move, only to return immediately to the tonic chord.

G | E | G | E | G | A | G | E

The music literally never gets going. Both the verse and chorus chord progressions underscore the song's images of sitting, waiting, wasting time, watching the tide and the ships "roll in" only to see them "roll away again." The protagonist is in a state of suspended animation, lonesome and far from home yet unable to break his inertia ("So I guess I'll remain the same").

The bridge is the only section of the track that employs primarily diatonic harmony (until the F chord at 1:39). It preserves the feeling of inertia by repeating a G–D–C progression three times in a row but nevertheless provides a welcome contrast to the persistent chromaticism. The straightforward harmony accompanies Redding's move to a higher register and a climactic emotional peak. He does not, however, break into testifying. Rather, his reserved tone opens up into an intimate expression of his plight. The bridge's poignancy is echoed in Redding's whistling during the coda, a section Cropper assumed would be filled with the sort of vocal improvisation that Redding usually performed at the end of a track. Unplanned and unforeseen, this lonely, whistled tune would prove to be Redding's final farewell.

Listening Guide

"(Sittin' on) The Dock of the Bay" (Otis Redding, Steve Cropper), Volt (mono). Also appears on the album *The Dock of the Bay*.
Recorded at Stax Studio, Memphis, November 1967
Otis Redding (voice), Booker T. Jones (piano), Steve Cropper (guitar), Donald "Duck" Dunn (bass), Al Jackson, Jr. (drums), Wayne Jackson (trumpet)
Producer: Steve Cropper
Charts: Hot 100 #1, Top Selling R&B Singles #1, Top LP's #4, Top Selling R&B LP's #1
Key: G
Meter: 4/4

Time	Section	Lyric Cue	Listen For
0:00	Intro (4)		Fade-in: bass riff, acoustic guitar, water sounds.
0:09	Verse 1 (8)	"Sitting in the morning sun"	Voice, piano, drums.
			All chords are major, connected by chromatic passing tones in the bass to create a rising and falling motion.
0:27	Chorus 1 (8)	"Sitting on the dock"	Signature guitar riff accompanies voice; water sounds.
			Static harmonic progression.
0:46	Verse 2 (8)	"I left my home"	Horn arrangement moves in parallel chromatic motion with the bass.
			Seagull sounds.
1:05	Chorus 2 (8)	"So I'm just going"	Similar to chorus 1.
1:14			New horn accompaniment.
1:23	Bridge (8)	"Looks like nothing's going to change"	Full instrumental texture.
			Diatonic harmony.
1:39		"So I guess"	F chord.
1:42	Verse 3 (8)	"Sitting here resting"	Similar to verse 1 with added seagull sounds.
2:00	Chorus (8)	"I'm just going to sit"	Similar to chorus 2.
2:19	Coda (fade)	Whistling	Redding whistles over the bass riff from the intro combined with the chord change (G–E) from the chorus. Instrumental texture is the same as the intro with added drums.

14.4. "I GOT THE FEELIN'" (1968)

JAMES BROWN

James Brown was a unique force in music. His various nicknames—Godfather of Soul, Hardest Working Man in Show Business, Mr. Dynamite, Soul Brother Number One—attest to his ambition and achievements. Unaffiliated with the soul powerhouse labels Motown, Stax, or Atlantic, Brown was nevertheless a perennial R&B chart presence. A songwriter, singer, dancer, band leader, pianist, record producer, and icon of black identity, his legacy of influence has spanned generations of performers from the young Michael Jackson to Prince to Bruno Mars.

Brown first entered the charts in 1956 as frontman for the Famous Flames, a doo wop group from Toccoa, Georgia, with a track called "Please, Please, Please." By the late 1960s, as one of soul music's biggest stars, he was on the leading edge of a new musical style that would come to be known as funk (see Stevie Wonder, "Superstition"). Relying on complex rhythms and rhythmic textures, Brown's funk tracks often de-emphasize melody, harmonic progression, and lyrics. Instead they focus on intricate rhythmic interplay among riffs and densely syncopated percussion. Brown's vocals are visceral expressions of energy peppered with screams, grunts ("Unh!"), and short exclamations ("Get up!" "Ain't it funky!"). (As a matter of context, it is worth listening to Brown's vocal skill with standard song repertory on the album *Gettin' Down to It*.) The result is infectious. It is impossible to listen to a James Brown track and not *move*.

"I Got the Feelin'" is based on the blues chord progression, but the song employs it freely to provide a structure that is clear, yet flexible. Recall that the common twelve-bar blues progression follows a pattern of I (four bars), IV (two bars), I (two bars), V (two bars), I (two bars), with the V chord serving as the climactic point of each chorus. Brown adapts this to his own purpose. Chorus one follows the chord sequence but changes the proportions:

I (12 bars), IV (4 bars), I (4 bars), V (6 bars)

Chorus two delays the arrival of the V chord by repeating the I and IV chords:

I (12 bars), IV (4 bars), I (12 bars), IV (4 bars), I (4 bars), V (6 bars)

Each chord is associated with a discrete musical idea. So, in addition to the chord progression forming an organized harmonic flow aimed at the climactic V chord, it also presents a series of modules, each containing contrasting musical events.

MODULE 1 (I)

The I chord supports the track's main riff, a repeating two-bar loop, which is the track's most rhythmically complex section. To get inside of what is going on, listen first to some individual elements. In the loop's first bar, the horns stress the offbeats, playing chords on the "and" of beats two and three. The guitar doubles the horns but plays one more offbeat note on the "and" of beat four.

By contrast, in the loop's second bar, the horns shift from chords to melody and from offbeat to onbeat. First, we hear a three-note melodic fragment that begins on beat two and ends on beat three. And then a four-note fragment that begins on beat four and ends in the next bar, overlapping the beginning of the loop. This second fragment has a dual quality, beginning on the beat but ending on the offbeat. This duality serves as a link between the two bars of the loop, one highlighting offbeats, the other onbeats.

The kick and snare drum parts lay down a highly kinetic, richly syncopated groove. But they hit in a couple of key spots that help to keep the groove in focus. The kick, along with the bass, plays on the downbeat (its normal position) at the beginning of each loop repetition (i.e., every other bar). The snare, though mostly doubling the offbeat horn accents and tapping out skittering sixteenth notes, usually hits on the second beat (its normal backbeat position) of the second bar of each loop. Through most of the track, these two moments are the only places we hear kick and snare in their conventional positions. The drum kit—played here by the great funk drummer Clyde Stubblefield—has clearly moved beyond its normal timekeeping role to provide the track a complex rhythmic personality.

MODULE 2 (IV)

When we move to the IV chord, the texture thins out and the beat becomes clearer. The drums remain syncopated, but the guitar clearly articulates the downbeat and the horns play only once per bar, doubled by the snare drum.

MODULE 3 (V)

The V chord has two bars of horns playing in unison, setting up the cadence. Again, they are doubled by the snare drum. The next four bars are left to Brown's a cappella "Baby, baby, baby."

Now that you've dug down into the mechanics of the arrangement, zoom out with your ears and listen to how it all flows together. And don't forget to dance.

Listening Guide

"**I Got the Feelin'**" (James Brown), King Records (mono). Also appears on the album *I Got the Feelin'*.
Recorded at Vox Studios, Los Angeles, January 1968
James Brown (voice), Waymon Reed, Joe Dupars (trumpet), Levi Rasbury (trombone), Alfred "Pee Wee" Ellis (alto saxophone), Maceo Parker (tenor saxophone), St. Clair Pinckney (baritone saxophone), Jimmy Nolen, Alphonso "Country" Kellum (guitar), Bernard Odum (bass), Clyde Stubblefield (drums)

Producer: James Brown
Charts Hot 100 #6, R&B Best Sellers #1, Top LP's #135, Top Selling R&B LP's #8
Key: F
Meter: 4/4

Time	Section	Lyric Cue	Listen For
0:00	Intro (4)		Main riff: 2-bar loop.
			Horns play off-beat chords in bar 1; on-beat melodic fragments in bar 2.
			Aggressively syncopated drums.
0:07	**Chorus 1** (12+4+4+2+4)	"I got the feelin' "	I chord (12) main riff.
0:30		"Hey yeah"	IV chord (4) simpler texture.
			Guitar plays on downbeats.
			Horn chords answer guitar.
0:37		"Good God"	I chord (4) main riff.
0:45		"Alright!"	V chord (2) cadence figure in horns.
		"Baby, baby, baby"	Solo voice (4).
0:57	**Vamp** (2)	"I got the feelin' "	Main riff.
1:00	**Chorus 2** (‖:12+4:‖+4+2+4)	"Baby"	I (12)
1:23		"Baby!"	IV (4)
1:30		"No, no"	I (12)
1:52		"Hey baby"	IV (4)
2:00		"Baby"	I (4)
2:07		"Alright!"	V (2)
		"Baby, baby, baby"	Solo voice (4).
2:19	**Break** (7 to fade)		Saxophone solo.
			Main riff.

NOTES

    1. Ray Charles and David Ritz, *Brother Ray: Ray Charles' Own Story* (New York: Da Capo Press, 2004), 177.

    2. Quoted in Craig Werner, *A Change Is Gonna Come: Music, Race and the Soul of America* (Ann Arbor: University of Michigan Press, 2006), 72.

    3. Quoted in Leo Sacks, *The Best of Wilson Pickett* CD booklet (Atlantic Records, 1992), 1.

4. Jerry Wexler and David Ritz, *Rhythm and the Blues: A Life in American Music* (New York: Knopf, 1993), 143.

5. Quoted in Sacks, *The Best of Wilson Pickett*, 4.

6. Wexler and Ritz, *Rhythm and the Blues*, 172.

7. Wexler and Ritz, 175.

8. Wexler and Ritz, 172.

9. Quoted in Jann Wenner, "Booker T. and the MG's," in *The Rolling Stone Interviews Vol. 1* (New York: Warner, 1971), 134.

10. Quoted in "Lady Soul Singing It like It Is," *Time*, June 28, 1968, 63.

11. Quoted in "Lady Soul Singing It like It Is," 62.

12. Quoted in Wexler and Ritz, *Rhythm and the Blues*, 206.

13. Wexler and Ritz, 207.

14. Wexler and Ritz, 203.

15. Wexler and Ritz, 206.

16. Wexler and Ritz, 207.

17. Quoted in Mark Bego, *Aretha Franklin: The Queen of Soul* (New York: Skyhorse), 76.

18. Quoted in Rob Bowman, *Soulsville U.S.A.: The Story of Stax Records* (New York: Schirmer Trade Books, 1997), 132.

19. Quoted in Jonathan Gould, *Otis Redding: An Unfinished Life* (New York: Crown Archetype, 2017), 427.

FURTHER READING

Bowman, Rob. *Soulsville, U.S.A.: The Story of Stax Records.* New York: Schirmer Trade Books, 1997.

Guralnick, Peter. *Sweet Soul Music: Rhythm and Blues and the Southern Dream of Freedom.* Edinburgh: Mojo, 2002.

Hirshey, Gerri. *Nowhere to Run: The Story of Soul Music.* New York: Da Capo Press, 1994.

Wexler, Jerry, and David Ritz. *Rhythm and the Blues: A Life in American Music.* New York: Knopf, 1993.

FURTHER LISTENING

Ben E. King, "Stand By Me" (Atco, 1961)
Booker T. and the MG's, "Green Onions" (Stax, 1962)
Solomon Burke, "Cry to Me" (Atlantic, 1961)
Ray Charles, "What'd I Say" (Atlantic, 1959)
Gladys Knight and the Pips, "Every Beat of My Heart" (Vee-Jay, 1961)
Sam and Dave, "Soul Man" (Stax, 1967)
Percy Sledge, "When a Man Loves a Woman" (Atlantic, 1966)
Joe Tex, "Hold What You've Got" (Dial, 1964)
Carla Thomas, "B-A-B-Y" (Stax, 1966)
Ike and Tina Turner, "A Fool in Love" (Sue, 1960)

15

COUNTERCULTURE
Psychedelic Rock

In the summer of 1966, a Texas band called the 13th Floor Elevators released an album titled *The Psychedelic Sounds of the 13th Floor Elevators*. The title crystallized a gathering movement of artistic experimentation that included such records as the Beatles' "Tomorrow Never Knows," the Beach Boys' "Good Vibrations," and the Byrds' "Eight Miles High." Such unusual songs and sounds would become associated with late-1960s psychedelic culture, a loose agglomeration of social and artistic trends informed by the use of hallucinogenic drugs and a vague association with South Asian (especially Indian) mysticism and music. These musical forays into uncharted pop territory were fueled by the general cultural upheaval of the time—the assertion of an anti-establishment counterculture—and specifically by the increasing prevalence of drug use among rock musicians and their audience, as well as a youthful quest for meaning beyond the conventional norms of Western society. They were also the result—drugs or no drugs—of rock musicians' increasing artistic ambition.

Psychedelic rock was also known as "acid rock," which aptly describes its overt connection to a specific category of drug. Hallucinogens such as LSD and mescaline were seen to have mind-expanding properties that produced extraordinary sensory perception. Prominent LSD users such as novelists Aldous Huxley and William Burroughs reported that music enhanced their trip and helped them to recall the experience after the drug wore off. Indeed, any music can transport a listener to imaginary realms and create a distorted sense of time, which is, in a sense, a psychedelic type of experience. This quality of altered perception could be further enhanced sonically with the use of recording studio techniques that had been developing throughout the postwar era of pop record production. Psychedelic rock historian Jim DeRogatis notes that "circular, mandala-like song structures; sustained or droning melodies; altered and effected instrumental sounds; reverb, echoes, and tape delays that created a sense of space, and layered mixes that rewarded repeated listening by revealing new and mysterious elements" were all techniques that evoked the psychedelic.[1]

While the recording studio provided ideal resources for crafting extraordinary aural experiences—sometimes referred to as "headphone music"—live performing was an important incubator. In long jam sessions, often playing over an extended **drone** (a sustained pitch in the bass) or multiple blues choruses, musicians improvised extensively. Modal jazz, free jazz, Indian, and Latin music were among the new influences feeding stylistic developments in a climate of ongoing experimentation. As performances became longer and style palettes more diverse, records offered listeners ever more complex, immersive musical encounters. If the term "psychedelic rock" implied a drug connection, its deeper and more lasting significance was an expansion of artistic possibility.

15.1. "WHITE RABBIT" (1966)

JEFFERSON AIRPLANE

Jefferson Airplane spearheaded international awareness of the San Francisco rock scene, which included the Grateful Dead, Big Brother and the Holding Company (with Janis Joplin), and Quicksilver Messenger Service. With a flourishing hippie movement, a bohemian artist tradition that included the Beat poets and novelists, plentiful drugs, and myriad bands to supply the soundtrack, San Francisco was at the epicenter of psychedelic culture. Jefferson Airplane was the first of San Francisco's psychedelic bands to reach the pop charts. They were early headliners at Bill Graham's legendary Fillmore Auditorium concerts, and they were on the front page of the first issue of *Rolling Stone*. In short, they led the San Francisco counterculture's advance on the pop mainstream.

By the time the group released its hit album, *Surrealistic Pillow*, in 1967, it consisted of six members: Grace Slick, Paul Kantner, Marty Balin, Jorma Kaukonen, Jack Casady, and Spencer Dryden. The band brought together a range of talent and sensibility, melding musical styles and cultural ideology. As *Rolling Stone* editor and publisher Jann Wenner wrote, "They were both architects and messengers of the psychedelic age, a liberation of mind and body that profoundly changed American art, politics and spirituality. . . . Together they were unbeatable."[2]

"White Rabbit" is one of two hit singles that appear on *Surrealistic Pillow* (along with "Somebody to Love"). The song's lyrics invoke Lewis Carroll's *Alice's Adventures in Wonderland* with surrealistic imagery, in keeping with the psychedelic implications of the album's title. Grace Slick, who wrote the song, said she wanted to call out the hypocrisy of the older generation's criticism of psychedelic drugs when they themselves "were the original experimenters with the ups, downs, and sideways manufactured by the 'legal' drug dealers."[3] She used imagery from *Alice in Wonderland* because its popularity as a children's classic represented what Slick considered a mixed message. She intended to "remind our parents . . . that *they* were the ones who read all these 'fun with chemical' children's books to us when we were small." Alice "is the biggest druggie of them all. . . . The girl is thoroughly ripped all the way through the book."[4]

On the other hand, the lyrics' exotic and fanciful images and rebellious attitude embodied the contemporary rock zeitgeist. Adding to the track's exotic tone are its Spanish inflections: a bolero-type rhythm and a Phrygian modal effect created by juxtaposing two major chords a half step apart (F#–G). The bass outlines both of these features at the outset, joined after two bars by the snare drum doubling the bolero rhythm. The snare is panned left and its reverb is featured prominently on the right, creating a sense of deep shadow cast across the stereo field. The lead guitar emerges from the snare shadow playing Phrygian-flavored melodic lines, its own reverb image panned to the left. Around 0:19 the bass slides to the left, joining the snare and making way for the voice.

Grace Slick's entrance is restrained in a spooky way, as though concealing something. The voice claims the center of the stereo field, along with its reverb, which evokes a large space. From this hushed opening a crescendo begins to grow, rising gradually through the course of the track as Slick's character reveals an ever more forceful personality. The cadence at the end of verse one provides the first indication that the quiet opening was only a departure point. Now the lilting bolero rhythm is replaced by heavier accents and a pointed command: "Go ask Alice." The chords finally move from the hypnotic Phrygian loop to a strong III–IV–I (C–D–A) cadence. (Note that C is a triad built on the flatted third in the tonic key of A.)

In verse two the bolero returns but Slick's character remains more assertive than in verse one. The cadence for verse two follows the same progression as the first but is now thickened with an added organ part (L). As the track enters the bridge, the texture is in full rock mode, with heavy backbeat accents reinforced by guitars, and Slick is in full voice.

The harmonic rhythm is the same as in the verse (two bars per chord), but the Phrygian feel is replaced by diatonic harmony. The last four bars of the bridge make a dramatic return to the F♯ and a final "Go ask Alice" as the bolero rhythm returns. Now, however, as the track begins moving to its final climax the bolero is overlaid with the heavy backbeats. This layered rhythm continues into verse three, where the final cadence (with different words) brings the track's intensity to its highest level with a driving guitar and bass rhythm, snare flams pounding the backbeat, and Slick almost shouting, "Feed your head!"

Listening Guide

"White Rabbit" (Grace Slick), RCA Victor (stereo). Also appears on the album *Surrealistic Pillow*.
Recorded at RCA Studios, Hollywood, November 1966
Grace Slick (voice, organ), Jorma Kaukonen (guitar), Paul Kantner (guitar), Marty Balin (guitar), Jack Casady (bass), Spencer Dryden (drums)
Producer: Rick Jarrard
Engineer: Dave Hassinger
Chart Position: Hot 100 #8, Top LP's #3
Key: A
Meter: 4/4

Time	Section	Lyric Cue	Listen For
0:00	Intro (12)		Bass (C) plays F♯–G loop in bolero rhythm.
0:05			Snare (L, reverb R) joins bolero rhythm.
0:09			2 guitars (R): rhythm and lead (reverb L). Lead plays Phrygian-flavored melodic lines.
0:19			Bass moves gradually to the left side.
0:28	Verse 1 (8+4)	"One pill makes you larger"	Voice alone at the center of the mix with spacious reverb.
0:45		"Go ask Alice"	Cadence (A–C–D–A); bolero suspended.
			Bass moves to center.
0:55	Verse 2 (8+4)	"And if you go"	Voice is more assertive.
			Bolero and Phrygian chord loop return.
			Bass moves back to left.
1:13		"Go ask Alice"	Cadence; organ (L).

continued on next page

Time	Section	Lyric Cue	Listen For
1:22	Bridge (8+4)	"When the men"	Heavy backbeat, reinforced with added guitar (L) and organ.
1:40		"Go ask Alice"	Bolero and chord loop return in bass and rhythm guitar (R) overlaid with backbeat guitar (L) and organ.
1:49	Verse 3 (8+8)	"When logic and proportion"	Layered bolero and backbeat texture continues.
2:06		"Remember . . . feed your head"	Loudest and heaviest section. Driving rhythm; voice almost shouting. Extended cadence.

15.2. "THE END" (1966)

THE DOORS

The world we suggest is of a new Wild West. A sensuous evil world.[5]

—Jim Morrison

The Doors emerged from an eclectic and energized Los Angeles music scene centered in and around clubs on the Sunset Strip. The scene included members of such bands as Iron Butterfly, Love, Buffalo Springfield, and the Byrds. The critical seed for the Doors' formation lay in frontman Jim Morrison's notebooks of poetry written during a fever of creativity while living on a rooftop in Venice, California, during the summer of 1965. Morrison wrote poems as if they were song lyrics set to imaginary music played by an imaginary band, which he called the Doors.

The poems began turning into actual songs when Morrison sang some of them to his friend and fellow film student Ray Manzarek, a skilled keyboardist who fleshed out the musical sketches. With the subsequent addition of John Densmore on drums and Robby Krieger on guitar, the Doors began playing the Los Angeles clubs, working their way up to a regular booking at the Strip's premier spot, the Whisky a Go Go, in the summer of 1966.

The group's sound was unique, beginning with its unusual lineup. Amid ubiquitous psychedelic rock bands spotlighting long guitar solos, the Doors instead featured the organ. They had no bass player. And while Krieger's original guitar styling was a key element of the sound, his parts were often embedded in a composite texture. Manzarek, Densmore, and Krieger all had varied musical backgrounds and brought together influences ranging from jazz to flamenco to Indian music to Kurt Weill. The Doors' grooves rocked, but they were also supple and nuanced. The band's stunning debut album balanced funky blues ("Back Door Man") and aggressive rock ("Break on Through") with shimmering ballads ("Crystal Ship") and hooky, if moody, pop ("Light My Fire"). The lyrics were both earthy and literary, possessed of a haunted aggression that Morrison enacted vividly, both on stage and on record. In a town where the Beach Boys proffered a sunny version of the California dream, the Doors explored its other side.

"The End" grew out of the extended improvisations featured in the Doors' live shows. Although the song had taken shape through many performances at the Whisky a Go Go, it remained a piece of spontaneous interactive music making performed live in the studio without overdubs. The Doors played it twice; parts of each take were spliced together to create the final track. It begins with an intro and a short song analogous to a "head" in jazz, the section that presents the thematic material prior to beginning improvisation. After this opening section the track moves into a free-form narrative that works its way gradually to a climax, ending with a brief return to the opening material. The lyrics of the dramatic climax refer to the story of Oedipus, who killed his father, married his mother, and lived with the consequences. As Morrison enacts his modern version of the tortured character, the music grows louder, faster, and more dissonant.

The track unfolds over a drone (D), its melodic character determined not by major or minor scales but by melodic fragments treated in the manner of an Indian raga with blues connotations. Unlike a raga or mode, however, which can serve as resources for any number of performances, the pitch treatment here is specific to this piece of music. The notes are fairly limited and appear chosen to create a sense of ambivalence, setting C against C♯ and F against F♯. In the intro, for example, we hear the guitar play the motive C♯–D repeatedly over the D drone. Yet after the first line from the voice ("This is the end") the harmony changes to C ("Beautiful friend"), abruptly canceling the C♯ only to bring it back with the next chord change. Also, throughout the track we will hear the guitar's C♯ juxtaposed against a C♮ in the organ's melodic fragments and in the vocal. C and F, of course, are blue notes in D, which accounts for the blues feeling that runs through the track, especially in Morrison's vocal part.

The guitar intro also presents the F–F♯ conflict, which in relation to the drone pitch, D, provides a shifting minor-major feeling. We hear F first (at 0:18), which suits the track's moody atmosphere. It is played in a high register. At 0:22 F♯ sneaks in as part of a quick arpeggio and a rising melodic fragment in a lower register. Immediately the guitar returns to F♮ in the high register. This is essentially how the pitches will interface throughout the track: always in the guitar part, F in the high register, and F♯ usually in the low register and often as part of an arpeggio.

The basic musical elements of the piece are laid out in the intro and part one. After that, the track ebbs and flows through a series of sections while the D drone provides a basis for free-form improvisation. Morrison's lyrics follow a dark stream of consciousness filled with disturbing, fragmentary images. Part four brings the track's climax with all band members engaged in an improvised dialogue. The tempo increases and the music becomes dissonant, the sounds of the guitar and organ distorted amid growing textural and emotional agitation. Finally, the groove collapses, followed by a return to the track's opening music as Morrison's character drifts back into introspection. In one final metaphor, the voice sings the minor third (F) and is answered on guitar by the major third (F♯). The track's pervasive tone of ambivalence persists right to its final sound.

Listening Guide

"The End" (The Doors), Elektra Records (stereo). Appears on the album *The Doors*.
Recorded at Sunset Sound Recorders, Hollywood, August 1966
Jim Morrison (voice), Ray Manzarek (organ), Robby Krieger (guitar), John Densmore (drums)
Producer: Paul Rothchild
Engineer: Bruce Botnick
Charts: Top LP's #2
Key: D
Meter: Mostly 4/4

Time	Section	Lyric Cue	Listen For
0:00	Intro		Stereo space framed with guitar, wind chimes (R), and cymbal roll (L).
0:11			Guitar plays C♯–D motive and minor third (F♮) in upper register.
0:22			Major third (F♯) in lower register followed by F♮ in upper register.
0:32			Drum kit/percussion (L).
0:35			Keyboard bass groove.

Time	Section	Lyric Cue	Listen For
0:54	Part 1 Song	"This is the end"	Subdued vocal entrance.
0:56			Drone note moves from D to C and back.
1:12		"Of our elaborate"	Organ chords: C–G–D.
			Phrases elongated with interspersed bars of 6/4.
1:36			Drums become more prominent (L).
1:43		"Can you picture"	New chord sequence: C–D–G–D.
2:09			Drum roll.
2:13	Part 2		Improvisation over D drone.
2:54		"Lost in a romance"	Voice sings quasi-improvised fragments focused on the fifth (A) above the drone.
3:01			Organ begins playing melodic figures.
3:35			Instrumental (no voice).
3:54		"There's danger"	Voice returns.
5:47		"The blue bus"	New vocal melody.
6:10			Instrumental.
6:27	Part 3	"The killer awoke"	Begin spoken Oedipus section.
7:25		"Father . . . I want to kill you"	
7:34		"Mother, I want to . . . [SCREAM]"	
7:43			Instruments answer scream then die away.
8:13		"Come on baby"	Intensity builds gradually.
8:46	Part 4		Tempo increases slightly, groove picks up momentum with rhythmic figures in guitar and organ parts.
9:03			Improvised jam, including voice; tempo increases.
9:50			Music becomes dissonant and distorted; groove collapses.
10:20	Part 5		Similar to **part 1**.
10:33		"This is the end"	Opening song returns in shortened version with new lyrics.
11:30		"This is the end"	Voice sings minor third (F) answered by major third (F#) in guitar.

15.3. "SUNSHINE OF YOUR LOVE" (1967)

CREAM

Cream was one of the first rock "supergroups," which meant simply that all three of its members were already known from previous projects before they joined to form the new band. Bassist Jack Bruce had played with Blues Incorporated, the Graham Bond Organisation, and Manfred Mann; Ginger Baker had played with Bruce in the Graham Bond Organisation; and guitarist Eric Clapton had been a member of the Yardbirds and then John Mayall and the Bluesbreakers. All three were skilled musicians with a range of musical experience—blues, R&B, and jazz, as well as rock. Their power trio format (one guitar, bass, drums) was a relatively new one for rock, employing advances in electronic amplification to produce extremely loud guitar and bass sounds. It would become a standard band format, exemplified by such groups as the Jimi Hendrix Experience, Blue Cheer, and Grand Funk Railroad.

Although Cream played some traditional blues repertory amplified to modern rock's sonic proportions, they also reworked blues language to create their own brand of heavy psychedelic rock. "Sunshine of Your Love," from their second album *Disraeli Gears*, is a good example. The track is based on a recurring bluesy riff and alludes to twelve-bar blues structure. But the form is stretched out from twelve to twenty-four bars and overlaid with a verse-chorus form indicated by the lyrics, which have a distinctly psychedelic vibe. Proportionally the verse is analogous to the first eight bars of a conventional blues chorus (though doubled to sixteen), while the chorus is equivalent to the last four (doubled to eight). The chord changes I–IV–I–V occur in all the right places for a blues progression, but the move to V, which is the chorus, is treated like a separate section with its own texture and lyric refrain ("I've been waiting so long").

The track is lean in its arrangement but densely muscular in its sonic effect. The group played in the studio as they did on stage—together in the same room and with minimal overdubbing. The sound was extremely loud, seriously hampering the engineer's ability to isolate microphones and separate the instruments from one another. "I'd say the room itself was 30 or 40 percent of the sound of that record," said engineer Tom Dowd, "just because the band was so loud."[6]

The groove has an unusual "inside out" feel, reversing the rhythmic placement of snare and bass drums so the snare plays on beats one and three, the bass on two and four. The drums seem, in effect, to be playing *against* the guitar and bass riff. The choruses switch back to a normal backbeat groove, though it is somewhat disguised by the many drum fills. The rhythmic effect is paradoxical, both heavily beat-oriented and somehow off-balance at the same time.

The track's other key feature is the riff that runs through each verse. It is a blues reduction, an essence magnified by loudness and the weight of the guitar-bass doubling. It permeates the track with a blues feeling yet runs counter to authentic blues in its crystalline minimalism and its mantra-like repetition. Like the drum groove, it is paradoxical—blues and not blues.

At the break the guitar solo furthers this ambiguity. It begins with a stylistically incongruous quote from the Rodgers and Hart song "Blue Moon," a ballad written in 1934 and recorded by scores of pop singers. Picking up on the track's general rhythmic ambivalence, the guitar finds its own groove somewhere between the drums and the guitar-bass riff. The solo's narrative has two contrasting sections, analogous to the song's verse-chorus form. The pitches in the "verse" section (the first sixteen bars, 2:01–2:34) have a major mode orientation and the rhythmic phrasing is elastic. The "chorus" section (the next eight bars, 2:34–2:50) shifts to a minor-mode blues and a tighter rhythmic feel coordinated with the bass and rhythm guitar.

Listening Guide

"Sunshine of Your Love" (Eric Clapton, Jack Bruce, Pete Brown), Atco Records (stereo). Also appears on the album *Disraeli Gears*.
Recorded at Atlantic Studios, New York City, May 1967
Jack Bruce (bass, voice), Eric Clapton (guitar), Ginger Baker (drums)
Producer: Felix Pappalardi
Engineer: Tom Dowd
Charts: Hot 100 #5, Top LP's #4
Key: D
Meter: 4/4

Time	Section	Lyric Cue	Listen For
0:00	**Intro** (8)		Guitar (L), bass (C), drums (R); guitar and bass play unison riff; drums play "inside out" groove.
0:17	**Verse 1** (16)	"It's getting near dawn"	Voice in (C).
0:50	**Chorus** (8)	"I've been waiting"	Harmony voice. Riff out; texture change.
1:07	**Riff** (2)		Similar to **intro**.
1:11	**Verse 2** (16)	"I'm with you"	Similar to **verse 1**.
1:44	**Chorus** (8)	"I've been waiting"	Similar to previous **chorus**.

continued on next page

Time	Section	Lyric Cue	Listen For
2:01	Break (24)		Guitar solo (C) begins with quote from "Blue Moon," then "major" blues.
			Texture as in verses.
2:34			Texture as in **choruses**; lead guitar tightens rhythm and shifts to "minor" blues.
2:50	Riff (4)		Similar to **intro**.
2:59	Verse 3 (16)	"I'm with you"	Similar to previous **verses**.
3:32	Chorus (4+8+fade)	"I've been waiting"	Begins with 4 bars of repeated lyrics, then follows format of previous **choruses**.

15.4. "PURPLE HAZE" (1967)

JIMI HENDRIX

Jimi Hendrix was an authentic bluesman. He knew the traditional repertory and could navigate the language with rhetorical skill and a virtuoso guitar technique. B. B. King, Albert King, and Freddie King—who Hendrix referred to as the three kings—were his musical mentors. But Hendrix was a restless musical spirit and an ambitious recording artist. He freely incorporated whatever struck his fancy, and he used the studio to develop complex textures for which the blues was only a starting point. His debut album, *Are You Experienced*, ranged from the hard-driving "Manic Depression" to the ethereal "May This Be Love."

The fish-eye photo on the US album cover featured the three-man Jimi Hendrix Experience in mod psychedelic garb. Everything about the record—its sound palette, its arrangements, its guitar lines, its attitude—was unlike anything in the blues-based psychedelic guitar scenes in San Francisco and London. "We don't want to be classed in any category," said Hendrix. "If I must have a tag, I'd like it to be called 'Free Feeling.' It's a mixture of rock, freak-out, blues and rave music."[7]

Hendrix was discovered in 1966 by Chas Chandler, former bassist for the British group the Animals and then a manager. Hendrix's flamboyant hippie bluesman image made it difficult to find a niche in an American music industry that offered a fairly prescribed set of possibilities for a black guitarist. He had done what was expected: played as a sideman for the likes of Little Richard and Curtis Knight on touring shows. But he much preferred fronting his own band, Jimmy James and the Blue Flames. Decked out in flamboyant attire, he fell to his knees, played guitar with his teeth, and colored his original riffs and solos with distortion and feedback. Chandler heard Hendrix playing at the small Cafe Wha? in New York's Greenwich Village and recognized a bold artistic persona. He signed Hendrix and took him to London, where Chandler had the contacts to jumpstart what he felt certain could be a superstar career. Within months Hendrix had formed a band with Noel Redding (bass) and Mitch Mitchell (drums). The trio began recording almost immediately, and by the spring of 1967, *Are You Experienced* was ready for release. That summer Hendrix made a triumphant return to the US with a tour, an album, and a performance at the Monterey Pop Festival that left no doubt a major rock figure had arrived.

The opening of "Purple Haze" is one of rock's iconic musical moments. Bass and guitar play octave intervals in quarter notes, setting the track's mood with an assertive rhythmic march. If the rhythm is assertive, then the pitches are aggressive, the bass and guitar notes separated by the dissonant interval of an augmented fourth, or tritone. After two bars, the drums enter and, as the bass continues the marching octave figure, the snare drum joins in with steady quarter notes. Meanwhile the guitar breaks into a blues melody covering an expansive range: two octaves and a third. It is a typical Hendrix move, using blues language to create rock spectacle. The intro ends with four bars of vamp on the chords that underpin the verse.

The mix of instrumental sounds has little stereo separation, creating a dense image that leans slightly off-center toward the left. At the beginning of verse one the voice appears alone on the right side, along with its heavy echo and reverb treatment. This separation of voice and instruments is the track's primary stereo configuration, but at the break, as the track slides into a more chaotic texture, a second voice appears on the far left side of the mix.

Two key elements in the break enhance the track's psychedelic feel: (1) a mysterious stereo vocal image and (2) a whimsical, non-bluesy guitar solo. The second voice (the one on the left) is heavily reverberant. It is pitched lower and is less prominent in the mix than the main voice, which remains on the right. The second voice's words are indistinct, but throughout the first part of the break the two voices carry on random dialogue between the right and left sides of the mix. The guitar solo has a similarly disjointed quality, which is enhanced tonally by an electronic device, the Octavia. This effect duplicates pitches an octave higher. The note doublings, however, are not consistently balanced. At times either the high or the low note is louder. Again, there is a sense of randomness to the sound.

The break falls into two sections. The first introduces the chaotic texture, which resonates with the protagonist's sense of disorientation.

In the second section, which begins at 1:37, things snap back sharply into focus with the reintroduction of the blues melody from the intro, accompanied again by the march rhythm. The voices, too, become more strictly rhythmic.

This alternation of a complex, "hazy" texture and a sharply delineated one is among the track's structural principles. Before the break, we hear this same type of contrast between the intro and the verse. Whereas the intro presents a tight, focused texture with all instruments locked in a clear rhythm matrix, the verse is much freer and denser rhythmically. The verse's more complex texture drops out at the climactic line "'Scuse me while I kiss the sky." On the turnaround that follows, the bass and guitar play in unison, briefly pulling the texture back together before moving into verse two, where the hazy complexity returns.

Listening Guide

"Purple Haze" (Jimi Hendrix), Reprise Records (stereo). Also appears on the album *Are You Experienced*.
Recorded at De Lane Lea and Olympic Studios, London, February 1967
Jimi Hendrix (voice, guitar), Noel Redding (bass), Mitch Mitchell (drums)
Producer: Chas Chandler
Engineer: Eddie Kramer
Chart Position: Hot 100 #65, Top LP's #5
Key: E minor blues
Meter: 4/4

Time	Section	Lyric Cue	Listen For
0:00	Intro (2+8+4)		Bass and guitar play octaves a tritone apart.
0:05			Guitar breaks into a blues melody.
			Bass continues with quarter notes doubled by snare drum.
			Mix has little stereo separation.
0:24			Vamp; denser texture.
0:32	Verse 1 (8+1)	"Purple haze"	Voice (R) with heavy echo and reverb.
0:46		"'Scuse me"	Voice alone.
0:49			Turnaround: Guitar and bass in unison.
0:52	Verse 2 (8+1)	"Purple haze"	Similar to **verse 1**.
1:06		"Whatever it is"	Voice alone.
1:09			Turnaround.

Time	Section	Lyric Cue	Listen For
1:13	**Break** (11+8)	"Help me"	Second voice (L) in lower register, at lower volume, and with heavy reverb.
			"Dialogue" between the 2 voices on opposite sides of the mix.
1:19			Guitar solo (C) with Octavia effect.
1:37			Texture snaps back into rhythmic focus.
			Intro guitar melody.
			Rhythmic voices.
1:55	**Verse 3** (8+1)	"Purple haze"	Similar to previous **verses**.
2:07		"Is it tomorrow"	Voice alone.
2:11			Turnaround
2:14	**Coda** (16 to fade)	"Help me"	Similar texture to **break**.

NOTES

1. Jim DeRogatis, *Turn on Your Mind: Four Decades of Great Psychedelic Rock* (Milwaukee, WI: Hal Leonard, 2003), 12.
2. Jann Wenner, Foreword to Jeff Tamarkin, *Got a Revolution: The Turbulent Flight of the Jefferson Airplane* (New York: Atria Books, 2003), xv.
3. Grace Slick with Andrea Cagan, *Somebody to Love: A Rock-and-Roll Memoir* (New York: Grand Central, 1999), 106.
4. Slick and Cagan, 107–08.
5. Jim Morrison, Elektra Records promotional biography, cited in Tom Baker, "Morrison," *Spin*, August 1990, 28.
6. Quoted in Dan Daley, "Cream's 'Sunshine of Your Love,' " *Mix*, September 2001, 188.
7. Quoted in Harry Shapiro and Caesar Glebbeek, *Jimi Hendrix: Electric Gypsy* (New York: St. Martin's Griffin 1990), 129.

FURTHER READING

DeRogatis, Jim. *Turn on Your Mind: Four Decades of Great Psychedelic Rock.* Milwaukee, WI: Hal Leonard, 2003.
Manzarek, Ray. *Light My Fire: My Life with the Doors.* New York: G. P. Putnam's Sons, 1998.
Shapiro, Harry, and Caesar Glebbeek. *Jimi Hendrix: Electric Gypsy.* New York: St. Martin's Press, 1990.
Tamarkin, Jeff. *Got a Revolution!: The Turbulent Flight of the Jefferson Airplane.* New York: Atria Books, 2003.

FURTHER LISTENING

13th Floor Elevators, "Dust" (IA, 1966)
Beatles, "Strawberry Fields Forever" (Capitol, 1966)
Byrds, "Eight Miles High" (Columbia, 1966)
Donovan, "Hurdy Gurdy Man" (Pye, 1968)
Grateful Dead, "St. Stephen" (Warner Bros., 1969)
Love, "The Red Telephone" (Elektra, 1967)
Pink Floyd, "Astronomy Domine" (EMI, 1967)
Steppenwolf, "Magic Carpet Ride" (ABC Dunhill, 1968)
Vanilla Fudge, "You Keep Me Hangin' On" (ATCO Records, 1967)

16

BACK TO THE ROOTS
Country Rock

In 1968, signs of country music began emerging on the psychedelic landscape. In part it was a return-to-roots idea; many psychedelic rockers were former folk musicians and had a leftover fondness for plainspoken tunes and simpler arrangements. The Byrds, for example, followed the synthesizer-tinged textures on *The Notorious Byrd Brothers* album with *Sweetheart of the Rodeo*, which contained covers of songs by the Louvin brothers, Merle Haggard, and Woody Guthrie. They recorded in Nashville, country music's creative center, and the album's signature sound was no longer the electric twelve-string but the steel guitar. Grateful Dead lead guitarist Jerry Garcia took up steel guitar himself and joined New Riders of the Purple Sage. Two former members of Buffalo Springfield, Richie Furay and Jim Messina, formed Poco. Byrds bassist Chris Hillman and new Byrds member Gram Parsons left the group after *Sweetheart* to form the Flying Burrito Brothers. Bob Dylan stripped down his mid-1960s sound and he, too, moved his recording operation to Nashville to make his *John Wesley Harding* and *Nashville Skyline* albums. His backing band—the Hawks, rechristened the Band—went out on their own with the album *Music from Big Pink*. Seeking to capture what they called "a woody, thuddy sound," they blended roots sounds with cutting-edge rock in a strikingly original stylistic fusion. Linda Ronstadt, former singer for the folk-rock trio Stone Poneys, became a country-rock superstar, and the backing band for her 1971 summer tour became the Eagles. It seemed by the turn of the decade that many rock musicians wanted, as Joni Mitchell wrote in her song "Woodstock," to "get back to the land."

Country rock is less a cohesive genre than an indication of the influence of country music among far-flung rock bands. There may be a stylistic gulf between, say, the Flying Burrito Brothers and the Band, but both in their own ways tip their hat to America's southern and southwestern traditions. Of the tracks discussed in this chapter, only one ("Lay Lady Lay") uses steel guitar, a sine qua non of country music. But all represent new sounds on the rock stage with clear southern roots.

16.1. "LAY LADY LAY" (1969)

BOB DYLAN

Dylan's *John Wesley Harding* album was a departure from his previous two albums, *Highway 61 Revisited* and *Blonde on Blonde*. In contrast to the folk-rock opulence of those albums, the new one was stripped to the bone. The songs were shorter and more circumspect in their lyric imagery. The electric guitars and organ were gone. The drums were a subtle presence. The instrumental centerpieces were acoustic guitar and harmonica, as on Dylan's earliest records. Recorded toward the end of his eighteen-month hiatus from pop celebrity, the sessions took place in Nashville, where he had finished recording *Blonde on Blonde* at the urging of producer Bob Johnston. Although the city provided Dylan with a new and more relaxed setting than his customary New York sessions, other than a bit of steel guitar on the last two tracks of *John Wesley Harding* there was nothing to indicate that his work was influenced by his trek to the capital of country music.

But the next album, *Nashville Skyline*, made an explicit connection. Aside from its suggestive title, the record included a symbolic performance: a duet between Dylan and Johnny Cash, one of country music's biggest stars at the time, on Dylan's "Girl from the North Country." Many Nashville studio musicians participated in the recording sessions, and the album is filled with country-style guitar picking, slide guitar, and steel guitar. But the songs were Dylan's, which meant that the country influence was mixed with assorted other bric-a-brac from the restless artist's trove of musical memories. Regardless of whether the album was one of Dylan's more substantial efforts, his stature nevertheless made it a signal event, calling further attention to the ascendancy of country rock. And in the harmonically exotic love song "Lay Lady Lay," country musicians were themselves pushed into new territory.

"Lay Lady Lay" was the album's hit single. It centers around a repeating two-bar harmonic progression (A–C♯ minor–G [the flatted seventh]–B minor). The progression has a "falling" quality produced by the descending chromatic line (A–G♯–G–F♯) played by steel guitar and organ.

The line is also doubled at times by the bass. The melancholic sound of the steel guitar underscores a general sense of lethargy as the chord progression cycles around, going nowhere.

The verse consists of a series of four-bar phrases in an *aaba* pattern. Each *a* phrase repeats the "falling" progression twice—once with words and once without, leaving plenty of space for the musical atmosphere to sink in. The contrasting *b* phrase uses a different chord progression (E–F♯minor–A), which moves toward, instead of away from, the tonic chord. This phrase has a brighter quality than *a* (in part because its first chord, E, contains a G♯, which raises the flatted seventh scale degree, G, back to its diatonic position) and so provides a brief respite from the chromatic mantra of the descending line. It also has a different rhythmic texture featuring drums instead of the light percussion that accompanies the *a* phrases. A sudden burst of words further propels the *b* phrase's musical motion.

The bridge is an expanded variant of the *b* phrase. The chords are slightly different but they, too, relieve the persistent chromaticism of the *a* phrase and move toward the tonic chord A. The feel, again, is brighter and the drum texture is similar to *b*.

The track has an unusual percussion groove accompanying the *a* progression, which complements the unusual harmonic progression. The part came about by accident. Drummer Kenny Buttrey, usually quick to invent an appropriate drum part, had no ideas for this song, so he asked Dylan and producer Bob Johnston for direction. Neither had any definite ideas either, but Dylan recommended bongos and Johnston suggested cowbell. Thinking to "show 'em how bad their ideas're gonna sound," Buttrey rigged up the bongos and cowbells and to his surprise the part came to him spontaneously as the tape rolled. "It came from nowhere," he later recalled. "To this day it's one of the best drum patterns I ever came up with."[1] And though the percussion part seemed to fit the *a* phrases, Buttrey had the presence of mind to delineate the *b* phrases and the bridge by switching to drums. It was one of the happy accidents that often happens when good musicians gather in a recording studio.

Listening Guide

"Lay Lady Lay" (Bob Dylan), Columbia Records (stereo). Also appears on the album *Nashville Skyline*.
Recorded at Columbia Music Row Studios, Nashville, February 1969
Bob Dylan (voice, guitar, harmonica), Pete Drake (steel guitar), Charlie Daniels (guitar), Norman Blake (guitar), Bob Wilson (organ, piano), Charlie McCoy (bass), Kenny Buttrey (drums)

Producer: Bob Johnston
Engineers: Charlie Bragg, Neil Wilburn
Charts: Hot 100 #7, Top LP's #3
Key: A
Meter: 4/4

Time	Section	Lyric Cue	Listen For
0:00	Intro (4 bars)		Steel guitar, acoustic guitar 2, bass (L). Acoustic guitar 1 (C). Organ, percussion, acoustic guitar 3 (R). "Falling" chromatic line and chord progression.
	Verse 1 (16)		
0:13	*a* (4)	"Lay lady lay"	"Falling" progression.
0:25	*a* (4)	"Lay lady lay"	
0:37	*b* (4)	"Whatever colors"	Diatonic chords; new harmonic progression. Change from percussion to drums.
0:50	*a* (4)	"Lay lady lay"	Similar to previous *a* phrases.
1:03	Verse 2 (16)	"Stay lady stay"	Similar to **verse 1**.
1:51	Bridge (8)	"Why wait any longer"	Similar texture to *b* phrase, diatonic harmony.
2:16	Verse 3 (16+3)	"Lay lady lay"	Similar to previous **verses**.
3:05	Outro		Rising chord progression.

16.2. "CHEST FEVER" (1968)

THE BAND

The Band was a group of four Canadians and an American from Arkansas. They had played together as the Hawks since the early sixties backing rockabilly singer Ronnie Hawkins and then Bob Dylan. When Dylan went into temporary retirement in Woodstock, New York, in 1966, the Hawks followed. With no gigs or recording commitments, Dylan, Robbie Robertson (guitar), Richard Manuel (piano), Rick Danko (bass), Garth Hudson (organ), and Levon Helm (drums) got together each day in a house they named Big Pink to play music just for themselves. They played old songs, new songs, half-finished songs, free-form jams, whatever came to mind. Away from any commercial pressure or fan expectations, they all just had "a really good time writing music, hanging out," as Robertson put it.[2] Dylan finally rejoined the pop world when he went to Nashville to record the songs for *John Wesley Harding*. The Hawks took a new name, the Band, and set out to make a record of their own, something that captured the vibe of their informal down-home sessions even as it introduced an extraordinary new sound. They would call it *Music from Big Pink*.

The five men were exceptionally skilled musicians with years of nightly gigs and relentless rehearsal under their belts and a deep grasp of rock and roll, R&B, blues, folk, and country music, which they combined seamlessly in their own modern rock blend. They shared a single-minded commitment to musical craft. "We drove ourselves as near to perfection as we could get,"[3] said Richard Manuel. Moreover, they were keenly attuned to one another. "We'd been back-to-back for a long time," said Levon Helm. "We were birds of a feather. We all had a common appreciation of music, art, and nature, and our chemistry had been tried and tested under fire."[4] The time spent steeping in America's musical melting pot gave the Band's music a sense of timelessness. It *felt* old, historic, even as it roared with electronic sound. It was "a sound bordering on country and reminiscent of the Procol Harum [a British prog rock group]," read a confusing *Billboard* review.[5] A *Life* magazine reviewer called it "clear, cool, country soul that wash[es] the ears with a sound never heard before."[6] *Rolling Stone* alluded to the group's blend of the musical present and past with the quip, "The Band is the only rock and roll group that could have warmed up the crowd for Abraham Lincoln."[7]

The uniqueness of the sound lay in the extraordinary musical empathy among the group's members. The group chemistry was so cohesive that the spotlight never remained long on any single member, yet each stood out. The lead vocal was often passed around in the course of a song. Vocal harmonies were not cleanly synchronized or blended; rather, each voice sang or shouted the line in its own way, giving the impression of an old-time revival meeting. In their instrumental parts, too, each man often seemed to occupy a distinct musical space, yet all were solidly tethered to a central musical axis. The result was both loose and tight at the same time. And the mix of styles the Band invoked was a portrait of rock itself. Here was a group, said admirer Eric Clapton, that "finally kind of amalgamated all of the influences."[8]

"Chest Fever" is the most aggressively rocking track on *Music from Big Pink*. On such tracks as "Long Black Veil" (recalling the hit version by country star Lefty Frizzell) or the largely acoustic "The Weight," the group showcases an obvious country influence. "Chest Fever," on the other hand, is a rock and roll evocation of the hell-raising attitude at the core of country's honky-tonk ethos. It begins with an organ solo whose first gesture echoes the opening of J. S. Bach's Toccata in D minor (BWV

565). A distortion effect lends the sound an ominous edge. After a brief, rhythmically free solo, the organ settles into a lumbering four-chord riff. The drums provide a solid foundation as guitar, piano, and bass take their places in the communal groove, each announcing an individual presence before piano and guitar fall into unison with the organ riff.

Piano, guitar, and organ continue their unison riffing during the verse, while the bass dances to its own rhythm, cutting across the groove with displaced accents. From here to the end of the chorus the track leads the listener through a progression of texture and rhythm changes. At the pre-chorus the bass falls into a more stable pattern of accents on beats one and three, interspersed with sixteenth-note subdivisions, while the unison piano/organ/guitar texture breaks into discrete components (the organ drops out altogether).

At the chorus the bass drops the frisky sixteenth-note subdivisions and finally joins the drums' relentlessly solid rhythmic core, playing a simple eighth-note figure. Meanwhile, the piano and guitar also lock more tightly into the groove while the organ pads the texture with sustained notes. The texture and groove progressions finally lead to a point of dissolution at the end of the chorus ("She receives") and then begin anew, building again from the foundational riff.

The beginning of the bridge is startling. The texture and groove once again dissolve but this time the music drifts into a different dimension, morphing into the sound of a ragtag street band. The scene is suddenly surreal. Dusty musicians in some nineteenth-century frontier town seem to have taken over the track with their forlorn horns and fiddle, and the protagonist (in the voice of Richard Manuel) has turned pitiful. At the end of eight bars, the character changes as Levon Helm takes over to finish Manuel's "I don't think I'm going to last" with a shouted "very much longer!"

The organ riff jolts the track back to the present, setting up a rocking organ solo, which is accompanied by yet another texture-groove variant. The bass now lends a distinct funk flavor as all chord progression stops and the group concentrates on rhythmic interaction. Meanwhile, a leftover horn has somehow traveled back from the other dimension, adding its own funky rhythm to the jam. One final trip through the riff–verse–pre-chorus–chorus sequence and the track draws to a close with a fadeout on the riff texture.

Listening Guide

"Chest Fever" (J. R. Robertson), Capitol Records (stereo). Appears on the album *Music from Big Pink*.

Recorded at A&R Studios, New York City, February 1968

Robbie Robertson (guitar, voice), Richard Manuel (piano, voice), Rick Danko (bass, voice), Garth Hudson (organ), Levon Helm (drums, voice), John Simon (baritone horn), other instruments played by members of the Band

Producer: John Simon

Engineer: Shelley Yakus

Chart: Top LP's #30

Key: E

Meter: 4/4

Time	Section	Lyric Cue	Listen For
0:00	**Intro** (Free Meter+8)		Organ (with distortion) plays in free meter; deep reverb tails to the right.
0:33			Riff.
0:37			Drum groove.
0:41			Piano (L), guitar (R), bass (R).
0:48			Piano and guitar join organ riff.
0:52	**Verse 1** (7)	"I know she's a tracker"	Lead voice, Manuel (L); harmony voice, Helm (R).
			Riff answers vocal phrases.
			Displaced bass accents.
1:09	**Pre-Chorus** (4)	"She was just there"	Texture change: Bass moves to regular accents on beats 1 and 3 with sixteenth-note subdivisions.
1:19	**Chorus** (8)	"And as my mind"	Texture change: Bass switches to simpler eighth-note groove.
			Danko and Robertson add harmonies (C).
1:33			Texture and groove dissolve.
1:38	**Riff** (4)		Texture begins to build as in **intro**.
1:47	**Verse 2** (7)	"She's been down"	Similar to **verse 1**.
2:05	**Pre-Chorus** (4)	"She was just here"	Similar to **pre-chorus 1**.
2:14	**Chorus** (8)	"And as my mind"	Similar to **chorus 1**.
2:33	**Bridge** (8)	"It's long, long"	Ragged-sounding ensemble of instruments, including baritone horn, fiddle, and saxophone.
			Manuel's voice moves to center of the mix.
			Groove shifts to triplet swing.
2:53	**Riff** (4)		Similar to **intro**.
3:03	**Organ Solo** (16)		Quasi-funk jam; tonic harmony throughout.

continued on next page

Time	Section	Lyric Cue	Listen For
3:40	**Riff** (6)		Similar to **intro**.
3:54	**Verse 3** (7)	"She's stoned"	Similar to **verse 1**.
4:11	**Pre-Chorus** (4)	"She was just there"	Similar to **pre-chorus 1**.
4:20	**Chorus** (8)	"And as my mind"	Similar to **chorus 1**.
4:39	**Coda** (2+8 to fade)		Brief reference to opening organ solo; riff to fade.

16.3. "FORTUNATE SON" (1969)

CREEDENCE CLEARWATER REVIVAL

> I was trying to figure out what part of Louisiana you boys are from. When I found out you were from Berkeley, I burned all your records.[9]
>
> —Donald "Duck" Dunn

Stax bass player Donald "Duck" Dunn was a funny guy and his quip was meant as an accolade. To Dunn, a quintessential southern musician, Creedence Clearwater Revival's deceptively authentic southern sound seemed to upend the normal musical order of things. In fact, however, the band hailed not from Berkeley but El Cerrito, California, not far in distance but a world apart. Nevertheless, if this sleepy, white working-class suburb had little in common with the countercultural doings ten miles down the road, it was virtually a different planet from the bayous and cotton fields of Louisiana and Mississippi. Still, Dunn's impression is understandable. Creedence's guiding light, John Fogerty, raised on records and radio, had developed a style of singing, playing, and songwriting infused with southern spirit, both blues and country. With the haunted sounds of "Born on the Bayou" and "Green River," the rockabilly stomp of "Bad Moon Rising," and the forlorn "Lodi," Creedence brought a modern rock honky-tonk sound to top-forty radio, with fourteen hits in less than four years.

Fogerty was the band's lead guitarist, singer, songwriter, and producer. While his was the band's guiding vision, however, the other members—brother Tom Fogerty, Stu Cook, and Doug Clifford—made up a solid ensemble. All but Tom, who joined later, had played together since junior high school. If Fogerty was the most ambitious and dedicated, Cook and Clifford completed a cohort of musical buddies who grew up together in a rock and roll band and worshipped many of same musical heroes. By the time of their debut album *Creedence* in 1968, they had been playing together for nearly ten years.

Fogerty's songs and the band's records have a chiseled quality with everything solidly in its place. Unlike the sprawling tracks of many contemporary San Francisco bands, Creedence's many hit singles are short, distilled blasts of elemental rock and roll. Fogerty likes to tell a story about how, as an eight-year-old boy, he was captivated by the R&B instrumental "Lost Dreams" (1956) by Ernie Freeman. The record remained a favorite, which somewhat explains Fogerty's approach. "Lost Dreams," too, is elemental—a simple thirty-two-bar tune played once on piano with loudly thumping kick and snare drums dominating the accompaniment. The record's melancholy mood owes as much to its sound as its melody and harmonies. Working in an age of multitrack recording, Creedence's tracks are more complex in texture, but Fogerty never loses sight of the lesson learned from "Lost Dreams": The trick to imparting a musical essence is knowing how to do just enough.

"Fortunate Son" is a perfect example. The track asserts its fundamental elements at the outset: drums, bass, guitar riff. The snare groove is basic; its only quirk is a slapback echo (an allusion to rockabilly style) placed to the right of the snare, creating a continuous bounce across the stereo field. The bass pulses with steady eighth notes. At Fogerty's vocal entrance the guitar texture is spilt between rhythm on the right and lead on the left. Fogerty sings in a primitive, angry growl, his grainy blues tone reflecting that of the guitars. The verse and chorus are nearly identical in their harmonic phrases, the only difference being a switch from ♭VII to V.

Verse: I–♭VII–IV
Chorus: I–V–IV

These descriptions hold for the entire track with the exception of the break, which remains on the tonic while introducing a new, though related and equally simple, guitar riff.

But within this framework Fogerty introduces subtle textural touches that enhance the sound. For example, although the opening guitar riff is straightforward, the sound—created by four guitars—is constructed for a particular sonic effect. Two guitars, one on each side of the stereo field, play a descending series of sixth intervals. As the guitars sustain their last notes, two other guitars, again, one on each side, finish the riff with a bluesy answer in a lower register. They, too, sustain their last note while the first two guitars begin to repeat the riff. The entire riff can be played on a single guitar, but by splitting it up this way Fogerty makes it much more effective. Using a pair of guitars for each of the riff's two fragments, he spreads the guitar tone across the stereo field. And by splitting the riff into these two fragments, he allows each of them to overlap, creating a seamless continuity of sound.

Similarly, the break is musically simple yet sonically rich thanks to a four-guitar arrangement. A low register guitar part (L) doubles the bass's tonic drone while a new riff (thirds now instead of sixths) dominates the left side of the mix. The riff is doubled on the right side by a third guitar mixed at a lower volume. When the riff repeats, this volume increases so that the left and right sides are in balance. The repeat is further delineated by adding a fourth guitar, this one on the right side and in the low register doubling the drone guitar on the left, but adding a different, more distorted sound.

The song lyrics, written at the height of the Vietnam war, reflect Fogerty's working-class roots and his anger at having been drafted for a military adventure of vague purpose (prior to Creedence's success). In the protagonist's mind, it was rarely those with political connections or money who went to the war, and the biggest flag wavers were often those who made the least sacrifice. Fogerty's stark words and enraged delivery stand as an enduring indictment of elitism and its life-and-death consequences—all delivered in just over two minutes of vital rock and roll.

Listening Guide

"Fortunate Son" (John Fogerty), Fantasy Records (stereo). Also appears on the album *Willy and the Poor Boys*.
Recorded at Wally Heider Recording, San Francisco, 1969
Musicians: John Fogerty (voice, lead guitar), Tom Fogerty (rhythm guitar), Stu Cook (bass), Doug Clifford (drums)
Arranger and producer: John Fogerty
Engineer: Russ Gary
Charts: Hot 100 #3, Top LP's #3
Key: G
Meter: 4/4

Time	Section	Lyric Cue	Listen For
0:00	Intro (2+8)		Bass (L) plays repeated eighth notes on tonic.
			Kick and snare (C); snare echo (R).
0:04			Guitar riff 1: 2 guitars, L&R, sixths.
0:10			Guitar riff 2: 2 guitars, L&R, blue third.
0:18	Verse 1 (8)	"Some folks are born"	Rhythm guitar (R); lead guitar (L) answers vocal phrases.
			I–♭VII–IV–I chord sequence.

Time	Section	Lyric Cue	Listen For
0:33	**Chorus 1** (8)	"It ain't me . . . no senator's son"	I–V–IV–I chord sequence.
0:47	**Verse 2** (8)	"Some folks are born"	Similar to **verse 1**.
1:02	**Chorus 2** (8)	"It ain't me . . . no millionaire's son"	Similar to **chorus 1**.
1:16	**Break** (8)		Bass as in **intro**.
			Drums out.
			Guitar riff (L) doubled at lower volume (R); guitar 3 doubles bass part (L).
1:23			Riff repeats, riff guitars balanced in volume.
			A fourth guitar doubles guitar 3 with fuzz tone (R).
			Drums in.
1:30	**Verse 3** (8)	"Some folks are born"	Similar to **verse 1**, but no guitar on left.
1:43			Enter guitar on left.
1:45	**Chorus 3** (8)	"It ain't me . . . no fortunate son"	Similar to **chorus 1**.
2:00	**Chorus** (fade)		

NOTES

1. Quoted in Clinton Heylin, *Bob Dylan: The Recording Sessions 1960–1994* (New York: St. Martin's Griffin, 1995), 75.

2. Quoted in Rob Bowman, *Music from Big Pink* CD booklet (Capitol Records, 2000), 5.

3. Quoted in Barney Hoskyns, *Across the Great Divide: The Band and America* (New York: Hyperion, 1993), 73.

4. Quoted in Hoskyns, 167.

5. "Album Reviews," *Billboard*, July 13, 1968, 77.

6. Alfred G. Aronowitz, "Country Soul from Bob's Backup Band," *Life*, July 26, 1968, 12.

7. "The Band in Concert," *Rolling Stone*, February 7, 1970. Accessed July 19, 2021. https://theband.hiof.no/history/The_Band_in_Concert_1969.pdf. This site has a wealth of articles on the Band scanned from the original sources.

8. Biography.com editors, "Eric Clapton—The Band's Influence," Eric Clapton interview, Accessed July 18, 2021. https://www.biography.com/video/eric-clapton-the-bands-influence-2080111524.

9. Reported by band member Doug Clifford, quoted in Hank Bordowitz, *Bad Moon Rising: The Unauthorized History of Creedence Clearwater Revival* (Chicago: Chicago Review Press, 2007), 77.

FURTHER READING

Einarson, John. *Desperadoes: The Roots of Country Rock*. New York: Cooper Square Press, 2001.

Hoskyns, Barney. *Across the Great Divide: The Band and America*. New York: Hyperion, 1993.

Kealing, Bob. *Calling Me Home: Gram Parsons and the Roots of Country Rock*. Gainesville: University Press of Florida, 2012.

FURTHER LISTENING

Byrds, "You Ain't Going Nowhere" (Columbia, 1968)
Eagles, "Desperado" (Asylum, 1973)
Flying Burrito Brothers, "Sin City" (A&M, 1969)
Gram Parsons, "Return of the Grievous Angel" (Reprise, 1974)
New Riders of the Purple Sage, "Whatcha Gonna Do" (Columbia, 1971)
Tom Petty and the Heartbreakers, "Louisiana Rain" (Backstreet, 1979)
Poco, "Honky Tonk Downstairs" (Epic, 1970)
Linda Ronstadt, "I Can't Help It (If I'm Still in Love with You)" (Capitol, 1974)
Rod Stewart, "Gasoline Alley" (Mercury, 1970)

17

TROUBADOURS
The Singer-Songwriter

The singer-songwriter was a holdover from the urban folk scene of the late '50s and early '60s, but the genre had evolved significantly by the late '60s. It was no longer focused on folk repertory and songs of social or political relevance. These songwriters looked inward, writing about relationships and their perspectives on the world using poetic imagery and metaphor. A 1971 *Time* magazine cover story put it this way: "What all of them seem to want most is an intimate mixture of lyricism and personal expression—the often exquisitely melodic reflections of a private 'I.'"[1] Moreover, the musical arrangements were not restricted to the small acoustic ensembles that were the hallmarks of folk music. Although acoustic guitar or piano were usually featured, singer-songwriters might also include electric instruments, drums, and even orchestras in their arrangements. And they might draw on diverse styles such as jazz, R&B, or pop. If folk music was their heritage, there was no question that the music of the singer-songwriters was yet another flavor of rock.

Nothing, however, was to detract from a candid and heartfelt presentation. Glitz and showmanship were downplayed. Although there were some musical similarities among artists, the genre's stylistic influences varied widely and included Tin Pan Alley, blues, country, R&B, and, of course, the commanding presence of mid-1960s Bob Dylan. But whatever the stylistic traces, the singer-songwriter aimed to express a personal take on life experience, even if that expression was through an assumed character. Accordingly, leading figures included such diverse artists as Leonard Cohen, Jim Croce, Laura Nyro, Elton John, Melanie, Carly Simon, Gordon Lightfoot, Cat Stevens, Carole King, Randy Newman, Jackson

Browne, and Paul Simon, as well as the three artists discussed in this chapter. These artists represent compelling personalities closely identified with the protagonists in their songs.

17.1. "BOTH SIDES NOW" (1969)

JONI MITCHELL

> Joni Mitchell's songs are the product of her fascination with changes of heart, changes of mind, changes of season and changes of self.[2]
>
> —Ellen Sander, *New York Times*

Before she became a star performer, Joni Mitchell had a well-established reputation as a songwriter. Her poetic lyrics and flowing melodies appeared on records by such well-known folk performers as Buffy Sainte-Marie, Tom Rush, and Judy Collins. Collins's hit album *Wildflowers* (1968) contained two of Mitchell's songs, "Michael from Mountains" and "Both Sides Now," the latter a top-ten pop single. So by the time of Mitchell's own debut album, *Song to a Seagull* (1968), she was already a respected artist among her peers and a small group of fans. The record introduced her to a broader public as a singer whose distinctive style brought out the emotional drama of her complex lyrics and a unique guitar stylist who favored resonant open tunings and unusual chord changes.

"Both Sides Now," from Mitchell's second album, *Clouds*, is a song of innocence and experience. In a series of vignettes, Mitchell sketches a set of before-and-after contrasts that juxtapose impressions of naive wonder with world-weary insights. Moving from the metaphor of "clouds" to "love" and finally "life," the song's protagonist relates her experience of each from both perspectives. The song's verses are divided into two eight-bar sections, the first filled with images of enchantment, the second expressing a tone of disillusion. As if to underscore that both are part of the same reality, the music for both sections is identical.

The chorus returns each time to the attractiveness of illusion, with the melody rising to its highest point three times in succession, perhaps expressing a persistent longing ("*Both* sides now, *up* and down, *still* somehow"). Though she knows better, it is the naive illusion that sticks in the protagonist's mind. But as she acknowledges in the refrain lyric, that simply means that she doesn't really know clouds or love or life "at all."

"I feel my music with a solitary voice and a solitary guitar," Mitchell once said.[3] "Both Sides Now" is a good example of what she meant. She sings and plays in the tradition of the lone troubadour, yet her guitar provides a rich textural accompaniment with varying shades of harmony. The open tuning provides a ringing resonance and the near-constant drone of the tonic pitch (F♯) softens the chord progression and inflects a mild, shimmering dissonance. Instead of the chords moving solidly from root to root, they seem to float suspended above the tonic. Most of the pitches are diatonic, but at the end of each section in the verses, two quick blues notes sound—♭7 (E) and ♭3 (A)—injecting a faint association with the blues and its eloquent exploration of life's troubled uncertainty.

The song's limited harmonic palette of I, IV, and V chords is unusual compared with other tracks on *Clouds*. ("Songs to Aging Children Come" is an especially good example of Mitchell's complex harmonic sensibility.) But as one Joni Mitchell scholar put it, "She exploits the redundancy for expressive purpose."[4] In other words, the song's world-weary tone is effectively expressed in the plainest way, capturing some of the protagonist's feeling of resignation. A comparison with Judy Collins's bouncy folk-rock version of "Both Sides Now" is instructive. While Collins's singing is wistful, the arrangement is peppy. Arranged for guitar, bass, drums, strings, and a bright organ riff, the track is lovely in its own pop way but conveys little of the existential depth of Mitchell's spare version.

Listening Guide

"**Both Sides Now**" (Joni Mitchell), Reprise Records (stereo). Appears on the album *Clouds*.
Recorded at A&M Studios, Hollywood, 1969
Joni Mitchell (voice, guitar)
Producer: Joni Mitchell
Engineer: Henry Lewy
Charts: Top LP's #31
Key: F♯
Meter: 4/4

Time	Section	Lyric Cue	Listen For
0:00	Intro (4)		Open tuning (E, B, E, G♯, B, E), capo on second fret.
0:11	Verse 1 (8+8)	"Rows and flows"	Two sides of clouds.
			Innocence.
0:31		"But now they only"	Experience.
			Guitar plays blues inflection at the end of each 8-bar phrase.

continued on next page

Time	Section	Lyric Cue	Listen For
0:50	**Chorus 1** (10)	"I've looked at clouds"	Melody reaches its highest point three times in succession.
1:14	Vamp (3)		
1:22	**Verse 2** (8+8)	"Moons and Junes"	Two sides of love. Innocence.
1:42		"But now it's just another show"	Experience.
2:01	**Chorus 2** (10)	"I've looked at love"	Similar to **chorus 1**.
2:26	Vamp (3)		
2:33	**Verse 3** (8+8)	"Tears and fears"	Two sides of life. Innocence.
2:53		"But now old friends"	Experience.
3:13	**Chorus 3** (10)	"I've looked at life"	Similar to previous **choruses**.
3:37	Vamp (3)		
3:45	**Chorus 3** (10)	"I've looked at"	Repeat.
4:07	Vamp (8)		

17.2. "FIRE AND RAIN" (1969)

JAMES TAYLOR

In 1970 James Taylor became the face of the singer-songwriter genre with the commercial success of his second album, *Sweet Baby James*, and its hit single "Fire and Rain." He was featured in a *Time* magazine cover story and costarred in the film *Two-Lane Blacktop*. As the *Time* article put it, he was "the man who best sums up the new sound of rock—as well as being its most radiantly successful practitioner."[5] Taylor's "new sound" incorporated traces of folk rock and country rock and blues in a personal style that highlighted his finger-picked guitar and cool yet sweet vocals. His lyrics were a combination of reflexive rumination and poetic imagery, reflecting his early difficulties with mental illness and drug addiction. The song "Knockin' Around the Zoo," for example, is a story drawn from Taylor's experience as a patient at the McLean psychiatric hospital in Cambridge, Massachusetts, where he spent several months when he was a teenager.

"Fire and Rain" also weaves together images born of Taylor's personal experience in an expression of sadness and beauty. Of the song's three verses, the first two deal with painful memories: the suicide of a friend named Suzanne (verse one) and Taylor's struggle with heroin and depression (verse two). Verse three shifts to musing on the road traveled to his newfound success. It includes a reference to the failure of his early band, the Flying Machine. The chorus is a poignant refrain whose first two lines invoke symbols of life's pain (the "fire" of electroconvulsive therapy and the "rain" of the cold shower that follows) and beauty (endless "sunny days"). The last two lines leave the listener with a sense of impermanence and loss. Amid "lonely days" the protagonist "always thought" that he would see his friend (presumably Suzanne) again. But now that hopeful expectation is gone forever.

Described this way, the song sounds bleak, which is not in fact the case. The atmosphere is lightened partly by the symbols of hope Taylor invokes—the help of Jesus and a reference to the future ("things to come"). But the brightest ray of sunshine is the musical setting and Taylor's performance. The delicate finger picking in the intro sets a gentle, reflective tone, complemented by the piano playing of Taylor's friend, Carole King. Taylor's voice is clear and forthright, reporting the fact of the tragedy without becoming part of it himself. The words of verse one are in themselves heartbreaking, yet Taylor's restraint allows listeners to feel their own emotions.

The music does have a particular twist, however, that underscores the melancholy lyrics. A persistent use of the flatted-seventh scale degree (B♭) infuses the chord progressions with a shadowy hue. The note is used in two ways: (1) to change the V chord from major (its normal state) to minor and (2) as the root of a flatted VII chord. One or the other occurs in each four-bar harmonic phrase of the verses. The eight-bar intro, which is simply once through the chord changes of the verse, is a good place to hear this. In the first of the four-bar phrases, the second chord (V) is G minor, instead of the normal G major. In the second four-bar phrase the G major is restored but the following chord—the third chord in the progression—is B♭, which again suggests a darker color.

C major scale: C, D, E, F, G, A, B   Flatted 7th scale degree: **B♭**
V chord: G–B–D (normal)   V chord with alteration: G–**B♭**–D
VII chord: B–D–F (normal)   VII chord with alteration: **B♭**–D–F

The chorus leaves this harmonic ambivalence behind, lightening the mood with a soulful melody sung over a diatonic chord progression that repeats three times. The chords are unambiguous in their harmonic direction and mood, arriving each time on the tonic with an affirmative little guitar riff. But in the final phrase of the chorus ("always thought") we are put back into the shadows with the B♭ chord. The move seems to knock the chorus off balance. While each preceding phrase is directed firmly at a tonic resolution, the final phrase is left hanging on an unresolved dissonance, a glimpse perhaps into the protagonist's lingering malaise.

Listening Guide

"Fire and Rain" (James Taylor), Warner Bros. Records (stereo). Also appears on the album *Sweet Baby James*.
Recorded at Sunset Sound, Hollywood, December 1969
Musicians: James Taylor (voice, guitar), Carole King (piano), Bobby West (bass), Russ Kunkel (drums)
Producer: Peter Asher
Engineer: Bill Lazerus
Charts: Hot 100 #3, Top LP's #3
Key: C
Meter: 2/4

Time	Section	Lyric Cue	Listen For
0:00	Intro (4)		Phrase 1: guitar (L), G minor chord.
0:06			Phrase 2: piano (R), B♭ chord.
0:12	Verse 1 (4+4)	"Just yesterday"	Voice (C) in subdued style.
			Bowed bass (L&R).
			Phrasing as in **intro**.
0:37	Chorus 1 (8+1)	"I've seen fire"	Drums enter.
			Bass changes from half notes to quarter notes, doubling harmonic rhythm.
			Diatonic chord progression.
0:56			B♭ chord leading to unresolved dissonance.
1:03			1-bar extension features tom fills.
1:05	Verse 2 (4+4)	"Won't you look down"	Similar to **verse** 1 (with drums).
1:31	Chorus 2 (8+1)	"Oh, I've seen fire"	Similar to **chorus** 1.
			Bass in octaves: low (L), high (R).
2:00	Verse 3 (4+4)	"Been walking"	Similar to previous **verses**.
			Bass drone on tonic throughout.
2:25	Chorus 3 (8)	"Oh, I've seen fire"	Similar to previous **choruses**.
2:50	Coda (fade)		Based on **chorus** extension.
			Dissonance extended through fade.

17.3. "HEART OF GOLD" (1971)

NEIL YOUNG

Like Joni Mitchell, Neil Young came to America from Canada, settling in Los Angeles in 1966. By the end of the '60s, Neil Young had been a key player in three successful musical projects: Buffalo Springfield; Crosby, Stills, Nash, and Young; and his own solo career with his band Crazy Horse. He was a leading figure in folk rock and country rock. His individualism and his tendency to write from a personal viewpoint, often accompanied in concert only by his acoustic guitar, also made him a natural fit for the singer-songwriter genre.

"Heart of Gold" was recorded in Nashville over a winter weekend while Young was in town to appear on *The Johnny Cash Show*. Also appearing on the show were James Taylor and Linda Ronstadt, who Young asked to contribute backing vocals on the recording. The track is a study in minimalism, from its lyrics to its musical content to the restrained performances by the session musicians. It comes across as an unadorned confession of detachment mingled with the protagonist's hope for some elusive emotional connection. The lyrics sketch the song's theme, but its fuller significance is fleshed out by the musical accompaniment. The chord progression is simple and to the point, as is the drum groove. The very starkness evokes the protagonist's state of mind.

In between vocal sections, a solo harmonica plays to the same chordal accompaniment as the voice and takes up almost as much playing time. The harmonica's prominence makes it feel like an extension of the songwriter's voice, wordlessly expressing the inner feelings that the protagonist finds so difficult to communicate ("These expressions I never give").

With its spare instrumentation of harmonica, guitar, bass, and drums, the track's intro creates a texture reminiscent of Dylan's *John Wesley Harding* album (which uses the same Nashville drummer). It feels both rustic and somehow old-fashioned. The opening gesture is a two-bar acoustic guitar riff in E minor, which is followed by the first of three harmonica solos in G major (intro, interlude one, interlude two), each one a gentle evocation of lonesome introspection. The intro is capped off with another iteration of the E minor riff. Bookending the harmonica's major-mode phrases with the minor-mode riff sets the tone for the song's ambivalent mood.

The vocal melody in the verse is even simpler than the harmonica's, repeating the same two-bar melodic phrase three times. The voice and harmonica share the same chord changes for these first six bars, but then comes a refrain ("keeps me searching"), which replaces the E minor guitar riff. The refrain music is unique to the voice. It slows the harmonic rhythm (one chord per bar instead of two) as it brings the verse to its conclusion. It also stays in the major mode.

Verse Harmonic Rhythm
First 3 phrases: ‖: vi–IV | V–I :‖
Refrain: ‖: vi | I | IV | IV–I :‖

The riff, then, is associated with the harmonica and the refrain with the vocal, which adds to the formal delineation between interludes and verses. In the track's coda, however, these two musical ideas merge. The voices take over from the guitar to sing the minor-mode riff, but they use the lyrics from the refrain. After three riff repetitions, they continue on into the final cadence of the actual refrain to end the track.

The steel guitar part is arranged in a similar fashion. Through most of the track, it is conspicuous only during the verses, its crying sound an effective counterpoint to the voice. During the harmonica interludes, it fades to the distant background. In the coda, however, the steel guitar joins the voices throughout, playing along with both riff and refrain.

The centerpiece of the track, of course, is Young's voice, one of rock's most distinctive. Fellow singer-songwriter Rickie Lee Jones described it as "hesitant, whiny, masculine and feminine."[6] Her description aptly captures the tenuousness and sadness in Young's sound. The vocal persona suits the song's taciturn yet hopeful protagonist, who comes across as both vulnerable and purposeful in his continuing search for a heart of gold.

Listening Guide

"Heart of Gold" (Neil Young), Reprise Records (stereo). Also appears on the album *Harvest*.
Recorded at Quadrafonic (now Quad) Sound Studios, Nashville, February 1971
Neil Young (voice, guitar, harmonica), James Taylor (voice), Linda Ronstadt (voice), Teddy Irwin (guitar), Ben Keith (steel guitar), Tim Drummond (bass), Kenny Buttrey (drums)
Producers: Elliot Mazer, Neil Young
Charts: Hot 100 #1, Top LP's #1
Key: G
Meter 4/4

Time	Section	Lyric Cue	Listen For
0:00	Intro (4+8)		Riff (minor).
			Guitar 1 and snare (L).
			Kick drum and bass (C).
			Guitar 2 (riff, R).
0:11			Harmonica melody (major, C).
0:29			Riff.
0:34	Verse 1 (10+4)	"I want to live"	Vocal (C).
			Steel guitar (L).
			Rhythm guitar (R).
0:51	Refrain	"That keep me searching"	Steel and rhythm guitar suddenly quieter; focus on voice.
0:57			Guitars louder for cadence.
1:02	Refrain		Repeat refrain.
1:13	Interlude 1 (8)		Harmonica melody.
			Texture similar to **intro**.
			Steel guitar recedes to mix background.
1:30			Riff; steel guitar out.
1:36	Verse 2 (10+4)	"I've been to Hollywood"	Similar to **verse 1**.
			Steel guitar returns.
2:15	Interlude 2 (6)		Harmonica melody.
			Texture similar to **intro**.
			Steel guitar recedes.
2:32	Coda (10)	"Keep me searching"	Voices sing riff three times with refrain lyrics.
			Steel guitar (L) returns.
2:49		"I've been a miner"	Refrain music (major).

NOTES

1. "James Taylor: One Man's Family of Rock," *Time*, March 1, 1971.
2. Ellen Sander, "Three Who Sing Their Own Songs," *New York Times*, December 29, 1968, 24 D.
3. Quoted in Susan Gordon Lydon, "In Her House, Love," *New York Times*, April 20, 1969, 32 D.
4. Lloyd Whitesell, *The Music of Joni Mitchell* (New York: Oxford University Press), 144.
5. "James Taylor," *Time*.
6. Quoted in Jimmy McDonough, *Shakey: Neil Young's Biography* (New York: Anchor Books, 2003), 15.

FURTHER READING

McDonough, Jimmy. *Shakey: Neil Young's Biography*. New York: Anchor Books, 2003.

White, Timothy. *Long Ago and Far Away: James Taylor—His Life and Music*. London: Omnibus Press, 2001.

Whitesell, Lloyd. *The Music of Joni Mitchell*. New York: Oxford University Press, 2008.

FURTHER LISTENING

Leonard Cohen, "Suzanne" (Columbia, 1967)
Elton John, "Your Song" (MCA, 1970)
Carole King, "You've Got a Friend" (A&M, 1971)
Kris Kristofferson, "Me and Bobby McGee" (Monument, 1970)
Van Morrison, "Moondance" (Warner Bros., 1970)
Laura Nyro, "Stoned Soul Picnic" (Columbia, 1968)
Carly Simon, "You're So Vain" (Elektra, 1972)
Cat Stevens, "Where Do the Children Play" (A&M, 1970)
Townes Van Zandt, "Pancho and Lefty" (Tomato, 1972)

18

GRAND AMBITION
Progressive Rock

Progressive, or prog, rock developed as an offshoot of psychedelic rock. As we have seen, psychedelic rock exemplified rock musicians' expanded aesthetic scope and artistic ambition. Tracks like the Doors' "The End," the Beatles' "Strawberry Fields Forever," the Nice's "Ars Longa Vita Brevis," and the Mothers of Invention's "Who Are the Brain Police" all demonstrate unprecedented approaches to pop music. Whether in their length, narrative structure, harmonic and melodic design, rhythmic complexity, expanded instrumentation, or innovative studio techniques, an increasing number of rock tracks explored new pop frontiers. The impulse to push boundaries was widespread among musicians of diverse stylistic orientation. Led Zeppelin, Queen, and David Bowie, for example, occupy distinct positions on rock's style spectrum, but all have their prog moments.

In the UK, which was prog's first creative hotbed, Western classical music provided inspiration and musical resources for such early prog groups as Procol Harum, the Moody Blues, Pink Floyd, and King Crimson. The classical connection meant expanded instrumental palettes, unconventional—sometimes through-composed—forms, longer compositions, and richer and freer pitch resources, sometimes to the point of atonality (absence of any key center). It might even mean performing classical repertory in a rock way, as in Emerson, Lake, and Palmer's *Pictures at an Exhibition* (Mussorgsky) or Yes's "Cans and Brahms" (Brahms Symphony No. 4, third movement).

Also similar to classical music was prog's drift away from dancing toward a pure listening experience. This was perhaps the sharpest divergence with rock's roots. Prog represented "the vital expression of a bohemian middle-class intelligentsia," as Yes and King Crimson drummer Bill Bruford put it. He also located its provenance. "Art schools, colleges, and universities contributed mightily, but if you want to understand why the style grew and flourished in England rather than the U.S.A, look no further than that powerful cultural agent, the Anglican Church."[1] Just as so many American musicians had gained their earliest musical experience in church, young English musicians absorbed the sounds of the choral and organ music of the Anglican tradition. It was a long way from the blues or gospel, yet prog was unmistakably rock. It was yet another fulfillment of rock and roll's promise and an illustration of its central premise. The music had begun in a spirit of omnivorous inclusion, absorbing musical influences indiscriminately—revising, reinterpreting, reimagining, and reinventing guided by creative whim and the audience feedback from the commercial marketplace. Prog simply showed once again that rock and roll's power to absorb and reshape musical influence had few limits.

18.1. "THE COURT OF THE CRIMSON KING" (1969)

KING CRIMSON

"The Court of the Crimson King" is the last song on King Crimson's debut album, *In the Court of the Crimson King*. The record is a landmark of prog rock. Designed as a concept album, its five tracks unfold as a listening journey. The song lyrics often paint a picture of alienation in the midst of a dystopian society (e.g., "21st Century Schizoid Man," "Epitaph"). The music shows traces of jazz and folk as well as psychedelic rock and employs both classically influenced compositional techniques and avant-garde improvisation. The album's sound palette is widely diverse, featuring woodwinds nearly as prominently as guitars and enlisting the sampled sounds of the Mellotron, an electro-mechanical instrument whose keys triggered playback of sounds recorded on pieces of tape. The orchestral strings we hear in the choruses of "The Court of the Crimson King," for example, are in fact Mellotron sounds. The album's tracks are long—the shortest just over six minutes, the longest more than twelve. The music offers little to get up and dance to; it's better to put on the headphones and listen to its expansive story unfold.

For all its iconic status, *In the Court of the Crimson King* was a one-off project. The young band that produced it—Robert Fripp, Greg Lake, Michael Giles, Peter Sinfield, and Ian McDonald—would barely survive its subsequent North American tour. The project was a hugely ambitious undertaking produced by studio novices with the help of the experienced engineers at Wessex Studio in London. Limited to eight tracks, the band made extensive use of track bouncing to add layer upon layer to achieve the effect they were after. One engineer recalled that to create the large choral effect of the chorus in "The Court of the Crimson King," each note of the chords was triple tracked by voices and then bounced down to one track. If the chord was a triad, this would mean nine vocal tracks bounced down to three. Then those three were bounced down to one, leaving the other seven tracks free to continue the process.

The track-building was meticulous. The vocal part for "The Court of the Crimson King," for example, was recorded line by line, according to lyricist Peter Sinfield. And since the limited track space meant that different instruments might share the same track, strategic choices had to be made about allotting sounds because any EQ applied to a track would affect all the sounds it contained. Further, when it came to the mixing process, the music's complexity required that the mix be recorded a few bars at a time and then spliced together.

The lyrics for "The Court of the Crimson King" are filled with symbolism, suggesting a mythic past. Their metaphoric meaning is open to interpretation, but a general sense of unease pervades the track. Interestingly, the chorus, which we hear five times, has no lyrics—only massed voices singing "ahh," evoking perhaps the gathering of souls in the court of the Crimson King.

Considering its ten-minute length, the track is based on a surprisingly simple song. It uses a straightforward verse-chorus form that contrasts the verse's minor-mode sonority with the major-mode sound of the chorus. The verses have two chords; the choruses have three. Still, the track presents an intricate narrative by revisiting the same elements from different perspectives. For example, though each of the four verses is identical in phrase structure, harmony, and melody, each has a distinct instrumental arrangement. Similarly, although the track's two instrumental breaks are based on the same two-chord sequence, the rhythm and texture change significantly from break one to break two. The metronomic pulse and monophonic Mellotron melody in break one give way to a nearly pulseless free variation in break two, played by the bass and flute with added guitar counterpoint. Break two is also longer and ends with a different transitional section aimed at a different destination (i.e., break one transitions to a chorus and break two, to a verse).

Through most of the track, starting with its first appearance in the intro, the chorus music is the most consistent. Amid the many variations in the track's arrangement, the chorus provides a solid, reliable refrain whose only variable is its textural density (it tends to become a bit fuller with repetition). Yet its persona feels somehow conflicted. Although its harmonic sonorities are major, the chords D, C, and B, when arranged in series, belong to no major key. They belong to E minor. So even as the music moves away from the stark moodiness of the verses, it never sheds a looming minor-mode aura.

Eventually the chorus suffers a graphic dissolution, perhaps a reflection of the album's overall theme. After a grand cadence that seems to end the track, a pause is followed by the return of the chorus music, but now it is transformed into a disjointed parody of itself. The symphonic and choral splendor is gone, replaced by the Mellotron sounding now like a group of recorders playing the melody haltingly. This odd-sounding iteration of the once grand theme feels like a sad epitaph. It is soon interrupted by a return of the full chorus texture, but the sound is no longer stately. It has turned into a psychedelic jam session filled with strident sounds and dissonance. Finally, it is abruptly switched off. After another stretch of silence, the track fades to an end amid strange, inhuman electronic sounds.

Listening Guide

"The Court of the Crimson King" (Ian McDonald, Peter Sinfield), Atlantic Records (stereo). Also appears on the album *In the Court of the Crimson King*.
Recorded at Wessex Sound Studios, London, July–August 1969
Robert Fripp (guitars), Ian McDonald (Mellotron, organ, harpsichord, flute, voice), Greg Lake (bass, lead voice), Michael Giles (drums, percussion, voice)
Producers: King Crimson
Engineer: Robin Thompson
Charts: Hot 100 #80, Top LP's #28
Key: E minor
Meter: 4/4

Time	Section	Lyric Cue	Listen For
0:00	Intro (8)		**Chorus** music.
			Mellotron (L) plays melody.
			Guitar (R) plays pulsing quarter note chords.
			Bass (C), drums (LCR).
			Three chords: D–C–B (major-mode sonority but no major key).
0:11			Second Mellotron (R) doubles turnaround line.

Time	Section	Lyric Cue	Listen For
0:29	**Verse 1** (4+3)	"The rusted chains"	Texture thins to voice (C) and acoustic guitar (L).
			Minor-mode sonority (E minor).
0:44		"The purple"	Chord change.
			Bass (C).
			Flute trills (R).
0:51			Last bar is in 6/4 so that "King" falls on **chorus** downbeat.
0:57	**Chorus 1** (8)	"King" then "Ahh"	Similar to **intro**.
			Choral vocals (L+R) double Mellotron melody.
1:25	**Verse 2** (4+3)	"The keeper of the city"	Similar to **verse 1**; adds drums.
			Bass out.
1:39		"The black queen"	Chord change; bass in.
1:52	**Chorus 2** (8)	"King" then "Ahh"	Similar to **chorus 1**.
2:17			Guitar transitions to steady eighth-note pulse (R).
2:20	**Break 1** (8+2)		Eighth-note pulse taken by organ (R), feels like tempo has doubled.
			Bass doubles pulse in sixteenth notes.
			Sixteenth notes on cymbals.
			Mellotron melody (L).
			First two chords from the **chorus** (D and C), looped four times.
2:46			Arrive on third chord of **chorus** (B).
			Transition.
2:53	**Break Chorus** (8)	"Ahh"	Similar to **chorus 1**.
3:20	**Verse 3** (4+3)	"The gardener plants"	Similar to **verse 2**; harpsichord-type sound (R) doubles guitar.
			Bass out.
3:34			Chord change; bass in.
3:47	**Chorus** (8)	"King" then "Ahh"	Similar to **chorus 1**.
4:14	**Break 2** (22)		Flute and bass (C) begin free variation on material from **break 1**.
			Cymbals (L), guitar (R).
4:33			Electric guitar (R).
5:09			Flute refers to Rimsky-Korsakov's *Scheherazade*.
5:24	Transition		Return to E minor

continued on next page

Time	Section	Lyric Cue	Listen For
5:31	Verse 4 (4+3)	"On soft grey mornings"	Guitar plays sixteenth-note figure (L).
5:45		"The yellow jester"	Bass (C), harpsichord (R), flute (C) enter.
5:58	Chorus (12)	"King" then "Ahh"	Similar to **chorus** 1, extended by 4 bars (1 phrase).
6:43	Coda		E major chord; false ending.
			Cymbal patter.
7:17			Disjointed version of main **chorus** riff.
			Two Mellotrons, low (L) and high (C), reverb (R).
7:58	Jam (24)		Begin final jam on **chorus** music. Mellotron and organ overdubs spread across stereo field.
9:22			Cutoff, 19 seconds of silence.
9:41			Sounds.

18.2. "ROUNDABOUT" (1972)

YES

"Roundabout," from Yes's fourth album, *Fragile*, is the most elaborate of our prog examples and it makes a good case study. It exemplifies prog's classical influences, its symphonic scope, and the virtuosity of its performers. The narrative is not only long but complex in its meter, rhythm, arrangement, and formal design. And the difficult musical parts are handled with expert technique by band members Jon Anderson (voice), Steve Howe (guitar), Chris Squire (bass), Rick Wakeman (keyboards), and Bill Bruford (drums).

The intro sets the scene with an ominous crescendo. The sound is unfamiliar, otherworldly. (It's actually a backward recording of a piano note.) At the crescendo's peak, a guitar harmonic sounds, followed by a meditative fragment of music. The guitar sound is that of a nylon string classical guitar, unusual for a rock record and clearly an allusion to classical music. After a second piano note, the guitar leads to the start of the track's A section, which kicks in with a jolt, placing its initial accent on the eighth note before the downbeat. This beginning instantly announces one of the track's central themes: rhythmic urgency in the form of syncopation. The bass riff adds another recurring motive: fast instrumental runs.

The track makes strategic use of repetition—of sections, riffs, lyrics, and textures—to control its sprawling form. In its broad outline, the form is ABA. But each of the large sections has several components and its own distinct feel. Unlike a conventional bridge, the B section is sufficiently distinct and lasts long enough to be a strong disruptive presence. And before it returns to the A section, the track has an extended instrumental that is itself in two parts (interlude and break). Immersed in the break's jamming organ solo, we find ourselves far from where we started and with no certainty that the music of the A section will ever return.

The A section, along with its irregular vocal phrasing, mixed meter, and tricky instrumental parts, has three verses and two bridges. The verses are underpinned by the riff that follows the guitar intro. Its hyperactive bassline drives a groove peppered with syncopated accents. The bridges change the groove and the key (from E minor to G Mixolydian). The rhythm is much more straightforward, the beats are clearly articulated, and the arrangement introduces a new riff on electric guitar and increased synthesizer activity. Together, these parts of the A section offer a wealth of musical interest, but after the second bridge an energetic new riff suddenly kicks off the B section, which introduces yet another set of elements.

The B section makes a striking contrast to the A. Both feature a signature melodic figure, but whereas the A riff has a unified, if complicated, groove, the B riff cuts across the rhythmic flow in a way that creates an acute tension. Guitar and bass play quarter-note triplets (three attacks over two beats) while the drums play sixteenth notes. This means that three notes (bass and guitar) play against eight (drums). The rhythmic agitation continues throughout the section and through two verses of new lyrics. Then, with the B riff still playing, we hear the words and melody from verse one of the A section. The effect is disorienting not only to the listener but seemingly to the track as well. It breaks down into an interlude that recaps the guitar intro, now accompanied by a synthesizer. In another surprise, this guitar leads to the voice singing a fragment from the bridge of the A section accompanied now by Mellotron flutes.

As if to restore some order to what has become a meandering mixture of formal elements—with musical bits from the intro, A, and B sections bleeding into one another—the track launches into a vigorous organ solo. The drums and bass that fell silent in the interlude now come back with renewed energy to restore the groove and propel what feels like a funk jam. In addition to its immediate musical appeal, this section serves as a conceptual connection between the track's experimental character and rock music's fundamental roots.

But if the break simplifies the formal complexity, it also leaves us far from a sense of closure. So, it's a relief when, as the break comes to its end on a sustained B (V, or the dominant, of E minor), it delivers us back into the A section. The return is welcome, but it has taken a long time and the music has gone through transformation. We are reminded of the journey's effect in a subtle last gesture. The track's farewell is a reprise of the intro guitar lick that kicked off riff A. Recall that it was initially played by a nylon string (i.e., classical) guitar. Now the sound is that of a steel string, and the chord it leads to is not E minor but E major.

Listening Guide

"Roundabout" (Jon Anderson, Steve Howe), Atlantic Records (stereo). Also appears on the album *Fragile*.
Recorded at Advision Studios, London, September 1971
Jon Anderson (vocal), Steve Howe (guitars), Rick Wakeman (organ, Mellotron), Chris Squire (bass), Bill Bruford (drums)
Producers: Yes, Eddie Offord
Engineer: Eddie Offord
Charts: Hot 100 #13, Top LP's #4
Key: E minor/G Mixolydian
Meter: 4/4 and mixed

Time	Section	Lyric Cue	Listen For
0:00	Intro		Backward-tape piano sound crescendos to guitar harmonic; nylon-string guitar (classical music reference).
	A		
0:44	Riff A (8)		Kick drum and bass accents fall on pickup to downbeat.
			Bass plays riff (C).
			Acoustic guitar chords in harmonics (L).
0:50			Electric guitar run (R).
0:58	Verse A1 (12)	"I'll be the roundabout"	Voice (C).
			Mixed meter: 4/4 (4) + 6/4 (1) + 4/4 (2) + 2/4 (3) + 4/4 (2).
1:12			Organ enters (L).
1:18	Riff A (4)		Kick drum and bass accents fall on pickup to downbeat.
1:23			Vamp ends with sudden synthesizer interruption (R+L).

Time	Section	Lyric Cue	Listen For
1:25	Verse A2 (12)	"The music dance"	Similar to **verse A1**, with thicker acoustic guitar texture.
			Added backing vocal (R).
1:35			Organ (L) supports transition to **bridge A1**.
1:45	Bridge A1 (12+2) Phrase 1	"In and around the lake"	Strong downbeat arrival; groove change; bass, drums, organ out.
			Key changes to G Mixolydian.
			Mixed meter: 4/4 (2) + 6/4 (1) phrase.
			Rhythm guitar (R).
			Backing vocals (L+R).
1:52	Phrase 2		Organ in (L).
1:58	Phrase 3		Drums and bass in; bass and kick syncopated.
2:05	Phrase 4		Full band.
2:11		I'll be there with you"	4/4 transition to A (2).
2:15		**Riff A** (8)	Kick drum and bass accents fall on pickup to downbeat.
			Back to E minor.
2:20			Organ (L) and synth (R) run.
2:26	Interruption		Organ doubled by guitar (R) play fast variation on **intro** guitar lick.
2:29	Verse A3 (12)	"I will remember you"	Similar to **verse A2**.
2:49	Bridge A2 (12+3)	"In and around the lake"	Similar to **bridge A1**; drums and bass play throughout; organ out.
2:56			Organ in (L).
3:21	Interruption/ Transition (2)		Organ (now R) doubled by guitar (now L) play fast variation on **intro** guitar lick.
	B		
3:25	Riff B (4+4)		E minor.
			Guitar and bass play quarter note triplets in unison (C).
			Steady quarter note beat on kick (R).
			Sixteenth notes on toms (L).

continued on next page

Time	Section	Lyric Cue	Listen For
3:39	**Verse B1** (4+4+4)	"Along the drifting cloud"	Choral vocals (L+R); i.e., no lead.
4:00	**Riff B** (4+4)		Organ plays counterpoint to riff (C). Guitar (L) and bass (R) move out of the center of the mix.
4:14	**Verse B2** (4+4+4)	"Go closer hold the land"	Organ line moves to outer edges of the stereo field (L+R). Guitar and bass back to center.
4:36 4:51	**Verse A1 over Riff B** (8+4)	"I'll be the roundabout"	Voices (**verse A1**) and instruments (**riff B**) layer music from different sections of the track. Breakdown texture; pulse is kept faintly by synthesizer arpeggiator (R).
4:57 5:33	Interlude	"In and around the lake"	**Intro** reprise with synthesizer arpeggiator (L). **Bridge A1** fragment without rhythmic articulation. Mellotron flutes (R).
5:50 6:15 6:30 6:42 6:56	**Break** (41 Divided as Shown) A		G Mixolydian. R&B-style organ solo based on **bridge** music (12). Guitar (L), bass/drums (C), organ (R). Guitar interlude (L+R), 4/4 (8). Organ solo based on **bridge** (8). Guitar interlude, 4/4 (8). Texture changes to rhythmic unison (5).
7:05	**Verse** (12)	"I'll be the roundabout"	Kick drum and bass accents fall on pickup to downbeat. E minor. Similar to **verse A1**. Choral vocals.
7:25	**Bridge** (12+3)	"In and around the lake"	Similar to **bridge A2**. Choral vocals.
7:55	**Coda** (18)		E Dorian. Mixed meter: Alternating 4/4 and 3/4. Vocal counterpoint with syncopation. Acoustic guitar texture ends with the same flourish as the **intro**, but now the sound is a steel string guitar (not nylon) and the final chord is E major (not E minor).

18.3. "MONEY" (1973)

PINK FLOYD

Pink Floyd was among the most eclectic of the early prog bands. Their records ranged from classical orchestra music to light jazz, cabaret to blues, tunes to sound effects, all combined in original stylistic mosaics. Using both composition and improvisation they committed to tape whatever their musical imaginations could conjure. And though they twisted or outright ignored pop conventions, they managed to win a vast international pop audience. Though they would soon lose their initial frontman and chief songwriter Syd Barrett to mental illness, the rest—Roger Waters, David Gilmour, Richard Wright, and Nick Mason—would go on to produce a unique catalog of rock music.

"Money" is the opening track on side two of *The Dark Side of the Moon*. One of the biggest-selling records of all time, the album spent 736 consecutive weeks on the *Billboard* charts. The songs convey perspectives on human experience stitched together to impart a sense of conceptual coherence. The album's continuous narrative flow is underscored by running the tracks together and sprinkling sound effects and speech fragments across the span of the album.

"Money" is a prog rock blues workout. Despite the odd vocal phrasing, Gilmour's vocal has a convincing blues feel, as does his guitar solo and Dick Parry's saxophone solo. The entire track is structured around some version of a twelve-bar blues, though never in a traditional way. To begin with, the meter is 7/4, which gives the groove an unbalanced feeling foreign to idiomatic blues. Like a blues chorus, the verses are divided into three parts, each four bars long. But the first two parts remain on the tonic chord (no move to IV). The last part moves to V and then IV, like a conventional rock blues, but changes meter with each chord (8/4 for V, 6/4 for IV), creating an even more unbalanced metric feel. So, each verse is structured as follows:

A   4 bars of 7/4 (I)
B   4 bars of 7/4 (I)
C   1 bar of 8/4 (V), 1 bar of 6/4 (IV), 2 bars of 7/4 (I)

In the saxophone solo, the blues chord progression continues, but it's treated differently. At first it sounds more conventional than the verse. The first two parts of the blues chorus, though the number of bars is doubled from the normal eight to sixteen, retain the proportion of I to IV that we expect. We seem to be in the midst of a stretched-out blues chorus where each of the three phrases is doubled from four to eight bars, but each chord is in its right proportional place. If it continued to follow this conventional plan, the arrangement would produce a twenty-four-bar chorus. However, when the harmony moves to V, which should last for two bars, it lasts for only one. We've suddenly shifted from the twenty-four-bar expanded blues to a normal twelve-bar blues mid-chorus. This disorienting switch compresses the end of the sax solo, ending it abruptly and rushing the track into the guitar solo after only twenty bars. The rushed feeling is intensified by also compressing the meter. Recall that the verse's C phrase has a mixed meter of 8/4 (V) + 6/4 (IV) + 7/4 (I). But now, when we arrive back on I, the meter changes to 4/4 and the track shifts its groove.

The guitar solo covers three blues choruses. Things seem to be normalizing now. The meter change to 4/4 and the driving swing groove have a more idiomatic rock feel. The first two choruses are each a full twenty-four-bars (a doubled twelve-bar structure), but there is still something odd about the move to V. The V chord should be followed by IV before returning to I, but instead the phrase is interrupted by a descending B minor scale followed by four bars of a placeholding vamp. Again, the conventional proportions of a blues chorus are undermined. At the end of the third chorus of guitar solo, the disruption caused by the B minor scale is put to good use as a way of transitioning back into the 7/4 bass riff.

As you listen to the track, notice the importance of the bass as a unifying element. Amid the track's rhythmic trickery, everything coalesces around the persistent walking quarter-note rhythm. Notice, too, how the sound effects in the intro flow into the track's groove. The cash register sounds are not random. They fall on specific beats prefiguring the track's tempo and 7/4 meter.

Listening Guide

"Money" (Roger Waters), Harvest Records (stereo). Also appears on the album *The Dark Side of the Moon*.
Recorded at Abbey Road Studios, London, June 1972–January 1973
David Gilmour (guitar, voice), Richard Wright (keyboards), Roger Waters (bass), Nick Mason (drums), Dick Parry (saxophone)
Producers: Pink Floyd
Engineer: Alan Parsons
Mix supervision: Chris Thomas
Charts: Hot 100 #13, Top LP's #1
Key: B minor
Meter: Mixed

Time	Section	Lyric Cue	Listen For
0:00	Intro		Sound effects loop sets up tempo and 7/4 meter (L+R).
0:12			Bass and guitar play riff in unison (C).
0:26			Texture: drums (C), keyboard with Dorian inflections (R), rhythm guitar (L), tremolo guitar (C).
			Irregular rhythmic accents.
0:40	**Verse 1** (12)	"Money, get away"	Blues phrasing (8+4).
1:08			V (8/4) – IV(6/4) – I(7/4).
			Voice and guitar (L) double bassline in unison.
1:21	**Verse 2** (12)	"Money, get back"	Similar to **verse 1**.
1:48			V–IV–I
2:03	**Sax Solo** (20)		Blues phrasing stretches out in first 16 bars, then compresses in final 4 bars.
			Wah-wah effect on keyboard.
			8 bars of I.
2:28			4 bars of IV.
2:42			4 bars of I.
2:55			4 bars: V (8/4)	IV (6/4)	I (4/4)| I (4/4).
3:02			Groove transition.
3:05	**Guitar Solo** **Blues Chorus 1** (24)		4/4 meter.
			Standard 12-bar blues chorus but doubled to 24 bars.
			Lead guitar double-tracked (L+R).
			More active keyboard.
3:38			Interruption: Descending B minor scale.
3:48	**Blues Chorus 2** (24)		Texture shifts to sparse and dry.
			"Small" guitar (L).
4:20			Interruption; full texture.
4:23	**Blues Chorus 3** (20+2)		Lead guitar with heavy reverb (LCR).
5:01			Interruption.
5:05			7/4 riff returns for 2 bars before vocal entrance; similar to **intro** texture.
5:11	**Verse 3** (10)	"Money, it's a crime"	Similar to **verse 1**, keyboard retains wah-wah.
			Cuts off final two bars; elides with **coda**.

continued on next page

Time	Section	Lyric Cue	Listen For
5:44	Coda		Shift to 4/4.
			Music fades as speaking voices come to the fore.
			Organ segues to next track.

NOTE

1. Bill Bruford, "Reflections on Progressive Rock," in *The Rock History Reader*, ed. Theo Cateforis, 2nd ed. (New York: Routledge), 159.

FURTHER READING

Bruford, Bill. *Bill Bruford: The Autobiography. Yes, King Crimson, Earthworks and More.* London: Foruli Classics, 2013.

Povey, Glenn. *Echoes: The Complete History of Pink Floyd.* Chicago: Chicago Review Press, 2010.

Macan, Edward. *Rocking the Classics: English Progressive Rock and the Counterculture.* New York: Oxford University Press, 1996.

FURTHER LISTENING

David Bowie, "Station to Station" (RCA, 1976)
Emerson, Lake, and Palmer, "Knife Edge" (Island, 1970)
Genesis, "Firth of Fifth" (Charisma, 1973)
Gentle Giant, "River" (Vertigo, 1972)
Jethro Tull, "Aqualung" (Reprise, 1971)
Kansas, "Aperçu" (Kirshner, 1974)
Moody Blues, "Legend of a Mind" (Deram, 1968)
Queen, "Bohemian Rhapsody" (EMI, 1975)
Rush, "2112" (Anthem, 1976)
Frank Zappa and the Mothers of Invention, "Inca Roads" (DiscReet, 1975)

19

HEAVY SOUNDS
Hard Rock

At the end of the 1960s, a mix of psychedelic and blues-based styles began to coalesce as a new rock genre. Termed "hard rock" or heavy metal, the genre featured a larger-than-life sound and an aggressive attitude. The guitar, usually heavily distorted, was the featured instrument; vocals were high-pitched and gritty; drum grooves packed an especially heavy wallop; songs often grew from riffs; and the whole thing was extremely loud, pushing amplification technology to the limit. The prototypes were such bands as Cream, MC5, Blue Cheer, and the Jimi Hendrix Experience, but as the genre came into its own in the 1970s it was defined by such groups as Led Zeppelin, Alice Cooper, Aerosmith, AC/DC, Van Halen, Black Sabbath, and Kiss. While hard rock and heavy metal would eventually become distinct genres (differentiating, for example, Metallica from AC/DC), through most of the '70s the two terms were used interchangeably.

The effect of hard rock is often achieved by simplifying musical gestures and limiting textural clutter. (Think, for example, of the iconic riff from Deep Purple's "Smoke on the Water.") What remains is amplified to outsized proportions, creating a texture that is both heavy and spacious. The guitar riff is key. A central component of rock and roll since Chuck Berry's records in the 1950s, the riff is hard rock's essential vehicle. Short and catchy, it can be blown up to huge sonic dimensions, setting ecstatic listeners to simulated head banging and transcendent flights of air guitar. The drum groove is similarly heavy, aimed at laying down a loud, rock-steady beat. The bass is fat, complementing the kick drum in filling out the low-end with a menacing rumble. Any other instrumental sounds are decorative. The elemental sound of hard rock is that of guitar, bass, and drums. Atop the thunderous instrumental accompaniment, the lead singer belts out the song with a hypercharged energy.

19.1. "BLACK DOG" (1971)

LED ZEPPELIN

Jimmy Page was a prolific studio guitarist in London during the 1960s, playing on all sorts of records in all sorts of pop styles. When he decided to form a band of his own—after the breakup of the Yardbirds, in which he briefly held the guitar spot previously occupied by Eric Clapton and then Jeff Beck—he was already a virtuoso guitarist and an experienced studio hand savvy in the ways of the music business. Unlike earlier British bands like the Beatles and the Rolling Stones, which more or less fell together through happenstance, Zeppelin (initially called the New Yardbirds) was deliberately assembled. Like Cream and Traffic, Zeppelin, though not a "supergroup," drew from a pool of young rock professionals the likes of which had never existed before. Teamed with the tough-minded manager Peter Grant, Page recruited John Paul Jones (bass), Robert Plant (voice), and John Bonham (drums) with a particular sound and direction in mind. After completing a series of previously contracted Yardbirds dates, the group recorded a self-financed album under its new name. Atlantic Records in New York signed the band based on these recordings and released the album without alteration. It was a top-ten hit within the year.

The contract with Atlantic stipulated Zeppelin's artistic control, which allowed the group to develop according to its own aesthetic vision without record company interference. With Page as producer and the others contributing excellent musicianship, as well as songwriting and arranging skills, Zeppelin combined blues, heavy rock, acoustic folk, progressive rock, and hippie mysticism to create a distinctive new style. All of these traits are on display on Led Zeppelin's fourth album, which though officially untitled is often referred to as *IV* or *ZOSO*. From the stomping blues of "When the Levee Breaks" to the psychedelic folk of "Going to California," from the hard driving "Rock and Roll" to the all-acoustic "Battle of Evermore" to the textural complexity of "Four Sticks" to the album's expansive centerpiece "Stairway to Heaven," *Led Zeppelin IV* represents the band in all its diversity, power, and brilliance.

"Black Dog" is the album's leadoff track. Its basic structure is a call-and-response between Robert Plant's unaccompanied wails and a unison guitar and bassline filled with tricky displaced accents. This line is usually referred to as a riff, and for convenience we'll refer to it that way as well. But it is worth noting that the line is in fact longer and more complex than a typical riff.

The song has four verses grouped into two larger sections (one and two; three and four) separated by an extended B section. Verses one and two, and then three and four, make complementary pairs.

Verse one consists of three short bursts of blues singing followed by three puzzling riff responses (riff A). The sense of rhythmic uncertainty in this riff is caused by a pickup phrase—played by guitar (with layered overdubs), bass, and snare drum—that carries past the downbeat, reaching its first accented note on the "and" of beat one. The accent is doubled by the first kick drum hit, which further obscures the downbeat, leaving listeners with a sense of metric instability. The riff is only eight beats in length, so before normal metric order can be restored the instruments are out and we're back to the solo voice. After the third of these riff responses, the guitar and bass continue with a variant of the riff transposed down a fourth. The drums now hold down a strong 4/4 beat but this hardly helps settle things down. The riff extension has even trickier displacements of accent that seem to pit the guitar and bass against the drums in a battle of syncopation.

The extension leads directly into one more iteration of riff A, followed by a shift into a double-time drum groove with excited activity on the toms and crash cymbal. The guitar now plays a new riff (riff B) with a bit of major-mode flavor, and the voice finally joins the band ("Oh yeah"). Altogether, verse one is nearly a minute long.

Verse 1 Structure
voice–riff A–voice–riff A–voice–riff A with transposed extension–
riff A–riff B (double time)

Verse two is considerably shorter. It has only two call-and-response segments, after which the voice sings "Ah, ah" repeatedly as the music seems to come to a stop. At this point there is no riff response, no riff extension, and no move to the double-time groove. Instead a furious drum fill blasts into the B section ("Hey baby"), which is based on a new riff (riff C). Unlike the previous riffs, which are more melodic, this one is primarily rhythmic. The bass and guitar are joined by the snare drum in a high-energy unison gesture that, again, features persistent syncopation.

Verses three and four follow the same plan as verses one and two. The track culminates in a long guitar solo, which is based on the material in the preceding B section. In typical Zeppelin fashion, "Black Dog" is at once primal and complex.

Listening Guide

"**Black Dog**" (Jimmy Page, Robert Plant, John Paul Jones), Atlantic Records
    (stereo). Also appears on the album *Led Zeppelin IV*.
Recorded on location at Headley Grange, Headley, England, winter 1971

Robert Plant (voice), Jimmy Page (guitar), John Paul Jones (bass), John Bonham (drums)
Producer: Jimmy Page
Engineer: Andy Johns
Charts: Hot 100 #15, Top LP's #2
Key: A minor
Meter: 4/4 with some mixed meter

Time	Section	Lyric Cue	Listen For
0:00			Random sounds
0:06	Verse 1	"Hey hey mama"	Solo voice (C) with echo and reverb (R).
0:12			Riff A: Guitar (doubled L and R) and bass (C) play in unison.
			Snare drum doubles on pickup phrase; kick arrives on "and" of beat 1.
0:18		"Ah ah child"	Solo voice.
0:24			Riff A.
0:29		"Hey hey baby"	Solo voice.
0:35			Riff A.
0:41			Riff A transposed and with displaced accents.
0:47			Riff A.
0:53		"Oh yeah"	Riff B; double-time groove.
1:04	Verse 2	"I gotta roll"	Solo voice.
1:09			Riff A.
1:15		"Eyes that shine"	Solo voice.
1:20			Riff A.
1:27		"Ah, ah"	Solo voice with echo.
			Drum fill.
1:40	B Section	"Hey baby"	Riff C.
2:04	Verse 3	"Didn't take too long"	Solo voice.
2:09			Riff A.
2:15		"Spent my money"	Solo voice.
2:21			Riff A.
2:26		"I don't know"	Solo voice.
2:32			Riff A.

Time	Section	Lyric Cue	Listen For
2:38			Riff A transposed and with displaced accents.
2:45			Riff A.
2:50		"Oh yeah"	Riff B; double-time groove.
3:01	Verse 4	"All I ask for"	Solo voice.
3:06			Riff A with added guitar harmony.
3:12		"Need a woman"	Solo voice.
3:18			Riff A with added guitar harmony.
3:23		"Ah, ah"	Solo voice with echo.
			Drum fill.
3:37	Guitar Solo (24 to fade)		Based on B section music.

19.2. "SWEET EMOTION" (1975)

AEROSMITH

During the 1960s, Boston was a rock and roll backwater. A lively local scene produced a number of spirited bands but none managed to win a larger audience, despite a post–Summer of Love initiative by MGM Records to promote the "Bosstown Sound." The failure of groups such as the Beacon Street Union and Ultimate Spinach to win commercial success led to an industry notion of the "Boston curse." In the 1970s, however, the situation would change. Aerosmith was among the first wave of musicians who would go from the small clubs in and around Boston to international stardom. Over the course of the decade, Aerosmith was joined by the likes of the J. Geils Band, Boston, and the Cars.

The album *Toys in the Attic* was Aerosmith's third. While the first two albums put the band on the map, it was *Toys* that made them rock stars. Its leadoff single "Sweet Emotion" was the band's first top-forty hit. The album sold eight million copies and became an iconic hard rock record with widespread appeal. Another of the album's hit singles, "Walk This Way," was later covered by the hip-hop group Run-DMC as part of a rap-rock fusion project. "I used to rap over it when I was twelve," recalled Run-DMC member Joe Simmons.[1]

In typical Aerosmith style, "Sweet Emotion" is a riff fest. Four distinct one-bar riffs shape the track's architecture as each is associated with a specific section.

Riff A is played by the bass, appearing first in the intro and then the choruses.

Riff B is a guitar riff that plays off the vocal phrases during the verses.

Riff C is an instrumental hook doubled by multiple guitars and bass. It plays in the interludes between each pair of verses and before the chorus. It also leads into the coda.

Riff D, which is a heavy transformation of riff A, accompanies the guitar solo in the coda.

The track is a study in contrasts as it moves from one section to the next. The introductory chorus is almost dreamlike with its hypnotic bass riff A (reinforced with bass marimba) and long sustained tones in the voices. Each vocal phrase takes four bars to deliver just two words: "sweet emotion." The vocal harmonies are lush and spread wide across the stereo field. At the arrival of the verse and riff B, we switch instantly from the chorus's ethereal texture to the sound of a no-nonsense, aggressive bar band. The chorus's wide stereo image collapses as the guitar, bass, drums, and voice crowd into the center of the stereo field. Riff B provides a heavy rock energy, which is matched by Steven Tyler's clipped, declamatory vocal. Like the riff, the vocal phrases are all one bar in length.

Verses one and two are separated by an interlude and riff C, which provides another set of contrasts. In one sense, this riff is related to riff B in its heavy rock attitude, but the texture is completely different. The stereo image is again wide, with the riff doubled by guitars on the right and left sides. This more expansive riff is further enhanced by the bass doubling. The interlude's drum part is more active, and the backbeats are augmented with a kind of sucking sound, which, according to producer Jack Douglas, was created by mixing in backward recordings of handclaps, hi-hat, and the band chanting "Thanks Frank," referring to Aerosmith manager Frank Connelly.

The track's contrasting textures provide bookends to the overall narrative. The intro has a strangely psychedelic vibe, with the guitar's talk box effect creating a spectral atmosphere. At the other end of the track, in the coda guitar solo, the band plays a high-intensity blues jam. In both cases the guitar sets the tone, but again it presents dramatically contrasting characters.

Listening Guide

"Sweet Emotion" (Steven Tyler, Tom Hamilton), Columbia Records (stereo). Also appears on the album *Toys in the Attic*.
Recorded at the Record Plant, New York City, March 1975
Steven Tyler (voice), Joe Perry (lead guitar), Brad Whitford (rhythm guitar), Tom Hamilton (bass), Joey Kramer (drums), Jay Messina (bass marimba)
Producer: Jack Douglas
Engineer: Jay Messina
Charts: Hot 100 #36, Top LP's #11
Key: A
Meter 4/4

Time	Section	Lyric Cue	Listen For
0:00	Intro (14)		Riff A; bass (C). Guitar with talk box. Bass marimba. Wide, dynamic stereo field.
0:36	Chorus 1 (8)	"Sweet emotion"	Voices wide L and R; sustained tones fill 4 bars. Riff A continues. Drums (C).
0:56	Verse 1 (8)	"Talk about things"	Riff B; stereo image mostly centered. 1-bar phrases in both voice and guitar.
1:15	Interlude 1 (4)		Riff C; stereo field widens suddenly. Bass and guitars in unison. Texture thickens (more guitars, more drum activity). "Sucking" sound on backbeats.
1:25	Verse 2 (8)	"Some sweat hog"	Riff B; similar to **verse 1**.
1:44	Interlude 2 (8)		Riff C; similar to **interlude 1**, but twice as long.
2:03	Chorus 2 (8)	"Sweet emotion"	Riff A; similar to **chorus 1**, with added guitar part that previews riff D.
2:22	Verse 3 (8)	"I pulled into town"	Riff B; similar to **verse 1**.
2:42	Interlude 3 (4)		Riff C; similar to **interlude 1**.
2:51	Verse 4 (8)	"Stand in the front"	Riff B; similar to **verse 1**.
3:10	Interlude 4 (8+1 bar of 6/4)		Riff C; similar to **interlude 1** with stop-time and added 2-beat extension.

continued on next page

Time	Section	Lyric Cue	Listen For
3:33	**Coda** (25 to fade)		Riff D; a transformation of riff A.
			Also, similar texture to riff C, i.e., wide stereo image; guitars doubled L+R; bass doubles guitars.
			Guitar solo.
			Heavy blues jam.

19.3. "HIGHWAY TO HELL" (1979)

AC/DC

AC/DC's first album, *High Voltage*, was released in 1975, but the band's roots extend back to the 1960s Australian group the Easybeats, whose song "Friday on My Mind" was an international hit in 1966. Easybeats member George Young is the older brother of Malcolm and Angus Young, who would comprise the two-guitar lineup for AC/DC some years later. When the younger brothers took their turn at the family rock and roll business, George Young and fellow Easybeat Harry Vanda took the production reins for the first five AC/DC albums. (Another Young brother, Alex, was a member of the band Grapefruit, signed to the Beatles' Apple label.)

AC/DC is a loud, hard-rocking, straight-ahead band, and the Young-Vanda production team aimed to capture the visceral power of the live shows without studio artifice. But although AC/DC attracted a loyal following as a live band, their records failed to crack the top one hundred in sales. Finally, in 1979, Atlantic, the band's record company, insisted on a new direction in the studio. The Young-Vanda team was to be replaced, and after an ill-fated tryout with former Hendrix engineer Eddie Kramer, the band settled on Mutt Lange, a South African producer on the rise. Lange had produced records for such artists as Graham Parker, the Boomtown Rats, and the Outlaws but had no hard rock tracks in his resume. He did, however, have an uncanny knack for bringing bands of whatever genre to a sonic peak. Without changing anything about AC/DC's basic approach, he produced, in *Highway to Hell*, the band's first top-twenty album. Aside from its own success, the record set the stage for two even more successful Lange-AC/DC collaborations: *Back in Black* and *For Those About to Rock (We Salute You)*.

"Mutt knew what FM stereo sounded like and we didn't," said Angus Young.[2] While Lange knew better than to change the band's essential chemistry, he zeroed in on AC/DC's hooks and amplified them to irresistible proportions. Avoiding the potential risk of diminishing the band's intensity with too much recording studio refinement, Lange used studio techniques to create a recorded image that better reflected the band's live impact. The album's title track, "Highway to Hell," a signature AC/DC number, is an excellent example. Three of the band's characteristic elements—guitar riff, gutty lead vocal, gang chorus—are highlighted to maximum effect. The rock is hard, but the delivery of the hook is a thing of pop perfection.

The track begins with a distorted guitar riff of the kind Angus Young seemed to produce at will—short and apparently simple yet clever and catchy, its persistent syncopation a source of momentum through the song's verses. The riff is made up of three chords (A, D, and G). It sits on the right-hand side of the mix and almost sounds as if it is played by a single instrument. It certainly could be, but instead two guitars, separated slightly in the stereo field, play the riff in unison. Listen to how the guitar that's further to the right has a brighter tone and is slightly louder. Still further to the right is the guitar reverb. These components add up to one composite guitar part with a larger than life presence, consuming the entire right side of the mix and demonstrating from the album's opening track AC/DC's new approach to record making. Under Lange's direction, they use studio techniques to mimic the effect produced in their live shows through volume and spectacle.

Guitar Riff Arrangement
Stereo Center
***   Guitar 1   Guitar 2   Reverb

After beginning with one of the band's central characteristics, the track continues with deliberation, adding the lean drum groove and Bon Scott's high-pitched growl. All through verse one we hear only essential AC/DC elements—fat riff, intense voice, heavy beat. Aside from the modest guitar reverb, the sounds are fairly dry, eliminating any distracting sonic artifacts. At the end of the verse the texture finally begins to expand. The harmony changes to V (E), holding it for two bars in preparation for an arrival on I (A) on the chorus downbeat. Another guitar fills out the left side of the stereo field, and the bass fills out the track's low-end. Coming out of this two-bar preparation, the chorus erupts with massed vocals in a classic example of the gang chorus. The hook has been set up perfectly to do its work. The gradual build from intro through the verse develops a momentum of expectancy, which makes the chorus arrival feel like the breaking of an irresistible wave.

Listening Guide

"**Highway to Hell**" (Angus Young, Malcolm Young, Bon Scott), Atlantic Records (stereo). Also appears on the album *Highway to Hell*.

Recorded at Roundhouse Studios, London, winter 1979; mixed at Basing Street Studios, London.

Bon Scott (voice), Angus Young (lead guitar), Malcolm Young (rhythm guitar), Cliff Williams (bass), Phil Rudd (drums)

Producer: Robert John "Mutt" Lange

Engineer: Mark Dearnley

Mix engineer: Tony Platt

Charts: Hot 100 #47, Top LP's #17

Key: A

Meter: 4/4

Time	Section	Lyric Cue	Listen For
0:00	Intro (8)		Composite guitar riff (R), syncopated.
0:10			Drums play heavy, unadorned groove.
0:18	Verse 1 (17)	"Living easy"	Voice, guitar riff, drums.
0:50			V chord; bass (C), second guitar (L).
0:53	Chorus (8+1)	"I'm on the highway"	Massed vocals.
			After pause, half a beat is added leading into verse.
1:12	Verse 2 (17)	"No stop sign"	Similar to **verse 1**.
1:47	Chorus (8+4)	"I'm on the"	Similar to previous **chorus**.
2:02			Groove suspended.
2:12	Break (8)		Guitar solo; full texture as in **chorus**.
2:28	Chorus (16+ Outro)	"I'm on the"	Double **chorus**.
			Lead guitar continues, answering vocal phrases.
3:00			Free rhythm; "live"-type ending.

NOTES

1. Quoted in Ed Kiersh, "Run-D.M.C. Is Beating the Rap," *Rolling Stone*, December 4, 1986.

2. Quoted in Martin Huxley, *AC/DC: The World's Heaviest Rock* (New York: St. Martin's Press, 2003), 95.

FURTHER READING

Christie, Ian. *The Sound of The Beast: The Complete Headbanging History of Heavy Metal.* New York: Harper Entertainment, 2003.

Shadwick, Keith. *Led Zeppelin: The Story of a Band and Their Music 1968–1980.* San Francisco: Backbeat Books, 2005.

Weinstein, Deena. *Heavy Metal: The Music and Its Culture.* New York: Da Capo Press, 2000.

FURTHER LISTENING

Alice Cooper, "Billion Dollar Babies" (Warner Bros., 1973)
Black Sabbath, "Paranoid" (Vertigo, 1970)
Blue Cheer, "Summertime Blues" (Philips, 1967)
Deep Purple, "Smoke on the Water" (Warner Bros., 1973)
Free, "All Right Now" (Island, 1970)
Kiss, "Rock and Roll All Nite" (Casablanca, 1975)
Motorhead, "Ace of Spades" (Bronze, 1980)
Van Halen, "Eruption" (Warner Bros., 1978)
ZZ Top, "La Grange" (London, 1973)

20

EVERYBODY DANCE
Disco

Disco is a shortened form of the French word *discothèque*, which is a nightclub where patrons dance to records. The idea of public dance gatherings without live music dates at least to the 1940s, and by the late 1950s such well-known clubs as Chez Régine in Paris and the Peppermint Lounge in New York hosted dancers nightly. The later 1960s saw a decline in the mainstream popularity of discos. By the early 1970s, the dance club scene was largely an underground phenomenon, particularly vibrant in New York City clubs frequented by gay men. There was at first no specific disco music genre, but, determined to keep dancers on the floor, DJ's choices in records ran to R&B and Latin styles. Through the decade's early years, disco remained on the periphery. When *Rolling Stone* finally took notice in the summer of 1973, DJs were identified as influential figures. "The best discotheque DJs are underground stars," the reporter wrote, "discovering previously ignored albums, foreign imports, album cuts and obscure singles with the power to make the crowd scream and playing them overlapped, non-stop so you dance until you drop."[1]

Record companies and mainstream press outlets were slow to grasp either the significance or the influence of the growing scene. It was the DJs who noticed audience response on a nightly basis and who helped to drive developing trends. Initially they spun whatever they could find that kept people on the dance floor. Many records featured in discos overlapped with radio hits—the O'Jays' "Love Train," the Pointer Sisters' "Yes We Can Can," the Temptations' "Papa Was a Rolling Stone"—but DJs also played obscure discs little heard in America outside the clubs. One early club hit, for example, was "Soul Makossa" by the Cameroonian saxophonist Manu Dibango, which was released in France and discovered in a West

Indian shop in Brooklyn by DJ David Mancuso. The underground nature of the early disco scene afforded a stylistic freedom often denied by the music industry's usual strictures.

But as disco spilled into the mainstream, record companies realized that dance clubs had become important venues for promoting their wares. They began catering to DJs and dancers with remixed versions of singles that ran longer than the radio versions and were distributed on 12-inch 45-rpm records. The discs were longer than the 7-inch singles used for radio play and retail sale, and they highlighted the track's rhythmic elements. Moreover, the term "disco" began to imply not only a place to dance but a musical style.

The new genre was a flavor of R&B distinct from contemporary funk and 1960s soul. A continuous steady groove was paramount, often provided by a kick drum pulsing on each quarter note, the same four-on-the-floor rhythm we heard in Stevie Wonder's "Superstition." The instrumental overlay was often elaborate, with strings, horns, and backing voices providing lush accompaniments to the lead vocal or instrumental melody. Glitzy style was prized. Lyrics were secondary, though the words of many disco tracks had a definite emotional impact (e.g., "I Will Survive," "Heaven Must Be Missing an Angel"). Aside from the mandatory beat, producers were free to experiment with sounds, stylistic mixture, and electronic artifice. Any music was fair game for disco-fication, including the theme from the first movement of Beethoven's Symphony No. 5 (Walter Murphy's "A Fifth of Beethoven"). A good example of the disco makeover is Gloria Gaynor's version of the Jackson 5's "Never Can Say Goodbye," which strips the original of its laid-back swing feel and substitutes a four-on-the-floor groove adorned with full disco orchestra.

In 1974 a number of records broke out of the clubs and onto the pop charts. Several reached number one, including Barry White's "Love's Theme" (with the Love Unlimited Orchestra) and "Can't Get Enough of Your Love, Babe," MFSB's "TSOP (The Sound of Philadelphia)," the Hues Corporation's "Rock the Boat," and Carl Douglas's "Kung Fu Fighting." This trend continued through the decade as disco's popularity spread around the globe, leaving its mark on fashion (hot pants, platform shoes), film (*Saturday Night Fever*), and celebrity culture (New York's Studio 54 dance club). Musically, disco became a style unto itself, with its own dedicated stars: Sylvester, La Belle, Donna Summer, and the Village People all rose to the top of the pop charts as disco artists.

On the other hand, beginning in the mid-1970s many established stars began aiming their records at the dance floor. Among the first was Diana Ross, whose 1976 record "Love Hangover" reached number one on the pop charts. The Bee Gees, a folk-pop group in the 1960s, were recast as disco stars with such hits as "Staying Alive," "Night Fever" (both of which appeared in the film *Saturday Night Fever*), and "Tragedy." Even consummate rockers like Rod Stewart, David Bowie, Paul McCartney, and the Rolling Stones succumbed to the lure of the beat. By the time disco waned at the end of the 1970s, its influence was permanently embedded in the musical landscape.

20.1. "BAD LUCK" (1975)

HAROLD MELVIN AND THE BLUE NOTES

Harold Melvin and the Blue Notes, accompanied by the group of studio musicians known as MFSB (Mother Father Sister Brother), unwittingly provided disco DJs with an archetypal track in their 1973 recording "The Love I Lost." It was not intended as a disco record, for there was no such thing at the time. It was simply another R&B record aimed at radio and retail. But it perfectly embodied the necessary ingredients for a disco hit. MFSB drummer Earl Young described the groove as a variation on the characteristic Motown snare rhythm, which hit on every quarter-note beat. Young moved the steady beat from the snare to the kick drum, producing the four-on-the-floor rhythm that would become disco's standard groove.

The sound of the record was crafted by a recording team based in Philadelphia: producers Kenneth Gamble, Leon Huff, and Thom Bell; the MFSB musicians; and engineer Joe Tarsia. The team produced hits for such vocal groups as the Blue Notes, the Spinners, the O'Jays, the Stylistics, and the Delfonics, creating what came to be known as the Sound of Philadelphia. The Philadelphia style is conceptually akin to the Motown sound, a sophisticated urban black pop music featuring a combination of lush instrumentation (including strings, brass, and woodwinds) and funky groove. The sound gained widespread exposure through MFSB's 1973 recording "TSOP (The Sound of Philadelphia)," which was used as the theme song for *Soul Train*, a TV show launched by Don Cornelius featuring contemporary black music.

Like "The Love I Lost," "Bad Luck" became a disco favorite largely on the strength of its irresistible groove. Aside from the steady kick drum rhythm, the track owed some of its dynamic propulsion to an unusually prominent open hi-hat on the "and" of beats one and three. Though this hi-hat technique would become another disco staple, it only gained attention through a serendipitous studio accident.

The track was recorded not at Sigma Sound—longtime home of Gamble and Huff productions—but in a small room in the building housing Gamble and Huff's Philadelphia International record label, simply called Studio B. "Bad Luck" was among the first tracks Tarsia recorded in Studio

B, and according to assistant engineer Jim Gallagher, the team was still figuring out how to best position microphones in the unfamiliar room. "We weren't accustomed to exactly the way things were going to sound," recalled Gallagher. "It was still pretty experimental." During recording, the hi-hat bled into other microphones and its volume became difficult to tame in the mix. "It came out a little bit too bright and a little bit too close. . . . And because Joe didn't have a lot of control over it, that hi-hat remained very loud in the mix."[2] It was a "mistake" many others would emulate consciously.

In addition to the drum groove, "Bad Luck" is peppered with rhythmic action at the sixteenth-note level. The track opens with an active bass riff, which is doubled by electric guitars on either side of the stereo field. In its first bar the riff accents each beat as it scampers down an octave driven by sixteenths on the offbeats, but then it takes on a syncopated feel as the accents fall not on the beats but somewhere in between. Meanwhile, a piano vamp pumps out sixteenth-note syncopations of its own on the left side of the mix. This intro texture sets the kinetic scene for all that follows.

The verses have two four-bar phrases. In the first of these, the bass, though it drops the intro riff, continues its prolongation of the fifth scale degree (E, the dominant). As it repeats the note over four bars, it imparts a sense of anticipation as we await some kind of harmonic motion. In the second phrase, the bass releases the dominant harmony and the harmonic rhythm drives the phrase forward through a series of chords. Since none of these is the tonic, the phrase seems to be a pre-chorus leading toward a big tonic arrival. But because the verses come in pairs, the first time we hear the phrase it only leads once more to the dominant, leaving things unresolved as it restarts the verse. This delay in the anticipated resolution will ultimately add to the chorus's impact. In verse two, the phrase's pre-chorus function is finally realized as it drives through to the chorus and makes a satisfying arrival on the tonic (A). The arrival is further emphasized by delaying it for one added bar.

Verse 1
Phrase 1 (4 bars)   Dominant prolongation
Phrase 2 (4 bars)   Harmonic release (no tonic chord)

Verse 2
Phrase 1 (4 bars)   Dominant prolongation
Phrase 2 (**5 bars**) Harmonic release + one-bar extension

Chorus
Tonic arrival

The track's texture is filled out with horns and strings. The horn parts are primarily rhythmic and riff-based. When we first hear the horns in the verse they join the syncopated piano vamp. The strings play sustained tones or brief melodic lines. They are much lower in volume, so their role is mostly to provide the mix with a bit of sonic cohesion, sometimes referred to as "glue."

In addition to the orchestra, the chorus texture is further enhanced by massed backing vocals singing the title phrase. The lyrics in the chorus are divided into two call-and-response phrases, each with a different rhythmic feel. "Bad luck" is sung on two long notes (doubled by strings); the answering line, "That's what you got," is sung in a clipped rhythmic syncopation, joined by a horn riff. (Note: To better hear the orchestra's part in the chorus, listen to the choruses at 3:12–3:45, where the backing voices are out.)

Once the track's verse and chorus textures are set forth, the track's narrative proceeds with a series of variations based on eight-bar divisions. It's a modular-type technique that allows for a lot of repetition (important for the dance floor) while still providing musical interest, as outlined in the Listening Guide. In this six-and-a-half-minute album version the narrative ends with a long coda based on the verse music, over which lead singer Teddy Pendergrass turns his improvisatory style to testifying about current social circumstances including economic inflation and the impeachment of President Nixon. But the modular form allows for any number of rearrangements and any number of repeated sections. One dance club remix of "Bad Luck" is more than sixteen minutes long.

Listening Guide

"Bad Luck" (Vic Carstarphen, Gene McFadden, John Whitehead, Bobby Martin), Philadelphia International Records (stereo). This mix appears on the album *To Be True*.

Recorded at Philadelphia International Studio B, Philadelphia, 1975

Teddy Pendergrass (lead voice), Harold Melvin, Lawrence Brown, Jerry Cummings, Bernard Wilson (nominal voices, probably includes studio singers), Leon Huff (piano), Leonard Pakula (organ), Norman Harris, Roland Chambers, Bobby Eli (guitar), Ronnie Baker (bass), Earl Young (drums), Larry Washington (congas), Don Renaldo and others (strings), Sam Reed and others (horns)

Arranger: Bobby Martin
Producers: Kenneth Gamble and Leon Huff
Engineer: Joe Tarsia
Charts: Hot 100 #15, Hot Soul Singles #4, Top LP's #26, Soul LP's #1
Key: A
Meter 4/4

Time	Section	Lyric Cue	Listen For
0:00	Intro (8)		Kick and hi-hat play disco groove.
			Bass riff (C) doubled by guitars (R, L). Syncopated piano vamp (L).
0:17	Verse 1 (4+4)	"Look downhearted"	Voice (C).
			Horns (R) join piano vamp.
			Strings (L) play sustained tones.
0:25			Harmonic release.
0:33	Verse 2 (4+5)	"Losing your money"	Verse texture.
0:41			Harmonic release.
0:49			Extension.
0:52	Chorus (8)	"Bad luck"	Tonic arrival.
			Sustained notes, voices and strings (L).
		"That's what you got"	Answered by rhythmic riffs, voices, and brass (R).
1:08	Verse 3 (8)	"Played a number"	Verse texture.
1:24	Verse 4 (4+5)	"Losing your rhythm"	Verse texture.
1:42	Chorus (8)	"Bad luck"	Chorus texture.
1:59	Break (8)		New riff (R).
			Based on first phrase of **verse**, repeated.
2:14	Verse 5 (5)	"Law of average"	Release section only plus extension.
2:24	Chorus (8)	"Bad luck"	Chorus texture.
2:40	Chorus (8)	"Bad luck"	Chorus texture.
2:57	Chorus (8)	"Bad luck"	Chorus texture.
3:12	Chorus (8)	"Bad luck"	Backing voices out. Lead voice continues improvisation.
3:29	Chorus (8)	"Bad luck"	Backing voices out.
3:45	Chorus (8)	"Bad luck"	Full chorus texture; backing voices in.
4:01	Chorus (8)	"Bad luck"	Chorus texture.
4:17	Coda (8+56 to fade)		Intro riff: bass, drums, piano only (4).
			Voice begins testifying.
4:25			Guitar joins riff (4).
4:32			Begin series of 8-bar segments based on first phrase of **verse**, no harmonic release.
			Emphasized horn stabs.
4:50			Wah-wah guitar scratches (R).
4:58		"Cut down on smoking"	Backing voices.
5:17		"Opened it up"	Backing voices.
5:37			Strings (L) play variant of **break** riff.

20.2. "HE'S THE GREATEST DANCER" (1979)

SISTER SLEDGE

Sister Sledge was another product of the fertile Philadelphia R&B scene. Sisters Kim, Debbie, Joni, and Kathy Sledge began singing at the Second Macedonia Baptist Church as young girls and were performing at public events by the time they were teenagers. Their first pop success came with the 1974 single "Love Don't You Go through No Changes on Me," which featured prototypical disco elements, notably the orchestral arrangement by Bert DeCoteaux. A good illustration of disco's emergence as a distinct market, the record barely cracked *Billboard*'s Hot-100 but was a top-five club hit.

In 1979, the group's label, Atlantic Records, teamed the sisters with producers Bernard Edwards and Nile Rodgers, whose own group Chic had gained both a club audience and a larger pop following with their 1978 release "Le Freak," a number-one hit on both club and pop charts that sold some six million copies. (Chic repeated the dual number-one hit in 1979 with "Good Times.") The collaboration, which produced the Sister Sledge album *We Are Family*, was fruitful. The record would be the sisters' best seller, reaching number three on the *Billboard* album chart.

We Are Family is very much a Chic-like production, with the addition of the Sledge sisters' voices. All of the songs were written by Edwards and Rodgers and the duo played bass and guitar, as they did with Chic. They also employed their regular New York session musicians, recording engineer, and recording studio. In crafting their disco style, Rodgers and Edwards came up with distinctive approaches to their instruments. Edwards animates the low-end with bass playing that blends the instrument's harmonic and rhythmic functions in intricate lines. Rodgers's guitar style is a mix of syncopated sixteenth-note chord fragments and melodic riffs that make the rhythmic texture percolate. "He's the Greatest Dancer" is a good example of the duo's style. It begins with the basics: a drum groove, Edwards's bassline, and two Rodgers guitar parts, one featuring his chordal playing (R), the other melodic (L). The track stresses the groove as its three chords cycle repeatedly through a two-bar loop.

Once the feel is established, a piano part comes in spelling out fuller versions of the chords, followed eight bars later by long, swelling notes from the string section. In this album version of the mix, the intro cycles through the two-bar loop for nearly a minute, allowing time for the groove to sink in and the disco vibe to develop. Finally, the voices enter with an introductory chorus. The syncopated vocal melody is doubled by strings and answered by an edgy chord played by the strings and a synthesizer. The lyrics juxtapose a matter-of-fact observation ("He's the greatest dancer") with a breathless expression of amazement ("Oh, what! Wow!"). The chord, an F# diminished 7, reflects this breathlessness in harmonic terms. In its answer to "Oh, what! Wow!" the F# comes as a surprise to the ear because it's the only place F# occurs in the track. The rest of the time the F♮ is pervasive. The sudden contrast leaps out as an instrumental expression of the sisters' "Wow!"

The loop that underpins the intro and verse is based on a "syncopated" chord progression. That is, the chord change hangs over across the barline (see figure 20.1).

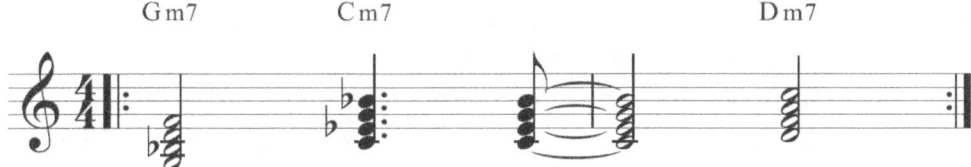

Figure 20.1. "He's the Greatest Dancer" Verse.

Because there is no chord change on the downbeat of the second bar, and the dotted quarter rhythm played on the C minor chord (see figure 20.2) typifies a groove that normally begins on beat one (not beat three),

Figure 20.2. "He's the Greatest Dancer" Rhythm.

this simple figure has a surprisingly strong disorienting effect. Order is restored at the chorus, where the rhythm moves to the downbeat (see figure 20.2). Notice, too, that the same chord—C minor 7—that falls on beat three in the verse falls on the downbeat in the chorus.

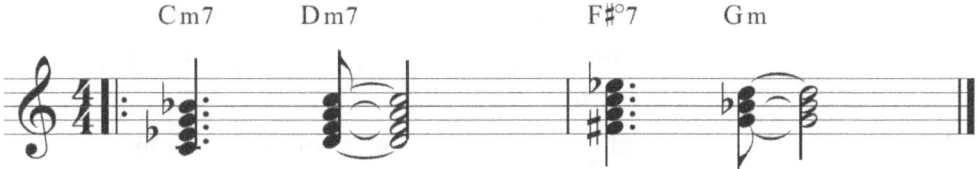

Figure 20.3. "He's the Greatest Dancer" Chorus.

The track's break is in the style of a dance-club break. It employs a dub mixing technique borrowed from Jamaican reggae producers. This involves dropping instruments in or out of the mix, creating sudden changes in the sonic texture simply by pressing the mute buttons on the recording console, thus muting instruments instantly. The break begins with sixteen bars of groove texture similar to the intro and verse. Then, as the music moves to the chorus, the texture suddenly reduces to strings, synthesizer, and drums. After two times through the chorus, the full instrumentation suddenly returns to play the chorus twice more. It is the suddenness of these changes (no transitions) that evokes the dub style.

Listening Guide

"He's the Greatest Dancer" (Nile Rodgers and Bernard Edwards), Cotillion Records (stereo). This mix appears on the album *We Are Family*.
Recorded at Power Station Studios, New York City, 1978
Kathy (lead), Kim, Debbie, Joni Sledge (voice), Nile Rodgers (guitar), Raymond Jones, Robert Sabino, Andy Schwartz (keyboards), Marianne Carroll, Cheryl Hong, Karen Milne (strings), Bernard Edwards (bass), Tony Thompson (drums)
Producers: Nile Rodgers and Bernard Edwards
Engineer: Bob Clearmountain
Charts: Hot 100 #9, Hot Soul Singles #1, Top LP's #3, Soul LP's #1
Key: G minor
Meter: 4/4

Time	Section	Lyric Cue	Listen For
0:00	**Intro** (8+8+8)		Disco groove.
			2-bar chord loop.
			Nile Rodgers guitar style (chords and single notes).
			Bernard Edwards bass style.
0:18			Piano highlights harmonic "syncopation."
0:36			Strings.
0:52	**Intro Chorus** (8)	"Oh, what! Wow!"	Backing voices, synth, and strings in unison.
			Dotted quarter harmonic rhythm shifts to downbeat.
			Synth and strings answer vocals with F# diminished 7 chord.
1:09	**Verse 1** (16)	"One night"	Lead voice accompanied by full **intro** texture.
			Four 4-bar vocal phrases.
1:43	**Chorus 1** (8)	"Oh, what! Wow!"	Similar to previous **chorus** with lead voice added.
2:00	**Verse 2** (16)	"The champion"	Similar to **verse 1**.
2:34	**Chorus 2** (8)	"Oh, what! Wow!"	Similar to **chorus 1**.
2:51	**Chorus** (8)	"Oh, what! Wow!"	Repeat.

Time	Section	Lyric Cue	Listen For
3:08	**Break** (16)		**Verse** texture; prominent guitar.
3:42	(16)		**Chorus** twice with dub effect.
			Strings, synth, and drums; bass and guitar out.
4:15	(16)		**Chorus** twice with full instrumentation.
4:50	**Chorus** (16)	"Oh, what! Wow!"	**Chorus** twice with voices.
5:23	**Coda** (22 to fade)		**Intro** texture.

20.3. "I FEEL LOVE" (1977)

DONNA SUMMER

Donna Summer grew up singing in church but rose to fame simulating sexual climax in a recording studio—twenty-two orgasms on a single track, according to *Time* magazine.[3] The track was "Love to Love You Baby," and in 1976 it put the unknown singer at the top of the pop charts. It was essentially a novelty record, but it would come to symbolize an era. It also launched one of disco's biggest, most enduring stars and cemented a collaborative relationship among Summer and her producers Giorgio Moroder and Pete Bellotte that would continue through the rest of the decade.

Surprisingly, since she worked in a genre where singles were the focus of attention, Summer's albums were often constructed as concept albums. The albums' themes were conceived by Bellotte, who was the primary lyricist in the Moroder-Bellotte partnership. "I Feel Love" is from a concept album called *I Remember Yesterday*. (Other Summer concept albums include *Love Trilogy* and *Four Seasons of Love*.) The tracks on the album suggest a progression through several decades of popular music styles, culminating with the futuristic "I Feel Love."

Aside from Summer's ethereal siren song, all the sounds we hear (even drum sounds) come from a Moog synthesizer. The "performance," too, is generated electronically using a **sequencer**, which is an electronic trigger that fires off sounds at defined time intervals. Thus, pitches and rhythms that would normally have been played by musicians were instead triggered by a machine. The synthesizer programmer devised a method of synchronizing the sequencer to the tape machine so that overdubs could be perfectly coordinated. The resulting metronomic rhythm takes disco's fascination with the steady pulse to a new level. The electronic groove would become a foundation for many genres to emerge during the 1980s, including hip-hop, techno, synth pop, and house.

The sequencer plays a two-beat riff throughout the track (note the way the riff is spread across the stereo field). It changes pitch to make the chords change, but the figuration itself remains the same. Song structure is based on a four-chord sequence, which plays in both the verse and chorus but unfolds at different rates of harmonic rhythm in each section. In the twenty-four-bar verse the harmonies unfold as follows: C (eight bars), E♭ (four bars), F (four bars), G (eight bars).

In the eight-bar chorus the harmonic rhythm is compressed to one chord per one bar: ‖: C | E♭ | F | G :‖. After the verse's long harmonic phrase, building gradually to its dominant chord, the chorus feels like an ecstatic rush.

With the sequencer pattern as a backdrop, the track is painted with the sounds of electronic filter sweeps and various percussive noises. Among the track's distilled musical resources is a two-note motive (E♭–E♮ over a C in the bass) that sweeps across the stereo field as it shifts the harmonic feel from minor to major. We first hear this in the intro. At 0:20, a minor third above the bass (E♭) sounds on the right side of the stereo field. Its filter sweep turns the sound from mellow to strident. At 0:28, a major third (E♮) sounds on the left and follows a similar timbral sweep.

There are several mixes of "I Feel Love" of varying length. The one described here, which is the album version, has a long interlude after the second chorus. During this section, there is no harmonic motion. The two-beat bass riff remains rooted on the tonic as various percussive synth sounds play across its surface. Club remixes of the track are even longer than this six-minute version, but this break is a good example of the sort of extensions that might be added to a track to give dancers more time to move with the beat.

On hearing "I Feel Love" for the first time, producer Brian Eno (David Bowie, Talking Heads, U2) proclaimed, "This is it, look no further. This single is going to change the sound of club music for the next 15 years."[4] Eno could not have known how prophetic his statement would prove to be. The immediate influence of the track was obvious on synth pop records of the early 1980s, but that was only the start of it. The electronic spirit of "I Feel Love" has been a continuous influence on electronic dance music for the past four decades.

Listening Guide

"I Feel Love" (Donna Summer, Giorgio Moroder, Pete Bellotte), Casablanca
    Records (stereo). Also appears on the album *I Remember Yesterday*.
Recorded at Musicland, Munich, Germany, 1977
Donna Summer (voice), Robbie Wedel (Moog programming)

Producers: Giorgio Moroder, Pete Bellotte
Engineer: Juergen Koppers
Charts: Hot 100 #6, Hot Soul Singles #9, Top LP's #18, Soul LP's #11
Key C
Meter: 4/4

Time	Section	Lyric Cue	Listen For
0:00	Intro (16)		Disco groove.
			Electronic sounds.
			Sequencer plays 2-beat loop spread across stereo field.
0:20			Minor third (R) with filter sweep.
0:28			Major third (L) with filter sweep.
0:42	Verse 1 (24)	"Ooh, it's so good"	C (8 bars)
0:57			E♭ (4 bars)
1:05			F (4 bars)
1:13			G (8 bars)
1:28	Chorus 1 (8)	"I feel love"	Same chords as **verse** compressed to four bars and repeated.
			Backing voices in.
1:43	Interlude 1 (8)		Similar to **intro**.
1:59	Verse 2 (24)	"Ooh, fallin' free"	Similar to **verse 1** with second voice added (L).
2:44	Chorus 2 (20)	"I feel love"	Similar to **chorus 1** with extension.
			Phrase repeats 5 times; first 4 with fading vocal.
3:14			Synth-only texture for last phrase.
3:22	Interlude 2 (24)		Bass loop repeats overlaid with percussive synth sounds.
4:06	Verse 3 (24)	"Ooh, I got you"	Similar to previous **verses**, with third voice added (R).
4:52	Chorus 3 (20)	"I feel love"	Similar to **chorus 2**.
5:30	Coda (fade)		Bass riff and electronic kick.

NOTES

1. Vince Aletti, "Discotheque Rock '72: Paaaaarty!" *Rolling Stone*, September 13, 1973, 60.
2. Quoted in John A. Jackson, *A House on Fire: The Rise and Fall of Philadelphia Soul* (New York: Oxford, 2004), 156.
3. "Show Business: Sex Rock," *Time*, December 29, 1975.

4. Reported by David Bowie, quoted in David Sheppard, *On Some Faraway Beach: The Life and Times of Brian Eno* (Chicago: Chicago Review Press, 2009), 249.

FURTHER READING

Echols, Alice. *Hot Stuff: Disco and the Remaking of American Culture.* New York: W. W. Norton, 2010.
Jackson, John A. *A House on Fire: The Rise and Fall of Philadelphia Soul.* New York: Oxford University Press, 2004.
Morgan, Johnny. *Disco: The Music, the Times, the Era.* New York: Sterling, 2011.

FURTHER LISTENING

Bee Gees, "Stayin' Alive" (RSO, 1977)
Chic, "Le Freak" (Atlantic, 1978)
Van McCoy, "The Hustle" (Avco, 1974)
Carl Douglas, "Kung Fu Fighting" (Pye, 1974)
Gloria Gaynor, "I Will Survive" (Polydor, 1978)
Hues Corporation, "Rock the Boat" (RCA, 1973)
K. C. and the Sunshine Band, "Get Down Tonight" (TK Records, 1975)
Diana Ross, "Love Hangover" (Motown, 1975)
Sylvester, "Dance (Disco Heat)" (Fantasy, 1978)
Village People, "YMCA" (Casablanca, 1978)

21

SCUFFING IT UP
Punk and New Wave

Punk rock began to coalesce as a distinct genre in the early 1970s in New York City. In downtown New York clubs like the Mercer Arts Center, CBGB, and Max's Kansas City—well off the mainstream music industry's radar—audiences heard fresh rock and roll from such bands as the New York Dolls, Ramones, Patti Smith Group, Television, and Blondie. Punk's immediate aesthetic predecessors were raw-sounding bands like the Stooges and MC5 from the Detroit area and the underground art-rock of the Velvet Underground from New York City, as well the collection of mid-1960s lo-fi garage bands included on the album *Nuggets* (Elektra) compiled by writer and guitarist Lenny Kaye and released in 1972. In the album's liner notes Kaye wrote, "Most of these groups were young, decidedly unprofessional, seemingly more at home practicing for a teen dance than going out on national tour. The name that has been unofficially coined for them, 'punk rock,' seems particularly fitting in this case, for if nothing else they exemplified the berserk pleasure that comes with being outrageous on stage, the relentless middle-finger drive and determination offered only by rock and roll at its finest."[1]

The New York punks also invoked the sounds of early 1960s rock—surf, girl groups, and the rougher side of the British Invasion (e.g., Kinks, Yardbirds, Them). Their general aim was to present a back-to-basics music that defied what the musicians saw as mainstream rock's stale commercialism. As the Ramones' Joey Ramone put it, "[Rock and roll] was a hodgepodge of Pink Floyd and ELP and all this crap, so basically what we did was we stripped it right down to the bone and we disassembled it and reassembled it and put all the excitement and fun and spirit, raw energy and raw emotion and guts and attitude back into it."[2]

The early punk scene was an underground phenomenon, with few venues for bands to play and little interest from record companies. Along with the clubs that did book the new bands, local fanzines like *New York Rocker* and *Punk* brought attention to the developing scene. Without commercial pressure, musicians were initially free to follow their instincts in crafting songs and styles with little regard for the hitmaking conventions of the day. In the punk scene a defiant attitude was far more important than musical competence. Unpolished performances, with freshness trumping virtuosity, harked back to rock and roll's raw essence as epitomized in tracks like Little Richard's "Tutti Frutti," the Kingsmen's "Louie Louie," or Sam the Sham and the Pharaohs' "Wooly Bully." The important thing was to make a noise. When these bands began to get record deals, they brought this attitude with them, changing a record industry that had become increasingly complacent in its corporate orientation.

21.1. "SHEENA IS A PUNK ROCKER" (1977)

RAMONES

The Ramones epitomized the punk principles of brevity and minimalism. With most songs lasting around two minutes and using a spare guitar/bass/drums lineup, the band led audiences on a loud, frenetic romp through a repertory that included originals "Rock and Roll High School," "Blitzkrieg Bop," "I Wanna Be Sedated," and "Teenage Lobotomy," as well as covers like the Trashmen's "Surfin' Bird," Joe Jones's "California Sun," and Bobby Freeman's "Do You Wanna Dance" (covered, too, in a hit version by the Beach Boys). Ramones shows were celebrations of the raw rock and roll spirit born in Little Richard's first howl of "A wop bop a loo mop." In a 1978 review, John Rockwell, the *New York Times* critic who covered the New York punk scene, described a typical Ramones show: "The songs themselves were short and aggressively simple, strung together in a mostly uninterrupted chain of howling feedback and twanging dissonance into one mosaic-like, half-hour set."[3]

The band members went by their assumed names Joey (vocals), Johnny (guitar), Dee Dee (bass), and Tommy (drums), all with the surname Ramone. They came from Forest Hills, Queens, where they had all attended Forest Hills High School. They wore ripped jeans, sneakers, and black leather jackets—a band of punk brothers set on reclaiming rock and roll's essence. Their music showed an affinity for records of the early 1960s, which they could channel with remarkable skill. Although the Ramones' brand of punk distills musical material to fundamentals, their records are well-crafted and savvy in their stylistic references. In part this is simply a reflection of the fact that, like all rock musicians, they grew up listening to lots of records. Their musical memories and aspirations were written in the language of rock and roll. In addition, however, Tommy Ramone had an interest in studio techniques and had worked in a recording studio. He served as coproducer for the band's first three albums before leaving the band.

"Sheena," whose lyrics refer to the comic book character "Sheena, Queen of the Jungle," borrows primarily from the sound of surf music, specifically the Beach Boys' "Little Honda," according to engineer Ed Stasium. We can hear this in the shouted "Go," which kicks off "Sheena," as it does "Little Honda." Similar, too, is the half-step ornament in the guitar and bass on the downbeat of each bar in the intro and the first half of the verse. A more general surf (or girl group) reference is the handclaps on the backbeat and the style of the backing vocals, which are sung here by three studio musicians.

The groove is typical of the Ramones: driving eighth notes in both guitars and bass, all played with forceful downstrokes. The rhythmic unison of the instruments helps to create a massive, pulsing wave of sound that recalls another 1960s figure: Phil Spector, who the Ramones would hire in 1979 to produce their fourth album, *End of the Century*. As in Spector's famous "wall of sound" production style (heard in the Ronettes' "Be My Baby"), the layers on "Sheena" are blended into a sonic slab whose individual elements draw only fleeting attention as your ear scans the texture. You may hear that the handclaps are more forward in the vamp than in the verse, or that the percussive pick attack of an acoustic guitar sharpens the sonic image as it holds its own amid the throbbing electric guitar distortion, or that the sheen of clanging cymbals hovers over the track's high-end. Or you may simply be swept along by the rush of sound. It works either way.

In addition to its intro, the track has three sections—verse, chorus, bridge—each of which has a distinct phrase structure and harmonic rhythm. Notice how the verse's harmonic rhythm accelerates as it moves into bar nine. After eight bars of mostly C harmony, the chords suddenly change every measure. The verse wraps up with a shortened recap of its opening but then adds a two-bar phrase extension, which sets up the chorus.

Verse 1. | C | C | C | C | G | G | C | C |
      2. | A minor | F | A minor | F | (harmonic rhythm accelerates)
      3. | C | C | G | G | G | G | (2-bar phrase extension)

The chorus is a two-bar chord loop repeated four times, and then the whole chorus is repeated. All in all we get eight repetitions of one of rock and roll's most basic chord sequences (I–IV–V). The chorus is both a catchy hook and a release of the musical energy built up in the verse.

Chorus: ‖: C | F G :‖ 4 times

The bridge also has its own harmonic rhythm, with each chord lasting two bars. In addition, it has the only non-diatonic chord in the song, the flatted seventh, which is B♭.

Bridge: | F | F | C | C | G | G | B♭ | B♭ |

This sharp distinction between the song's sections is consistent with the track's other musical elements and the song's lyrics. The form is straightforward, uncomplicated, and aimed at producing a point-blank musical impression.

Listening Guide

"Sheena Is a Punk Rocker" (Joey Ramone), Sire Records (stereo). Also appears on the album *Rocket to Russia*.
Recorded at Sundragon Studios, New York City, April 1977. Album remix at Power Station, NYC.
Joey Ramone (voice), Johnny Ramone (guitar), Dee Dee Ramone (bass), Tommy Ramone (drums), Michael Bonagura, Kathie Baillie, Alan LaBeouf (backing vocals)
Producers: Tony Bongiovi and Tommy Ramone
Engineer: Ed Stasium
Charts: Hot 100 #81, Top LP's #49
Key: C
Meter: 4/4

Time	Section	Lyric Cue	Listen For
0:00	Intro (4)	"Go!"	Sonic references from the 1960s: half-step guitar/bass riff.
			Wall of sound texture blending distorted guitars with drums; handclaps.
0:06	Verse 1 (8+10)	"Well the kids"	Lyric references from the 1960s: "surfboards," "discotheque," "au go go."
			Surf rock–style backing vocals.
0:17			Accelerating harmonic rhythm.
0:28		"Oh yeah"	2-bar phrase extension.
0:31	Chorus 1 (8+8)	"Sheena is"	2-bar chord loop.
			Backing vocals double "Sheena is."
			Double chorus.

Time	Section	Lyric Cue	Listen For
0:52	**Bridge 1** (8)	"Well she's a"	Beach Boys–style backing vocals.
1:01			♭VII chord.
1:03	**Vamp** (4)		Repeats intro riff and texture.
1:09	**Verse 2** (8+10)	"Well the kids"	Similar to **verse 1**.
1:33	**Chorus 2** (8+8)	"Sheena is"	Similar to **chorus 1**.
1:55	**Bridge 2** (8)	"Well she's a"	Similar to **bridge 1**.
2:06	**Vamp** (4)		Repeats intro riff and texture.
2:12	**Chorus 3** (8+8+8)	"Sheena is"	Three **choruses** to fade.

21.2. "CALL ME" (1980)

BLONDIE

Founded by Deborah Harry (voice) and Chris Stein (guitar) in 1974, Blondie eventually included Clem Burke (drums), Jimmy Destri (keyboards), and a series of bass players. Although the group was a regular at CBGB, it would emerge from the New York punk underground to gain worldwide superstardom as a new wave band. New wave bands (also referred to as "postpunk") grew from the punk ethos of social and musical rebellion, and many saw the term simply as an attempt by record company marketing departments to create a perceived distance from punk's grungy—and less commercial—image. But new wave groups in both the US and the UK tended to be more eclectic than pure punk bands, often incorporating a wider palette of pop styles—including disco and reggae—as well as the electronic sounds of synthesizers and drum machines. There are overlaps between the two genres, sometimes even within the work of a single band like the Clash, which can make distinctions confusing. But listening to the records, it is apparent that new wave is a more polished, if often ironic, brand of pop, with an affinity for modern trends in record production. In a 1977 *New York Times* piece, John Rockwell described Blondie's sound as a "a clever blend of punk-rock, progressive keyboard textures and 1960s nostalgia."[4] Along with such catchy original songs as "Heart of Glass" and "One Way or Another," the group recorded covers that included reggae ("The Tide Is High," Paragons) and doo wop ("Denis," originally "Denise," Randy and the Rainbows).

Blondie began their recording career with Richard Gottehrer, who, as the producer of the girl group track "My Boyfriend's Back" (Angels) and the three-chord number-one hit "Hang on Sloopy" (the McCoys), gave the band a tangible connection to the 1960s. After two albums with Gottehrer, Blondie began working with Mike Chapman, who would produce their breakout album *Parallel Lines* as well as the rest of their albums up until 1982, when the band went on a seventeen-year hiatus. "Call Me," however, was a one-off collaboration with disco producer Giorgio Moroder. The song was written by Moroder and Harry, and the track was created for the film *American Gigolo* as a reflection of its male prostitute character. Although the band initially devised and recorded the track's musical parts, Moroder, who was unaccustomed to working with bands, replaced many of their performances with those of studio musicians. In any case, "Call Me" was a landmark hit for the group, claiming the number-one position on *Billboard*'s Hot 100 for six weeks and cementing new wave music in the center of a stylistically reshaped record industry.

"Call Me" combines a heavy rock feel with a disco-style kick drum rhythm. The rock elements include the distorted electric guitars and the track's signature blues rock riff first heard in the intro. The disco feel is located in the four-on-the-floor kick drum and the featured synthesizer in the break. There is also a hint of reggae in the rhythm guitar part that plays on each backbeat with a triplet swing, as well as occasional places in the mix where all instruments except drums drop out briefly. This sort of muting—an instant on-off accomplished by pushing buttons on the mixing console—is another example of the dub technique we heard on Sister Sledge's "He's the Greatest Dancer."

As the track begins, an opening drum fill suggests a triplet orientation, which is confirmed immediately by an electronic sequencer (as heard on Donna Summer's "I Feel Love") pumping out a steady stream of triplets. Three guitar parts—one lead and two rhythm—play over this foundation (all guitars are doubled for a thicker texture). First, we hear four bars of the signature riff in the lead guitar along with rhythm guitar one playing chords. Then, rhythm guitar two enters playing single notes doubling the sequencer triplets. Both rhythm guitar parts are synchronized with the sequencer, creating a propulsive composite rhythmic texture that remains unchanged throughout the track.

Though they share this same driving rhythmic feel, the verse and chorus present an interesting musical contrast in their melodies and harmonic sequences. These coincide with Deborah Harry's change in vocal character as her relatively restrained performance in the verse is answered by an insistent shout in the chorus—"Call me!"

Verse-Chorus Melodic Contrast

The verse melody moves initially by step, following a D minor scale between the tonic note D and the A, a fifth higher, rising and falling within this range. The pre-chorus section repeats the rising part of this stepwise motive and extends the range up to B♭. The half step between A and B♭ helps create tension as the song builds to its chorus.

The chorus melody begins with a shout ("Call me!") on the D an octave higher than the one in the verse. From here the melody descends gradually back down to the D an octave below. But instead of moving by the steps of the minor scale (like the verse), it follows the pentatonic scale (i.e., no half steps).

So from verse to chorus we move from a predominantly *rising* melodic motion in D minor—with its half-step sonorities (E–F and A–B♭)—to a predominantly *falling* one that traces the D pentatonic scale with no half steps.

The harmonic contrast between verse and chorus involves a change in color as the chorus adds the major triad sonorities of F major and G major. Also, the harmonic root motion in the verse's first eight bars is *downward*, twice moving from D minor down to B♭. By contrast, the chorus's root progression moves *upward* through each phrase, supporting the chord progression D minor–F–G–B♭.

In the vamp after chorus two we feel an abrupt shift as the key changes suddenly to E minor in preparation for the bridge. As the music enters this new section, the rock guitars subside a bit as the synthesizer becomes gradually more prominent. In the bridge, the synth doubles the vocal melody, and then in the break that follows, it becomes the featured element.

Along with this change in sonic texture, the bridge also briefly relieves the metric regularity of the verse-chorus phrase structure as it supplies an unexpceted seven-bar harmonic phrase, which begins with a 6/4 bar (1:59, and again in the break at 2:31). The feeling this change imparts to the listener passes quickly, but its effect is real. The slight metric disruption forces the vocal phrases into an off-balance 3+4-bar arrangement that leads to a strong cadence. The arrival feels welcome. This obviously climactic moment restores the track's regular metric certainty undermined by the subtle disorientation of the preceding metric trickery.

Listening Guide

"Call Me" (Deborah Harry, Giorgio Moroder), Chrysalis Records (stereo)
Recorded at the Power Station, New York City, August 1979
Deborah Harry (vocal), Chris Stein (guitar), Jimmy Destri (keyboards), Frank Infante (bass), Clem Burke (drums), studio musicians recorded Westlake Studios, Los Angeles
Producer: Giorgio Moroder
Engineer: Harold Faltermeyer

Charts: Hot 100 #1
Key: D minor
Meter: 4/4

Time	Section	Lyric Cue	Listen For
0:00	**Intro** (8)		Signature blues-rock riff doubled by guitars and bass.
			Groove components:
			Four-on-the-floor kick drum.
			Triplet rhythm in sequencer.
			Rhythm guitar plays chords.
0:09			Second rhythm guitar plays single notes.
0:16	**Verse 1** (8+4)	"Color me"	Syncopated vocal melody moves stepwise up and then down the D minor scale.
0:29			Pre-chorus melody repeats rising scale twice, introducing a new pitch in the vocal (B♭).
0:36	**Chorus 1** (4+4)	"Call me"	Melodic contrast with the verse:
			Lyric is shouted on the D an octave higher.
			Melody descends on pentatonic scale over ascending chord sequence.
0:48			Dub effect.
0:49	**Vamp** (4)		Riff.
0:56	**Verse 2** (8+4+1) bars.	"Cover me"	Similar to **verse 1**; add vocal harmony for first 8
1:16			One-bar extension.
1:18	**Chorus 2** (8)	"Call me"	Similar to **chorus 1**.
1:31	**Vamp** (2+2)		Riff.
1:35			Key changes to E minor.
1:38	**Bridge** (4+4+4+7)	"Oo, oo, oo"	Synthesizer doubles vocal melody.
1:59		"Anytime, any place"	6/4 bar upon arrival back in D minor begins a 7-bar concluding phrase.
2:11	**Instrumental Break** (4+4+4+7)		Same chord sequence and phrase structure as **bridge**.
			Synthesizer plays variation of **bridge** vocal melody.
2:31			6/4 bar upon arrival back in D minor.
2:43			Brief dub effect.
2:44	**Chorus 3**		Similar to **chorus 2**.
			Repeat to fade.

21.3. "LONDON CALLING" (1979)

THE CLASH

British punk exploded in 1976 with the formation of such bands as the Damned, the Sex Pistols, the Buzzcocks, and the Clash. By 1978 the scene was splintering into a postpunk aftermath that saw a dizzying array of musical styles and innovations in record production. But punk's brief moment proved a powerful disruption, leaving an indelible mark on the music and attitudes of young people, particularly musicians and recording engineers. In contrast to the New York punk scene, UK punks not only projected a musical attitude but also reflected Britain's broader social and political circumstances. At a time of economic difficulty and political division, punk expressed a disaffected impatience with business as usual, including, of course, the music business. The result was sometimes a confrontational cynicism as heard, for example, in the Sex Pistols' "God Save the Queen" or the Clash's "White Riot." But above all, British punks shared their American peers' desire for a renewal of lo-fi rock and roll's vital energy.

The Clash had a classic rock lineup: two guitars (Joe Strummer, Mick Jones), bass (Paul Simonon), drums (Topper Headon, beginning with the band's second album). They produced some of punk's most enduring records, combining punk energy with pop savvy. The songwriting partnership of Strummer and Jones was the punk equivalent of Jagger and Richards. The band's eponymous first album (with drummer Terry Chimes) brims with catchy melodies (e.g., "Remote Control"), memorable guitar riffs (e.g., "Garageland"), and rousing gang vocals (e.g., "I'm so Bored with the U.S.A."). It also contains a cover of a reggae song, Junior Murvin's "Police and Thieves," announcing from the outset the band's interest in diverse musical idioms.

"London Calling" is the title track from the Clash's third album, an ambitious two-LP set that stands among rock's most significant works. Produced by Guy Stevens (Procol Harum, Mott the Hoople), the album ranges widely in its stylistic diversity, showing traces of rockabilly, reggae, hard rock, pop, and soul. "London Calling" has a desperate yet defiant feel. Amid lyric images of impending disaster, summarized metaphorically as London drowning, the protagonist claims to have no fear despite living in harm's way. Though he lives "by the river," he expresses no intention to seek higher ground. Is his defiance bold? Ironic? Hopeful? Hopeless? Is it a cry of courage, or of terror? The answer is perhaps all of the above, but the interpretation is left to you, the listener.

Accompanying Strummer's anguished vocal performance, the backing vocals make a haunting contrast. Their repeated hushed rendition of the words "London calling" has a spectral quality, enhanced by reverb and spread wide in the stereo field, while the lead voice is relatively dry and located firmly in the mix's center. In the chorus, the backing voices sing along softly on the second half of each line until finally they join Strummer in shouting the chorus's climactic phrase—"Live by the river"—still spread wide but no longer washed in reverb. Here, they sound more like a defiant gang that has risen to join their leader.

The track's musical tension is built around specific rhythmic and pitch motives. Rhythmically, the intro begins with four bars of a stiff march-like quarter-note pulse doubled by kick drum and guitars. Then the bass enters with a riff that prefigures the upcoming groove, which will overlay a triplet swing feel onto the steady pulse. The bass telegraphs this with a triplet played on the fourth beat of each bar. The message is confirmed by the triplet snare drum fill at the end of the intro, which breaks free of the intro's stiff rhythmic restraint and launches into the freer swing of the verse. This triplet swing will run through the track. It is driven by the bass but also reinforced by rhythm guitars and occasional snare drum hits and drum fills. It never feels like an easy swing, though. The steady martial pulse of the kick drum keeps the rhythmic energy tense.

The sense of the song lyrics is underscored by three half-step pitch relationships: E–F, B–C, and F–F$^\sharp$. The tensions these create are apparent both melodically and harmonically, sometimes in immediate juxtapositions, other times as markers of larger narrative structure.

To begin with, the song's first two verses have a clear Phrygian feeling (as in Jefferson Airplane's "White Rabbit") with the bassline moving from E to F in every phrase, even as the main guitar part remains stubbornly on an E minor chord. Another source of harmonic friction lurks deep in the mix, more felt than clearly heard. While the main guitar part (guitar one) sticks to the E minor chord, another one (guitar two) moves to an F major chord when the bass moves to F. Together, the E minor and F major guitars sounding simultaneously creates a dissonant note cluster: E, F, G, A, B, C.

The verse's Phrygian sound is also present in other parts of the track, but it moves in and out of focus. In the intro, for example, E minor is the primary sonority because the bass does not play F, and guitar two is mixed so quietly that although we can feel a faint Phrygian impression as it moves to F on every other bar, we can't quite identify why. Only when the bass plays F—which is only in the first two verses—can we be certain of the Phrygian presence. Otherwise it simmers as a submerged tension that runs through the track. Because the bass sticks with its intro riff for verse three, we do not hear a clear F in the last part of the track. The note remains present in guitar two, but has once again receded into the mix, leaving us with only a lingering feeling of unease.

The chorus changes the track's feel from Phrygian to minor by replacing the F with F♯. The change is apparent as soon as the chorus begins ("The Ice Age is coming"). The bass drops its triplet figure and incorporates the F♯ in a passing-note motion between the chords of E minor and G (see figure 21.1). This change is subtle, but it hints at the F♯'s big moment: its role as the third degree of the D chord that harmonizes the chorus's hook ("I live by the river"). These chorus cadences are the only times we hear the D chord. So, more than simply a change in harmonic color, the Phrygian (F♮) vs. minor (F♯) distinction is a structural marker separating verse and chorus.

Figure 21.1. "London Calling" Passing Note.

The B–C half-step relation is a persistent feature of the vocal melody in the verse. It repeats at the beginning of each four-bar segment, moving parallel with the bass's E–F. The backing vocals that begin each of the verse's four-bar segments with "London calling" seem to tug against the lead voice as they sing a descending E minor triad (B–G–E) followed immediately by the lead melody rising to C. This tug between falling and rising melodic movement pivoting on a half step repeats four times. Then, in the chorus, the C in the melody disappears. Strummer sings only pentatonic notes. Again, this contrast in pitch choices serves as a structural distinction between verse and chorus.

One further verse-chorus contrast is in the change of harmonic rhythm. Although both verse and chorus move repeatedly from E minor to G, the proportions of the progression vary. Remember that in the verse we hear one bar of F between the E minor and G chords. The four-bar progression is ‖: E minor | F | G | G :‖.

In the chorus, the E minor again moves up to G, but this time there is no chord between them—only the short F♯ passing note. The E minor to G motion is compressed, quickening the harmonic rhythm and propelling the track to the chorus's climactic phrase.

Listening Guide

"London Calling" (Joe Strummer, Mick Jones), Epic Records (stereo). Appears on the album *London Calling*.
Recorded at Wessex Sound Studios, London, August–September and November 1979
Joe Strummer (lead voice, rhythm guitar), Mick Jones (lead guitar, voice), Paul Simonon (bass, voice), Topper Headon (drums)
Producer: Guy Stevens
Engineer: Bill Price
Charts: Top LP's #27
Key: E minor
Meter: 4/4

Time	Section	Lyric Cue	Listen For
0:00	**Intro** (4+8)		Strict quarter-note groove played by kick and layered guitars.
			On every second bar we hear a faint Phrygian premonition as an F chord is played by a guitar buried in the mix while the focus is on the repeating E minor chord.
0:07			Bass riff prefigures triplet groove.
0:19			Triplet drum fill.
0:21	**Verse 1** (8+8)	"London calling to the faraway towns"	Triplet swing groove carried by the bass with rhythm guitar support low in the mix and occasional snare hits.
			Phrygian sound comes into focus as the bass plays F.
			Backing vocals sing descending E minor triad, followed by lead vocal ascending to C.
			Backing vocal reverb and stereo placement contrasts with drier lead vocal sound.
0:50	**Chorus 1** (9)	"The Ice Age is coming"	Aggressive guitar strums assert triplet groove.
			Bass introduces F# passing note, supplanting the Phrygian feel.
			E minor to G harmonic rhythm compresses.
1:04		"Live by the river"	Climactic D chord and gang vocal.
1:06	**Verse 2** (8+8)	"London calling to the imitation zone"	Similar to **verse 1** with added and varied guitar parts.
1:35	**Chorus 2** (9)	"The Ice Age is coming"	Similar to **chorus 1**.

Time	Section	Lyric Cue	Listen For
1:51	**Break** (8+8)		Drum breakdown.
			Guitars hold the quarter-note pulse.
			Phrygian bassline as in **verse**.
			Vocal screams.
2:05			Drum groove returns.
			Chaotic guitar break with multiple guitars, feedback, volume swells, and backward tape effects.
2:19	**Chorus 3** (9)	"The Ice Age is coming"	Similar to previous **choruses**.
2:35	**Vamp** (8)		Similar to **intro** with added vocal screams.
2:50	**Verse 3** (8+4)	"London calling, yes I was there too"	Intro music; verse harmonic phrase suspended.
			Phrygian F still faintly playing on guitar but submerged in the mix.
3:05			Lead voice out for last four bars.
3:15	**Outro**	"I never felt so much alike"	Groove dissolves. Morse code SOS signal (R).

NOTES

1. Lenny Kaye, *Nuggets* liner notes (Elektra Records, 1972).

2. Quoted in Mark Jenkins. "The Ramones: Time to Be Sedated? After Years on the Road and 16 Albums, The Punk Perennials Prepare to Call It Quits," *Washington Post*, August 6, 1995. https://www.washingtonpost.com/archive/lifestyle/style/1995/08/06/the-ramones-time-to-be-sedated-after-years-on-the-road-and-16-albums-the-punk-perennials-prepare-to-call-it-quits/192b94b9-41fc-4f7a-bc32-20d940c50b58/.

3. John Rockwell, "Ramones, Doyens of Punk Rock, in the Big Time," *New York Times*, January 6, 1978, C11.

4. John Rockwell, "Rock: Blondie," *New York Times*, January 24, 1977, 17.

FURTHER READING

Cateforis, Theo. *Are We Not New Wave?: Modern Pop at the Turn of the 1980s.* Ann Arbor: University of Michigan Press, 2011.

Savage, Jon. *England's Dreaming: Anarchy, Sex Pistols, Punk Rock, and Beyond.* New York: St. Martin's Griffin, 2002.

Heylin, Clinton. *From the Velvets to the Voidoids: A Pre-Punk History for a Post-Punk World.* New York: Penguin Books, 1993.

FURTHER LISTENING

Buzzcocks, "Boredom" (New Hormones, 1977)
Cars, "Just What I Needed" (Elektra, 1978)
Devo, "Q: Are We Not Men? A: We Are Devo!" (Warner Bros., 1978)
New York Dolls, "Personality Crisis" (Mercury, 1973)
Patti Smith, "Gloria" (Arista, 1975)
Sex Pistols, "Anarchy in the UK" (EMI, 1976)
Siouxsie and the Banshees, "Metal Postcard (Mittageisen)" (Polydor, 1978)
Slits, "Instant Hit" (Island, 1979)
Talking Heads, "Life During Wartime" (1979)
Television, "Venus" (Elektra, 1977)

22

A WHOLE NEW THING
Hip-Hop

As the 1980s dawned, the pop landscape was filled with new takes on established genres and revisions of earlier events. The disco beat pulsed (Eurythmics, "Sweet Dreams"), rockabilly rocked on (Stray Cats, "Rock This Town"), girl groups were back on the charts (Go-Go's, "We Got the Beat"), funk was as funky as ever (Prince, "1999"), folk rock rang out new songs on electric twelve-string guitars (Tom Petty and the Heartbreakers, "Here Comes My Girl"), and hard rock soared to new heights of popularity (Def Leppard, "Photograph"). British postpunk brought forth a second British Invasion, with bands like Human League, the Police, U2, and the Pretenders appearing around the clock on the new twenty-four-hour media outlet, MTV. Pop music celebrated its history, even as new artists, producers, and recording techniques emerged to further its stylistic evolution.

One genre to gain popularity in the early '80s, however, was brand new: hip-hop. Like doo wop, disco, punk, surf, and so many other rock idioms before it, hip-hop began as a marginal musical subculture. Developed at the grassroots, or, more specifically, in the streets of the South Bronx, its popularity took the mainstream music industry by surprise. Two things about hip-hop's central concept were radically different from any previous pop genres: vocals were spoken rather than sung, and tracks often used preexisting records in some way (e.g., "Rapper's Delight," by the Sugarhill Gang, is built on the break from Chic's "Good Times"; "That's the Joint," by Funky 4+1, unfolds over a riff taken from A Taste of Honey's "Rescue Me").

Hip-hop began as a dance party phenomenon. As disco DJs spun records at exclusive Manhattan clubs like Studio 54, others used their turntables and record collections to entertain dancers on playgrounds, in school gymnasiums, and in community centers uptown. These neighborhood DJs gradually became part of the show, not only selecting records to play but altering them on the fly. Noticing dancers' excitement when the singing dropped out and the rhythm took over—the breaks—DJs devised ways to extend these sections by using two turntables playing the same track. As one record finished playing the break, a second one, cued up to the break's beginning, would play it again as the DJ wound the first record back to play the break yet again. The technique—called "merry-go-round" by its inventor DJ Kool Herc—could be repeated at will, heightening the energy on the dance floor. Gradually, other techniques were added to the DJ's arsenal, including "scratching," by which the DJ moved a record back and forth, creating various effects that often included simultaneously manipulating a sound mixer. DJs became artists of record playing—turntablists—performers whose instrument was the turntable and mixer.

DJs were often joined by an MC (master of ceremonies), who introduced the DJ and provided patter to enhance the party atmosphere. The MC's stylized delivery developed into ever more sophisticated wordplay and rhyming—rapping. This became hip-hop's essential partnership: the DJ and the MC/rapper or a "crew" of rappers. Eventually the DJ's role would expand into full-blown record production teams, and the MCs would become extraordinarily skilled poets whose wordplay addressed a wide array of topics from parties to politics.

Moving from live music presentation to the recording studio, hip-hop DJs initially took a back seat as MCs recorded their raps over band performances. Record producers had yet to grasp the novel project of making records out of other records. But while many early hip-hop tracks were essentially rapping over funk- or disco-styled performances, some sought to emulate the creative aspect of the live events where DJs were the star performers and records were their creative resources. "The Adventures of Grandmaster Flash on the Wheels of Steel" is a record made entirely of other records. It illustrates hip-hop's reimagining of the terms "musician," "composer," and "song." Flash "plays" the turntables and mixer as he composes a new song made from preexisting material.

Hip-hop producers were among a creative vanguard—which included British postpunk engineers and producers—employing the technological innovations of the early 1980s in new ways of record making. For hip-hop, a genre obsessed with preexisting records, digital recording, or sampling, was especially useful. Digitally recorded sound could be manipulated and edited much more easily than magnetic tape. Moments of sound—samples—could be stored and replayed at the push of a button. They could be shortened to barely recognizable snippets, layered, looped, reversed, sequenced, and otherwise manipulated at the creator's whim. A new musical instrument facilitated this practice: the sampler, whose keys or pads allowed users to trigger sounds stored in digital memory.

Selecting, manipulating, and combining samples became a central element in hip-hop record production. It was a natural outgrowth of turntablism but offered a more elaborate range of possibility. Instead of manipulating two records in real time, sample artists composed tracks from a universe of records. Aside from drawing on records as musical material, their creations invoked specific historical characters and styles. In a practice referred to as "digging in the crates," producers regularly combed through record store racks looking for material—often old and/or obscure—to use in their tracks. Seeking out records both for their musical use and as potential signifiers—whether to signal something obvious to an audience or simply as a private allusion—DJs and sample artists cultivated a deep knowledge of pop music's recorded repertory and stylistic tradition.

22.1. "THE ADVENTURES OF GRANDMASTER FLASH ON THE WHEELS OF STEEL" (1981)

GRANDMASTER FLASH

Grandmaster Flash (Joseph Saddler) was among the first generation of turntable innovators. Along with such turntablists as DJ Kool Herc and Afrika Bambaataa, he developed many of turntablism's fundamental techniques. Together with his group of rappers, the Furious Five, his name would be one of the first to gain widespread recognition beyond the hip-hop subculture.

Flash's record label Sugar Hill Records was the most successful early hip-hop label. It was owned and operated by Sylvia Robinson, a music business veteran who had had her own chart success as a singer in the 1950s ("Love Is Strange") and 1970s ("Pillow Talk"). On most of the records under his name, Flash actually contributed little to the production (e.g., "The Message," "Freedom," "Birthday Party"). The voices on the records were those of the Furious Five, but the music was played by musicians in the studio. Eventually, however, Robinson agreed to release a recording of Flash himself. "The Adventures of Grandmaster Flash on the Wheels of Steel" is a recording of Flash's actual DJ performance. It was recorded as a continuous take, without overdubs or edits. It is a snapshot of a DJ at work, weaving his materials together on the fly into a coherent musical event that moves both dancers and listeners.

"Adventures" is based on the break from Chic's disco hit "Good Times" (1979). Like any musical idiom, hip-hop had its own conventions. The drum break from James Brown's "Funky Drummer," for example, has been sampled on well over a thousand records. Similarly, the break for "Good Times" was a staple of hip-hop dance parties. Flash uses it as a thematic thread that spans "Adventures," while other records come and go. The Bernard Edwards bassline has a distinctive beginning, with three repeated quarter notes followed by an upward motion. Flash selects other tracks whose basslines follow a similar pattern, establishing a thematic connection among the records: Spoonie Gee Meets the Sequence's "Monster Jam," Queen's "Another One Bites the Dust," and Blondie's "Rapture" (the repeated notes here are eighth notes).

Flash uses some older records—the Incredible Bongo Band's "Apache" (1973), the Hellers' "Life Story" from the obscure album *Singers . . . Talkers . . . Players . . . Swingers . . . & Doers* (1968), and the spoken-word album *The Official Adventures of Flash Gordon* (1966)—a testament to his eclectic record collection. He also uses some other Sugar Hill records: his own group's "Freedom" and "Birthday Party" and the Sugarhill Gang's "8th Wonder." Flash chooses a few word references to highlight himself: "Flash is fast, Flash is cool" from "Rapture," "Grandmaster cut faster" from "Freedom," "Flash, one time" from "Birthday Party," and the announcement "The official adventures of Flash" that opens the *Flash Gordon* album.

At the outset we hear two words chopped from the intro to Spoonie Gee's "Monster Jam": "You say." The words are repeated in a rhythmic stutter, in effect "performed" by Flash until he allows them to be pushed aside for the rest of the line. On "Monster Jam," this phrase is interrupted by a whistle blast that kicks off the groove. But in Flash's hands, the whistle instead drops us into a scene change. Suddenly it's Blondie's "Rapture" that briefly takes the spotlight to remind us that "Flash is fast, Flash is cool." Since Flash is in control, however, we actually hear "Flash is fa-[cut] / Flash is fa-[cut] / Flash is fast." After a moment of Deborah Harry's new-wave rap, Spoonie Gee recaps his previous phrase, but when he reaches the point where the whistle would blow, the familiar voices of "Good Times" launch us into that track's famous break. In effect, Flash has made the "Monster Jam" and "Rapture" fragments into an intro for his track's main theme, "Good Times."

Flash jams with the "Good Times" music, scratching in time, but the episode is short. "Good Times" will return again and again, but there is more thematic material to lay out. After an interlude where he plays the intro from the Incredible Bongo Band's "Apache" (four bars on the original record that Flash stretches to eight), we hear a bass fragment chopped and stuttering like Spoonie Gee's "You say." This turns out to be Queen's "Another One Bites the Dust." Flash has left the "Monster Jam" connection to the "Good Times" bassline implicit. We haven't heard the "Monster Jam" groove, only its intro. But the Queen connection is very clear, and even more so as it crossfades back into "Good Times" at 1:17. Many surprises await, but at this point the track's main theme is evident.

Flash skillfully employs an array of turntable techniques—which he terms "punch-phase, cut, cue, spin back, rub, and zuka-zuka"—to create the flow of musical action. But before he can do any of that he needs to enlist his crate skills, his knowledge of records. The tracks he selects must be closely matched in tempo, and they must fit the narrative he has in mind. They need to work together as he juxtaposes or superimposes them. On-the-fly edits need to happen without losing the groove. No matter how brilliant his manipulations, the dancing must go on. In the end, it's the flow that makes Flash's work so effective, and this begins by casting his experienced ear on a vast collection of records.

Listening Guide

"The Adventures of Grandmaster Flash on the Wheels of Steel," Sugar Hill Records (stereo)
Producers: Sylvia Robinson, Joey Robinson Jr.
Charts: Hot Soul Singles #55

Time	Lyric Cue	Listen For
0:00	"You say"	Spoonie Gee Meets the Sequence, "Monster Jam" (1980), repeats the first two words to produce a rhythmic intro.
0:11	"Fab Five Freddy"	Blondie, "Rapture" (1980), repeats and cuts the lyrics "Flash is fast."
0:22		"Monster Jam."
0:26	"Good times"	Chic, "Good Times" (1979).
0:33		Rhythmic scratching.
0:35		Incredible Bongo Band, "Apache" (1973).
0:42		Scratching.
0:51		Queen, "Another One Bites the Dust" bassline begins with fragment.
1:05		Scratching doubles bass riff in rhythmic unison.
1:18	"Good Times"	"Good Times."
1:35	"Grandmaster cut faster"	Grandmaster Flash and the Furious Five, "Freedom" lyrics overlaid on "Good Times."
1:52		Breakdown: fragments of "Good Times" string glissando.

continued on next page

Time	Lyric Cue	Listen For
1:57		"Good Times" groove resumes.
2:10		Scratches.
2:14		Grandmaster Flash and the Furious Five, "Birthday Party."
		String glissando from "Good Times" morphs into horn section of "Birthday Party." This section of "Birthday Party" includes a bassline similar to the one on "Good Times."
2:30	"Flash, one time"	Cuts in "good" (from "Good Times") as "Birthday Party" plays.
2:35	"Flash, two time"	Cuts in "good, good."
2:39		Scratches create transition to next section.
2:44	"Good times"	"Good Times" groove.
2:52		Cuts in bits of "Freedom."
3:33	"Why don't you tell me a story?"	Spoken intro from the Hellers' "Life Story" (1968).
4:03		The Sugarhill Gang, "8th Wonder" (1980) begins with turntable "stabs."
4:25		Begin scratching "Good Times" over "8th Wonder."
4:34	"Good times"	"Good Times."
4:43		Uses second copy of "Good Times" to double handclaps.
5:19	"The official adventures"	*The Official Adventures of Flash Gordon* (spoken-word LP), beginning of side one.
5:24	Party sounds, then "Hey, hey, everybody say"	Unknown source.
		Call-and-response between MC and crowd, continues to end.
5:57		Cuts in "good."
6:02	"Hey bro"	Unknown source.
6:05		Scratching.
6:14		Scratching.
6:27		"Good Times" intro (adds guitar and piano).
6:31		Scratching.
6:43	"Good times"	"Good times" break to fade.

22.2. "FIGHT THE POWER" (1989)

PUBLIC ENEMY

Although hip-hop began as party music, one of its breakout hits, Grandmaster Flash and the Furious Five's "The Message" (1982), was a serious rap about the struggles of inner-city life. This more sober side of the hip-hop ethos can be heard in the work of such 1980s New York artists as Boogie Down Productions (KRS-One), Eric B. and Rakim, and Public Enemy, whose beats and arrangements accompanied rhymes that spoke to contemporary social and political realities. Chuck D (Carlton Ridenhour) was Public Enemy's chief rapper. The confrontational tone of his lyrics is summarized in "Don't Believe the Hype," "Black Steel in the Hour of Chaos," "Burn Hollywood Burn," and "Welcome to the Terrordome." His words spoke, he said, of "oppression from a black point of view."[1] As fellow band member Hank Shocklee described it, Chuck D's booming voice amid Public Enemy's complex mosaic of samples and beats was like "the voice of God in a storm."[2]

"Fight the Power" was commissioned for the Spike Lee film *Do the Right Thing* (1989), which dealt with a Brooklyn neighborhood's hot summer of racial tension. The group was guided by Lee's insistence that he wanted a song that would serve as an anthem reflecting the film's topic. Chuck D's lyrics, inspired by the Isley Brothers' "Fight the Power" (1975), call listeners to "get down to business," not to "get careless" in standing up to a racist system with "nothing but rednecks for four hundred years." With "the music hitting your heart," and the crowd "swinging while I'm singing," he exhorts listeners to "fight the powers that be." The polemic tone of the words is lightened by the contribution of Public Enemy's second rapper Flavor Flav (William Drayton Jr.), who plays a sort of trickster character on Public Enemy records. He is "like lubrication to the whole machine," said Chuck D. He "keeps it from being like straight vodka with no chaser."[3]

Along with powerful rapping, Public Enemy mastered the art of sampling. As Chuck D put it, "Our music is all about samples."[4] The group called its production team the Bomb Squad. The Squad's job was to build sonic environments for the rap using drum machine beats and samples that were manipulated and combined in complex ways. With a record collection running well into the thousands, "digging in the crates" was central to the Squad's creative process. Squad member Hank Shocklee said of his brother Keith, another Squad member, that "he knows records like an encyclopedia."[5] This statement expresses an important aspect of the sampling ethos. Like an encyclopedia, the universe of records represents a repository of hip-hop artists' knowledge. Producers draw on this well of sonic tradition in crafting their original works. As they incorporate bits of earlier tracks, they situate their own tracks in a larger cultural context.

Public Enemy's use of samples is far more subtle than would be possible with live turntable manipulation. There are at least twenty records sampled on "Fight the Power" spanning more than twenty years—from Wilson Pickett's "Land of 1000 Dances" (1966) to Guy's "Teddy's Jam" (1988). Many of these are unrecognizable, having been chopped to minimal length, layered with other samples on multitrack tape, and manipulated in various ways in the recording studio (sped up, slowed down, reversed, etc.). Instead of presenting the samples as recognizable references, the aim is to infuse them deep into the fabric of the music—into its DNA, as it were—until they become the essential groove and flow of the track. The Listening Guide indicates several of the samples used, but this is meant only to illustrate some of the ways the Bomb Squad incorporated samples. It requires no specific knowledge of the track's references to get a sense of its immersion in the culture of black record making.

Like the track's samples, the lyrics also invoke other records. Aside from the Isleys, these references include James Brown's "I'm Black and I'm Proud" (1968) and "Funky Drummer" (1970), Bobby Byrd's "I Know You Got Soul" (1971), and Jesse Jackson's "Brothers and sisters!" shout from the Soul Children's "I Don't Know What the World Is Coming To" (1972), all of which embed "Fight the Power" firmly within black popular music tradition. And as Chuck D and Flavor Flav restate lyrics that occur in or relate to samples (e.g., "Funky drummer," "I know you got soul," "Get down," "Unh"), they bring the audience into a dialogue with that tradition.

Although the track is radically unconventional in its treatment of many musical elements, its song structure is straightforward: intro, three verses, four choruses, two breaks, and a coda. The verses are twelve, sixteen, and eighteen bars long, extending the loop repetitions to accommodate extra lyrics. The choruses and breaks are each eight bars long.

Verse and choruses each have their own one-bar loop, which share the drum groove but differ in texture and audible samples. For example, the chorus, which has a more turbulent low-end, makes recurring use (every bar) of samples from Sly and the Family Stone's "Sing a Simple Song" ("Let me hear you say") and Bob Marley's "I Shot the Sheriff" (only the "I" is clearly audible). The verses have a more streamlined texture with a sustained high-pitched sound on each downbeat. Samples that are not part of the loop come and go in an irregular way. They may be repeated at some point or occur only once. The relentlessly repeating loop serves as a canvas on which the recording team places sonic events to produce a desired effect.

Like any thematic element in a musical composition, samples may be developed in various ways. Notice, for example, how the sample of Afrika Bambaataa's "Yeah!" from "Planet Rock" makes a momentary appearance at 3:06, makes a longer one at 3:35, and then becomes a featured element in the coda starting at 4:20. Also, listen to how the brief "I Shot the Sheriff" sample buried in the chorus loop is highlighted in break two beginning at 4:00.

Sonically, "Fight the Power" is heavy and murky in the low-end, a hip-hop hallmark. Its texture is also infused with intentionally distorted sound. As Hank Shocklee said, "I wanted you to feel the concrete, the people walking by, the cars that are going by and the *vrroom* in the system. I wanted the city. I wanted that grittiness, the mugginess, the hot sticky, no-air vibration of the city."[6] Samples and electronic processing were the creative resources and tools for achieving Shocklee's desired soundscape. Speaking generally of the Squad's approach, he explained, "Part of the sound was in the dirt that we would get from the samples, whether it be hiss from the record or a crackle on top of the kick." In their creative abuse of technology, Public Enemy aimed to make listeners feel that "this was the street."[7]

Listening Guide

"Fight the Power" (Carlton Ridenhour, Eric Sadler, Hank Shocklee, Keith Shocklee), Def Jam Records (stereo). Also appears on the album *Fear of a Black Planet*.
Recorded at Greene Street Recording, New York City, June 1989
Chuck D (rapper), Flavor Flav (second rapper)
Producer: Bomb Squad
Engineer: Rod Hui
Charts: Hot Rap Songs #1, Top Pop Albums #10, Top R&B Albums #3
Key: N/A
Meter: 4/4

Time	Section	Lyric Cue	Listen For
0:00	Intro (13)	"Yet our best prepared"	Thomas Todd speech referring to black troops in Vietnam.
0:16		"Pump me up"	Trouble Funk, "Pump Me Up" superimposed with horns from Trouble Funk's "Saturday Night. Live! from Washington DC" (side one).
0:22		"Cha cha"	Dramatics, "Whatcha See Is Whatcha Get."
0:23		"Unh"	Wilson Pickett, "Land of 1000 Dances," sometimes answered by a second "Unh" further to the right side of the mix, which is probably a James Brown sample.
			Verse loop.
			Drum groove from James Brown, "Funky Drummer" break.
			Bass from James Brown, "Hot Pants."

continued on next page

Time	Section	Lyric Cue	Listen For
0:26		"Come on and get down"	Sustained high-pitched sound on each downbeat. West Street Mob, "Let's Dance" slowed down.
0:43		"Go home"	Rick James, "Give It to Me Baby."
0:45	Verse 1 (12)	"1989 the number"	Flavor Flav kicks things off, joined by Chuck D on "89."
0:52		"I know you got soul"	Bobby Byrd, "I Know You Got Soul."
1:13	Chorus 1 (8)	"Fight the power"	Chorus loop has more turbulent low-end texture.
		"Let me hear you say"	Sly and the Family Stone, "Sing a Simple Song."
		"I shot the sheriff"	Bob Marley, "I Shot the Sheriff."
1:31	Verse 2 (16)	"As the rhythm designed"	Verse loop.
1:42		"Oh damn"	Guy, "Teddy's Jam."
1:46		"Got to get over"	James Brown, "Funky President."
2:07	Chorus 2 (8)	"Fight the power"	Chorus loop.
2:26	Break 1 (8)		DJ Terminator X scratching over verse loop.
2:41			Syl Johnson, "Different Strokes" riff.
2:43	Break Chorus (8)	"Fight the power"	Chorus loop.
3:01	Verse 3 (18)	"Elvis was a hero"	Verse loop. First line repeated three times, emulating DJ loop technique.
3:06		"Yeah"	Afrika Bambaataa, "Planet Rock" fragment.
3:35		"Yeah"	"Planet Rock" longer sample.
3:42	Chorus 3 (8)	"Fight the power"	Chorus loop.
3:44		"Yes, yes ya'll"	Kurtis Blow, "AJ Scratch" or Spoonie Gee, "Love Rap."
4:00	Break 2 (8)	"I"	"I Shot the Sheriff" sample is highlighted and manipulated rhythmically.
4:19	Coda (8)	"What we got"	Verse loop.
		"Yeah"	"Planet Rock."

22.3. "LET ME RIDE" (1993)

DR. DRE

As hip-hop spread across the US, Los Angeles became a creative hotbed. In the late 1980s, successful records from the rapper Ice-T and the group

N.W.A. (which included Dr. Dre, Ice Cube, and Eazy-E) brought West Coast hip-hop to wide public attention with songs whose lyrics painted grim portraits of inner-city street life. The subgenre was dubbed "gangsta rap." Dr. Dre (Andre Young) took the confrontational attitude of gangsta rap and married it with the appealing musical sounds of funk, in particular Parliament, one of the most popular funk groups of the 1970s. With this musical blend—called G-funk (a reference to Parliament's P-Funk)—Dre's productions represented a hybrid tendency similar to other hip-hop records that included elements of rock, pop, and soul (e.g., Run-DMC's "Walk This Way," Coolio's "Gangsta's Paradise," Fugees' "Killing Me Softly"). The use of melodic hooks on such records completed hip-hop's crossover to the mainstream pop audience and the top of *Billboard's* Hot 100.

"Let Me Ride" uses the Parliament track "Mothership Connection (Star Child)" (1975) as its musical and historical reference point, using that song's chorus melody and lyrics for its hook. The adaptation is a new version (not a sample but an **interpolation**) performed by the singers Ruben and Jewell. Similarly, the bass part is an interpolation of the bassline from the coda of "Mothership Connection." This was typical of Dre's recording process—using live musicians to perform parts taken from earlier records.

But Dre includes samples as well, most notably two Moog synthesizer riffs, which are also taken from the coda of "Mothership Connection." The first of these is in the two-bar verse loop, and the other is in the chorus loop. (These samples are blended with other keyboards.) Another Parliament sample—a vocal performance—comes from a different version of the song called "Swing Down, Sweet Chariot," taken from a Parliament live album. This is heard in chorus three of "Let Me Ride." Further, the verse groove is based on a sample of the drum intro from Bill Withers' "Kissing My Love" (1972), and the chorus groove layers a sample of James Brown's "Funky Drummer" with a programmed drum machine.

Although "Let Me Ride" has an essential link to "Mothership Connection," the musical-historical connection extends further. The chorus tune and lyrics "Swing down, sweet chariot stop and let me ride" also appear on a gospel record by the Golden Gate Quartet called "Swing Down, Chariot" (1946), which itself was an adaptation of the African American spiritual "Swing Low, Sweet Chariot" dating to the late nineteenth century. Dre's rap, largely written by the rapper RBX (Eric Collins), portrays a character familiar from blaxploitation films of the 1970s, a savvy street hustler navigating dangerous terrain. Amid the harsh language of the street, invoking the old spiritual is perhaps an acknowledgment of the long tradition of hope amid pain represented by the black church.

The texture of "Let Me Ride" is far less dense than "Fight the Power." It has a chill airiness about it. The intro sets the mood and the 1970s vibe with only three elements, which enter sequentially: (1) a Moog synthesizer (favored by Parliament keyboardist Bernie Worrell), (2) a funk bassline, and (3) the sound of a wah-wah pedal. The verses and choruses each have their own loops, but they are closely related. The drum pattern and Moog melody are different, but the bassline and the Moog sound remain the same.

Verses and choruses are separated by one-bar breakdowns, where the groove pauses momentarily. These bars extend the meter to 6/4, adding a couple of extra beats for emphasis and variety. The breakdowns at the end of the verses feature Snoop Dogg, whose distinctive voice and diction add another flavor to the track. The breakdowns at the end of the choruses include the sound of record scratching. Both breakdowns share a sample, a short, percussive sound taken from King Tee's "Ruff Rhyme (Back Again)." This is most easily heard underneath Snoop's line "Rolling in my 6-4."

Dr. Dre is one of hip-hop's most successful producers. In addition to his own records, his production credits include Snoop Dogg, Eminem, and 50 Cent. Another obsessive record collector, he estimated his collection at 80,000 discs when he sold it in 2010. Like any serious hip-hop DJ or producer, he is a student of records and record making. But although he followed the hip-hop practice of embedding his work in a context of preexisting records, he sampled sparingly, opting instead to use musicians playing parts taken from the original recordings. This reflected a new reality in the record industry. Recordings are subject to copyright protection. Although fragmentary samples like those on Public Enemy's first two albums in the late '80s were hardly noticed by the record companies (who owned the copyrights), with hip-hop sampling's commercial success came a change in attitude. Suddenly, any sound at all taken from an existing record was subject to royalty payments. As a result, large-scale sampling became prohibitively expensive. Whatever the merits of the legal case, the upshot was to curtail a creative practice.

Listening Guide

"Let Me Ride" (RBX, Snoop Dogg), Interscope Records (stereo). Also appears on the album *The Chronic*.
Recorded at Death Row Studios, mixed at Larrabee Sound Studios, Los Angeles, June 1992
Dr. Dre (rapper, keyboards, drum programming), Snoop Dogg (second rapper), Ruben and Jewell (voices), Colin Wolfe (bass)
Producer: Dr. Dre
Engineer: John Payne

Mix Engineer: Greg Royal
Charts: Hot 100 #34, Hot Rap Songs #3, *Billboard* 200 #3, Top R&B Albums #1
Meter: 4/4
Key: G minor

Time	Section	Lyric Cue	Listen For
0:00	Intro	"Bitch"	Snoop Dogg.
			Elements of 1970s funk vibe:
			Funk bass interpolation of Parliament, "Mothership Connection."
			Moog synth (L).
			Wah-wah sound.
0:13	Verse 1 (20+1)	"Creeping down the back street"	Sample of drum groove from Bill Withers, "Kissing My Love."
			Sample of Moog riff from Parliament, "Mothership Connection."
1:05	Breakdown	"Rollin' in my 6-4"	Snoop Dogg's voice spread out in stereo.
			6/4 bar.
			Sample of King Tee, "Ruff Rhyme (Back Again)."
1:10	**Chorus 1** (8+1)	"Swing down"	Vocal melody interpolation of Parliament's "Mothership Connection."
1:30	Breakdown	"Just another"	6/4 bar, King Tee sample.
1:34	**Verse 2** (20+1)		Similar to **verse 1**.
2:25	Breakdown	"Rollin' in my 6-4"	6/4 bar.
2:29	**Chorus 2** (8+1)	"Swing down"	Similar to **chorus 1**.
2:50	Breakdown	"Check this out"	6/4 bar.
2:54	**Verse 3** (16+1)		Similar to **verse 1**.
3:35	Breakdown	"Rollin' in my 6-4"	6/4 bar.
3:39	**Chorus 3**	"Swing down"	Similar to **Chorus 1**.
			Sample of vocal from Parliament, "Let Me Ride."

NOTES

1. Quoted in Mark Dery, "Public Enemy: Confrontation," *Keyboard*, September 1990.
2. Quoted in Laura K. Warrell, "Fight the Power," *Salon*, June 3, 2002. https://www.salon.com/2002/06/03/fight_the_power/.
3. Quoted in Dery, "Public Enemy."

4. Quoted in Dery.

5. Quoted in Tom Moon, "Public Enemy's Bomb Squad," *Musician*, October 1991, 70.

6. Quoted in Kory Grow, "Riot on the Set: How Public Enemy Crafted the Anthem 'Fight the Power,'" *Rolling Stone*, June 30, 2014.

7. Quoted in Richard Buskin, "Public Enemy 'Black Steel in the Hour of Chaos,'" *Sound on Sound*, January 2010.

FURTHER READING

Chang, Jeff. *Can't Stop Won't Stop: A History of the Hip-Hop Generation.* New York: St. Martin's Press, 2005.

Coleman, Brian. *Check the Technique: Liner Notes for Hip-Hop Junkies.* New York: Villard, 2007.

Katz, Mark. *Groove Music: The Art and Culture of the Hip-Hop DJ.* New York: Oxford University Press, 2012.

FURTHER LISTENING

Arrested Development, "Mr. Wendel" (Chrysalis, 1991)
Beastie Boys, "Paul Revere" (Def Jam, 1986)
Kurtis Blow, "The Breaks" (Mercury, 1980)
De La Soul, "Me Myself and I" (Tommy Boy, 1989)
Grandmaster Flash and the Furious Five, "The Message" (Sugar Hill, 1982)
Ice-T, "6 in the Mornin'" (Techno Hop, 1986)
Run-DMC, "King of Rock" (Profile, 1985)
Salt-N-Pepa, "Push It" (Next Plateau, 1987)
Tupac Shakur, "Trapped" (Interscope, 1991)
Sugarhill Gang, "Rapper's Delight" (Sugar Hill, 1979)

GLOSSARY

AABA. A song form in four sections, typically thirty-two bars in length (eight bars per section).

accent. An emphasis placed on a particular note or beat.

ADSR. The phases of a sound's envelope: attack, decay, sustain, release.

ADT. Automatic double tracking. An electronic simulation of a doubled recording.

amplitude. The loudness of a sound.

arrangement. The combination of elements constituting a piece of music.

attack. The onset of a sound.

augmented. Describes an interval one half step larger than a perfect interval (fourth, fifth, octave), or an augmented triad. An augmented triad is made up of a root, a major third, and an augmented fifth.

backbeat. The second and fourth beats of a 4/4 measure.

beat. A regular pulse that serves as a foundation for rhythmic activity.

blue notes. Pitches evoking a blues feeling, typically the flatted third, fifth, and seventh of a major scale, as well as microtonal inflections achieved by bending or sliding between notes of the chromatic scale.

blue-eyed soul. A vocal performance style where white performers assume stylistic features typical of black performers.

bolero. A Spanish dance typified by a characteristic rhythm.

boogie-woogie. A piano-based blues genre in which the left-hand accompaniment consists of broken chords.

break. A change of musical focus from voice to instruments, often with an emphasis on rhythm.

bridge. A song or track's contrasting middle section.

broken chords. Chords whose constituent notes are played one at a time.

cadence. A concluding musical passage for a phrase, a section, or an entire piece.

chord. Three or more pitches sounding simultaneously.

chord progression. A series of harmonies based on triads.

chorus. 1. A section of a song.
2. One complete iteration of an AABA form.
3. One complete iteration of a twelve-bar blues sequence.
4. An electronic effect.
5. A large vocal ensemble.

chromatic. Notes that fall outside of a key. Chromatic notes may add harmonic color or enable modulation to a different key.

clef. A symbol indicating the pitches on a staff.

coda. The concluding section of a track following the end of the song. Compare to *outro* and *tag*.

comping. Rhythmic chordal accompaniment.

compound meter. A meter in which each beat is subdivided into three (e.g., 6/8, 9/8, 12/8).

conjunct motion. Melodic motion by step. Contrast with *disjunct motion*.

consonance. Harmonic intervals or chords that feel stable. Contrast with *dissonance*.

counterpoint. Two or more independent melodies occurring simultaneously.

decibel (dB). A unit of measurement for sound pressure level or loudness.

diatonic. The set of pitches comprising a major or minor scale.

diminished. Describes an interval one half step smaller than a perfect interval (fourth, fifth, octave), or a diminished triad. A diminished triad is made up of a root, a minor third, and a diminished fifth.

disjunct motion. Melodic motion by leap. Contrast with *conjunct motion*.

dissonance. Harmonic intervals or chords that feel unstable or tense. Contrast with *consonance*.

dominant. The fifth degree of a major or minor scale.

downbeat. The first beat of a measure.

drone. A note sustained or repeated for a long period of time, usually in the low register. A drone may sustain through an entire track (e.g., "Tomorrow Never Knows," the Beatles).

duple. A type of meter where accents occur on every other beat (4/4, 2/4). A rhythm that subdivides beats by an even number.

duration. The length of time a note is held.

dynamics. Degrees of loudness that shape a musical performance.

echo. The discrete repetition of a sound.

envelope. The overall dynamic shape of a sound as it occurs over time.

equalizer (Eq). A device that allows a user to boost or cut selected frequencies or frequency ranges in an audio signal. Used for tone control.

flat. A note lowered by one half step from its letter name.

frequency. The rate of a sound's vibration expressed in cycles per second. The frequency content of a sound affects perception of pitch and timbre.

fundamental. The lowest frequency of a sound.

groove. An overall rhythmic character.

harmony. Pitches sounding simultaneously.

harmonic rhythm. The pace of harmonic change in a chord progression.

head arrangement. A musical arrangement that is not written down.

hertz (Hz). A measurement unit for frequency. One Hz = one cycle per second.

hi-fi. Recordings and playback equipment claiming accurate representation of recorded sounds.

high-end. In audio production, the area of the frequency range from about 6 to 20k Hz.

improvisation. A spontaneous musical performance.

indie. An independent record company or radio station.

interlude. A brief section of music, usually without lyrics, separating larger sections of a song.

interpolation. On a hip-hop record, a performance (rather a sample) that imitates a previously recorded part.

interval. The distance between two notes, measured in half steps. (See interval chart, p. 10.)

introduction (intro). The beginning of a track, typically before the voice enters.

key. A collection of pitches that forms a major or minor scale, named for the tonic note.

legato. A way of playing whereby notes are connected smoothly to one another.

low-end. In audio production, the area of the frequency range from about 20 to 250 Hz.

lo-fi. Recordings and playback equipment that obviously, often willfully distort recorded sounds.

major. A scale that follows a specific pattern of steps (W–W–H–W–W–W–H). A triad consisting of root, major third, and perfect fifth.

measure (bar). One unit of a designated meter.

melisma. Multiple notes sung to a single syllable.

melody. A succession of notes.

meter. Beats organized according to a recurring pattern of accents.

mid-range. In audio production, the area of the frequency range from about 250 to 6 kHz. Typically subdivided into low (250–2 kHz), mid (2–4 kHz), and upper (4–6 kHz).

minor. A scale that follows a specific pattern of steps (W–H–W–W–H–W–W). A triad consisting of root, minor third, and perfect fifth.

mix. A specific arrangement of all the audio elements in a track.

mode. Any of seven scales, each with a particular sequence of whole and half steps (see pp. 15–17).

modulation. A change from one key to another.

mono (monophonic). A single channel of audio. Compare to *stereo*.

multitrack. A collection of audio bands that combine to make a single recording.

natural. A musical symbol that cancels a sharp or flat.

note value. A note's duration.

novelty. A song or track that employs some sort of quirky concept as an identifying feature.

octave. An interval in which one pitch is either double or half the frequency of the other.

outro. A brief add-on following a song. Compare to *coda*, *tag*.

overdub (overdubbing). 1. To add a performance or other sound to an existing recording.
2. Any performances or other sounds added to an existing recording.

overtone. Frequency content above a sound's fundamental.

pad. A sustained background part in an arrangement, often composed of chords.

pentatonic. A five-note scale without half steps, which may be configured to convey either a major or a minor character.

phrase. A coherent musical statement.

pickup. One or more notes preceding a downbeat.

pitch. A fundamental frequency so prominent compared to its overtones that it is perceived as a discrete note.

pre-chorus. A song section that builds anticipation for the song's chorus.

protest song. A song with a social or political topic, especially songs associated with the urban folk scene.

range. A span of notes covered by a melody or available to a voice or instrument.

refrain. A repeated section of music and/or lyrics.

register. A specific region of the frequency spectrum.

rest. A specified duration of silence.

reverb (reverberation, ambience). A blend of sound reflections off the surfaces of an enclosed or semi-enclosed space.

rhythm. A specific arrangement of attacks and durations.

riff. A short musical phrase that may serve as an introduction or a refrain.

root. The note on which a chord is based.

sampler. An electronic device that records and retains sounds.

scale. A collection of seven notes spanning an octave arrayed in a particular sequence of whole and half steps.

sequencer. A device that records and plays back performance data, including rhythm, pitch, and dynamics. A sequencer triggers the sounds contained in or generated by a sampler, drum machine, or synthesizer.

sharp. A note raised by one half step from its letter name.

simple meter. A meter in which each beat is subdivided into two (e.g., 2/4, 4/4.)

slapback echo. A short echo (about 70 milliseconds) typical of rockabilly music.

song. A piece of vocal music usually stipulating melody, harmony, and lyrics but containing no actual sound. In record making, a song is analogous to a screenplay in film making.

staccato. A way of playing a note or chord that shortens its duration and separates it from any following notes.

staff. A set of five parallel lines and the spaces between them used for pitch notation.

stereo. A system of sound localization using two-channel (left/right) audio recording and playback. Compare to *mono*.

stereo image. A track's arrangement of audio across the left/right stereo field.

stop-time. A brief suspension of groove.

strophic form. A song form in which each stanza, or verse, of lyrics is set to the same music.

style. The set of characteristic features associated with a specific artist or, more generally, a musical genre.

subdivision. Divisions of a beat. For example, an eighth note subdivides the duration of a quarter note beat into two attacks (see Note Values chart, p. 20).

syncopation. A displacement of accent to a measure's weaker beat or a beat's subdivisions.

synthesizer. A musical instrument that generates and combines tones electronically.

tag. The briefest addition at the end of a track. Compare to *coda, outro*.

tape speed. The rate at which a magnetic tape passes over a tape recorder's erase, record, and playback heads, measured in inches per second (ips).

tempo. The speed of a piece of music, often expressed in beats per minute (bpm).

texture. The composite sound created by interaction among a track's elements.

tie. A musical notation symbol joining note values to extend duration.

timbre. Tone color.

tonic. The first note of a scale and its tonal center.

track. 1. A finished recording.
        2. A single band of audio recording.

transpose. To move a musical piece or any part thereof from one pitch level to another (e.g., to transpose a song from one key to another).

tremolo. 1. Rapid repetition of a note.
           2. Electronic variation in amplitude.

triad. A three-note chord consisting of root, third, and fifth.

triplet. A note that subdivides a beat into three.

tritone. The interval of an augmented fourth or diminished fifth.

turnaround. A brief passage that ends one musical section and sets up a following one.

twelve-bar blues. A conventional blues form that prescribes a specific length and chord progression for each chorus.

vamp. A short, repeated musical passage.

verse-chorus. A song form in which strophic verses are followed by a refrain.

INDEX

a cappella, 79, 116, 134–35, 172, 227
A Taste of Honey, 319
A&M Studios, 259
A&R (artist & repertoire), 54, 170
A&R Studios, 251
Abbey Road Studios, 278
Abbey Road, 133, 140, 144–48, 151, 177
AC/DC, 32, 281, 288–90
accent, 19
accordion, 174, 176
acid rock. *See* psychedelic rock
acoustic sound, 5–6
ADSR. *See* envelope
ADT, 137–38, 139, 140, 141, 142, 143
Advision Studios, 274
Aerosmith, 281, 285–88
Afrika Bambaataa, 321, 326, 328
Aftermath, 153, 154, 155, 157
album, as coherent artwork, 134, 173
Aldon Music, 116–17, 118
Alice Cooper, 281, 291
Alice's Adventures in Wonderland, 232
All Summer Long, 171–72
Allison, Jerry, 84
AM radio, 147
American Gigolo, 310
amplification, 5, 28, 238, 281
amplitude (loudness), 5–6
Andantes, 202, 208
Anderson, Jon, 272, 274
Andrews Sisters, 40, 115
Angels, 115, 128, 309
Animals, 168, 240
Another Side of Bob Dylan, 190

Apollo Theater, 121
Applebaum, Stanley, 96
Are You Experienced, 240–42
Aretha: Lady Soul, 221
Armstrong, Louis, 40, 92
Arnold, Eddy, 47, 62
arpeggio (broken chord), 80, 132, 145, 218, 236, 104
arrangement, 26–28
arranger, 40, 44, 98, 110, 116, 153, 183, 216, 298
Arthur Godfrey's Talent Scouts, 50
Asher, Tony, 175
Atkins, Cholly, 198
Atlantic Records, 94, 215–16, 219–20, 225, 282, 288, 298
Atlantic Studios, 220–21, 239
attack, 6–7, 20
augmented fourth (tritone), 10, 122, 241
Australia, 183, 288
Autry, Gene, 92

Bach, J. S., 249
Bacharach, Burt, 117
Back in Black, 288
backbeat, 21, 64, 70, 80, 87, 91, 104, 108, 123, 145, 155, 163, 178, 185, 217, 227, 232–33, 238, 307, 310
Baez, Joan, 183, 197
baião, 95
Baker, Ginger, 238–39
Baker, LaVern, 48
Balin, Marty, 231, 233
ballad, 50, 59, 66, 104, 107, 109, 140, 154, 170, 223, 235, 239
Ballard, Florence, 200, 202

341

Baltimore, 50
Band, 248–52
banjo, 182–83
Barrett, Richard, 54
Barrett, Syd, 277
Barrow, Marlene, 208
Barry, Jeff, 117, 121, 123, 125–26
bass
  fuzz, 145
  musical role of 64, 68, 83, 91, 104, 125, 160, 161, 177–78, 227, 232, 241, 242, 247, 253, 273, 278, 283, 286, 295, 298, 302, 307, 314–15, 329
  pedals, 154
  sampled, 322
  sonic role of, 27, 28, 29, 31, 32, 133, 155, 162, 177–78, 201, 203, 281, 289
  stand up (upright), 41, 42, 63, 65, 67, 69, 80, 91, 157, 182
  synthesizer, 210, 302
Beach Boys, 14, 26, 157, 168–80, 230, 235, 306–307
Beach Boys Today, 174
beat, 19–20
Beatlemania, 129
Beatles, 14, 21, 25, 33, 82, 107, 129–50, 152, 153, 154, 157, 158, 171, 173, 177, 182, 189, 200, 215, 230, 223, 267
The Beatles (White Album), 133, 140–41, 143–44, 147, 151
bebop, 86
Beck, Jeff, 168, 282
Bee Gees, 293, 304
Beggar's Banquet, 159–61, 165, 177
Bell Sound Studios, 54, 56, 119
Bell, Al, 199
Bell, Freddie and the Bellboys, 80
Bell, Madeline, 163
Bell, Thom, 294
Bellotte, Pete, 301, 302–303
Bennett, Estelle, 121, 124
Bennett, Tony, 47, 107

Berlin, Irving, 35, 206
Berry, Chuck, 14, 48, 74–75, 83, 86–88, 130, 159, 165
Between the Buttons, 157
big band, 34–35, 92
Big Brother and the Holding Company, 222, 231
Billboard, 3–4, 35, 91, 94, 103, 115, 182, 184–85, 249, 277, 298, 310, 329
Black Sabbath, 32, 281, 291
Black, Bill, 66, 68, 81
Blackboard Jungle, 64
Blackmon, Thelma, 71
Blanc, Mel, 40
Blind Faith, 159
Blonde on Blonde, 157, 246
Blondie, 305, 309–12, 322–23
Blue Cheer, 238, 281, 291
blue notes, 14, 132, 159, 160, 235, 259
blue-eyed soul, 30
bluegrass, 67
blues, 14, 56, 74, 86, 90, 131, 132, 142, 152–53, 159–60, 166, 217, 220, 235, 238–39, 240–42, 249, 252, 282, 286
  chord progression, 25, 75, 226, 238, 277
  singing, 221, 224, 253, 277, 283
  twelve-bar form. *See* song form
Blues Incorporated, 238
Bob B. Soxx and the Blue Jeans, 121
Bobbettes, 115
bolero, 111–13, 232–34
Bomb Squad, 325–27
Bonham, John, 282, 284
Boogie Down Productions (KRS One), 325
boogie-woogie, 50, 68–69, 91, 93, 104–106
Bookends, 193–94
Booker T. and the MG's, 216, 222, 224, 229
Boomtown Rats, 288

Boston (band), 285
Boston, (city), 285
Bowie, David, 267, 280, 294, 302
brass, 38–39, 42–43, 90, 98–100, 139, 174, 204, 208–209, 294, 297
break, 21, 26–27
Brenston, Jackie, 62
bridge, 25
Brill Building, 115–18, 198
Bringing It All Back Home, 185
British Invasion, 151–52, 168–69, 200, 305, 319
 second, 319
Broadway, 35, 40, 116–18
broken chord. *See* arpeggio
Brooks, Gene, 56
Brown, James, 32, 214, 225–28, 322, 327–29
Brown, Lawrence, 296
Browne, Jackson, 257, 258
Bruce Jack, 238–39
Bruford, Bill, 268, 272, 274
Bryant, Boudleaux, 107–108, 111
Bryant, Felice, 107
Buffalo Springfield, 183, 197, 222, 234, 245, 263
Burke, Clem, 309, 311
Burke, Solomon, 214, 229
Burroughs, William, 230
Butler, Jerry, 101, 214
Buzzcocks, 313, 318
Byrd, Bobby, 326, 328
Byrds, 26, 107, 133, 153, 182, 184, 189–92, 197, 222, 230, 234, 244–45, 256

cadence, 18–19
Café Wha? 241
California, 169–70, 222, 234–35, 252
call-and-response, 120, 123–24, 149, 172, 202, 205, 220–21, 282–83, 296, 324
Canada, 248, 263

Capitol Records, 39–40, 70, 129, 169–71, 173
Capitol Studios, 71
Carey, Mariah, 218
Carroll, Lewis, 232
Cars, 285, 318
Carstarphen, Vic, 296
Casady, Jack, 231, 233
Cash, Johnny, 63, 72, 246, 263
cassette tape recorder, 159
CBGB, 305, 309
Cecil, Malcolm, 211
celesta, 83
cello, 95, 118, 137, 178–79
Chad and Jeremy, 107
Chambers Brothers, 207
Chantays, 169, 181
Chantels, 54, 115, 128
Charles, Ray, 96, 101, 214, 229
charts, 3–4, 33
Chess Records, 203
Chess Studios, 165
Chess, Leonard, 87
Chess, Phil, 87
Chessler, Deborah, 51, 53
Chez Régine, 292
Chic, 298, 304, 319, 322–23
Chicago, 165, 215
Chiffons, 117, 128
choir, 5, 38–39, 109, 162–65
chord, 22–23
chord progression, 22, 40, 86, 107, 125, 171, 175, 223–24, 232, 246–47, 259, 261, 299, 311, 315
 blues. *See* blues
 chromatic, 40, 105, 121, 246–47
 doo wop, 55, 94, 121
chord root, 22–23, 160, 175, 259, 261, 311
Chords, 49, 61
chorus (electronic effect), 28
chorus, multiple meanings of the term, 25, 26, 77
chromatic pitches, 24, 38, 40, 42, 104, 119, 121, 123, 124, 132,

chromatic pitches *(continued)*
    134, 138, 140, 175, 194, 223, 225, 246–47, 248
The Chronic, 330
Chuck D (Carlton Ridenhour), 325–28
Chudd, Lew, 90, 92
civil rights movement, 97, 184
Clapton, Eric, 141–42, 238–39, 249, 282
Clark, Gene, 189–90
Clark, Petula, 151, 153
Clark, Sanford, 72
Clarke, Michael, 191
Clash, 26, 309, 313–17
classical music, 33, 86, 95, 117, 130, 137, 157, 162, 177, 216, 267–68, 272, 274, 277
claves, 190–91
clavichord, 139
clef, 9
Cleveland, 76
Clifford, Doug, 252, 254
Clooney, Rosemary, 35, 47
Clouds, 258–59
Clovis, New Mexico, 83–84, 109
Coastal Studios, 65
Coasters, 94, 117
Cochran, Eddie, 62, 72
coda, 26, 41, 142, 155, 163, 174–75, 178–79, 194, 210–11, 224, 264, 286, 296, 326, 329
Cohen, Leonard, 257, 266
Cole, Doris, 117, 119
Cole, Nat "King," 206
Collins, Judy, 258–59
Colpix Records, 121
Columbia Records, 34, 49, 184, 192, 219
Columbia Studio A (Los Angeles), 175, 179
Columbia Studio A (New York), 187
comping, 65
congas, 41, 164, 208
conjunct motion, 18
consonance, 21–22
Cook, Stu, 252, 254

Cooke, Sam, 90, 97–100, 214
Cookies, 117, 130
Coolio, 329
Cornelius, Don, 294
countermelody, 39, 175, 177, 178
counterpoint, 42–43, 55, 94, 100, 162, 174, 176, 264, 269, 276
country music (style), 38, 40, 62–63, 64, 66, 69–70, 106–107, 109, 165, 249
country rock, 245–56, 260, 263
country two-step, 39, 68–69
Covay, Don, 214, 220–21
Crazy Horse, 263
Cream, 141, 238–40, 281–82
Creedence Clearwater Revival, 252–55
Creedence, 252
Crests, 61, 118
Crickets, 72, 83
Croce, Jim, 257
crooning, 50–51, 90, 92, 95, 102, 206
Crosby, Bing, 35, 43, 62
Crosby, David, 189, 191
Crosby, Stills and Nash, 197
Crosby, Stills, Nash and Young, 263
crossfade, 193, 195, 323
Crowns, 93
Crows, 49, 54, 61
Crudup, Arthur, 62, 66
Crystals, 96, 117, 128
Cummings, Jerry, 296

Damned, 313
Danko, Rick, 248, 251
Danny and the Juniors, 75
The Dark Side of the Moon, 277–78
Darling Sisters, 121
Dave Clark Five, 151, 153
David, Hal, 117
De Lane Lea Studios, 242
Death Row Studios, 330
Decca Records, 40, 49, 50, 64, 69–70, 118, 183
decibel (dB), 6
DeCoteaux, Bert, 298

deejay (disc jockey, DJ), 137, 207, 292, 293, 294, 320–21
Deep Purple, 281, 291
Def Leppard, 319
delayed backbeat, 217–18
Delfonics, 294
Delmore Brothers, 107
demo recording, 116, 125, 170, 216
Demps, Louvain, 208
Denby, Al, 60
Densmore, John, 234, 236
DeRogatis, Jim, 231
Destri, Jimmy, 309, 311
Detroit Symphony Orchestra, 205, 208
Detroit, 115, 198–200, 203, 206, 215, 219, 305
Dexter, Al, 62
diatonic, 24, 201, 259, 261
Dibango, Manu, 292
Dick Dale and the Del-Tones, 169, 181
diction, 51, 63, 70, 103–104, 162, 164, 166, 190, 330
Dimension Records, 116
diminished chord, 23, 299–300
diminished fifth, 10, 17
Dion, 183
Dion, Celine, 2
disco, 292–304, 309–10, 319–20, 322
disjunct motion, 18
Disraeli Gears, 238, 239
dissonance, 21–23, 51, 53, 121–22, 124, 259, 262, 270, 306
distortion
  instrument, 28, 32, 104, 105, 145, 149, 159, 160, 177, 236, 237, 250, 254, 255, 281, 289, 307, 308, 310
  recording, 49, 59, 154, 327
Dixie Cups, 117
DJ Kool Herc, 320–21
Do the Right Thing, 325
The Dock of the Bay, 224
dominant (scale degree 5), 98, 146, 163, 175, 178, 204, 273, 289, 295, 302

Domino, Fats, 20, 48, 74, 78, 90–92
Dominoes, 61, 94
Donays, 130
Donovan, 183, 197, 244
doo wop, 48–61, 63, 76, 90, 93–95, 103–104, 107, 116, 121, 169, 172, 214, 225, 309, 319
Doors, 157, 234–36, 267
The Doors, 157, 236
double tracking, 132, 135, 170–71
Douglas, Carl, 293, 304
downbeat, 19, 21, 32, 68, 80, 141, 186, 190, 201, 210, 227, 272, 283, 289, 299, 307, 326
Dozier, Lamont, 199–200, 202
Dr. Dre (Andre Young), 328–30
Drifters, 59, 90, 93–97
drone, 162, 231, 235–37, 254, 259, 262
drum machine, 325, 329
drums
  cymbals, 28, 196, 271, 307
  hi-hat, 28, 112, 195, 208, 209–10, 286, 294, 295, 297
  kick, 27, 28, 29, 31, 32, 201, 207, 209, 210, 227, 281, 293, 294, 310, 314
  snare, 21, 27, 28, 29, 31, 32, 55, 59, 64, 80, 81, 87, 98, 108, 118, 123, 154–55, 185, 201, 217, 220, 227, 232, 238, 241, 253, 314
  toms, 28, 149, 154–55, 195, 208, 275, 283
Dryden, Spencer, 231, 233
dub mixing, 299–301, 310, 312
dulcimer, 154
duple, 21, 68, 77, 84, 87, 99
duration, 20
Dylan, Bob, 32, 97, 137, 157, 183–92, 245–48, 257, 263
dynamics, 5–6

Eagles, 245, 256
easy listening, 95, 103
Eazy-E, 329

Easybeats, 288
echo (delay), 36–37, 43–46, 67–71, 87, 137, 141, 241–42, 253–54, 284–85. *See also* slapback echo
echo chamber, 36–37, 84, 122
The Ed Sullivan Show, 129
eight-track recording, 44, 147, 165
El Cerrito, California, 252
Electric Lady Studios, 211
electronic amplification, 5, 28, 238, 281
electronic processing, 3, 28, 32, 137, 139, 193, 327
Ellington, Duke, 34
Emerson, Lake and Palmer, 267, 280
EMI Records, 129–30, 135, 137
EMI Studios (Abbey Road), 133, 139, 142, 144, 148
Eminem, 330
End of the Century, 307
England, 129, 183, 192, 268
Eno, Brian, 302
envelope, 6–7
Epstein, Brian, 129
equalizer, 6
Eric B. and Rakim, 325
Ertegun, Ahmet, 94
Essex Records, 64
Essex, 115
Eurythmics, 319
Everly Brothers, 14, 21, 103, 106–109, 192
The Everly Family Show, 106
Evers, Medgar, 185
Exciters, 117, 128
Exile on Main Street, 159

Fair, E. and the Sensational Gladys Davis Trio, 220
Fairport Convention, 183
Falcons, 215
falsetto, 104, 169, 171
FAME studio, 219
Famous Flames, 225

Federal Records, 104
feedback (electronic), 241, 306, 317
fiddle, 70–71, 161, 182, 250–51
filer sweep, 302–303
Fillmore Auditorium, 223, 231
film music, 35, 38
Fitzgerald, Ella, 115
Five Satins, 49, 59–61
flamenco music, 235
flat VII chord, 131–32, 159–60, 216, 218, 223, 246, 247, 261, 308–309
flat, 11
Flavor Flav (William Drayton Jr.), 325–28
Fleetwoods, 103, 113
Florence, Alabama, 219
Floyd, Eddie, 223
Flying Burrito Brothers, 245–46, 256
Flying Machine, 261
FM radio, 133, 288
Fogerty, John, 252, 254
Fogerty, Tom, 252, 254
folk music (style), 36, 38, 44, 97, 166, 182–83, 245, 249, 257, 268, 282
folk rock, 153, 182–97, 215, 246, 260, 263, 319
For Those About to Rock (We Salute You), 288
Ford, Mary, 37, 43–45, 115
Ford, Tennessee Ernie, 47, 62
Four Aces of Western Swing, 63
Four Freshmen, 170
Four Seasons of Love, 301
Four Tops, 153, 199–200, 213
four-on-the-floor, 293–94, 310, 312
Fox Theater, 121
Fragile, 272, 274
Francis, Connie, 113, 115
Franklin, Aretha, 29, 218–22
Franklin, C. L., 219
Freddie and the Dreamers, 153
Freed, Alan, 76, 116
Freeman, Bobby, 89, 306

Freeman, Ernie, 253
Freeman, Jim, 60
French horn, 98, 100, 139, 162, 164, 175, 177, 207, 209
frequency range (register), 5–7, 27–28, 31, 95
Fripp, Robert, 268, 270
Frizzell, Lefty, 249
Fugees, 329
Fulfillingness' First Finale, 209
fundamental (pitch), 6
Funk Brothers, 198, 205, 208
funk music, 21, 207, 209, 226, 250, 273, 319, 329, 330
Funky 4+1, 319
Fuqua, Harvey, 206
Furay, Richie, 245

G-funk, 329
Gabler, Milt, 40–41
Gaither, Tommy, 53
gang vocals, 289, 313, 316
gangsta rap, 329
Ganser, Marge, 125–26
Ganser, Mary Ann, 125–26
Garcia, Jerry, 245
Garfunkel, Art, 192–96
Garnes, Sherman, 55–56
Gaye, Marvin, 14, 26, 206–209
Gaynor, Gloria, 293, 304
Geller, Harry, 38
genre, 2, 32, 40
Gershwin, George, 35
Gershwin, Ira, 35
Get Back, 144
Gibson Les Paul, 44
Giles, Michael, 268, 270
Gillespie, Haven, 38
Gilmour, David, 277–78
girl groups, 115–28, 130, 305, 319
glee club (style), 81
Go-Go's, 319
Goffin, Jerry, 116, 118–19
Going to a Go-Go, 205
Gold Star Studios, 122–23

Gold, Dave, 122
Golden Gate Quartet, 329
Goldner, George, 54, 56
Goodman, Benny, 34
Gordon, Jim, 175, 179
Gordon, Rosco, 63
Gordy, Berry, 115, 198–200, 203, 206–207, 209, 222
Gore, Lesley, 115
Gospel Cavaliers, 214
gospel music (style), 90, 95, 97, 162, 200, 214
Gospel Starlighters, 214
The Graduate, 193
Graham Bond Organisation, 238
Graham, Bill, 231
Grand Funk Railroad, 238
Grand Ole Opry, 64
Grandmaster Flash (Joseph Sadler), 320–24, 332
Grandmaster Flash and the Furious Five, 321, 323–24, 332
Grant, Peter, 282
Grateful Dead, 18, 182, 231, 244–45
Great American Songbook, 75
Green, Doc, 96
Green, Johnny, 75
Greenberg, Florence, 115, 117
Greenberg, Howie, 116
Greene Street Recording, 327
Greenwich Village, 183–84, 192, 241
Greenwich, Ellie, 115, 117, 121, 123, 125, 221
groove, 20–21, 27, 64, 68, 77, 87, 91, 94, 95, 118, 123, 141, 154, 155, 159, 162, 163, 171, 174, 178, 208, 209, 216, 217, 220, 223, 227, 238–39, 247, 250, 273, 277, 278, 281, 283, 289, 293, 294, 298, 307, 314, 326, 329
guitar
    acoustic, 67, 83, 135, 137, 141, 155, 159, 162, 165–66, 182, 193, 257, 263, 307
    baritone, 220–21

guitar *(continued)*
   electric, 27, 28, 29, 32, 70, 74, 80, 82, 102, 104, 108, 154, 155, 162, 166, 185, 190, 192, 273, 307
   electric sitar, 27–30
   Nashville tuning, 166, 167
   open tuning, 162, 258, 259
   twelve-string
      acoustic, 165
      electric, 132–33, 189, 190, 319
Gunter, Henry Louis "Hardrock," 62
Guthrie, Arlo, 197
Guthrie, Woody, 183, 245
Guy, 325, 328

Haggard, Merle, 245
Haley, Bill and His Comets, 40, 62–66, 74
Haley, Bill and the Saddlemen, 62, 64
Hall, Daryl and John Oates, 27
Hall, Jim, 110
Hall, René, 98, 99
Hall, Rick, 219
hallucinogenic drugs, 230
Hamilton, Tom, 287
Hammond organ, 154
Hammond, John, 219
handclaps, 81, 123, 126, 221, 286, 307
A Hard Day's Night (album), 130–31, 133
A Hard Day's Night (film), 131
harmonic rhythm, 55, 105, 155, 185–86, 201, 204, 233, 264, 302, 307, 308
harmonica, 32, 161, 246, 263–64
harmony, 21–23
   vocal, 50, 59, 82, 132, 135, 143, 148, 182, 312, 315
   See also consonance; chord; chord progression; dissonance
harp, 170
harpsichord, 35, 174, 176, 271–72
Harris, Addie "Micki," 117, 119

Harris, Wynonie, 62
Harrison, George, 129, 133, 135, 136, 139, 140–44, 148
Harrison, Wilbert, 117
Harry, Deborah, 309–11, 322
Hart, Lorenz, 40, 41
Harvest, 264
Hawkins, Ronnie, 248
Hawks, 245, 248–49
head arrangement, 216, 219
Headley Grange, 283
Headon, Topper, 313, 316
Hellers, 322, 324
Hello Broadway, 206
Helm, Levon, 248, 250–51
Help!, 136, 151
Hendrix, Jimi, 32, 184, 222, 238, 240–43, 281, 288
Henry, Clarence "Frogman," 78, 89
Her Satanic Majesty's Request, 158
Herman's Hermits, 151
hertz (Hz), 5, 7, 31
Hess, Jurgen, 139
Hicks, Jackie, 208
High Voltage, 288
high-end, 5, 31, 84, 112, 133, 135, 154–55, 161, 201, 307
Highway 61 Revisited, 185, 187, 246
Highway to Hell, 288
Hillman, Chris, 189–91, 245
hip-hop, 21, 285, 301, 319–32
hippie, 160, 215, 231, 240, 282
Hitsville, U.S.A. Studio A, 202, 205, 208
Hitsville, U.S.A., 198–99
Hobbs, Elsbeary, 96
Hodge, Alex, 103
Hohner Clavinet, 210–12
Holland, Brian, 199–200, 202
Holland, Eddie, 199–200, 202
Holly, Buddy, 26, 62, 72, 74, 82–85, 95, 103, 109, 113, 130
honky-tonk (style), 38, 109, 249, 252

hook, 37, 110, 121, 133, 157, 159, 160, 186, 190, 201, 286, 289, 307, 315, 329
House of God Pentecostal church, 206
House, Son, 74
Houston, Whitney, 218
Howe, Steve, 272, 274
Howlin' Wolf, 165
Hudson, Garth, 248, 251
Hues Corporation, 293, 304
Human League, 319
Huxley, Aldous, 230

I Remember Yesterday, 301, 302
Ice Cube, 329
Ice-T, 328, 332
Imperial Records, 90
improvisation, 30, 156, 224, 235–37, 268, 277, 297
In the Court of the Crimson King, 268, 270
In the Groove, 207, 208
In the Midnight Hour, 217
Incredible Bongo Band, 322, 323
independent record company (indie), 35, 49, 58, 75, 129, 199
independent record producer, 117
Indian music, 131, 222, 235
Ink Spots, 50–52, 92, 104
Inman, Autrey, 62
Innervisions, 209
interlude, 26, 38–39, 140, 149, 172–73, 204–205, 207–209, 263, 265, 273, 276, 286–87, 302, 322
interpolation, 329, 331
interval, 9–10
  in scales, 12–13, 16–17
  in melody, 18
  in triads, 22–23
introduction (intro), 26
Iron Butterfly, 234
Isley Brothers, 325

J. Geils Band, 285
J&M Studio, 78

Jackson 5, 293
Jackson, Chuck, 96, 101, 214
Jackson, Mahalia, 214
Jackson, Michael, 225
Jackson, Wanda, 26, 62, 69–72
Jagger, Mick, 152–53, 155, 157, 160, 163, 166
James, Elmore, 74
James, Inez, 45
Jan and Dean, 169, 181
Jardine, Al, 169, 172, 179
jaw harp, 179
Jaynetts, 117, 128
jazz, 37, 39–40, 50, 86, 206, 222, 231, 235, 238, 257, 268, 277
Jefferson Airplane, 222, 231–34, 314
Jelly Beans, 117
Jenkins, Gordon, 40–41, 92, 183
Jerk (dance), 217
Jimi Hendrix Experience, 222, 238, 240, 281
John Wesley Harding, 245–46, 249, 263
John, Elton, 257, 266
The Johnny Cash Show, 263
Johnson, Marv, 198
Johnson, Robert, 74
Johnston, Bruce, 175, 179
Jones, Brian, 152, 154, 155, 157, 160
Jones, Joe, 306
Jones, John Paul, 282–84
Jones, Mick, 313, 316
Joplin, Janis, 231
Jordan, Louis, 40, 50
Jordanaires, 81

Kantner, Paul, 231, 233
Kaukonen, Jorma, 231, 233
Kaye, Carol, 175, 179
Kaye, Lenny, 305
Kerr, Anita, 110
key, 8, 19, 172, 175, 178, 223, 311
King Crimson, 267–72
King, Martin Luther, Jr., 184–85
King Tee, 330–31

King, Albert, 240
King, B. B., 240
King, Ben E., 94–96, 229
King, Carole, 115–19, 257, 261–62, 266
King, Freddie, 240
Kingsmen, 30, 306
Kingston Trio, 183
Kinks, 144, 152, 168, 305
The Kinks Are the Village Green Preservation Society, 144
Kirshner, Don, 116, 118
Kiss, 281, 291
Knight, Curtis, 240
Knight, Gladys and the Pips, 101, 199, 200, 207, 213, 229
koto, 154
Kramer, Joey, 287
Krieger, Robby, 234–36

La Belle, 293
Laboe, Art, 59
LaBostrie, Dorothy, 76, 78
Lady Soul, 219
Laine, Frankie, 36–39, 55, 107
Lake, Greg, 268, 270
Larrabee Sound Studios, 330
Latin musical styles, 87–88, 117, 231, 292
Latin rhythm, 95–96, 118, 120
Leadbelly, 183
Led Zeppelin IV, 282–83
Led Zeppelin, 32, 44, 267, 281–84
Lee, Beverly, 117, 119
Lee, Brenda, 62, 73
Lee, Peggy, 36, 39–43
Lee, Spike, 98, 325
Leiber, Jerry, 75, 80–81, 94–96, 117, 125
Lennon, John, 129, 131–37 passim, 139–40, 142, 144–46, 148–49, 152–54
Leslie speaker, 139, 177, 179
Lester, Richard, 131
Let It Be, 144, 151
Let It Bleed, 159, 161, 163

Let's Get It On, 206
Lewis, Al, 92
Lewis, Gary and the Playboys, 153
Lewis, Jerry Lee, 63, 70, 75, 89
Life (magazine), 249
Lightfoot, Gordon, 257
Little Eva (Eva Boyd), 116–17, 128
Little Richard (Richard Penniman), 21, 48, 70, 74–79, 87, 92, 130, 223, 240, 306
Little Sandy, 184
Liverpool, 129, 146
London Bach Choir, 33, 162–63
London, 130, 144, 152, 240–41, 269, 282
Los Angeles, 76, 92, 103, 115, 169, 174, 189, 199, 234, 263, 328
loudspeaker, 5, 31, 36, 76, 122
Louvin Brothers, 107, 245
Love Me Tonight, 40
Love Trilogy, 301
Love Unlimited Orchestra, 293
Love, 234, 244
Love, Darlene, 121
Love, Mike, 169–73, 175, 178–80
low-end (frequency range), 3, 5, 27–28, 31, 94, 125, 154, 156, 201, 204, 217, 220, 281, 289, 298, 326–28
Lubbock, Texas, 82–83
Lymon, Frankie and the Teenagers, 25, 49, 54–57
Lynch, David, 103, 105
lyrics, 30–31
Lytle, Marshall, 65

Malcolm X, 98
Mamas and the Papas, 182, 183, 197, 222
Mancuso, David, 293
mandolin, 161, 182
Manfred Mann, 151, 238
Mann, Barry, 116–17
Manuel, Richard, 248–51
Manzarek, Ray, 234, 236
Mar-Keys, 222

March on Washington for Jobs and
    Freedom, 184
Margouleff, Robert, 211
marimba, 286
Marley, Bob, 326, 328
Mars, Bruno, 225
Martha and the Vandellas, 117,
    199–200, 213
Martin, Bobby, 296
Martin, Dean, 47, 74
Martin, Ed, 60
Martin, Janis, 62, 73
Marvelettes, 117, 128, 130
Mason, Nick, 277–78
Master Recorders, 92
Mauldin, Joe B., 84
Max's Kansas City, 305
Mayall, John and the Bluesbreakers,
    238
MC, 320
MC5, 281, 305
McCartney, Paul, 129, 131–40 passim,
    142–45, 147–48, 150, 152–54,
    294
McCoys, 309
McDonald, Ian, 268, 270
McFadden, Gene, 296
McGuinn, Jim (Roger), 133, 189–91
McGuire, Barry, 183
McPhatter, Clyde, 70, 93, 101
measure (bar), 19
Melanie, 197, 257
melisma, 30, 43, 53, 60, 107, 110
Mellotron, 268, 269, 270, 271, 272,
    273, 276
Melody Maker, 79
melody, 18–19
Melson, Joe, 111
Melvin, Harold and the Blue Notes,
    294–97
Memphis Recording Service (Sun
    Studio), 63, 66, 68
Memphis, 63, 67, 215–16, 219
Mercer Arts Center, 305
Merchant, Jimmy, 56
Mercury Records, 104

Merseybeat, 118
Messina, Jim, 245
Metallica, 32, 281
metaphor, 80, 184, 186, 193, 257–58,
    269, 313
meter, 19–20
  compound, 99
  irregular, 278–79
  mixed, 273, 275–76, 277–78
  simple, 99
MFSB (Mother Father Sister Brother),
    293–94
microphone, 5, 28, 159
  bleed, 122, 238, 295
  placement, 137
  and reverb, 36–37
mid-range, 5, 27–28, 31, 80, 201
Milburn, Amos, 50
Miller, Glenn, 34, 92
Miracles, 14, 26, 130, 199, 203–205,
    207
Mitchell, Joni, 32, 184, 245, 258–60,
    263
Mitchell, Mitch, 241, 242
mix, 31–32
mode, 15–17
  Aeolian, 15
  Dorian, 17, 138–39, 207–208,
      210–11, 276, 279
  Ionian, 15
  Locrian, 17
  Lydian, 15–16
  Mixolydian 16, 131–33, 273–76
  Phrygian, 17, 232–33, 314–15, 316,
      317
  See also scale
modulation, 24, 39, 172, 173, 195
mono (monophonic audio), 29, 133,
    147–48, 155, 170
Monterey Pop Festival, 215, 222, 241
Moody Blues, 267, 280
Moog synthesizer, 193, 210, 301,
    329, 330, 331
Moon Dog House, 76
Mooney, Ralph, 71
Moonglows, 103, 206

Moore, Johnny, 93
Moore, Scotty, 66, 67, 68, 80, 81, 111
Moore, Warren, 205
Morrison, Jim, 234–36
Morrison, Van, 266
Morse, Ella Mae, 40
Mothers of Invention, 267, 280
motive, 111, 194, 195, 196, 235, 236, 272
Motown Records, 91, 115, 198–200, 203, 206, 207, 209, 294
Mr. Tambourine Man, 189
MTV, 319
Muddy Waters, 74, 152, 165
multitrack, 37, 223, 253, 326. *See also* overdub
Murmaids, 117
Murphy, Walter, 293
Murray the K, 121
Murvin, Junior, 313
Muscle Shoals Rhythm Section, 219–20
Muscle Shoals Sound Studio, 165–66
Music from Big Pink, 245, 250
Music of My Mind, 209
musical genre, 1–2
Musicland Studio, 302
Mussorgsky, Modest, *Pictures at an Exhibition*, 267

N.W.A., 329
Nanker Phelge, 153
Nashville, 64, 83, 107, 108, 245, 246, 248, 263
Nashville Skyline, 245, 246, 247
Nathan, Syd, 104
natural, 11
Negroni, Joe, 56
Nelson, Benjamin, 97
Nelson, George, 51–53
Nelson, Ricky, 62, 73
Nevins, Al, 116
New Haven, Connecticut, 58

New Jersey, 117, 193
New Orleans, 48, 76–78, 90–92
New Riders of the Purple Sage, 245, 256
new wave, 309–10
New York City, 35, 50, 51, 79, 115, 116, 183, 184, 198, 216, 241, 292, 305
  Brooklyn, 121, 293, 325
  Manhattan, 41, 54, 117, 319
  Queens, 125, 306
  South Bronx, 319
  Washington Heights, 121
New York Dolls, 305, 318
New York Rocker, 306
New York Times, 184, 258, 306, 309
Newman, Randy, 257
Newport Folk Festival, 185
Nice, 267
Nitzsche, Jack, 124, 153, 155
non-diatonic pitches, 24, 52, 98, 163, 201, 202, 223, 308. *See also* chromatic pitches
note values
  eighth note, 20, 95, 136, 220, 272
  half note, 20, 146, 210–11
  Note Values chart, 20
  quarter note, 20, 95, 146, 210–11, 212, 217, 218, 241, 270, 275, 293, 314
  sixteenth note, 20–21, 84–85, 209, 227, 271, 273, 275
  triplet, 20–21, 60, 77, 80, 82, 91, 93, 104–106, 174, 176, 178, 180, 204–205, 209, 251, 273, 275, 310, 312, 314–16
  whole note, 20
The Notorious Byrd Brothers, 245
novelty song, 35, 37, 48, 301
Nuggets, 305
Nyro, Laura, 257, 266

O'Jays, 292, 294
octave, 7–8, 11, 18, 37, 44, 207, 241, 295, 311

Octavia, 241, 243
The Official Adventures of Flash Gordon, 322, 324
Ogdens' Nut Gone Flake, 144
Oldham, Andrew Loog, 152–53, 155, 158
Oldham, Spooner, 221
Oldies but Goodies, 59
Olympic Studios, 157, 160, 163, 242
oral tradition, 182
Orbison, Roy, 83, 109–13
orchestra, 38, 41, 98, 130, 183, 257, 277, 293, 296
organ, 28, 162, 177, 179, 190, 193, 194, 201, 232, 234, 236, 249, 250, 268, 273
Orioles, 50–53, 59, 103
Orlons, 115
Outlaws, 288
outro, 26, 132, 133
overdub, 37, 132, 141, 147, 192
overtone, 6
Owens, Buck, 71
Owens, Shirley, 117–19
Ozark Jubilee, 69

P-Funk, 329
pad, 28, 31, 32, 250
Page, Jimmy, 44, 282–84
Page, Patti, 36, 47, 115
Paragons, 309
Parallel Lines, 310
Paris Sisters, 115
Parker, Graham, 288
Parliament, 329, 330, 331
Parlophone Records, 130
Parris, Fred, 58, 60
Parsons, Gram, 245, 256
passing tone, 132, 134, 223, 225, 315, 316
Patterson, Lover, 96
Patti Smith Group, 305, 318
Paul, Les, 37, 40, 43–46
Payne, Leon, 66
Pendergrass, Teddy, 296

Penguins, 49, 59, 61, 103
pentatonic scale, 14–15, 210–11, 311, 315
Pepper, Buddy, 45
Peppermint Lounge, 121
percussion, 83, 123, 126, 162, 178, 193, 247
  Latin, 40–41
Perkins, Carl, 62, 63, 73, 75, 83, 130
Perry, Joe, 287
Pet Sounds, 157, 173, 175, 177
Peter and Gordon, 107, 151
Peter, Paul and Mary, 183, 184
Petty, Norman, 83–84, 109
Petty, Tom and the Heartbreakers, 256, 319
Petty, Vi, 83
Philadelphia International Records, 294
Philadelphia, 58, 64, 294, 298
Philles Records, 115, 121
Phillips, Dewey, 67
Phillips, Sam, 63, 66, 68, 81, 109
phrase, 18–19, 20, 21, 27, 29
piano, 27, 28, 29, 32, 59, 77, 78, 80, 87, 91, 104, 125, 132, 133, 145, 157, 162, 174, 179, 219, 250, 261, 272, 295, 298
  electric, 207
Pickett, Wilson, 32, 214–18, 223, 325, 327
pickup, 77, 80, 99, 104, 146–47, 185, 283
Pink Floyd, 244, 267, 277–80
pitch, 5–9, 11–12, 14–16, 18–19, 21–22, 37
Plant, Robert, 29, 282–84
Platters, 92, 95, 102–106
Poco, 245, 256
Pointer Sisters, 292
Police, 319
Pomus, Doc, 117
Porter, Cole, 35, 206
postpunk, 309, 313, 319–20
Powell, Maxine, 198

Power Station Studios, 300, 308, 311
power trio, 238
pre-chorus, 26, 28, 31, 32, 186, 190, 207, 250, 295, 310
Presley, Elvis, 25, 30, 62–63, 66–71, 74–76, 79–83, 86, 92, 102–103, 113, 131, 184
Preston, Jimmy, 64
Pretenders, 319
Price, Lloyd, 78
Prince, 225, 319
Procol Harum, 249, 267, 313
protest song, 183–84, 191
psychedelic rock, 230–44, 267–68
The Psychedelic Sounds of the 13th Floor Elevators, 230
psychedelic soul, 206
Public Enemy, 324–28, 330
punk rock, 305–306, 309, 313
Punk, 306
Pythian Temple, 41

Quadrafonic Sound Studios, 264
Queen, 267, 280, 322–23
Quicksilver Messenger Service, 231

raga, 235
Ramone, Dee Dee, 306, 308
Ramone, Joey, 305–306, 308
Ramone, Johnny, 306, 308
Ramone, Tommy, 306–308
Ramones, 305–309
Randy and the Rainbows, 309
rapper, 320, 325, 328, 329
Ravens, 103
RBX (Eric Collins), 329–30
RCA Studio (Hollywood), 99
RCA Studio (Nashville), 111
RCA Studio A (New York), 81
RCA Victor Records, 49, 79
Record Plant, 287
records
 components, 27–32
 crossover, 33, 48–50
 hi-fi, 58–59, 79

lo-fi, 49, 58–59, 74–75, 104, 125, 154, 159, 305, 313
novelty, 35–36, 301
postwar conception, 1
postwar sales, 34, 49
record producer
 Asher, Peter, 262
 Bartholomew, Dave, 78, 91–92
 Blackwell, Robert "Bumps," 76, 78
 Bleyer, Archie, 108
 Bongiovi, Tony, 308
 Chandler, Chas, 240, 242
 Chapman, Mike, 310
 Creatore, Luigi, 99
 de May, Sid, 53
 Dixon, Luther, 118–19
 Douglas, Jack, 286–87
 Edwards, Bernard, 298, 300, 322
 Foster, Fred, 112
 Gamble, Kenneth, 294, 296
 Gottehrer, Richard, 309–10
 Huff, Leon, 294, 296
 Jarrard, Rick, 233
 Johnston, Bob, 246, 247, 248
 Kugell, Marty, 58, 60
 Lange, Robert John "Mutt," 288, 290
 Martin, George, 130–31, 133–34, 136, 139, 144, 148
 Mazer, Elliot, 264
 Miller, Dave, 65
 Miller, Jimmy, 158, 160, 163, 166
 Miller, Mitch, 36, 37, 38, 109
 Moroder, Giorgio, 301, 302, 303, 310, 311
 Morton, George "Shadow," 125, 126
 Nelson, Ken, 70, 71
 Pappalardi, Felix, 239
 Peretti, Hugo, 99
 Ram, Buck, 103, 105
 Robinson Jr., Joey, 323
 Rodgers, Nile, 298, 300
 Rothchild, Paul, 236
 Sholes, Steve, 81
 Simon, John, 251

Sokira, Tom, 58, 60
Stevens, Guy, 313, 316
Stevenson, Mickey, 199
Stewart, Jim, 216, 218, 223
Usher, Gary, 191
Wexler, Jerry, 40, 94, 216–22
   passim
Whitfiled, Norman, 199, 206, 208
Wilson, Tom, 187, 192
recorder, 157, 270
recording engineer
   Arthur, Brooks, 126
   Botnick, Bruce, 236
   Bragg, Charlie, 248
   Britz, Chuck, 172, 176, 179
   Clearmountain, Bob, 300
   Dearnley, Mark, 290
   Dowd, Tom, 94, 96, 221, 238–39
   Emerick, Geoff, 137, 139, 147–48, 151
   Faltermeyer, Harold, 311
   Gallagher, Jim, 295
   Gary, Russ, 254
   Halee, Roy, 187, 195
   Hassinger, Dave, 99, 156, 233
   Horn, Lawrence, 198
   Hui, Rod, 327
   Johns, Andy, 284
   Johns, Glyn, 158, 160, 163
   Johnson, Jimmy, 166
   Koppers, Juergen, 303
   Kramer, Eddie, 242, 288
   Lazerus, Bill, 262
   Levine, Larry, 124
   Lewy, Henry, 259
   Malo, Ron, 165
   Matassa, Cosimo, 78
   Messina, Jay, 287
   Offord, Eddie, 274
   Parsons, Alan, 278
   Payne, John, 330
   Platt, Tony, 290
   Porter, Bill, 108, 112
   Price, Bill, 316
   Robyn, Bunny, 92
   Scott, Ken, 142
   Smith, Norman, 133, 136–37
   Stasium, Ed, 307–308
   Tarsia, Joe, 294–96
   Thomas, Chris, 278
   Thompson, Robin, 270
   Townsend, Ken, 137
   Ulrich, Ernie, 81
   Wilburn, Neil, 248
   Yakus, Shelley, 251
recording process, 63, 81, 83, 141, 144, 329
recording studio, 1, 36–37, 78
recording/mixing console, 37, 63, 68, 122, 147, 300, 310
Red Bird Records, 125
Red Hot and Blue, 67
Redding Otis, 30, 32, 222–25
Redding, Noel, 241–42
Reed, Herbert, 103, 105
Reed, Johnny, 53
Reeves, Martha, 199–200
refrain, 25, 38, 45, 59, 77, 83, 97–98, 99, 107, 108, 142, 186, 190–91, 193–94, 201, 210, 211, 220, 238, 258, 261, 264, 269
reggae, 299, 309–10, 313
rest, 20
reverb (reverberation, ambience), 3, 27, 29, 36–37, 41, 59, 83, 84, 94, 95, 98, 122–23, 170, 177, 185, 190, 232, 241, 289, 314
reverse (backward) tape effect, 139, 272, 274, 286, 317
Revolver, 130, 137, 139, 151, 157
rhythm and blues (R&B), 48–50, 214
Richards, Keith, 152–55, 157–60, 163, 165–68, 313
riff
   bass, 171, 238–39, 273, 278, 286, 295, 314, 315
   guitar, 56, 86–87, 159–60, 171, 189, 193, 238–39, 253–54, 263–64, 281, 282–83, 286, 289, 310

riff *(continued)*
   horn, 55, 217, 210–11, 226, 296
   keyboard, 207, 208, 210–11, 250, 329
   sequencer, 302
   vocal, 70, 178
Rimsky-Korsakov, Nikolai, *Scheherazade*, 271
Rip Chords, 169, 181
Ripp, Artie, 126
Robertson, Robbie, 248, 250–51
Robinson, Alan, 176
Robinson, Smokey (William), 56, 199, 203–206
Robinson, Sylvia, 321, 323
rockaballad, 103
rockabilly, 62–73, 76, 82–83, 109, 248, 252–53, 313, 319
Rocket to Russia, 308
Rockwell, John, 306, 309
Rodgers, Richard, 40–41
Rogers Robinson, Claudette, 203, 205
Rogers, Bobby, 203, 205
Rolling Stone, 231, 249
Rolling Stones, 14, 33, 82, 137, 152–68, 282, 294
Rolontz, Bob, 219
Ronettes, 121–24, 307
Ronny and the Daytonas, 181
Ronstadt, Linda, 245, 256, 263
Rose, Vincent, 92
Ross, Diana, 29, 200, 202, 293
round, 174
Roundhouse Studios, 290
Royal, Greg, 331
Rubber Soul, 130, 134–35, 147, 151, 173
Ruben and Jewel, 329, 330
Ruby and the Romantics, 115
Rudd, Phil, 290
Ruffin, David, 199, 213
Run-DMC, 1, 285, 329, 322
Rupe, Art, 76
Rush, Tom, 258
Russell, Larry, 45

Sadler, Eric, 327
Saint Bernadette Catholic Church, 58, 60
Sainte-Marie, Buffy, 258
Sam and Dave, 223, 229
Sam the Sham and the Pharaohs, 306
sampler, 28, 321
sampling, 320–21, 325–31 passim
San Francisco, 223, 231, 240, 253
Santiago, Herman, 56
Saturday Night Fever, 293, 294
saxophone, 55, 56, 91, 102, 104, 123, 201, 204, 210, 217, 277–78
scale, 7–17. *See also* mode
Scepter Records, 118
Scott, Bon, 289–90
scratching, 320, 322, 323, 324, 328, 330. *See also* turntablism
Second Macedonia Baptist Church, 298
Sedaka, Neil, 116
Seekers, 183
sequencer, 301–303, 310, 312
Sex Pistols, 313, 318
Sgt. Pepper's Lonely Hearts Club Band, 130, 140, 151, 158, 177, 215, 223
Shangri-Las, 115, 125–27
sharp, 11
Sharp, Alex, 53
sheet music, 7, 76, 182
Sheffield, Alabama, 165–66
Shirelles, 25–26, 115, 117–20, 130
Shirley and Lee, 78
Shocklee, Hank, 325, 327
Shocklee, Keith, 325
shuffle, 77–79, 90, 162
Shuman, Mort, 117
Sigma Sound, 294
Simmons, Joe, 285
Simon and Garfunkel, 31, 107, 192–96, 222
Simon, Carly, 257, 266
Simon, Paul, 29, 184, 194–95, 258
Simonon, Paul, 313, 316
Sinatra, Frank, 35, 74, 199, 206

Sinfield, Peter, 268–70
Sing Out!, 185
singer-songwriter, 32, 83, 257, 260, 263–64
Singers . . . Talkers . . . Players . . . Swingers . . . & Doers, 322
Sister Sledge, 21, 298–300, 310
sitar, 33, 130, 136, 139, 154
slapback echo, 67–71 passim, 253
Sledge, Debbie, 298, 300
Sledge, Joni, 298, 300
Sledge, Kathy, 298, 300
Sledge, Kim, 298, 300
sleigh bells, 174, 177
Slick, Grace, 231–33
Sly and the Family Stone, 206, 326, 328
Small Faces, 144
Smith, Beasley, 38
Smith, Huey, 77
Snoop Dogg (Calvin Broadus Jr.), 330–31
solid-state electronics, 147
Song to a Seagull, 258
song form, 24
    AABA, 25, 26, 41, 45, 54, 58, 107, 118, 132
    strophic, 24, 97
    twelve-bar blues, 25–26, 64–65, 70, 74–75, 77, 80, 83, 86, 226, 238, 277–78
    verse–chorus, 24, 26, 64, 70, 75, 77, 110, 121, 166, 177, 186, 190, 238–39, 269, 310–11, 315
Songs in the Key of Life, 209
Sonny and Cher, 153, 183
Soul Children, 326
soul music, 30, 32, 199, 214–29
Soul Stirrers, 97, 214, 215
Soul Train, 294
The Soulful Moods of Marvin Gaye, 206
sound, 5–6
sound effects, 27, 125, 126, 127, 139, 224, 225, 277, 278, 279
Sound of Philadelphia, 294
South, Joe, 221
Southern Tones, 214
Specialty Records, 76
Spector, Phil, 115, 121–24, 144, 148, 153, 170, 307
Spector, Ronnie (Veronica Bennett), 56, 121
Spencer Davis Group, 158, 168
Spinners, 294
Spoonie Gee Meets the Sequence, 322–23
Squire, Chris, 272, 274
staff, 9
Standord Records, 58
Starr, Ringo (Richard Starkey), 129, 133, 136, 142, 144, 148
Stax Records (Stax sound), 199, 215–16, 219–20, 223, 225
Stax Studio, 217, 224
steel guitar, 64, 65, 66, 70, 71, 245, 246, 247, 248, 264, 265
Stein, Chris, 309–11
stereo, 29, 31, 98, 133, 145, 147, 162, 165–66, 193, 210, 241, 253, 286, 289, 302
The Steve Allen Show, 80
Stevens, Cat, 257, 266
Stewart, Rod, 256, 294
Sticky Fingers, 159, 165–66
Stock, Larry, 92
Stoller, Mike, 80–81, 94–96, 117
Stone Poneys, 245
Stone, Sly, 206
Stooges, 305
stop-time, 21, 53, 55, 57, 60, 71, 77–79, 106, 147, 150, 287
Stray Cats, 319
string quartet, 33, 130, 137
strings, 38, 90, 94–95, 98, 110, 111, 122, 123, 137, 170, 174, 204, 293, 294, 295, 298, 300. *See also* cello; viola; violin
Strong, Barrett, 130, 206, 208, 213
Strummer, Joe, 313, 316

Stubblefield, Clyde, 227
Stubbs, Levi, 199
Studio 54, 293, 319
Studio Band, 78
studio musician
  accordion
    Fortina, Carl, 176
  bass
    Badie, Chuck, 99
    Baker, Ronnie, 296
    Bond, Jimmy, 179
    Cogbill, Tommy, 221
    Dixon, Willie, 87
    Drummond, Tim, 264
    Dunn, Donald "Duck," 217, 224, 252
    Fields, Frank, 78
    Guyton, Lawrence, 92
    Hall, Al, 56
    Huskey, Roy, 108
    Jamerson, James, 202
    Macho Jr., Joe, 187
    McCoy, Charlie, 247
    Moore, Bob, 110, 111
    Murray, Doug, 60
    Odum, Bernard, 227
    Osborn, Joe, 195
    Pohlman, Ray, 175, 179
    Ritz, Lyle, 175, 179
    Wolfe, Colin, 330
  cello
    Ehrlich, Jesse, 176, 179
    Jones, Norman, 139
    Sargeant, Emmet, 99
    Simpson, Derek, 139
  clarinet
    Marocco, Frank, 176
  drums/percussion
    Below, Fred, 87
    Benjamin, Benny, 202
    Blaine, Hal, 175, 179, 195
    Buttrey, Kenny, 247, 264
    Coleman, Cornelius, 92
    Dijon, Rocky, 163
    Fontana, D. J., 81
    Gregg, Bobby, 187
    Gussak, Billy, 64, 65
    Harman, Buddy, 108, 111
    Hawkins, Roger, 221
    Jackson Jr., Al, 217, 224
    Langhorne, Bruce, 187
    Mapp, Bobby, 60
    Palmer, Earl, 77, 78, 99
    Radocchia, Emil, 99
    Thompson, Tony, 300
    Washington, Larry, 296
    Young, Earl, 294, 296
  flute
    Green, Bill, 176
  French horn
    Hinshaw, William, 99
  guitar
    Adams, Justin, 78
    Atkins, Chet, 108
    Bartold, Norman, 99
    Blake, Norman, 247
    Bloomfield, Mike, 187
    Bradley, Harold Ray, 111
    Campbell, Glen, 179
    Chambers, Roland, 296
    Cropper, Steve, 215–17, 223–24
    Daniels, Charlie, 247
    Edenton, Ray, 108
    Eli, Bobby, 296
    Garland, Hank, 108
    Harris, Norman, 296
    Irwin, Teddy, 264
    Johnson, Jimmy, 221
    Kellum, Alphonso "Country," 227
    Maphis, Joe, 71
    Messina, Joe, 202
    Nelson, Walter, 92
    Nolen, Jimmy, 227
    Ryerson, Art, 65
    Shirley, Jimmy, 56
    White, Clifton, 99
  harmonica
    Morgan, Tommy, 178
  keyboards
    Battiste, Harold, 99

Cramer, Floyd, 108, 111
de Lory, Al, 179
Dickinson, Jim, 166
Glover, Curlee, 60
Grande, Johnny, 65
Griffin, Paul, 187
Griffith, Johnny, 202
Knechtel, Larry, 176, 179, 195
Kooper, Al, 163, 187
Leake, Lafayette, 87
Pakula, Leonard, 296
Randi, Don, 175, 179
Sabino, Robert, 300
Schwartz, Andy, 300
Stoker, Gordon, 81
Wilson, Bob, 247
saxophone
  Allen, Lee, 78
  Axton, Charles "Packy," 217
  Duconge, Wendell, 92
  Ellis, Alfred "Pee Wee," 227
  Hagans, Buddy, 92
  Hartman, Leonard, 176
  Horn, Jim, 176
  Laurence, Trevor, 211
  Love, Andrew, 217
  Mazzetta, Vinny, 60
  Migliori, Jay, 176
  Newman, Floyd, 217
  Parker, Maceo, 227
  Parry, Dick, 277, 278
  Pinckney, St. Clair, 227
  Reed, Sam, 296
  Silvers, Eddie, 92
  Terry, Mike, 202
  Tyler, Alvin "Red," 78
  Wright, Jimmy, 54, 56
steel guitar
  Drake, Pete, 247
  Keith, Ben, 264
  Williamson, Billy, 65
theremin
  Tanner, Paul, 179
trombone
  Blackburn, Louis, 99
  Ewing, John, 99
  Rasbury, Levi, 227
trumpet
  Dupars, Joe, 227
  Jackson, Wayne, 216, 217, 224
  Madaio, Steve, 211
  Reed, Waymon, 227
vibraphone
  Gitten, James, 202
  McCoy, Charlie, 111
viola
  Hyams, Harry, 99, 176
  Shingles, Stephen, 139
  Underwood, John, 139
violin
  Baker, Israel, 99
  Belnick, Arnold, 99
  Carroll, Marianne, 300
  Gilbert, Tony, 139
  Hong, Cheryl, 300
  Kurasch, William, 99
  Lipschultz, Irving, 99
  Malarsky, Leonard, 99, 176
  Milne, Karen, 300
  Neiman, Alexander, 99
  Pepper, Jack, 99
  Renaldo, Don, 296
  Sanders, Jelly, 71
  Sax, Sidney, 139
  Schaeffer, Ralph, 99, 176
  Sharp, Sidney, 99, 176
  Sharpe, John, 139
  Terwilliger, Darrel, 99, 176
  Zelig, Tibor, 99
voice
  Baillie, Kathie, 308
  Bonagura, Michael, 308
  Cher, 124
  Franklin, Carolyn, 221
  Franklin, Erma, 221
  LaBeouf, Alan, 308
  Troy, Doris, 163
  Workman, Nanette, 163
style mixture, 36, 38, 48, 62–64, 67, 86, 95, 109, 161, 240, 249, 293

style, 32–33
Stylistics, 294
Sugar Hill Records, 321–22
Sugarhill Gang, 319, 324, 332
Sullivan, Ed, 129
Sullivan, Niki, 84
Summer of Love, 215
Summer, Donna, 293, 301–302, 310
Sun Records, 63, 67–68, 79, 92, 109
Sundragon Studios, 308
Sunset Sound, 179, 236, 262
Sunset Strip, 234
Supremes, 153, 199–203
surf music, 118, 169, 172–73, 305, 307–308, 319
Surfaris, 169, 181
Surfer Girl, 170
Surrealistic Pillow, 231, 233
Swan Records, 129
Swan Silvertones, 215
Sweet Baby James, 260, 262
Sweet Inspirations, 221
Sweetheart of the Rodeo, 245
swing era, 34, 35, 36
swing, 49, 55–56, 65, 77, 210, 221, 278, 310, 314
Sylvester, 293, 304
syncopation, 19, 63, 102, 118, 272, 283, 289, 296
synthesizer, 27–29, 31, 193, 210, 211, 245, 273, 274, 276, 299, 300, 301, 309–12 passim, 329, 330

tabla, 136, 139
tag, 26, 46, 72, 86, 99, 100
Talking Book, 209, 211
Talley, Nedra, 121, 124
tambourine, 143, 149, 156, 177, 180, 190, 203, 205, 207, 208
Tamla Records, 205, 208, 211
tape echo. *See* slapback echo
tape head (erase, record, playback), 37
tape loop, 139, 320
tape recorder, 37, 44, 68, 122

tape speed, 37, 43, 44, 132, 141
tape splice, 92, 145, 235, 269
Tarplin, Marvin, 205
Taylor, James, 24, 30, 32, 260–62, 263, 264
Taylor, Mick, 166
Taylor, Zola, 103, 105
Teddy Bears, 103, 114
Television, 305, 318
tempo, 19
Temptations, 153, 199, 203, 206, 213, 292
Terrell, Tammi, 206
Them, 168
theremin, 179–80
Thomas, Carla, 223, 229
Thomas, Charlie, 96
Thornton, Willie Mae "Big Mama," 80, 117
Tiara Records, 117
tie, 95
Til, Sonny, 50, 53
timbre, 6, 27–28, 32, 37, 44, 132, 179
Time (magazine), 102, 130, 218, 257, 260, 301
timpani, 43, 90, 94, 98, 100
Tin Pan Alley, 35, 51, 54, 75, 104, 107, 116, 118, 206, 257
tonic, 8, 19
Town Hall, 184
Townsend, Pete, 44
Toys in the Attic, 285, 287
track, 3
Traffic, 159, 197, 282
transpose, 12, 15
Trashmen, 30, 181, 306
Treadwell, George, 93, 96
tremolo (electronic variation in amplitude), 108, 279
tremolo (rapid repeated notes), 45–46, 100, 112, 208
triad, 22–23
A Tribute to the Great Nat "King" Cole, 206

tritone. *See* augmented fourth
trumpet, 41–43, 210
tube electronics, 147
Tune Weavers, 114
turnaround, 26, 52, 53, 60, 77, 84, 85, 216, 218, 242, 243, 270
Turner, Tina, 115, 214, 229
turntablism, 320–25
  merry-go-round, 320
Turtles, 183
Two-Lane Blacktop, 260
Tyler, Steven, 286–87

U2, 302, 319
underscore, 98, 193
United Artists, 198
urban folk music, 182–84, 257

Valentines, 54
vamp, 26, 159, 160, 190, 210, 211, 216, 217, 241, 278, 295, 307, 311
Van Halen, 281, 291
Vanda, Harry, 288
Vee-Jay Records, 129
Velvet Underground, 305
Venet, Nick, 170
vibraphone, 111, 112, 113, 201
vibrato, 45, 46, 142
Village People, 293, 304
Village Voice, 130
Vincent, Gene and His Blue Caps, 62, 70, 73
viola, 137
violin, 41, 42, 120, 140, 204, 205, 207, 208, 209
Violinaires, 214, 215
voice, 29–30, 41, 45, 51, 55, 59, 67, 75, 83, 90, 91, 104, 106, 109, 111, 123, 132, 138, 142, 155, 163, 169, 171, 174, 190, 200, 202, 203, 207, 219, 241, 261, 264, 283, 325, 330
Volt Records, 215
Vox Studios, 227

Wagner, Bill, 170
Wagoner, Porter, 70
Wakeman, Rick, 272, 274
Walden, Phil, 223
walking bass, 65, 68
wall of sound, 122, 170, 174, 307–308
Wally Heider Recording, 254
waltz, 40, 41, 44, 67, 70, 71, 72, 178
Waring, Fred, 43
Washington, Dinah, 50
Waters, Roger, 277–78
Watts, Charlie, 152, 154–55, 157, 160, 166
We Are Family, 298, 300
Weavers, 40, 47, 183
Weber, Joan, 74
Wedel, Robbie, 302
Wednesday Morning, 3 A.M., 192
Weil, Cynthia, 115–17
Weill, Kurt, 235
Weiss, Betty, 125–26
Weiss, Mary, 125–26
Wells, David, 99
Wells, Mary, 115, 203, 206, 213
Wenner, Jann, 231
Wessex Studio, 269
Western Recorders, 172, 175, 179
Westlake Studios, 311
Weston, Kim, 206
What's Going On, 206
Whisky a Go Go, 234–35
White, Barry, 293
White, Ronnie, 203, 205
Whitehead, John, 296
Whitford, Brad, 287
Who, 44, 152, 222
Wildflowers, 258
Williams, Cliff, 290
Williams, Hank, 64
Williams, Tony, 103–105
Wills, Bob, 62
Willy and the Poor Boys, 254
Wilson, Bernard, 296

Wilson, Brian, 56, 169–70, 172–73, 175–76, 179
Wilson, Carl, 172, 174, 175, 176, 177, 179
Wilson, Dennis, 169, 172, 179
Wilson, Jackie, 101, 203
Wilson, Mary, 200, 202
Wilson, Murry, 169
Withers, Bill, 329, 331
Womack, Bobby, 99
Wonder, Stevie, 14, 199, 209–12, 226, 293
Woodstock, New York, 248
woodwinds, 38–39, 174, 178–79, 268, 294
Worrell, Bernie, 330
Wrecking Crew, 122, 124
Wright, Richard, 277–78
Wyman, Bill, 152, 154–55, 157, 160, 166

Yardbirds, 152, 168, 238, 282, 305
Yellow Submarine, 147, 151
Yes, 267–68, 272–76
Young, Angus, 288–90
Young, Faron, 69
Young, George, 288
Young, Malcom, 288, 289–90
Young, Neil, 21, 32, 263–65
Young, Paul, 27, 30
Younger Than Yesterday, 190–91

SONG INDEX

"Abraham, Martin and John," 183
"The Adventures of Grandmaster Flash on the Wheels of Steel," 320–324
"Ain't That a Shame," 48, 74, 91
"Ain't Too Proud to Beg," 206
"All I Have to Do Is Dream," 14, 21, 103, 106–109
"Am I Asking Too Much?" 50
"America," 192–96
"Another One Bites the Dust," 322–323
"Apache," 322–323
"Ars Longa Vita Brevis," 267
"As Tears Go By," 137, 154
"At the Hop," 75

"Baby Love," 200
"Back Door Man," 235
"Bad Luck," 294–297
"Bad Moon Rising," 252
"Battle of Evermore," 282
"Be My Baby," 121–24
"Be True to Your School," 170
"Be-Bop-A-Lula," 70, 73
"Bernadette," 200
"Bird Dog," 107
"Birmingham Bounce," 62
"Birthday Party," 321–322, 324
"Black Dog," 282–285
"Black Steel in the Hour of Chaos," 325
"Blitzkrieg Bop," 306
"Blowin' in the Wind," 32, 97, 183–184
"Blue Monday," 48
"Blue Moon of Kentucky," 66–69
"Blue Moon," 92, 239–240

"Blue Suede Shoes," 73
"Blueberry Hill," 20, 48, 91–93
"Born on the Bayou," 252
"Both Sides Now," 258–260
"Break on Through," 235
"Bring It on Home to Me," 97
"Brown Sugar," 165
"Burn Hollywood Burn," 325
"By the Light of the Silvery Moon," 92
"Bye Bye Love," 107

"California Dreaming," 183, 197
"California Sun," 306
"Call Me," 309–12
"Cans and Brahms," 267
"Carol," 87
"Catch a Wave," 170
"The Cattle Call," 47, 62
"A Change Is Gonna Come," 97–99, 108
"Chapel of Love," 121
"Chest Fever," 249–252
"Chicken Shack Boogie," 50
"Claudette," 109
"Come On-A My House," 35
"Come See about Me," 200
"Come Softly to Me," 103, 113
"Come to Me," 198
"Count Every Star," 103
"Country Honk," 165
"The Court of the Crimson King," 268–272
"Crazy Man, Crazy," 63–66
"The Cry of the Wild Goose," 37
"Cryin' thru the Night," 70
"Crying," 109–13
"Crystal Ship," 235

"Cupid," 97

"Da Doo Ron Ron," 121
"The Day Isn't Long Enough," 170
"Deep Purple," 95
"Denis," 309
"Denise," 309
"Do You Wanna Dance," 306
"Don't Be Cruel," 80
"Don't Believe the Hype," 325
"Don't Worry Baby," 171
"Don't," 103
"Downtown," 151, 153

"Earth Angel," 49, 59, 61, 103
"Eight Miles High," 190, 230, 244
"8th Wonder," 322, 324
"Eleanor Rigby," 14, 133, 136–140
"The End," 234–237
"Epitaph," 268
"Eve of Destruction," 183
"Everyday," 83
"Everytime You Go Away," 27–31

"Fever," 40
"A Fifth of Beethoven," 293
"Fight the Power," 324–328
"Fingertips," 209
"Fire and Rain," 24, 260–262
"For No One," 139
"For What It's Worth," 183
"Fortunate Son," 252–255
"409," 170
"Four Sticks," 282
"Freedom," 322, 323, 324
"Friday on My Mind," 288
"Fujiyama Mama," 70
"Fun, Fun, Fun," 170
"Funky Drummer," 322, 326–327, 329
"Funnel of Love," 70

"G.T.O." 169, 181
"Gangsta's Paradise," 329
"Garageland," 313

"Gee," 49, 54, 61
"Get Off of My Cloud," 154
"Girl from the North Country," 246
"The Girls on the Beach," 171
"Give Him a Great Big Kiss," 125
"God Only Knows," 26, 173–177, 179
"God Save the Queen," 313
"Going to a Go-Go," 203
"Going to California," 282
"Good Rockin' Tonight," 62
"Good Times" (Chic), 298, 319, 322–324
"Good Times" (Sam Cooke), 97
"Good Vibrations," 177–180, 230
"Goodnight Irene," 35, 183
"Got to Get You into My Life," 139
"Great Balls of Fire," 75
"The Great Pretender," 104
"Green River," 252
"The Gypsy," 50

"Half as Good a Girl," 70
"Hang on Sloopy," 309
"Harbor Lights," 92
"A Hard Day's Night," 25, 130–134
"Hard Headed Woman," 70
"A Hazy Shade of Winter," 193
"He's the Greatest Dancer," 21, 298–301
"Heart of Glass," 309
"Heart of Gold," 263–265
"Heaven Must Be Missing an Angel," 293
"Help Me, Rhonda," 174
"Here Comes My Girl," 319
"Here Comes the Sun," 140
"Hey Little Cobra," 169, 181
"Hey, Schoolgirl," 192
"Highway to Hell," 288–290
"Honey Love," 93
"Honky Tonk Women," 165
"Hound Dog," 25–26, 74–75, 79–82, 102
"How Much Is That Doggie in the Window?" 35

"I Can't Get Next to You," 206, 213
"(I Can't Get No) Satisfaction," 153–154
"I Can't Help Myself (Sugar Pie, Honey Bunch)," 200, 213
"I Cover the Waterfront," 75
"I Don't Know What the World Is Coming To," 326
"I Don't Want to Cry," 96
"I Feel Love," 301–303, 310
"I Found a Love," 215
"I Get Around," 14, 171–173
"I Got Rhythm," 35
"I Got You Babe," 183
"I Gotta Know," 26, 69–72
"I Heard It through the Grapevine," 14, 26, 206–209, 213
"(I Know) I'm Losing You," 206
"I Know You Got Soul," 326–328
"I Love You Because," 66
"I Met Him on a Sunday," 117
"I Never Loved a Man (the Way I Love You)," 219
"I Second That Emotion," 203
"I Shot the Sheriff," 326, 328
"I Wanna Be Sedated," 306
"I Want to Be Your Man," 152
"I Want to Hold Your Hand," 173, 183
"I Was Made to Love Her," 209
"I Will Survive," 293, 304
"I'm Black and I'm Proud," 326
"I'm Only Sleeping," 139
"I'm So Bored with the U.S.A.," 313
"I've Been Loving You Too Long," 223
"I've Got a Woman," 214
"Icy Heart," 64
"In Dreams," 110
"In My Room," 170
"In the Midnight Hour," 215–218
"In the Still of the Nite," 25, 58–61
"Is That All There Is?" 40
"Isn't She Lovely," 211
"It Ain't Me Babe," 183

"It Must Be Jesus," 214
"It's All Over Now," 165
"It's too Soon to Know," 50–53, 103

"Jailhouse Rock," 75
"Jigsaw Puzzle," 161
"Johnny B. Goode," 87
"Jumpin' Jack Flash," 155, 158–161, 177

"Killing Me Softly," 329
"Kissing My Love," 329, 331
"Knockin' Around the Zoo," 260

"Lady Jane," 154
"Land of 1000 Dances," 325, 327
"Lay Lady Lay," 246–248
"Le Freak," 298, 304
"Leader of the Pack," 125
"Learnin' the Blues," 74
"Let It Bleed," 165
"Let Me Go Lover," 74
"Let Me Ride," 328–331
"Let's Have a Party," 70
"Let's Spend the Night Together," 157
"Light My Fire," 235
"Like a Rolling Stone," 184–188, 192
"A Little Bird Told Me," 35
"Little Deuce Coupe," 170
"Little Honda," 171, 181, 307
"Living for the City," 211
"Locomotion," 116
"Lodi," 252
"London Calling," 26, 313–317
"The Lonesome Death of Hattie Carroll," 184
"Long Black Veil," 249
"Long Tall Sally," 70, 130
"Lost Dreams," 253
"Louie Louie," 30, 306
"Love Child," 200
"Love Don't You Go through No Changes on Me," 298
"Love Hangover," 293, 304
"The Love I Lost," 294

"Love Is Strange," 89, 321
"Love Me Tender," 102, 113
"Love Train," 292
"Love You To," 139
"Love's in Need of Love Today," 211
"Lover," 36, 39–43
"Lovin' Country Style," 70

"Mambo Italiano," 35, 47
"Manic Depression," 240
"May This Be Love," 240
"Maybe," 54, 115, 128
"Maybellene," 74
"Mean Mr. Mustard," 143–150
"Mean, Mean Man," 70
"Memories Are Made of This," 47, 74
"The Message," 321, 324, 332
"Michael from Mountains," 258
"Midnight Rambler," 161
"Misirlou," 169, 181
"Money Honey," 70, 93
"Money," 277–280
"Monster Jam," 322–323
"Mothership Connection," 329, 331
"Mr. Echo," 36, 47
"Mr. Lee," 115
"Mr. Spaceman," 190
"Mr. Tambourine Man," 189, 192
"Mrs. Robinson," 193
"Mule Train," 37
"My Back Pages," 26, 189–192
"My Boyfriend's Back," 128, 309
"My Cherie Amour," 209, 211
"My Girl," 206
"My Guy," 203, 213
"My Prayer," 92

"Never Can Say Goodbye," 293
"New San Antonio Rose," 62
"Night and Day," 35
"Night Fever," 293
"1999," 319
"19th Nervous Breakdown," 154
"No Expectations," 165
"Norwegian Wood," 33, 154
"Not Fade Away," 83

"Nowhere Man," 21, 130, 133–137
"Nowhere to Run," 200

"Octopus's Garden," 144
"One Step at a Time," 62, 73
"One Way or Another," 309
"Only a Pawn in Their Game," 185
"Only the Lonely," 109
"Only You," 102–106
"Ooby Dooby," 109
"Out in the Streets," 125
"Out of Nowhere," 75
"Oxford Town," 183

"Pain in My Heart," 223
"Pains of Life," 214, 220
"Paint It Black," 14, 153–57
"Papa Was a Rolling Stone," 292
"Peg O' My Heart," 36
"Peggy Sue," 26, 74, 82–85
"Penny Lane," 177
"Photograph," 319
"Pillow Talk," 321
"Pipeline," 169, 181
"Pistol Packin' Mama," 62
"Please Let Me Wonder," 174
"Please Mr. Postman," 96, 128
"Please Please Me," 129
"Please, Please, Please," 225
"Police and Thieves," 313
"Polythene Pam," 143–150
"Precious Lord," 219
"Pride and Joy," 206
"Purple Haze," 240–243
"Puttin' on the Ritz," 35

"Rapper's Delight," 319, 332
"Rapture," 322–323
"Reach Out I'll Be There," 199
"Remember (Walking in the Sand)," 125–127
"Remote Control," 313
"Rescue Me," 319
"Riders in the Sky," 40
"Rock and Roll High School," 306
"Rock and Roll Music," 14, 86–88

"Rock and Roll," 282
"Rock the Joint," 62, 64
"Rock This Town," 319
"Rocket 88," 62, 64
"Roll Over Beethoven," 86–87
"Roundabout," 272–76
"Ruby Tuesday," 154–155, 157–158
"Ruff Rhyme (Back Again)," 330–331
"Run Joe," 50
"Runaway Child, Running Wild," 206
"Running Scared," 110

"Save the Last Dance for Me," 96
"Save the Life of My Child," 193
"School Day," 86
"Sh-Boom," 49, 61
"She Came In through the Bathroom Window," 143–150
"She Knows Me Too Well," 174
"She Loves You," 129–30
"Sheena Is a Punk Rocker," 306–309
"Shop Around," 203
"Sincerely," 103
"Sing a Simple Song," 326, 328
"(Sittin' on) The Dock of the Bay," 222–225
"Sixteen Candles," 61, 118
"Sixteen Tons," 47, 62
"Smoke on the Water," 281, 291
"So Long (It's Been Good to Know Ya)," 183
"So You Want to Be a Rock 'n' Roll Star," 190
"Some Things Just Stick in Your Mind," 165
"Somebody to Love," 232
"Someday We'll Be Together," 200
"Something," 140
"Songs to Aging Children Come," 259
"Soul Makossa," 292
"The Sound of Silence," 192
"St. Therese of the Roses," 95
"Stairway to Heaven," 282
"Stand by Me," 96, 229
"Star Dust," 95
"Staying Alive," 293

"Step by Step," 70
"Strawberry Fields Forever," 177, 244, 267
"Street Fighting Man," 160
"Stubborn Kind of Fellow," 206
"Stupid Cupid," 115
"Sun King," 143–150
"Sunshine of Your Love," 238–240
"Surf City," 169, 181
"Surfer Moon," 170
"Surfin' Bird," 30–31, 181, 306
"Surfin' Safari," 170
"Sweet Dreams," 319
"Sweet Emotion," 285–288
"Swing Down Chariot," 329
"Swing Down Sweet Chariot," 329
"Swing Low, Sweet Chariot," 329
"Sympathy for the Devil," 160, 161

"Take It or Leave It," 154
"Teddy's Jam," 325, 328
"Teenage Lobotomy," 306
"Tennessee Waltz," 35–36, 47
"That Lucky Old Sun (Just Rolls around Heaven All Day)," 36–39, 44
"That'll Be the Day," 72, 82–83
"That's All Right," 62, 66–67, 76
"That's How Strong My Love Is," 223
"That's the Joint," 319
"Then He Kissed Me," 96, 121, 128
"There Goes My Baby," 94–97, 118
"These Arms of Mine," 223
"This Diamond Ring," 153
"This Ole House," 35
"The Tide Is High," 309
"Time Is on My Side," 165
"The Times They Are A-Changin'," 192
"To Know Him Is to Love Him," 114
"Tom Dooley," 183
"Tomorrow Never Knows," 139, 230
"Tonight's the Night," 118
"Too Fat Polka," 35
"The Tracks of My Tears," 14, 26, 203–205

"Tragedy," 294
"True Love Ways," 83, 103, 113
"Try a Little Tenderness," 223
"TSOP (The Sound of Philadelphia)," 293–294
"Tutti Frutti," 21, 74–79, 87, 306
"Tweedle Dee," 48
"21st Century Schizoid Man," 268
"Twilight Time," 95, 103
"Twistin' the Night Away," 97

"Unchain My Heart," 96
"Under My Thumb," 154
"Uptight," 209

"Vaya con Dios," 42–46

"Wake Up Little Susie," 107
"Walk This Way," 285
"The Way You Do the Things You Do," 206
"We Got the Beat," 319
"The Weight," 249
"Welcome to the Terrordome," 325
"Well Alright," 83
"Wendy," 171
"(We're Gonna) Rock Around the Clock," 64, 74
"What'd I Say," 214, 229

"When the Levee Breaks," 282
"While My Guitar Gently Weeps," 140–143, 147
"White Rabbit," 231–234, 314
"White Riot," 313
"Who Are the Brain Police," 267
"Who's Sorry Now?" 113
"Whole Lotta Shakin' Goin' On," 70
"Why do Fools Fall in Love?" 55–57
"Wild Horses," 154–155, 165–167
"Will You Love Me Tomorrow," 25–26, 115, 117–120
"Wipe Out," 168, 181
"With God on Our Side," 183
"Woodstock," 245
"Wooly Bully," 306
"Words of Love," 130

"Yellow Submarine," 139
"Yes We Can Can," 292
"Yesterday," 33, 136–37
"You Can't Always Get What You Want," 33, 155, 161–164, 177
"You Can't Have My Love," 70
"You Can't Hurry Love," 200
"You Gotta Move," 165
"You Send Me," 97
"You've Really Got a Hold on Me," 203

www.ingramcontent.com/pod-product-compliance
Lightning Source LLC
Chambersburg PA
CBHW081328230426
43667CB00018B/2860